Latin America and the Caribbean in the Global Context provides state-of-the art analysis interpreting the transformations of the region's place in world politics and the global economy through the lenses of contemporary theories of international relations. Fundamental issues such as the quality of democratic governance and transnational drug trafficking, the region's quest for greater autonomy in a world scene marked by the war against terrorism, China's rise as a global power and challenges to US hegemony receive particularly acute treatment.

William C. Smith, *Professor of Political Science, University of Miami, Editor,* Latin American Politics and Society

It is extremely fortunate that this book brings to the forefront a core argument that is seldom considered by mainstream IR studies and comparative policy: the relevance and contribution of Latin America and the Caribbean to both world politics and democratic dynamics. The authors combine theory and practice, a historical and contemporary perspective covering multiple key issues across the whole area, with a singular purpose that they have been able to achieve: to thoroughly demonstrate why the post Cold war changing reality of LAC is significant; first to itself, to the Inter-american system, and to global affairs. In the end, Bagley and Horwitz show that the study and understanding of the region can be academically rigorous and intellectually empathetic.

Juan Gabriel Tokatlian, *Universidad Torcuato Di Tella,* *Buenos Aires, Argentina* ii

LATIN AMERICA AND THE CARIBBEAN IN THE GLOBAL CONTEXT

Current perspectives on Latin America's role in the world tend to focus on one question: Why is Latin America and the Caribbean always falling behind? Analysts and scholars offer answers grounded in history, economic underdevelopment, or democratic consolidation. Horwitz and Bagley, however, shift the central question to ask why and to what extent does Latin America and the Caribbean (LAC) matter in world politics, both now and in the future.

This text takes a holistic approach to analyze Latin America's role in the international system. It invokes a combination of global, regional, and sub-regional levels to assess Latin America and the Caribbean's insertion into a globalized world, in historical, contemporary, and forward-looking perspectives. Conventional international relations theory and paradigms, introduced at the beginning, offer a useful lens through which to view four key themes: political economy, security, transnational issues and threats, and democratic consolidation. The full picture presented by this book breaks down the evolving power relationships in the hemisphere and the ways in which conflict and cooperation play out through international organizations and relations.

Betty Horwitz was a Lecturer in the Department of International Studies at the University of Miami, where she received her Ph.D.

Bruce M. Bagley is Professor in the Department of International Studies at the University of Miami. His research interests are in U.S.-Latin American relations, with an emphasis on drug trafficking and security issues.

LATIN AMERICA AND THE CARIBBEAN IN THE GLOBAL CONTEXT

Why care about the Americas?

Betty Horwitz and Bruce M. Bagley

NEW YORK AND LONDON

First published 2016
by Routledge
711 Third Avenue, New York, NY 10017

and by Routledge
2 Park Square, Milton Park, Abingdon, Oxon OX14 4RN

Routledge is an imprint of the Taylor & Francis Group, an informa business

© 2016 Taylor & Francis

The right of Betty Horwitz and Bruce M. Bagley to be identified as authors of this work has been asserted by them in accordance with sections 77 and 78 of the Copyright, Designs and Patents Act 1988.

All rights reserved. No part of this book may be reprinted or reproduced or utilised in any form or by any electronic, mechanical, or other means, now known or hereafter invented, including photocopying and recording, or in any information storage or retrieval system, without permission in writing from the publishers.

Trademark notice: Product or corporate names may be trademarks or registered trademarks, and are used only for identification and explanation without intent to infringe.

Library of Congress Cataloging in Publication Data
Names: Horwitz, Betty, 1956- author. | Bagley, Bruce Michael, author.
   Title: Latin America and the Caribbean in global context : why care about what happens in the Americas? / Betty Horwitz and Bruce Bagley.
   Description: New York, NY : Routledge, 2016. | Includes bibliographical references and index.
   Identifiers: LCCN 2015034325| ISBN 9780415877442 (hbk) | ISBN 9780415877459 (pbk) | ISBN 9780203855508 (ebk)
   Subjects: LCSH: Latin America–Foreign relations. | Caribbean Area–Foreign relations. | Latin America–Politics and government. | Caribbean Area–Politics and government. | Latin America–Economic conditions. | Caribbean Area–Economic conditions.
   Classification: LCC F1415 .H67 2016 | DDC 327.8–dc23
LC record available at http://lccn.loc.gov/2015034325

ISBN: 978-0-415-87744-2 (hbk)
ISBN: 978-0-415-87745-9 (pbk)
ISBN: 978-0-203-85550-8 (ebk)

Typeset in Bembo
by Taylor & Francis Books

WE DEDICATE THIS BOOK TO OUR COMPANIONS AND CONFIDANTS, OUR SPOUSES OF OVER FORTY YEARS AND COUNTING, ROBERTO HORWITZ AND ANNETTE LOUISE TRAVERSIE BAGLEY. WE WOULDN'T BE HERE WITHOUT THEIR LOVE AND SUPPORT.

CONTENTS

List of illustrations	xiii
Acknowledgments	xiv

PART I
Why Do Latin America and the Caribbean Matter? 1

1 Why Care About What Happens in Latin America and the
Caribbean (LAC)? 3

Introduction 3
Location, Location, Location, and a Complicated Relationship 5
Organization of the Book 8

2 The Insertion of Latin America and the Caribbean in
World History 14

Introduction 14
Spain and Portugal Explore the World: Opportunism and
Epidemic Outbreaks 15
The Era of Colonialism 16
Napoleon, Europe, and Independence from Spain and Portugal 19
Latin America's Importance During the Era of
Corporate Capitalism 24
Latin America, the Caribbean and the American Century 25

3 A Theoretical Framework to Understand Latin America in
World Affairs 34

Introduction 34
Realism 35
Institutionalism 36

CONTENTS

Liberalism 37
Constructivism 39
The English School 41
Critical Approaches 41
Underdevelopment and Dependency Theory: Made in
 Latin America 42
Using Theoretical Tools to Understand the Americas 43

PART II
Latin America and the Caribbean: Power and Political Economy
53

4 Economic Power: Commodity Lottery Booms and Busts
55

Introduction 55
Growth and Inequality, Dependent Development, and
 Orden y Progreso 56
The Commodity Lottery 57
Latin America in the Twentieth Century 58
World War II, Import Substitution (IS), Economic Growth
 and Protectionism 61
The Cold War and a Realist World Order 62
The Golden Era of Import Substitution 64
Debt-led Growth and Globalization 66
The "Lost Decade" of Economic Growth 69

5 Latin American and Caribbean: Political Economy in the
Twenty-First Century
85

Introduction 85
Latin America and the Caribbean Enter the Twenty-First
 Century 87
Economic Growth and the 2008 Global Downturn 88
Made in China or Hecho en Mexico, *or Brazil, Chile, Peru,*
 or Colombia 91
Latin America Looks to the East 96

CONTENTS

PART 3
Security and Democracy   103

6 Power: Political Institutions and Democracy   105

Introduction 105
How Caudillismo *Helped Establish a State 106*
The Caudillo *Tradition and Presidentialism in Latin America 109*
The Importance of the "Third Wave" of Democratization
in LAC 110
A "How To" Guide to Democracy for Latin America and
the Caribbean 114

7 Electoral Democracies in Latin America and the Caribbean   121

Introduction 121
Electoral Democracies 122
Latin America's Two Lefts 125
The Pragmatic Center and the Ghost of Caudillismo's *Past 132*

8 Challenges to Democracy: Drug Trafficking, Organized Crime
and Terrorist Networks in LAC   141

Introduction 141
The Globalization of Drug Consumption 142
Partial Victories Against Drugs 144
Proliferation of Areas of Cultivation and Smuggling Routes (the
Balloon Effect) 146
Dispersion and Fragmentations of Criminal Drug Trafficking
Organizations (the Cockroach Effect) 148
Transnational Criminal Organizations and Terrorism in LAC
and Beyond 152
Iran's Activities in Latin America 156
Reaction to Terrorism and Regional Cooperation 160
Failure of Political Reform or State Building (the
Deinstitutionalization Effect) 161
The Inflexibility and Ineffectiveness of Regional and International
Drug Control Policies 163
The Failure of U.S. Drug Policies 163
The Search for Alternatives: The Debate over Legalization,
Decriminalization, and Harm Reduction 164

CONTENTS

PART IV
Latin America and the Caribbean on the World Stage   177

9 Latin America and the Caribbean and the Development of the
   Inter-American System   179

   Introduction 179
   The Inter-American Context 181
   The Inter-American System and LAC Independence 182
   World War II, Security and the Birth of the
   * Inter-American System 183*
   The Cold War and U.S. Supremacy 185
   Security Cooperation 188
   9/11and the Global War on Terrorism (GWOT) 190
   The Americas: A Community of Democracies 193
   Reimagining Hemispheric Regionalism: The Economy 200

10 We Should Care about Latin America and the Caribbean   215

   Introduction 215
   LAC: A Tale of Two Economies 217
   Brazil and Mexico: Friends or Foes? 219
   Latin America and the Caribbean: A Tale of Two Lefts 222
   Latin America and the Caribbean, and the U.S. 225
   Why Latin America and the Caribbean Matter 230

   Bibliography   241
   Index   261

LIST OF ILLUSTRATIONS

Figures

1.1	Growth outlook	7
4.1	Percentage of World GDP (last 500 years)	59
5.1	GDP growth for Latin America and the Caribbean, 2002–2012	89
5.2	GDP growth, 2013 and 2014	93
5.3	Growth is expected to gradually accelerate in all subregions except the Caribbean	94
5.4	Countries with large shares of commodity exports will be more sensitive to commodity price declines	95
7.1	Chile GDP annual growth rate	126
7.2	Brazil's GDP per capita and real GDP growth	127
7.3	Brazil's DP annual growth rate	128
7.4	Venezuela's GDP annual growth rate	129
7.5	Bolivia's GDP growth rate	130
7.6	Argentina's GDP annual growth rate	132
10.1	Brazilian and Mexican GDP	223
10.2	Venezuela's foreign exchange rates	229

Tables

3.1	Theories in brief	46
4.1	Summary of theories and events	74
5.1	Summary of theories and events	99
6.1	Military coups, autogolpes, and illegal interruptions to democracy (including failed elections) in Latin America, 1900–2009	112
8.1	Proliferation of Mexican cartels, 2006–2010	150

ACKNOWLEDGMENTS

We are grateful to Routledge Publishers for their encouragement, advice and comments. We are thankful for the help of Rocio Alejandra Rivera Barradas and Yulia Vorobyeva, Ph.D. students of the Department of International Studies at the University of Miami and Clara L. Diaz, for their help with our graphics and tables, and Rosa Schechter for her counsel.

Part I

WHY DO LATIN AMERICA AND THE CARIBBEAN MATTER?

Let's think about the whole earth
pounding with love on the table.
I don't want blood to soak
the bread, beans, music,
again: I want the miner,
the little girl, the lawyer, the doll
manufacturer to accompany me,
let's go to the movies and set out

to drink the reddest wine.

I don't want to solve anything.

I came here to sing
so that you'd sing with me.

"Let Woodcutter Awaken" from *Canto General*, by Pablo Neruda, translated by Jack Schmitt.
© 2011 by the Fundacion Pablo Neruda and the Regents of the University of California. Published
by the University of California Press.

1

WHY CARE ABOUT WHAT HAPPENS IN LATIN AMERICA AND THE CARIBBEAN (LAC)?

Introduction

For the last two hundred years, most observers of world affairs wrote off the nations of Latin America and the Caribbean (LAC) as minor actors on the world's economic and political stages.

It is true that once they gained their independence from Spain and Portugal during the second decade of the nineteenth century and through the nineteenth and most of the twentieth centuries, LAC remained poor, underdeveloped, plagued by internal conflicts and territorial disputes with neighbors, dependent on commodity exports, prone to dictatorial or authoritarian regimes, and essentially subordinate to the dominant power of the United States.

They were, in effect, "rule takers" rather than "rule makers" in the international system, constantly overshadowed by American hegemony.

The central argument of this book is that by the second decade of the twenty-first century, LAC and its role in and importance to the international system has changed dramatically for the better. Today, some of the countries of LAC are significantly more important—in both global economic and security terms—than at any time in the region's history. LAC is increasingly able to exercise national and regional autonomy in international affairs.

Furthermore, if recent history is any indication, the U.S. is likely to continue to be the major economic, political, and military power in the world, albeit less engaged than in the past. Its low rate of exports, its increasing self-reliance (especially in terms of energy), and its experiences over the past decade will cause it to be increasingly cautious about economic and military involvement in the world.

This may be perceived as a decline in U.S. hegemony both worldwide and in the Western Hemisphere. This relative disengagement, however, can work to the advantage of the Western Hemisphere, and LAC in particular. Specifically, it can help countries like Brazil, Mexico, Colombia, and Chile position themselves to take advantage of their close ties to the U.S. as they emerge as increasingly relevant and independent actors on the international stage.

The objectives of this volume are to explain how this transformation has come about, to examine how far it has proceeded to date, and to analyze what role(s) the major countries of the region can be expected to play in the international system over the coming decades of the twenty-first century.[1]

As the mature phase of globalization approaches 2030, Brazil and Mexico are consistently finding themselves among the 15 largest economies in the world, while Colombia finds itself positioned among the first 30.[2]

As part of the Western Hemisphere, these nations are likely to grow into a role as global economic actors. With its size and growing GDP, Brazil[3] (and possibly Mexico[4]) could become a very real contender to China as a center of manufacturing. Both nations could emerge as principal leaders in Latin America, and they're not alone; countries such as Uruguay, Chile, and Colombia could become part of the world's most advanced economies in the next 15 to 20 years.

Latin America has shed its past stagnation and instability and is emerging as a key engine of world economic growth, an area of relative political stability, and, considering the length of time that has passed since the 1978 electoral defeat of Joaquín Balaguer in the Dominican Republic, an example of democratic solidification.[5]

Certainly not all is said and done, but the last two decades has seen deepening global connections and economic growth in Latin America, hand in hand with government pragmatism and democratic strengthening.[6]

Many feared that the inclusion of disenfranchised groups would lead to the creation of authoritarian regimes with a leftist populist slant (such as the one in Venezuela) that would upset economic gains. Instead, more consensual, pragmatic, and centrist politics have taken hold, as seen in Colombia, Brazil, Chile, and Peru.

The poor performance of the authoritarian Latin American left paired with a broader engagement in global affairs on issues such as energy, security, finance, technology, manufacturing, and trade have discouraged any radical departures in economic issues.

Of course, Latin America is not yet free of its past troubles and still faces major obstacles in its quest to play a major role on the world stage. The region remains plagued with extremely high rates of poverty and continues to present the worst wealth and income inequality patterns in the world.

LAC's economic development faces headwinds due to its heavy dependence on the primary production of oil, minerals, and agricultural commodities and its limited diversification in basic industries, high technology, and key service sectors such as banking, insurance, and research and development.

That being said, the principal obstacles to Latin America's growth are internal and political in nature: deeply rooted social and political exclusion, criminal violence, and weak political institutions ultimately erode not only the economic competitiveness but also the democratic practices and institutions. These hurdles could potentially stifle or thwart Latin America's advancement toward a greater role in the global system over the first half of the twenty-first century.[7]

Whether or not Latin America, led by key countries such as Brazil and Mexico, will realize its promise in the twenty-first century remains very much an open question.

There are important reasons to believe it will, however, especially when LAC is compared with other regions of the developing world. Side by side with other nations, LAC's obstacles appear manageable.[8] Much of LAC seems to be moving in the direction of poverty alleviation and institutional consolidation.

If LAC manages to continue its positive trajectory in the coming decades, it will assuredly rise to a more prominent role in world affairs.

This book is based on the premise that its future matters a great deal, both to the LAC itself and to the rest of the world.

Location, Location, Location, and a Complicated Relationship

LAC may not be the largest, fastest-growing, most populated, or even most dangerous area in the world, but LAC's prime global position has kept it as an active participant in the struggle for supremacy among world powers.

For the past two hundred years, its proximity to the U.S. made LAC the territory where Washington could impose its foreign policy priorities and experiment with different strategies before implementing them anywhere else. As Washington's backyard, LAC has had an important role to play in the development of the international capitalist system in place today.

Take Mexico: the U.S.'s GDP is nine times that of its neighbor to the south, so the two nations present the largest income gap between any two contiguous countries in the world. Yet because of the North American Free Trade Agreement (NAFTA), the entire region of North America (Canada, the U.S., and Mexico) has the potential to become the most crucial of the continental regions worldwide.[9]

Mexico, together with Central America, constitutes a growing demographic powerhouse with which the U.S. has had a complex and mutually dependent relationship. This relationship will become even more complex in the future, be it through increasing trade ties, legal and illegal immigration, or organized crime.

Case in point: the scheduled 2014 widening project of the Panama Canal in order to open the Caribbean Basin to megaships from East Asia. From Texas to Florida to Central America and the Caribbean, the economic fates of port cities will be closely intertwined.[10]

5

Indeed, LAC's location is one of a kind. Still, in spite of its considerable size, prime location and close relationship with the U.S., it has not been able to establish itself at the forefront of progress. Compared to other regions of the world, LAC's economic performance is not particularly impressive.[11]

In spite of its enviable location, LAC countries seem to be perpetually unable to seize the moment.[12] In contrast to its Southeast Asian counterparts, the economies of Latin American nations have traditionally grown only slightly faster than the world overall.

Furthermore, there is a great variance in the absolute size of the different Latin American economies. GDP is highly concentrated in only a few.[13] For this reason, it is very difficult to try and gauge the importance of LAC as one unit.

Countries such as Mexico, Brazil, and even Chile cannot be considered in the same league as Honduras or today's Venezuela. What happens (for good or bad) in countries like Brazil or Mexico affects the rest of the world a great deal more than what happens in countries like Nicaragua or Jamaica.[14]

LAC is an enigma. In looking at the profound inequality that permeates every aspect of its political, economic, and social canvas, LAC should be considered among the poorer and more disadvantaged regions of the globe.[15] Yet it's still not in the same league as, say, South Saharan Africa.[16]

Ironically, and true to its contradictory nature, the region has achieved a per capita income of approximately $8,403,[17] placing it solidly among the upper tier of the middle-income economies. This puts Latin Americans among the higher middle tiers of the world's economies, despite the fact that the majority of people still live in poverty.

A closer look reveals that, first, not all Latin American countries have grown or will grow at the same rate. Second, Latin American economies have not been able to sustain a substantial rate of economic growth for a long enough period of time to benefit everyone. The general populations of LAC have yet to enjoy the benefits that stem from economic growth.

Thanks to the sustained economic development enjoyed by many Latin American countries in the last ten years, however, there are reasons to be hopeful. This time around, LAC may seize the moment.

These days, business communities and governments seem to be more willing and able to take advantage of the prolonged period of economic growth and commodity exports by coupling them with good macro-economic policies. In Brazil for example, more that 40 million people have risen out of poverty in the last 30 years.[18]

In Mexico, just half a century ago, 80 percent of the population was poor. Today, Mexicans are joining what is considered to be the global middle class in great numbers, and the nation may be able to drastically reduce its level of poverty within a generation.[19]

If LAC is able to ride the effects of the 2008 economic debacle and adjust to a rapidly changing economic environment, it may wean itself off its dependence on commodities. There are grounds for optimism, but only time will tell.

WHY CARE ABOUT LAC?

Also true to its contradictory nature, LAC is considered to be relatively peaceful in spite of the growing problems of organized crime and drug trafficking in countries like Honduras or Guatemala.

In Washington's eyes, the increasingly powerful drug cartels may lead the U.S. to question whether they represent an overwhelming threat to host LAC governments, but compared to Al Qaeda in Afghanistan or other similar terrorist groups such as ISIS in Iraq or Yemen, these cartels don't pose an existential threat to the U.S. or the rest of the world—at least not yet.

As we mentioned at the beginning, whether LAC, led by key countries such as Brazil and Mexico, will achieve its promise in the twenty-first century remains very much an open question.

The evidence suggests, however, that if it manages to keep moving towards economic growth, fiscal responsibility, poverty alleviation, and institutional consolidation, there are important reasons to believe it will. Many Latin American countries have come a long way during the first decade of the twenty-first century.

Whether these nations succeed or fail in becoming relevant players in world affairs will have important implications for the future of the international system of today's world.

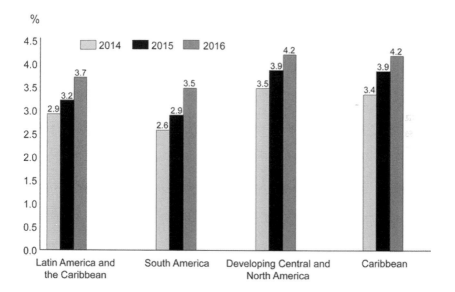

Figure 1.1 Growth outlook
Source: World Bank, "Global Economic Prospects: Latin America and the Caribbean," January 2014 (www.slideshare.net/WB_Research/outlook-lacjanuary2014?next_slideshow=1).

Organization of the Book

To examine all of the aforementioned questions, this book is divided into four parts.

Part I, *Why Do Latin America and the Caribbean Matter?*, includes three chapters.

Chapter 1 questions whether LAC matters in world affairs and why it matters to the international system in general and to the U.S. in particular—for better or worse. This is the main theme this book intends to examine and respond to.

Chapter 2 begins with a historical overview of how LAC was inserted in the international system, helping readers understand how and why it ended up as a "rule-taker" in world affairs. Beginning in 1492, the chapter will continue with LAC's role in the world system from colonial times through the first half of the nineteenth century.

This approach aims to provide an explanation as to why newly independent LAC states ultimately failed to play a significant role in the international system and modernize their economies, societies, and politics in the nineteenth and twentieth centuries. This Latin American story demonstrates how LAC has remained the eternal land of promise, and how it may be able to break the underdevelopment patterns in the near future.

Chapter 3 proceeds with a theoretical framework that allows for a comprehensive approach to the different problems afflicting the region. The review of the relevant aspects of International Relations (IR) theory addresses LAC in terms of fundamental concepts such as the use of power—or the lack thereof. The purpose of this conceptual discussion is to illustrate how IR theory clarifies Latin America's past and present roles in the global political economy and in world politics.

This book's core contention is that Realism, Liberalism, Institutionalism, the English School, Marxism together with Dependency Theory, and Constructivism serve as important tools to understand the problems of the international relations of the region (both past and present) and must be invoked in combination to interpret and explain Latin America's role in the international system.

Part II, *Latin America: Power and Political Economy*, continues to analyze how and why Latin America played a rule-taker's role in the international system by concentrating on the use of economic power, which has remained the clearest manifestation of the use of force in the Americas. This section is composed of two chapters.

Chapter 4 explores the obstacles that the major LAC countries, as commodity and primary products exporters, confronted in carving out a role for themselves in the modern capitalist global economy and in consolidating democratic political regimes during the twentieth century.

In this chapter there's a particular emphasis on the post-World War II period, paying particular attention to the role of Latin Americans as commodity providers to developing economies, which afforded them both great opportunities and formidable obstacles for development.

Chapter 5 examines how LAC crossed the threshold of the twenty-first century, and whether or not Latin Americans took advantage of and learned from previous experiences, both good and bad. Particular attention is paid to the latest commodity boom and which LAC nations have used this opportunity to get ahead through particular internal capabilities, responsible fiscal policies, and their knowledge of how to use the international economic system to their advantage.

The chapter then examines how many Latin American economies have overcome their roles as simple rule-takers in the international system by using economic influence to pursue their interests—and how many have failed to do so. The emphasis of this chapter is on understanding where LAC societies are now and how they've learned to effectively use economic power to compensate for their lack of coercive capabilities.

Part III, *Security and Democracy*, proceeds to analyze why Latin Americans have had mixed results in the way their states and political systems have developed. This section is composed of three chapters.

Chapter 6 begins with a historical overview, exploring the bumpy path LAC societies took in order to gain some degree of effective governance and become (to a greater or lesser degree) democratic.

Subsequently, Chapter 7 concentrates on exploring the nature of the particular LAC electoral democracies. The chapter examines the different kind of democratic arrangements that exist in the Americas today, veering either to the right or to the left but mostly to the center of the political spectrum.

This chapter also explains why and how the traditional authoritarian tendencies that emerged with the newly independent LAC states in the early nineteenth century have survived and adapted to become part of many democratic regimes, and how, in other instances, they've rendered weak and ineffective states.

Lastly, Chapter 8 examines the great challenges to LAC democratic regimes and economies from drug trafficking, organized crime and even terrorism, all of which can derail some or all of the LAC positive trends.

The different chapters in this section complement the LAC portrait in the previous section on political economy. A historical overview and analysis of the political arrangements and security threats that characterize LAC nations affords a more comprehensive image of why the Americas are the way they are. This allows for an understanding of why Latin American nations matter—for good when it comes to their role in the economic international system, as participants in one of the most stable neighborhoods in the world, and as part of the Western camp in the international political arena, and for bad by providing a space where all organized crime groups including drug producers and traffickers can coexist with legality.

Part IV, *Latin America and the Caribbean in the World Stage*, the final section of this book, aims to bring together all the themes presented in this volume to understand the role and importance of LAC in the world stage today. This section is composed of two chapters.

Chapter 9 begins by exploring how LAC has participated in world affairs as part of the Inter-American System. In this chapter, LAC's basic cooperative approach to foreign policy is reviewed, with special attention paid to their persistent search for effective collective security and economic and normative arrangements in the hemisphere.

The aim of this chapter is to go beyond the realms of political economy, security, and internal institutional and political arrangements to gain a better understanding of how Latin Americans have attempted to use these resources to cooperatively manage their position in world affairs.

Finally, Chapter 10 concludes this volume by analyzing the present status, importance, and future role or roles of LAC states in world affairs. This chapter builds on the thorough examination of the LAC trajectory in this volume and pays particular attention to the role of LAC in the international economic system, especially as a U.S. partner.

This is done mainly through the lens of political economy, but without forgetting LAC principal domestic political trends; LAC current and future security problems and arrangements; and the new forms of regional cooperation emerging in the face of new economic and security challenges in the twenty-first century.

In addition, the importance of the spread of democratic ideals and values in the region is addressed, as is the acceptance of democratic processes as legal and binding; and the solidification of democratic institutions nationally and regionally.

These, as well as external influences coming from within the hemisphere and beyond, help IR students understand the dynamics of economic development, institutional strength, and democratic solidification throughout the region and see how LAC societies are navigating the fast-changing international environment, aiming to become potential U.S. partners and thus, important players in world affairs.

Throughout this volume it's established that whether Latin America fulfills its promise or fails to confront its many problems is extremely important. One way or the other, the path or paths taken by LAC and the Caribbean in the near future cannot be ignored. If Latin America slowly joins the club of rule-makers and leaves behind its role of rule-taker in the twenty-first century, it will have great consequences for not only for the U.S. but also the international system as a whole.

What follows in the chapters below is an exploration of where LAC has come from, where it is today, and which alternative path or paths the key countries and the region may follow over the remainder of the twenty-first century.

WHY CARE ABOUT LAC?

The discovery of the Americas is the first step in the understanding of the complicated relationship between this region, its northerly neighbors, and the rest of the world.

Notes

1 With a total regional population of about 525.2 million, rapid economic growth, and declining levels of poverty in a number of countries in the last two decades, the LAC region is expanding its share of global trade (fueled, especially, by rising demand in China). In its February 23, 2015, Decade Forecast for 2015–2025, *Stratfor* points out that the world has been restructuring itself since 2008 when Russia invaded Georgia and the subprime financial crisis struck. It is their view that we have entered a period in which the decline of the nation-state is accelerating and power is no longer held by states devoted to armed factions that can neither defeat others nor be defeated. More important for LAC, China has completed its cycle as a high-growth, low-wage economy and has entered its "new normal" phase. This includes much slower growth and an increasingly powerful dictatorship to contain divergent forces created by slow growth. China will continue to be an important global economic engine, but it will have to share this role with a new group of dispersed regions, including Southeast Asia, East Africa, and parts of Latin America.

2 For more, see Center for Economic and Business Research (CEBR), *World Economic League Table 2015*, December 26, 2014 (www.cebr.com/reports/worl d-economic-league-table-2015/).

3 Among the ten largest economies in the world, Brazil is now a major global actor and could even surpass Mexico. To achieve this goal Brazil's government has proposed an ambitious plan to boost its infrastructure. Brazil, with a population of almost 200 million, has also assumed a leadership role in the World Trade Organization's (WTO) Doha Round of trade negotiations, often playing a spoiler role. In addition, in partnership with Turkey and against U.S. wishes, Brazil advanced an alternative solution to the Iranian nuclear issue. The success of these two initiatives has been mixed. Nevertheless, Brazil has emerged as a key voice in the newly empowered Group of 20 (G20) and a leading contender for a permanent seat on the United Nation's Security Council in any future reorganization of this body. For more, see Joe Leahy, "Appetite for Construction", *Financial Times*, August 29, 2012, 6.

4 Mexico, on the other hand, is quickly closing in on China and becoming more competitive in terms of manufacturing exports, especially to the U.S. It's becoming the preferred center of manufacturing for multinational companies looking to supply the Americas and, increasingly, beyond. None of this means that Mexico is going to replace China as the world's first choice for manufacturing, but from what appeared to be a dark future as a result of NAFTA's unintended consequences and in spite of the drug war, Mexico has moved into a position that has made the next few years look very bright. Today, Mexico exports more manufactured products than the rest of Latin America put together. During the first half of 2011, for example, Mexico accounted for 14.2 percent of manufactured goods to the U.S., the world's largest importer. In 2005, Mexico's share was just 11 percent. Surprisingly, China, which had gained a huge portion of the U.S. import market for many years, has started to lose ground. From a high of 29.3 percent of the total at the end of 2009, it has now shrunk to 26.4 percent. Furthermore, while winning a bigger slice of the

WHY DO LATIN AMERICA AND THE CARIBBEAN MATTER?

U.S. market, Mexico has diversified its customers. A decade ago, about 90 percent of the country's exports went to the U.S. Last year, the figure fell to less than 80 percent. For more information, see Adam Thomson, "China's Unlikely Challenger," *Financial Times*, September 20, 2012, 7.

5 After the assassination of General Trujillo there followed a series of conflicts and coup attempts due to the vacuum in the Dominican Republic. As a result of the evident emergence of the Soviet threat in the Caribbean, the decision was made to intervene through the Organization of American States (OAS) and the U.S. Department of Defense (DOD) to topple the democratically elected leftist candidate Juan Bosch. Unilateral U.S. military operations began on Tuesday, April 1965. Joaquín Balaguer returned from exile and in 1966 gained the support of the military and the elites to assume the presidency, a post he held until 1978 when he lost the election to Antonio Guzmán and left office. For more see José Antonio Moreno, *El Pueblo en Armas; Revoluvión en Santo Domingo* (Madrid: Editorial Tecnos, 1973) and Major Lawrence M. Greenberg, *United States Army Unilateral and Coalition Operations in the 1965 Dominican Republic Intervention* (Washington, DC: Analysis Branch, U.S. Army Center of Military History, 2015).

6 Recent public opinion surveys such as *Latinobarómetro* and Americas Barometer show higher levels of support for democratic systems of government throughout the region, even when the state of democratic governance in Latin America has been mixed. Michael Shifter and Jorge I. Domínguez (eds), *Constructing Democratic Governance in Latin America* (Baltimore, MD: Johns Hopkins University Press, 2013). Nevertheless, as Scott Mainwaring and Aníbal Pérez-Liñán point out in "Cross-Currents in Latin America," *Journal of Democracy*, vol. 26, no. 1 (2015), 114–127, there are reasons for concern that in countries with weak governance and poor economic performance the quality of democracy is persistently low.

7 Yet it is heartening that, for example, Latin American authorities are increasingly recognizing the need to address basic problems that have kept LAC behind. Latin America has generally relaxed the obstacles for political participation and social inclusion. Moreover, political authorities have acknowledged the need to concentrate on reforming and strengthening their government institutions and promoting greater learning for their children, particularly among the poor. Peter Kingstone, *The Political Economy of Latin America: Reflections on Neoliberalism and Development* (New York: Routledge, 2011) and Jeffrey Puryear and Tamara Goodspeed, "How Can Education Help Latin America Develop?" *Global Journal of Emerging Market Economies*, vol. 3, no. 1, 2011.

8 For instance, Tunisia, Egypt, and Libya exploded in 2011, revealing the dramatic economic, social, and institutional failures of key Middle Eastern and North African regimes during the twentieth century. Most of sub-Saharan Africa is still deeply mired in underdevelopment and poverty, dependence, and dictatorship. On the other hand, in Asia, economic development has generally been high and sustained, but democratic consolidation has lagged far behind, especially in China, India, and Pakistan.

9 Javier Reyes and Charles Sawyer, *Latin American Economic Development* (New York: Routledge, 2011) point out that not only does Latin America share a huge border with the most powerful country in the world, it also covers half of the Western Hemisphere's total area and has approximately 530 million people or about 59 percent of the whole population of the Americas. Looking at the entire globe, Latin America covers just about 14 percent of its total area and has just about 7.9 percent of its population. At first glance the conclusion may be that Latin America doesn't matter all that much, but consider its prime location and things look very different.

10 For more see Robert D. Kaplan, *The Revenge of Geography; What the Map Tells Us About Coming Conflicts and the Battle Against Fate* (New York: Random House, 2012).

11 Latin America's total economic output was a little over 7.7 percent of the total world economic output. According to the IMF, in 2010 the world's GDP was $63 trillion. In terms of economic trade, Latin America accounted for close to 6 percent of the total worldwide. For more see: IMF, *World Economic Outlook*, April 2012 (www.imf.org/external/pubs/ft/weo/2012/01/weodata/index.aspx); ECLAC, "Latin America and the Caribbean in the World Economy: The Region in the Decade of the Emerging Economies 2010–2011" (http://reposi torio.cepal.org/bitstream/handle/11362/1182/S2011521_en.pdf?sequence=1), 21.

12 Indeed, when looking at its performance, including during periods of strong economic expansion (the 1950s and 1960s for example) Latin America grew at an accelerated pace but only reached 5.9 percent of the world economy. Recently, after yet another period of strong economic expansion with a high demand for its commodities, in 2009 Latin America comprised only 7.7 percent of the total GDP worldwide. For more see ECLAC, "Latin America and the Caribbean in the World Economy: The Region in the Decade of the Emerging Economies", United Nations/ECLAC, 2011 (http://repositorio.cepal.org/bit stream/handle/11362/1182/S2011521_en.pdf?sequence=1).

13 ECLAC, *Statistical Yearbook for Latin America and the Caribbean 2011* (Statistics and Economic Projection Division, ECLAC, LC/G.2513-P/B, United Nations), 81.

14 Inequality, Latin America's quintessential characteristic, permeates every aspect of the region, both among the Latin American states and within the countries themselves. This makes some countries much more important than others on a global stage. For example, the world paid more attention to Mexico's smooth and lawful presidential election in 2012 than to the unraveling of the democratically elected Lugo regime in Paraguay, though both happened simultaneously. What's more, Washington is more likely to pay attention to the actions and decisions of UNASUR under the current Venezuelan leadership than worry about the possible undoing of CARICOM if and when Jamaica decides to exit the block.

15 The total output of LAC is approximately $5 trillion. When the economies of the 32 countries of Latin America are ranked by size of GDP, Brazil and Mexico come out in first place with GDPs of $2 and $1 trillion, respectively. Argentina and Venezuela trail in second place with a substantial drop in GDP of approximately $370 billion. Colombia and Venezuela come next with $288 and $239 billion, respectively. After that, only Chile and Peru follow, with GDPs of $200 and $157 billion. Ecuador follows in a distant fourth place with a GDP roughly one-third the size of Peru. Lastly, the other 22 countries lag behind in a relatively tight cluster of GDP between $7 billion and $40 billion.

16 According to the UNDP, Latin America/the Caribbean is the most unequal region. www.un.org/apps/news/story.asp?NewsID=35428&Cr=latin+america&Cr1.

17 ECLAC, Statistical Yearbook for Latin America and the Caribbean 2011 (Statistics and Economic Projection Division, ECLAC, LC/G.2513-P/B, United Nations), 82.

18 Economic and Social Council at the UN. SOC/4789 (www.un.org/News/Press/docs/2012/soc4789.doc.htm).

19 For more information, see Luis de la Calle and Luis Rubio, *Mexico: A Middle Class Society, Poor No More, Developed Not Yet* (Washington, DC: Washington Institute, Woodrow Wilson Center for Scholars, 2012), see www.wilsoncenter. org/sites/default/files/Mexico percent20A percent20Middle percent20Class per cent20Society.pdf.

2

THE INSERTION OF LATIN AMERICA AND THE CARIBBEAN IN WORLD HISTORY

> Men make their own history, but they do not make it as they please. They make it under already existing circumstances, given and transmitted from the past.
>
> Karl Marx (1852)[1]

Introduction

The current international system is the product of an evolutionary process that has consistently spread across the globe over the last five hundred years. With very few exceptions, all the nations of the word today are part of one global capitalist system. This is due to a historical process that can be traced to a single symbolic event: the discovery of the Americas in 1492.

When Columbus set sail to find a new route to the East, the process of exploration and discovery wasn't really a new phenomenon. In fact, explorers and travelers in Europe and Asia had been looking for adventure, new lands, and fortunes for many years. In the thirteenth century, for example, Marco Polo reached at least Russia (if not China), encountering the Mongols on his way. What's more, recent archeological discoveries in Newfoundland suggest that Vikings may have already reached the New World by around 1000 CE.

Curiosity and ambition seem to be part of the human DNA. So what was different in 1492?

When Columbus reached the New World, what followed wasn't just the discovery of new and exotic cultures and the writing of interesting travelogues that people could read back home—the European determination to discover new trade routes to the Far East unleashed the violent conquest and colonization of the Americas.[2]

Consequently, the expeditions of explorers such as Hernán Cortés and Bernal Díaz del Castillo (both of Spain) ended up linking the European powers to their new possessions in such a way that what happened on either side of the Atlantic profoundly affected both continents, despite their physical separation by a vast ocean.

The drive that propelled Portugal and Spain to search for gold and spices served to intimately bond the destinies of two completely different regions, histories, peoples, and cultures. This dramatically changed world history, as the relationship between the European powers and their respective colonies would institute different development paths, which would eventually set North America (Canada and the U.S.) apart from the rest of the continent.

To paraphrase Karl Marx: historical circumstances set the stage for human interaction. This chapter highlights the social structures that emerged after 1492 as a result of this contact.

By setting the stage on which the Latin American colonial societies emerged and developed in contrast to their northerly neighbors, this chapter begins to explain why LAC was on a path to underdevelopment very early on.

Indeed, the particular link that tied Spain and Portugal to their American colonies set the course for the development of Latin American society structures that were not prepared to face an independent future.

Spain and Portugal Explore the World: Opportunism and Epidemic Outbreaks

In 1492, in an attempt to break free from economic dependence on the rest of Europe, the Spanish and Portuguese crowns set sail to look for new commercial ocean routes and sources of wealth.

Aiming to dominate the spice trade, the Portuguese crown was the first to launch its pioneer exploration to find new and faster routes to Asia. In 1488, Portuguese explorers sailed around the Southern tip of Africa, and in 1497, under the command of Vasco de Gama, they traveled around the cape to East Africa. Four years later they conquered the South Seas and with the arrival of Pedro Álvares Cabral on the coast of Brazil in 1500, the Portuguese crown made its mark on the Americas.

Not to be left behind, the united Spanish crowns of Castile and Aragon also launched an expedition in 1492. Under the command of Cristobel Columbus, the purpose was to seek a shorter route to India, and, as Americans well know, they inadvertently stumbled on a whole new continent.

Using Cuba as a base, Spanish explorers continued to search through the mainland for sources of treasure as well as a shortcut to India. By 1513 Vasco Nuñez de Balboa had crossed the Isthmus of Panama and reached the Pacific Ocean. More importantly, Hernán Cortés left Cuba in a hurry in 1519 and began his conquest of Mexico.

Following in Cortés' footsteps, Francisco Pizarro set out to conquer the Incan empire in 1530. These adventurers were certainly driven by a desire to find new sources of wealth for their sovereigns, but most of all they were driven by a profound yearning to find the fame and fortune that was unattainable to them back home. In their quest for glory these explorers set in motion a bloody conquest.[3]

How these adventurers actually succeeded in taking over great empires is astonishing. For example, disobeying the orders of Cuban governor Diego Velásquez and backed by only about 550 soldiers and 16 horses, Hernán Cortés set sail in haste, escaping prison and arriving on the shores of Meso-America in February of 1519.

Within two years, Cortés and his forces dismantled the entire Aztec empire, gaining control of its territories. They did so by recognizing the biggest weakness of the young empire: the resentment of the newly subjugated peoples toward their new Aztec masters. They also exploited the legend of the return of Quetzalcoatl.

Most significantly, however, Cortés benefited from the pox epidemic that dominated the local population—an epidemic that the adventurers themselves had introduced.

The story of the conquest of the Incan empire was extraordinarily similar.

In 1527, Francisco Pizarro arrived in what is now Peru with his band of just 175 poorly armed men, finding the Incas in the middle of a civil war. They too, brought a pox, and it claimed the life of the Inca emperor, Huayna Capac, and his heir, leaving two half-brothers, Atahualpa and Huáscar, who fought for control of the empire.

By 1532 Atahualpa had emerged victorious. In 1533, Pizarro set a trap by asking Atahualpa and his men to meet with him unarmed, which Atahualpa agreed to. Pizarro then captured and held him for ransom. Once the ransom was paid, he executed Atahualpa, naming his brother Manco Capac as nominal ruler. By 1535, after looting the Incan empire, Pizarro consolidated his control over the Incas.

The Portuguese also profited from arriving in a time of turmoil. They landed in Porto Seguro (what is now Brazil) in 1500 while on their way to India. Unlike the organized and highly stratified Aztec or Incan empires, however, the native population that Álvares Cabral found was divided between hundreds of tribes and language groups across the Amazon Basin.

Cabral attempted to subjugate these populations by keeping them from uniting against him, an impossible feat. Yet in the end, just as in Mexico and Peru, the native population could not prevent the devastation caused by the diseases imported first by the Europeans, then by the African slaves brought in to work in their stead. In Brazil, what the force of arms could not achieve was accomplished by disease.[4]

The Era of Colonialism

Colonial Latin America emerged as a result of a violent and bloody process that decimated and subjugated existing populations while allowing Spain, and to a lesser degree Portugal, to become world powers.

As was true for all colonial powers worldwide at that time, Spain and Portugal imposed the policy of mercantilism on their colonies, distorting their trade and production patterns for hundreds of years to come.[5] The production and export of these commodities and primary goods were, and continue to be today, an important part of the economy of the region.

Throughout the mercantile era, LAC was forcibly bound to the European economies as a supplier of natural resources and primary products, suffering, as a result, from the many commodity booms and busts.

The new Portuguese properties lacked both mining resources and settled populations. Moreover, the Portuguese empire was commercial rather than colonial. Thus, to encourage an externally oriented global economy when they settled the Brazilian coast, the Portuguese first incorporated these territories as part of a maritime monarchy, awarding territory to the nobility through grants and trading licenses.

For a while, this approach was successful. The Portuguese crown supervised an economic system that imported and re-exported timber, sugar, and wine from Madeira and the Azores, gold from the Guinea coast, spices from India, and first dyewood and forest products then sugar, gold, gems, and hides from Brazil.

Over time, however, increasing French and Dutch competition for control on the continent forced the Portuguese to shift strategies from trading to sugar cultivation. Portugal adopted the colonial practices espoused by Spain that were already in place in Barbados, Cuba, Jamaica, and the south of the U.S. These territories had in common climates suitable for the production of extensive-scale economies, and African slaves were imported to replace the decimated local population.

In the New Spain, the Spanish conquistadors immediately imposed a strictly hierarchical society under the authority of a viceroy, the direct representative of the Spanish monarch. The viceroy was vested with executive, legislative, judicial, ecclesiastical, and military powers to rule over the colonies and supervise all traffic of goods and services between the colonies and Spain.

The viceroyalties imposed a rigid monopoly over the local economies and discouraged the production of goods that might compete with the Spanish economy.[6] Interestingly, while filling Spanish coffers, Latin America's precious metals revolutionized all the other European economies. In the rest of Europe, banking prospered, commerce expanded, and as a result of increasing demand, prices of precious metals (particularly silver) soared, especially in the Netherlands.

Ironically, Spain, known for its role in this economic system as "the basket of Europe," failed to reinvest the profits of this newfound wealth to strengthen its own economy and develop its industry.[7]

The colonial practices adopted by Spain and Portugal in the Americas created strictly stratified societies. In Brazil there were the *engenhos de açucar*, massive plantations based on an enslaved labor force. In New Spain there were haciendas (plantations) and *encomiendas*, where indigenous people were required to provide tribute and labor to the *encomenderos* or *hacendados*, who in turn were responsible for their welfare, acculturation, and Christianization. The Spanish absolutist system recognized some rights known as *fueros*, exercised by selected groups such as the Church, the *criollos*, or the military, and managed the native population through *caracas* or *caciques*, local native political bosses.

These institutions formed highly hierarchical societies where inequality became a permanent feature, prevalent not only among *encomenderos* or *hacendados* and the rest of the population but also among the elites.[8]

In due course, LAC established a caste society in which a small group of landowners, officials, and clergy ruled over large native and *mestizo* (born in the Americas from Spanish and Native American descent) populations. These inequalities also existed where government control rested in the hand of Spanish (born in Spain or *peninsulares*) or Portuguese envoys, whose rights and position were considered superior to those of the *criollos* or Creoles (born in the Americas from Spanish descent), the Spanish or Portuguese populations born in the Americas.

By the 1700s, Spain and Portugal were in irreversible decline.[9] In Spain, the effects of the general 1602 European recession and the Thirty Years' War (1618–1648) greatly affected its economy, provoking a distance between the Spanish crown and *criollos* and *mestizos* in the colonies who felt affected by these distant conflicts that had nothing to do with them.

With its economy collapsing, the Portuguese crown became increasingly dependent on England, while Brazil was becoming wealthier and more autonomous. Finally, in order to survive and keep the empire intact and as part of the 1703 War of the Spanish Succession, Portugal formally linked the Portuguese metropolitan and colonial economies to that of England through the Treaty of Methuen.

After three hundred years Spain and Portugal had failed to use their newfound colonial fortunes to modernize their internal structures and, by extension, the structures of their colonies, where local elites started thinking about the benefits of autonomy.[10]

During the eighteenth century the population of Spanish America was able to reverse the many losses that the conquest and colonization processes inflicted on them. Even Spain's isolated northern territories enjoyed a surge in agricultural and mining production. New towns and missions were founded in what are now California, Arizona, New Mexico, and Texas.[11] Finally, the American colonies were starting to grow, and to do so in a dramatic way.

Meanwhile, *criollo* elites had become aware of the relative freedom enjoyed by Britain's North American colonies, and witnessed their official gaining of independence in November 1783. The elites in New Spain also took note and could not help but become restless. They too yearned to gain some degree of autonomy or even full independence from the Spanish crown, which was in their view draining their resources without giving them much in return.

On the other side of the Atlantic, with the slogan "*Liberté, Egalité, Fraternité*," the French overthrew the ancient absolutist monarchy in 1787. Then, following suit in 1791, a group of black slaves led the Haitian slave revolt in the French colony of Hispaniola.

The birth of the United States of America and the republic of Haiti on one side of the Atlantic, together with the French Revolution and the advance of Napoleon Bonaparte in Europe, unleashed a wave of independence movements in the Americas.[12]

Napoleon, Europe, and Independence from Spain and Portugal

The discovery and colonization of the Americas linked Europe to their conquered lands so that a crisis on either side of the Atlantic ended up profoundly affecting both. Histories, cultures, and peoples were by then intimately intertwined.

Spain and Portugal were already starved for resources when Napoleon Bonaparte began advancing in Europe. In New Spain, *criollos* started showing signs of resentment when the Spanish crown started to assert its authority through the Bourbon reforms in order to replenish its coffers. The resentment became particularly acute when Spain decided to expel their educators, the Jesuit order.

Aside from the fact that they were keenly aware of the birth of two new states in the Americas (the United States and Haiti), the dissatisfaction among colonial elites reflected the growing influence that the European Enlightenment was having on everyone.[13]

Portugal, on the other hand, had been losing its gains in trade, metropolitan manufacture, financial institutions, and even population growth for some time, so much so that by the 1700s it was but an appendage of its colony in America. In order to be able to assert its power and authority over its empire, the Portuguese crown was forced to tie its fortune to that of England through the 1703 Methuen Treaty. This treaty obliged Portugal to reduce tariffs on English textiles in return for England's favored treatment of Portuguese wines.

Interestingly, this agreement came with a military component, compelling Portugal to participate in the War of the Spanish Succession on behalf of England against France and Spain; Napoleon Bonaparte retaliated by invading Portugal.

Once the French invaded, instead of defending their territory, the Portuguese court elite fled, escorted by English warships, to Rio de Janeiro, effectively exporting the Portuguese empire to Brazil. As a result of this, in 1807 Rio de Janeiro became the de facto capital of the Portuguese empire, thus accomplishing a peaceful transfer of independence with the de facto transfer of the monarchy.[14]

In 1808, after occupying Portugal, Napoleon and his French army proceeded to invade Spain. Taking advantage of a power struggle within the Bourbon dynasty, Napoleon captured and exiled King Ferdinand VII and placed his brother, Joseph Bonaparte, on the Spanish throne. The Spanish people rebelled against French control, offering yet another example of revolution to the Spanish Americans.

Most *criollos* initially remained loyal to Ferdinand VII, proclaiming independence in the Americas on his behalf. But some *criollos* and *mestizos* saw the Napoleonic conflicts as an opportunity to gain full independence.[15]

The original plan of the *criollo* leadership was to achieve a rather painless transition of power. Void of Spanish control, they aimed to take over their local governments and, if possible, adopt republican ideals without dramatically transforming their societies.[16] But this plan was flawed. The Latin American societies were very different from those of their British counterparts. The principles that inspired independence movements in New Spain needed to be adapted to colonial structures fit only to export commodities and primary goods.

These conditions meant that the new leaders in Spanish America needed to decide what to do about their populations, the majority of whom remained poor, subjugated, and without equitable legal rights. In the leaders' view, the majority of citizens—*mestizos*, Indians, and black slaves—weren't capable of participating equally in the new economic and political order.

The reality was that the new leaders of Latin American independence found it difficult to embrace U.S. republican and French revolutionary ideals while maintaining their privileged status and property rights.

There was a liberal faction of *criollos* and *mestizos* in support of fully independent representative republics, but the majority of conservative landowning elites who had participated in the struggle were reluctant to implement changes to the existing social structure. Landowning elites did not fully support these governments, which remained weak and ineffective and in dire need of strong men to keep the peace. A strong government was deemed unnecessary because once the conflict ended, *criollo* landowners returned to their estates, which functioned as self-sufficient units providing them with both power and autonomy. As soon as a particular strong man or *caudillo* became too powerful, the *criollo* landowners would rise up and seek *mestizo* support to topple them. This established a conflict of interests that would define the nature of politics all over the region.[17]

In order to gain autonomy, the colonial elites had first enlisted the support of black slaves and more importantly, *mestizos*, using independence from Spain as a common cause. When all was said and done, however, the Spanish American elites (even those within the liberal factions) did not really consider these groups to be worthy of equal rights. In their view, the ideals of the Enlightenment and self-government were meant to be exclusive.

As a result of this fundamental disagreement, two factions, liberal and conservative, would emerge as polarizing political parties that became a permanent feature of Latin American societies, politics, and governments—to this day.

The Napoleonic Wars inspired Latin American elites to seek independence that, once achieved, had disastrous consequences for Spain and Portugal.

By failing to evolve, and without the riches provided by their colonies, these empires began to crumble. By 1824, following the Napoleonic adventure, Spain had lost all of its mainland territories, retaining only Cuba and Puerto Rico. Moreover, by 1826, after prolonged fighting, Spanish America finally became independent, while the Portuguese empire had already been (de facto if not de jure) exported to Brazil.[18]

Into this new world order the British Empire, France, and eventually the U.S. emerged as world powers ready and able to take advantage of a new phenomenon: the Industrial Revolution. This required new sources of supply for raw materials.

To satisfy the demand for commodities and primary goods for their newly built factories, these more advanced economies turned once again to Latin America. The newly independent nations possessed vast natural resources coveted by industrializing nations, but they lacked the capacity to fully take advantage of either.

The two sides of the Atlantic became even more interdependent and the nature of LAC economies was set for a significant time to come.

In the increasingly integrated world economy being shaped by the Industrial Revolution, LAC colonial social structures were only geared to extract and export natural resources or, at best, produce and export agricultural or primary goods. This left Latin Americans at a disadvantage, unable to participate on equal terms with more industrializing societies that were developing a manufacturing capacity. This is why Latin America experienced negligible economic growth.[19]

Instead of developing mechanized power, the new Latin American economies (like the southern U.S.) remained linked to external sources of demand and supply and relied on the large-scale production of staples by a large, coerced labor force.[20]

The inability to rapidly transform LAC economic structures reflected the nature of *criollo* elites, who either couldn't or wouldn't address the social inequity in their new nations. This growing gap was replicated in the political arena, as liberals and conservatives kept fighting instead of compromising. Governments remained weak while disputes continued.

Instead of building necessary infrastructure such as railroads or durable institutions such as courts, militaries, or police, elites clashed over whether their countries should become monarchies or republics and whether their regimes should be parliamentary or presidential, centralized or federalist, liberal or conservative.

Most importantly, however, elites continued to oppose measures that promoted more egalitarian values in line with the industrialized societies they were supposedly trying to emulate. The protracted process of creating these separate and independent countries left only one stable institution in place: the large land estate.[21]

As a result, instead of compromise and gradual state formation, the history of LAC during the nineteenth century was defined by coups, revolts, and constant interruptions of power, leaving these emerging states fragmented and vulnerable to outside intervention by both the U.S. and Europe.

Mexico, for example, was overwhelmed by battles between liberal and conservative factions, which left the country divided and without effective government or central control. This is why the northern part of the Mexican state of Coahuila and Tejas (Texas) decided to declare its independence from the government of President Antonio López de Santa Anna.

To protect its borders, the U.S. Congress voted to annex the Texas Republic, sending troops led by General Zachary Taylor to the Rio Grande in December 1845. The inevitable clashes between Mexican troops and U.S. forces provided the justification for the U.S. invasion that resulted in Mexico losing more than half of its territory, an event that resonates in the Mexican collective memory to this day.[22]

In the Southern Cone, the Republic of Gran Colombia was also being torn apart by internal strife. It eventually broke down when persistent confrontations between *caudillos* (strongmen) and political factions revealed the instability of the state; even Simón Bolívar could not keep it whole.[23] The Central American Federation fared no better. By 1841, plagued by the conflict between liberals and conservatives, the leaders partitioned their federation into five countries.[24]

The new Empire of Brazil collapsed in a series of regionalist revolts under Pedro I, leaving the monarchy effectively neutralized. Then, in 1840, at the age of fourteen, Pedro II was called to the throne. By encouraging coffee production instead of sugar and by making significant gains in railroad, telegraph, and cable construction, Pedro II established Brazil as a viable nation.

In contrast to the rest of LAC, Pedro II successfully headed over 36 different cabinets as a constitutional monarch. He did so by astutely alternating support between the Liberal and Conservative parties, ensuring that both enjoyed an equal amount of time in power and providing orderly, nonviolent transitions between them.

Neither party, however, was an accurate reflection of the interests of the many different groups in Brazil. The Liberal and Conservative parties only

THE INSERTION OF LAC IN WORLD HISTORY

represented the landholding oligarchy and as a result the Brazilian Congress never really addressed issues that affected other sectors of Brazilian society.[25]

Argentina, on the other hand, developed as a rural economy based on wage goods coming from the *estancias*. These goods, derived from cattle and agriculture, were brought to Buenos Aires for processing, readied for consumption and export. This economic structure created a rivalry between two elite groups: the rural *estancieros* and the urban and more industrial *porteños*.

During the early years of the nineteenth century this rivalry between the more modernized province of Buenos Aires and the rest of the country began to adversely affect economic progress and political stability. This was only resolved—at the expense of democratic institutions—when the *caudillo* Juan Manuel de Rosas became the unchallenged dictator of Argentina.

His downfall came only when he tried to forcefully incorporate Uruguay and Paraguay, prompting an international intervention by Britain and France. Nevertheless, a precedent had been set.

Fueled by admiration for those who pursued and killed the native population only to replace them with European immigrants, the *caudillo* tradition remained strong.

Even when the Republic of Argentina began to turn itself into an exporter of staple goods, its preference for authoritarianism and *caudillo* figures made the nation—one of the most developed and wealthy countries in the Americas at the outset of the twentieth century—into a quintessential cautionary tale.[26]

Dealing with constant rebellion, political instability, and mounting public debts paired with poor taxation, LAC governments and institutions remained weak. Ever-changing administrations, framed by constantly shifting constitutions that seemed out of touch, needed to fend off external interventions while trying to maintain a semblance of order.

To that end, governments tuned to strong authoritarian figures or *caudillos* who were able to take the reins of government by force and find the money and government positions to reward their followers.[27] By not paying attention to the important task of building strong finances and government institutions, these men and the elites behind them became complicit in keeping their executive, legislative, judicial, and military institutions weak.[28]

In its quest to play a major role on the world stage, the region faced significant obstacles as a result of its internal structural limitations. As rule-takers in a rapidly changing global economic system that was contingent on their geography and geological diversity, Latin Americans would concentrate on developing economies based upon extraction, processing (when possible), and transportation of their primary products to the closest exit port. The proceeds would allow for the acquisition of capital and consumer goods from more developed countries.

Whether this state of affairs was a blessing or a curse depended on what kind of commodities the nation in question possessed; it was like a lottery, determining the way in which a country was ultimately linked to the world economy. In other words, the type of economy a country developed depended upon the type of commodities available to it to either extract or extract and process.

Depending upon the resources they possessed, countries adopted one of two strategies. The first required further processing of a product, locally, before export. This was the case with Argentina. In processing meat, it developed linkages to other sectors of the local economy, stimulating some industrial development and urbanization. A second strategy was the one used by Central America (bananas) and Peru (guano), which required extraction and immediate export, offering little or no stimulus to other local industries or urbanization.

Furthermore, even if commodities only required extraction, nations still needed luck in the lottery, because some commodities were far more valuable than others. Countries like Mexico had oil and gold, which had no substitute and for which there was steady demand. Other countries, many of them in the Caribbean, depended on commodities such as cotton, which regularly faced competition from other fabrics, resulting in price fluctuation.[29]

Economic underdevelopment coupled with endemic inequality and weak state institutions left LAC states vulnerable to foreign intervention.

Spain, for example, made an unsuccessful attempt in the 1860s to re-establish colonial rule in the Dominican Republic and the islands off the coast of Peru, succeeding only in putting down an independence struggle in Cuba between 1868 and 1878. In the end, it kept Cuba and Puerto Rico as its only colonial foothold in the Americas.

In 1861, France took advantage of the U.S. Civil War and invaded Mexico. With the support of the conservatives, Napoleon III imposed Maximilian of Hapsburg as emperor, supported by French troops. By 1872, however, once the U.S. conflict was over, the U.S. helped Benito Juárez return to power and restore the republic.

Furthermore, territorial disputes (including the tragic War of the Triple Alliance between Argentina, Brazil and Uruguay against Paraguay, 1865–1870) only exacerbated the difficult position of Latin American states.[30]

Nevertheless, by the end of the nineteenth century, things began to improve.

Latin America's Importance During the Era of Corporate Capitalism

By the late 1800s, Latin Americans found themselves in a stable regional environment that was linked even more closely to the rest of the world. The spread of railroads, steamships, telegraph, refrigeration, and other technology revolutionized production, distribution, transportation, and trade. It also provided the basis for a truly global financial market, all of which served to bind Latin America ever more tightly to the international system and, more importantly, to the U.S.

This affluence was again led by a large global demand for commodities that Latin American states were able to produce, trade, and transport more efficiently. From wool, wheat, meat, and hides from Argentina to nitrates from Chile, Peru, and Bolivia and coffee and rubber from Brazil, Latin America was able to take advantage of the world's prosperity, even with the boom and bust cycles normal in a commodities market.

By the beginning of the twentieth century, the conditions in Latin America were improving to such a degree that immigrants from all over the world began to arrive in great numbers. These immigration waves not only fueled the economic expansion of their host countries but more importantly served to create new ties between populations around the globe, fostering economic synergy and trade.

Between 1870 and 1914 (referred to by many as the first era of globalization and by others as the era of corporate capitalism), the government of country after country in LAC transitioned from authoritarian colonial regime to authoritarian republic in a more modern setting. Latin American nations became presidential states in which political freedoms were suppressed, while local oligarchies, which were tied to foreign interests, benefited from the rapid worldwide economic expansion.[31]

Thanks to its success in achieving greater stability by providing the rule of law and upholding property rights, Latin America was able to contribute to a period of rapid economic growth with Britain and U.S. at the forefront. The U.S. in particular, emerging victorious after the Spanish-American war, continued to reassert its authority in the continent, such as during the border dispute between British Guiana and Venezuela, or throughout Panamanian independence efforts, in order to control the construction and management of the Panama Canal.[32]

As in the case of U.S. intervention in Central America to protect the interests of the United Fruit Company (with the excuse of keeping order and stability in the region), LAC became the region where the U.S. exercised its hegemonic power and tried out foreign policy doctrines (sometimes by force) before implementing them elsewhere.

Essentially, LAC became a testing ground for the U.S. It would extract acquiescence from Latin American authorities by using foreign investment and financial aid—without excluding the possibility of military intervention.

Latin America, the Caribbean and the American Century

What followed was the well-known story of two world wars and a catastrophic global depression that Latin America was not entirely able to avoid.

By the end of the 1920s, Latin American countries had fallen prey to the frequent devaluations that were making imports more expensive. LAC economies should have reaped some benefit because their cheaper currencies made their products more attractive and competitive for export. But instead of reaching a broader market, their exports encountered greater protectionism from industrialized nations, leading to a significant drop in their earnings.

This protectionist stance forced many Latin American countries to start making changes in favor of developing domestic consumption for their local manufacturing industries. Consequently, between 1914 and 1945, LAC became better prepared to ride the disruption of World War II by developing modern industrialization sectors to satisfy domestic demand.

The growth in manufacturing based on domestic consumption and the protection of local manufacturing was at first mainly driven by international circumstances. Monumental shifts such as the weakening of the British Empire and the end of the old international economic system based on the gold standard, were profoundly changing the geopolitical landscape in both economic and political terms. A new international economy began to emerge.

This new structure was based on foreign exchange rates and a system of tariffs that made imports more difficult and expensive to obtain and domestic manufacturing more attractive. Gradually, protectionism was seen as a way to further domestic consumption and manufacturing, and as a result, tariffs began to rise as a matter of policy.

By the end of World War II it became clear that the corporate capitalism model of the "golden age" had run its course and a new corporate model gradually took its place. The ideas of John Keynes, emphasizing the role of the state in the economy through different spending strategies and social programs, swept the industrializing world and formed the basis for many of the strategies that were tried during the twentieth century.

Seen as social contracts, "New Deals," or in the case of Latin America, as part of the Import Substitution Industrialization (ISI) policies, these different development plans aimed to create a global environment in which state interventions could establish an environment of certainty.

With the defeat of fascism, the aftermath of World War II paved the way for a power shift from Europe to the Americas, specifically to the U.S. A new world paradigm began to materialize, heralding the benefits of a mixed economy and the establishment of an institutional framework that could facilitate coordination and cooperation.

In response, Latin America was forced to switch from an economy based on commodity exports to a model based on fixed foreign exchanges, import substitution, and protection for small local manufactures. After World War II, the policies that originated during the Great Depression as a collection of defensive measures began to coalesce into a highly coherent plan of economic development.

Known as Import Substitution Industrialization (ISI), this strategy was adopted by LAC as the main post-war policy for economic development. It is interesting to note that the defensive measures LAC was forced to enact during and after World War I provided the basis for what was to become a Latin American doctrine.

Nevertheless, LAC still faced significant obstacles before it could emerge as an important player in world affairs. In spite of its enviable location and its efforts to develop some local industrial capacity, LAC economies still depended heavily on the primary production of oil, minerals, and agricultural commodities.

The greatest obstacles to Latin America's emergence as a key region, however, were internal and political, inheritance of a complicated history. These obstacles—deeply rooted social and political exclusion, weak political institutions and rule of law, and an engrained authoritarian streak—would continue to erode not only the region's economic competitiveness but also its democratic practices and institutions.

These obstacles combined—LAC's proximity and close relationship to the U.S., overwhelming dependence on commodities to foster economic growth, acute inequality and political exclusion, and the nature of internal politics that rendered governments weak—have made LAC the eternal land of promise, a region that has yet to achieve its full potential.

Main points:

- As a result of European discovery and conquest, Latin Americans inserted in world economic structure as "rule-takers."
- The land structures established in colonial Spain and Portugal establish unequal societies and economies based on commodities and primary goods.
- After independence, landowners, and wealthy *criollos* (creoles, Spanish descent) and *peninsulares* (Spanish born) support the development of weak governments dependent of *caudillos* that can be deposed when too powerful.

Notes

1 Karl Marx, *The Eighteenth Brumaire of Louis Bonaparte*, 1852 (www.marxists.org/archive/marx/works/1852/18th-brumaire/ch01.htm).
2 William I. Robinson, *Latin America and Global Capitalism* (Baltimore, MD: Johns Hopkins University Press, 2008), 6–20, examines the relationship of Latin America to the rest of the world in terms of the dynamic of expansion built into capitalism, both extensively and intensively. He posits that today's "global moment" is the product of a capitalist system that has developed through different stages—namely, the mercantile, competitive industrial, and corporate or monopoly epochs of evolution. Each epoch succeeded in expanding the system further and linking more member-states through capitalist institutions.

WHY DO LATIN AMERICA AND THE CARIBBEAN MATTER?

3   There are many accounts that deal with the Spanish and Portuguese explorations and conquests. Two examples are Stanley J. Stein and Barbara H. Stein, *The Colonial Heritage of Latin America* (New York: Oxford University Press, 1970) and Eric R. Wolf, *Europe and the People Without History* (Berkeley, CA and London: Berkeley University Press, 1997).

4   Rex A. Hudson, *Brazil: A Country Study*, 5th edition (Washington: GPO for the Library of Congress, Library of Congress Federal research Division, October 1998).

5   The Merriam-Webster dictionary defines mercantilism as an economic system developing during the breakdown of feudalism to unify and increase the power and especially the monetary wealth of a nation by strict governmental regulation of the entire national economy, usually through policies designed to secure an accumulation of bullion, a favorable balance of trade, the development of agriculture and manufactures, and the establishment of foreign trading monopolies. Colonial possessions suffer the imposition of trade restrictions that benefit the dominant nation. Portugal imposed mercantilist policies that were similar to Spain's, but the fact that mineral wealth was not discovered initially resulted in the early development of a colony based primarily on producing agricultural products such as sugar or tobacco. Because of this, the mercantilist policies of the Portuguese crown were never as rigorous as the ones imposed on the rest of Latin America. Moreover, these policies ended much sooner because of the trade relations between Brazil, Portugal, and the U.K. Reyes and Sawyer, *Latin American Economic Development* (New York: Routledge, 2011).

6   In contrast to their British counterparts, the Spanish and Portuguese conquistadors were mostly uneducated *hidalgos* or lower-rank members of the military who had fought and expelled the Muslims to unite the kingdoms of Seville and Granada and continued fighting during the Counter-Reformation. Consequently, they brought with them a militarized feudalism and intolerant Catholicism and imposed a system of full control over the surviving conquered native peoples in a strictly hierarchical society. The new Spanish possessions, both in the Caribbean and on the mainland, came under the centralized authority of Spanish viceroyalties and were strictly monitored by envoys or *visitadores*. At first the new Spanish territories were divided between the viceroyalties of New Spain and Peru, both established in 1535. The viceroyalty of New Spain included what are now Mexico, Central America, Florida, and the southern United States. The viceroyalty of Peru included present-day Chile, Argentina, Bolivia, Peru, Ecuador, Colombia, Venezuela, and Panama. Later on, the viceroyalty of Peru was subdivided, creating in 1717 the viceroyalty of New Granada and, in 1776, the viceroyalty of La Plata. To impose Spanish economic protectionism, all commercial endeavors to and from their new territories were centralized and monopolized through the House of Trade or *Casa de Contratación de Sevilla*. Furthermore, the Spanish crown established a special body of laws to manage and subjugate the native population: the *Leyes de Indias*. In so doing, through large amounts of forced labor (*mitas*), the viceroyalties provided Spain with gold from places like Colombia and, most importantly, silver, mostly from Mexico and Potosí. Hudson, *Brazil: A Country Study*.

7   Instead of reinvesting its profits to strengthen their economy, Spain used its silver to pay for Asian goods and other luxuries for its kings and nobles. Most importantly, large amounts of the silver were used to pay for the costly Spanish wars, campaigns against heresy, and the administration of its global empire. Stein and Stein, *The Colonial Heritage*; Wolf, *Europe and the People*.

8   Stein and Stein, *The Colonial Heritage*; Hudson, *Brazil: A Country Study*. Also Stanley L. Engerman and Kenneth L. Sokoloff, *Economic Development in the*

THE INSERTION OF LAC IN WORLD HISTORY

Americas since 1500: Endowments and Institutions, NBER Series in Long-Term Factors in Economic Developments (New York: Cambridge University Press, 2012).

9 By the end of the eighteenth century, the effects of the reforms and tightening of financial controls introduced during the Bourbon regimes of Carlos III and Carlos IV had started to strain their economies.

10 By the late 17th century, taking advantage of Spain and Portugal's weaknesses, English, Dutch, and French raiders started targeting Spanish trading ships that had to stop in the Caribbean. By 1638, with an expanding worldwide empire, the British occupied what is now Belize. Then in 1670 England took over control of Jamaica, a center of Caribbean raiding, piracy, and bootlegging. In addition, the English, Dutch, and French all occupied Guiana—what is now Suriname, French Guiana, and Guyana.

11 That is why in 1762, as a result of the British victory in the Seven Years War, Spain ceded Florida to Britain. In exchange and as compensation, Spain received from France the huge territory of Louisiana. To counteract British expansion in the Americas, France and Spain allied again in 1779 to support the American Revolution against Britain. Interestingly, following Britain's loss, Spain recovered Florida.

12 Influenced by the events in North America and, more importantly, the Declaration of the Rights of Man and of the Citizen in France, the slave majority rose under the leadership of a religious leader called Boukman on August 22, 1791. By January 1, 1804, after a bloody revolution, Haiti, the second republic in the Western Hemisphere, was born. For more see Laurent Dubois, *Haiti: The Aftershocks of History* (New York: Metropolitan Books, Henry Holt and Company, 2012).

13 For example, between 1780 and 1783 in Peru, a *mestizo* leader José Gabriel Condorcanqui, taking the name Túpac Amarú, launched a rebellion that was difficult to suppress. In Nueva Granada, the *visitador* Juan Francisco Gutiérrez de Piñeres (an inspector sent by the Spanish crown), encountered violence and unrest provoked by increasing Spanish taxation. By 1781, this violence had spread and turned into widespread upheaval, the insurgents succeeding in occupying Bogotá. This turmoil was exacerbated even further by the poor response by Spain to the British naval blockades that followed the 1763 British occupation of Havana. Feeling pressured and neglected, *criollos* and *mestizos* grew restless. For more see *The Cambridge History of Latin America: Volume I, The Colonia Era and the Short Nineteenth Century* and *The Cambridge History of Latin America: Volume II: The Long Twentieth Century,* ed. Victor Bulmer-Thomas, John Coastworth, Roberto Cortes-Conde (Cambridge and New York: Cambridge University Press, 2006); Victor Bulmer-Thomas, *The Economic History of Latin America since Independence,* 3rd edition (New York: Cambridge University Press, 2014).

14 Once established in Rio and granting preferential tariffs to Britain, King João opened Brazil's trade, effectively abolishing Portugal's monopoly in its American territories. As a result, Brazil opened up not only to commerce with other countries but also to visitations by foreign scholars and, more importantly, immigration. Finally, in 1821, the British persuaded King João to return to Portugal as a constitutional monarch, which he did, but not before leaving his elder son, Pedro, on the throne in Brazil. Once in charge, King Pedro successfully resisted Portugal's efforts to reinstate previous economic restrictions. Celebrating his triumph and being proclaimed Pedro I, Emperor of Brazil, Pedro declared Brazil's independence in 1822. Hudson, *Brazil: A Country Study*;

WHY DO LATIN AMERICA AND THE CARIBBEAN MATTER?

Thomas E. Skidmore and Peter H. Smith, *Modern Latin America* (Oxford and New York: Oxford University Press, 2005).

15 Independence declarations on behalf of the Spanish king started to be pronounced in 1810 in Argentina and Mexico, followed by the peoples and town councils of Caracas. By 1811, many other cities including Cartagena and Bogotá in Colombia, Santiago in Chile, and Quito in Ecuador were following their example. But these independence movements were not homogeneous. Hudson, *Brazil: A Country Study*; Stein and Stein, *The Colonial Heritage*; Engerman and Sokoloff, *Economic Development in the Americas*.

16 Beginning in 1810, Miguel Hidalgo y Costilla followed by José María Morelos y Pavón in Mexico, Francisco de Miranda and Simón Bolívar in what is now Venezuela, Colombia, and Ecuador, Bernardo O'Higgins and José de San Martín in Chile and Peru, José Gervasio Artigas in Uruguay, and Antonio José de Sucre y Alcalá in Peru and Alto Peru (Bolivia) started fighting to achieve some sort of autonomy with the Spanish *criollo* class at the helm. Fernando López-Alvez, *State Formation and Democracy in Latin America, 1810–1900* (Durham, NC and London: Duke University Press, 2000), Stein and Stein, *The Colonial Heritage*.

17 These social structures based on autonomous and independent rural units (such as the *haciendas*) afforded few channels for social mobility for *mestizos* who, inspired by the examples of the U.S., French and Haitian revolutions and Enlightenment ideals, were looking for advancement in their new countries. *Criollo* leaders had recruited them to fight against the metropolis, making military skill the means by which *mestizo* groups could gain social recognition. As a result, the military, government service, and political arenas became the routes for the *mestizo* class to attain social advancement. This social dynamic explains much of the turbulence during the nineteenth century, which was characterized by a strange vicious cycle. The new republics finished the wars of independence with military establishments led and supported by *mestizos* who, to get ahead, needed to stay in the army or move to serve in government. Landowning elites did not fully support these governments, thus rendering them weak and ineffective and in dire need of strong men to keep the peace. A strong government was deemed unnecessary because once the conflict had concluded, *criollo* landowners returned to their *haciendas*, which functioned as self-sufficient units providing them power, and autonomy. As soon as the strong man or *caudillo* and his government became too powerful, the *criollo* landowners would rise up and seek *mestizo* support to topple the regime. This pattern would play itself out time and again after internal conflicts or inter-state confrontations and wars were concluded. In the tradition of colonial *cacicasgos*, once the sources of conflict, internal or external, were resolved through military means, landed elites left government tasks to the *caudillos* as dictators and *mestizos* as government officials.

18 Despite the victory of Spanish America, success remained elusive. Fighting among local and regional factions in what were essentially civil wars complicated the final goals of the Spanish American elites. These independence movements may have achieved separation from the Spanish crown but they failed when aiming for unified and stable states. The unification ideals of Simón Bolívar never materialized, and the Mexican empire under Agustín de Iturbide failed after two years. Even more so, the Central American landed *criollo* class, which had at first decided to come under Iturbide's jurisdiction, backtracked as soon as Iturbide abdicated in 1823, while Guadalupe Victoria and Antonio López de Santa Anna declared Mexico a republic. Central American elites in the modern-day Central American states from Guatemala to Costa Rica (Panama was part of

THE INSERTION OF LAC IN WORLD HISTORY

Gran Colombia) then opted to join and form the independent United Provinces of Central America. Skidmore and Smith, *Modern Latin America*, 32–4.

19 The Pampas region of Argentina (cattle hides and wool) and copper-rich Chile probably began growing earlier than Brazil and the other former Spanish colonies. However, Mexican GDP per capita fell substantially. Bulmer-Thomas, Coastworth, and Cortés Conde, *The Cambridge History of Latin America*, vols I and II.

20 In contrast, the northern U.S. and Canada had, over time, promoted balanced agricultural, ranching, and industrial diversification, structures that proved conducive to democratic development and consolidation. Stein and Stein, *The Colonial Heritage*, 135.

21 After independence, the new Latin American countries continued to be linked to the European economies through their agricultural and mining production exports. The new Spanish American republics faced great difficulties as they embarked on independence during the 1820s. Still, by the 1830s, 19 independent nations had been born in the Americas. Canada and most of the Caribbean remained under British, French, and Spanish rule. On the Central and South American mainland, British Honduras (Belize) and the Guineas (English, Dutch, and French) remained as colonial enclaves. Victor Bulmer-Thomas, *The Economic History of Latin America since Independence*, 2nd edition (Cambridge: Cambridge University Press, 2003).

22 The clashes between Mexican forces and U.S. troops provided the justification for a Congressional declaration of war on May 13, 1846, and in August of 1847, U.S. forces captured Mexico City. The end of this war still resonates within the nation of Mexico. On February 2, 1848, the Treaty of Guadalupe Hidalgo was signed. It provided that Mexico cede 55 percent of its territory, present-day Arizona, California, New Mexico, Colorado, Nevada, and Utah, in exchange for ten million dollars as compensation for war-related damage to Mexican property. For more see Daniel C. Levy and Kathleen Bruhn, *Mexico, The Struggle for Democratic Development* (Berkeley and Los Angeles: University of California Press, 2006).

23 Gran Colombia, originally comprising Colombia, Panama, Venezuela, and Ecuador, was organized at the Congress of Cúcuta in 1821 as a centralized representative republic with its capital in Bogotá. Continual local confrontations between *caudillos* and political factions showed the instability of the state. Not even Simón Bolívar could keep Gran Colombia whole. Secession movements like José de Sucre's in Peru and Alto Peru (Bolivia) in 1825 and rebellions such as José Antonio Páez's in Venezuela in 1826 tore Gran Colombia apart. After ruling as dictator from 1828 to 1830, Bolívar tried to appease the dissenters, calling for a convention to frame a new constitution, but to no avail, and by 1830 the end of Gran Colombia put an end to Bolívar's dream. For more see John Lynch, *Simon Bolivar: A Life* (New Haven, CT: Yale University Press, 2006).

24 Afflicted by the conflict between liberals and conservatives, the leaders of these nations abandoned their unification ideals, partitioning their federation into five countries and leading them toward fragmentation and chronic instability (Bulmer-Thomas, 2003, 2–15; Skidmore and Smith, *Modern Latin America*, 36–40).

25 Even though Brazil succeeded in remaining whole, its political leadership failed to include the still subjugated and poor majority. Finally, unable to change his way of ruling, weakened by illness, and increasingly marginal to public affairs, Pedro II was overthrown by a military coup in 1889. Hudson, *Brazil: A Country Study*.

26 During the beginning of the nineteenth century, the fierce rivalry between the relatively more modern province of Buenos Aires and the rest of the country

31

began to spin out of control, making federalism a contentious issue for Argentina. This rivalry was resolved at the expense of democratic institutions when the *caudillo* Juan Manuel de Rosas returned victorious in 1835 (from the wars against the Indians) as an unchallenged dictator. His downfall only came when he tried to incorporate the provinces of Paraguay and Uruguay, which prompted France, Britain, Uruguay and Paraguay to declare war on Rosas, defeating him in 1854. At that moment, the Republic of Argentina was recognized by a new constitution under the government of Justo José Urquiza, yet the *caudillo* tradition remained strong in Argentina, fueled by admiration for those who pursued and exterminated the Indian populations in the Pampas. In need of labor, the Republic of Argentina fomented immigration, aiming to try and develop as a European society, while in the Argentinean Pampas the only indigenous inhabitants left were being exterminated. By 1879, the remaining Indians were either killed or driven south into Patagonia in a campaign commanded by General Julio Roca, who in 1880 (thanks to these extermination campaigns) was elected as president with dictatorial powers. The Republic of Argentina began to develop as an exporter of staple goods, but the lack of vision would eventually catch up with the nation's elite. A lack of investment in industrial development and infrastructure together with the fear of the spread of communism among urban workers propelled political elites to curtail political freedom and participation. Their economic short-sightedness and their preference and support for a dictatorial system under the command of *caudillos* such as Roca made Argentina one of the Americas' most developed and wealthy countries at the end of the nineteenth century, a quintessential cautionary tale of the twenty-first century. John Lynch, *Argentine Caudillo, Juan Manuel de Rosas* (Oxford: Rowan & Littlefield, 2001).

27 Support for a lawful resolution of disputes was not seen as a priority by *criollo* landowners who possessed their own autonomous production units and were ultimately making the political decisions. As soon as these strong bosses or dictators started abusing their power and going against the interests of the landed elites, *hacendados* and *estancieros* would leave their properties to topple and replace them. Without much thought given to the importance of building strong functioning states or to writing constitutions that would respond to their countries' needs, Latin American elites kept supporting governments that would respond only to their immediate interests, hindering the establishment of truly functioning governments and bureaucracies and exacerbating the perennial inequality that is so characteristic of Latin America even today. Skidmore and Smith, *Modern Latin America.*

28 Instead of looking for ways to develop peaceful alternations of power, landed elites and the *caudillos* they supported became entangled in the same cycle of violence each time they became dissatisfied, leaving their countries vulnerable to outside intervention. Skidmore and Smith, *Modern Latin America.*

29 Victor Bulmer-Thomas, *The Economic History of Latin America since Independence*, 2nd edition (Cambridge: Cambridge University Press, 2003), 14–15.

30 Under Francisco Solano López, Paraguay suffered a devastating defeat and was allowed to survive as an independent country only after losing some of its territory and most of its adult male population. Bolivia also suffered dearly by joining Peru in the War of the Pacific (1879–1883). As a result of their defeat, Bolivia became landlocked by losing its Pacific coastline. Along with Peru, Bolivia lost territory to Chile that was rich in nitrates. Bulmer-Thomas, *The Economic History of Latin America since Independence*, 48.

31 Britain and the U.S. in particular, provided the much-needed Foreign Direct Investment (FDI) in exchange for the political stability imposed by Latin American autarkies, with some measure of success. From 1870 to roughly 1930, the eight major economies of Latin America grew at a rate roughly equal to that of the U.S. overall. In fact, until World War II, the big eight Latin American economies grew faster than the average of all the advanced countries that later formed the Organization for Economic Co-operation and Development (OECD). But true to its contradictory nature, this growth did not trickle down to the population at large and thus the inequality plaguing Latin American populations persisted. John Coastworth, "Economic History of Latin America," in *Handbook of Latin American History*, ed. José C. Moya (New York: Oxford University Press, 2010), 407–423.

32 Under the peace agreement signed in December 1898, Cuba became independent and the United States gained sovereignty over Puerto Rico. The Philippines and Guam (Spanish colonies in Asia and the Pacific) also became U.S. protectorates. After the Spanish American War the U.S. continued to reassert its authority in the continent. In 1899, the U.S. forced Britain, already under pressure with the Boer War in South Africa, to compromise in the border dispute between British Guiana and Venezuela. The U.S. was increasingly able to assert its influence in the hemisphere while Latin America was once again falling behind. Furthermore, the U.S. was able to reassert control in the region when, in 1903, it supported the independence of Panama and asserted control over the construction and management of the Panama Canal. Bulmer-Thomas, *The Economic History of Latin America since Independence*, 46–50.

3

A THEORETICAL FRAMEWORK TO UNDERSTAND LATIN AMERICA IN WORLD AFFAIRS

> Political science falls into four parts: first, the individual man's governance of himself; second, the governance of the household; third, the governance of the city; and fourth, the governance of the large nation or of the nations.
>
> Moses Maimonides, *Logic* (1160)[1]

Introduction

One way to make sense of the complex social reality we live in is to utilize theories. Essentially, theories are tools that aim to make sense of our complex reality by offering a simplified version of any given aspect of the human story.[2]

The tool to better understand how nations relate to each other is the collection of explanations offered by International Relations (IR). As a relatively new discipline, IR resorts to a variety of theoretical approaches, some from IR itself, some from other disciplines such as history, economics, sociology and even psychology. IR combines them in order to pinpoint any given problem they deem necessary to address. Together, they function as frameworks that help clarify the main issues influencing world affairs, allowing for a better understanding of the facts.

Because of the complexity of our social reality and because IR is a relatively young discipline, few academics or decision-makers either believe in or lean on any individual theory. Nor do they think that by explaining one single phenomenon, problem, threat, or issue they can explain the entirety of a complex social structure. In other words, IR theories are almost always internally and externally contested.

To offer an explanation of any given issue affecting world affairs and gain a better understanding of the international environment as a whole, academics and policy-makers tend to emphasize the use of one of the following: power, economic interests, or ideological beliefs.[3]

34

A THEORETICAL FRAMEWORK

Realism

For Realists, the international system is defined by anarchy, or the absence of central authority.[4] States are sovereign, autonomous units, and it's not possible for any cohesive international structure to oversee them. They can only be bound by coercion or their own consent.

In such an anarchic system, state power is the only variable of interest because it's the only factor that allows independent states to defend themselves and aid in their own survival. Realism and its variants such as structural Realism, Neorealism, and coercive/defensive Realism explain power in a variety of ways, all of which translate into strong states forcing weaker states to (paraphrasing Thucydides) do what they must. Put simply, through Realism, coercive material capacity, which is the determinant of international politics, can be understood in terms of military capacity, economic might, or even diplomatic capabilities.

Although all (structural Realists, Neorealists, and the offensive or defensive variations) agree that power is what best helps us explain world affairs, Realists diverge in their belief about the way power influences human conduct. The offensive Realists for example, maintain that in order to ensure survival, states will seek to maximize their power relative to others. So, to be safe, a state needs to pursue a strategy of hegemony. Defensive Realists, on the other hand, believe that domination is an unwise strategy for survival. Hegemony is a strategy that can only bring constant conflict among states, and to avoid it, defensive Realists emphasize the benefits of seeking a balance of power among states, diminishing the risk of war.[5]

Put simply, power, whether seen through the lens of polarity or distribution of power, is a key concept for Realist theories—a concept that renders a dim view of international law and institutions. In their view, these rules cannot contain behavior unless they can offer a direct benefit to the states' material interests.[6]

The pessimistic Realist vision of the world rests on four assumptions. First, survival is the principal goal of the state and as a result, foreign invasions and occupations are the most pressing threats a state can face. Even when domestic interests, a shared history, commitment to national ideals, or prevalent cultural norms offer cooperative goals, the anarchic nature of the international system requires that states constantly ensure that they have enough power to defend themselves. States needs to advance the material interests necessary for survival above all else. Second, Realists hold states to be rational actors, meaning that if the goal is survival, decision-makers will act to maximize the likelihood of the state's continued existence. Third, Realists assume that all states have some military capacity and that no state can know its neighbors' precise intentions. Fourth, in such circumstances, it is the great powers—the states with most economic clout, and, even more importantly, military might—which are key to maintaining peace and order.[7]

35

Realism is the theory most often used to explain LAC's position in the international system throughout most of its independent history. During the nineteenth and most of the twentieth centuries, LAC countries, victims of their colonial pasts, have been rule-takers in an international system. Moreover, they have been overshadowed by Washington's hegemony.

During the second half of the twentieth century in particular, Latin Americans had no choice but to remain subordinate while U.S. policy-makers focused their efforts on confronting the Soviet threat in the region. International organizations (IOs) such as the Organization of American States (OAS) and the Inter-American Bank or international law such as the Rio Treaty were used by Washington to ensure the acquiescence of other states.

In Washington's view, these instruments were there to provide military and economic assistance to ensure the cooperation of LAC states. This assistance came with the understanding that Washington could resort to the use of force, as was the case in 1954, when the U.S. ousted Guatemala's newly elected leftist leader Jacobo Arbenz Guzmán, and in 1965, when the U.S. again intervened in the internal affairs of the Dominican Republic, this time to avoid "another Cuba."[8]

But looking at the world only through the use of force provides only a partial understanding of LAC's role in international affairs, especially today when the cost of military interventions is becoming too high. Economic interference, particularly in the Western Hemisphere, is becoming an increasingly effective way to encourage positive behavior among states.

Institutionalism

Like Realists, Institutionalists assume the international system to be anarchic and states to be self-interested, rational actors seeking to survive while attempting to improve their material conditions. They believe that a condition of anarchy results in an uncertainty that permeates relations between states and state actors.

In contrast to Realism, Institutionalism relies on microeconomic theory and game theory to reach its own conclusion: under certain circumstances, cooperation between nations is possible and, more than that, preferable.

When considering issues such as trade, for example, it becomes clear that cooperation can be more useful than confrontation. This is why Institutionalists reject the inevitability of the use of coercive power between states and accept cooperation as a rational, self-interested strategy. By identifying and pursuing common interests, states and state actors can effectively assure predictability, order, peace, and prosperity.[9]

Institutionalists argue that institutions—defined as a set of rules, norms, practices, and decision-making procedures that shape human interaction—can overcome the uncertainties that undermine cooperation.

First, institutions extend interactions to more than one round, fostering relationships and confidence between the parties. So instead of agreeing to one negotiation at a time, countries may benefit from repeated interactions with the same parties, facilitated by institutions. These partnerships may continue to extract the benefits of cooperation in the long term, succeeding, for example, in lowering trade tariffs.

Second, institutions increase information about the behavior of state and state actors, making the judgments of decision-makers (and their compliance with agreed-upon rules) more predictable.

Third, because of the available information and compliance with common rules of behavior, institutions can greatly increase efficiency. By not negotiating on an ad hoc basis but instead through institutions that increase confidence, states can reduce the transaction costs of coordination by providing a centralized forum where state and state actors can meet. They also provide "focal points" (established rules and norms) that allow a wide array of states to quickly settle on a certain course of action.

Institutionalists thus believe institutional cooperation is a rational choice, based on the same assumptions that lead Realists to be skeptical of international law and institutions. For Institutionalists, reciprocity and reputation play a role in designing a functional international system.[10]

In LAC, the Washington Consensus adjustments adopted by many countries in the late 1980s and early 1990s are a case in point. At the time, Latin American states were responding to pressure by the U.S. economic foreign policy priorities. When Latin American leaders adopted the IMF and the World Bank neoliberal economic adjustments, however, they understood the need to come together and work through institutions and agreements such as NAFTA, to make their economies more competitive.

This is why the governments of Victor Paz Estensoro in Bolivia, Carlos Menem in Argentina, and Carlos Salinas in Mexico accepted the imposition of free market policies. In so doing, they effectively abandoned their statist economic strategies based upon long-standing import substitution models.

These leaders could not foresee the unintended consequences these policies would bring, however, such as the weakening of authoritarian government structures. The collateral damage in the shape of economic crises (such as the 1994 "Tequila Slammer" or Argentina's 2002 debt default) ended up exacerbating the existing regional and economic inequalities, with dire consequences for the young and weak democracies established as a result of the "third wave" of democratization.[11]

Liberalism

Liberalism makes for a more complex and less cohesive body of theories than Realism and Institutionalism. Realism and Institutionalism both assume that states are rational actors with the same goals and behaviors, all seeking to gain advantage in the pursuit of their interests.

In contrast, Liberalism's basic insight is that the choices states make are not defined by outside logic but rather by their national characteristics.

In other words, to understand the behavior of states, scholars and policymakers must also gain an understanding of their individual, internal characteristics. It's these characteristics that determine what interests states may pursue. When looking at countries such as China or Iran, for example, it cannot be assumed that they aspire to adopt the characteristics of more liberal states.[12]

One of the most prominent developments within Liberal theory has been the phenomenon known as democratic peace. First imagined by Immanuel Kant, democratic peace envisions the absence of war between liberal states (defined as mature democracies). This idea, that implies that the legacy of Liberalism on foreign affairs is the possible foundation of a liberal community of republican democratic states that are more likely to preserve a peaceful world order has been subjected to extensive debates and analysis that is not yet totally proven.[13]

Liberal theorists have tried to raise the importance of democratic institutions to another level but have yet to provide a compelling theory as to if or why democratic states are less likely to fight each other than autocracies.

In today's world, however, globalization and individual exchanges among state and non-state actors across state boundaries (be they multinational corporations, NGOs, terrorist groups, or drug cartels) complicate the Liberal view of a community of democracies that opt for the establishment of a purely peaceful environment. Increasingly, alongside the interests pursued by states working through formal structures, other forces are shaping our world order. More and more, the demands of individuals, social groups (legal and illegal) are becoming fundamental forces that shape our world order. This phenomenon requires a state with the capacity to quickly respond to such forces and adapt its role as primary actor on the world stage.

New thinkers are aiming to adapt traditional IR theories to understand the role and importance of both state and non-state actors in an environment where economic interests do not necessarily create for a more peaceful global environment. For example, Andrew Movarsick at Princeton University has developed a more general theory of Liberal IR theory based on three assumptions: first, elite individuals and private groups, not states, are the fundamental actors in international affairs; second, states are the representatives of some dominant subset of a domestic society whose interests they serve; third, because of the global nature of our world, the configurations of these preferences across the international systems determine state behavior. Thomas Piketty, on the other hand, tries to understand through a Marxist lens how capital accumulation in an interconnected economic structure has affected social and economic inequality in the past and even more so today.[14]

In short, the main contribution of Liberalism is to suggest states are not simply "black boxes" seeking to survive and prosper in an anarchic system. They are configurations of individual and group interests which then project those interests onto the international system through a particular kind of government. Survival may be a key goal, but commercial interests or ideological beliefs are also important.[15]

At the outset of the twentieth century, for example, most Latin American states were oligarchic republics, primarily concerned with achieving economic growth.

Classical Liberalism affirmed that Latin American elites were the stewards of progress. They were charged with identifying and implementing policies to better extract and export their commodities, which would in turn develop their economies and, eventually, their societies.

For instance, Porfirio Díaz in Mexico believed it was possible to engineer policies that would inevitably result in order and, consequently, progress: *orden y progreso*. The Mexican government assumed that the benefits of the economic elites would eventually trickle down to the rest of the population, who were tasked with waiting patiently. What happened instead was revolution.

The main contribution of modern Liberalism is the understanding that to succeed, governments and elites need to know what kind of state their particular society requires. At present, Latin American political elites have come to consider the promotion and defense of democratic institutions and norms as the best way to maintain power, mainly because governments are considered legitimate only if they're the result of an election. Democracy has come to be accepted by both the U.S. and Latin American states as an important institution for binding the Western Hemisphere.

At the same time, the widespread acceptance of democracy has allowed Latin American elites to take advantage of an international environment regulated by institutions, not only to defend their legitimate right to power but also to shape state behavior. Events such the UPD electoral monitoring of the 2001 election of Peru's President Alejandro Toledo, for example, reveal a growing acceptance by Latin American policymakers of the importance of democratic norms for defending their interests.

Addressing differences through institutional means ends up being not only efficient but also cost effective. Democracy is still considered the best way to bind states and social actors to peacefully solve disputes. It's no longer the only alternative, however. As the cases of China or Singapore have shown, it is no longer the sole option for achieving economic development.[16]

Constructivism

Rather than one theoretical tradition, Constructivism is a set of assumptions about the world involving human motivation and agency. Its counterpart is not Realism, Institutionalism, or Liberalism but, rather, Rationalism.

For Constructivists, the variables of interest to IR scholars such as military power, trade relations, international institutions, or domestic preferences are less important than the social meaning they're given. This meaning is constructed from a complex mix of history, ideas, norms, and beliefs, which must be together understood to explain state behavior. The main contribution Constructivism makes to IR is the understanding that "Anarchy is what states make of it" (Wendt).[17]

For example, in the eyes of Constructivists, nuclear weapons in the arsenals of the U.S. or Britain present a different kind of danger to those in the hands of Iran. This is because all states base their decisions on specific historical and strategic assumptions.

In other words, Constructivists contend that international relations occur in a social context where issues of cultural norms, identity, and belief and the subjective perception of friends and foes become key determinants of state behavior. Constructivists distinguish between the "logic of consequences" (in which actions are logically chosen to maximize interests of a state) and the "logic of appropriateness" (in which rationality is heavily mediated by social norms).

Perhaps because their basic focus is on beliefs and ideology, Constructivists tends to emphasize the role of non-state actors in world affairs. More than any other theoretical tool, Constructivism concentrates on actors such as international organizations, NGOs, human rights advocates, and religious and extremist groups.[18]

In LAC, Constructivism comes in the shape of the concept of securitization (meaning that a particular issue is presented as an existential threat, requiring emergency measures and even justifying the use of force), a different perception of what constitutes a threat.[19] The Bush administration's insistence that Latin America and the Caribbean make the threat of global terrorism their first priority—over their own national and sub-regional concerns—has severely limited progress on collective security issues.

By grouping together terrorism with all forms of transnational crime, corruption, drug and human trafficking, and money laundering, the U.S. disengaged from many commitments necessary to undermine the growing power and influence of drug cartels in the Americas.

On the other hand, the acceptance of democracy by Latin American elites and their acquiescence to an international environment regulated by international institutions has shaped state behavior and made the hemisphere not only more democratic but also more stable.

Events such as the adoption of Resolution 1080 and the 1991 Santiago Commitment to Democracy reveal that a complete internalization of democratic norms only happens when all sectors of society deem these norms as the best or even only option (logic of appropriateness) for achieving their goals.

A THEORETICAL FRAMEWORK

The English School

The English School does not seek to create testable hypotheses about state behavior, as other traditions do. Instead, its goals are more in line with those of a historian. For example, Hendley Bull argued that international law was one of five central (constitutive) institutions mediating the impact of anarchy to build a hierarchical international structure. For the English School, history matters. It is not enough to simply understand the balance of power, as realists suggest, because the international system is intrinsically historical. Within this theory, atemporal approaches to the study of IR are inadequate.[20]

In other words, the English School proposes that to explain the structure and workings of the international system, it's crucial to understand how the balance of power came about, where it is today, and, possibly, where it is going. It is also important to understand domestic politics, as well as norms and ideologies. All of this matters when it comes to understanding the role of LAC in world affairs, particularly in regard to the development of the hierarchical nature of the Inter-American System.[21]

The English School shares many assumptions with Constructivism regarding the primacy of norms and ideas, but it also emphasizes the importance of international society and the social meanings of world politics (Hendley Bull).[22]

The English School mainly differs from Realism and Neorealism in its attention to the relevance of norms, common understandings and mutual expectations in understanding international politics. It differs from Liberalism and Institutionalism approaches in stressing the importance of the historically evolved sense of community among states. Lastly, it differs from Constructivism in its interest in the evolution of the institutions of international society, the special importance it attaches to international law as concrete historical practice, and the extent to which it draws attention to brute material facts as constraints on practice as well as its analysis.

Critical Approaches

Critical theories such as Colonialism, Feminism, etc., are a direct assault on the positivist approaches that have dominated social theoretical traditions. Among them, Marxism, Structuralism, and World System theories are mostly concerned with the ways in the state exercises its power and authority over its populations. These theoretical approaches challenge the right of the state to exercise a monopoly on the use of force, which both Realism and Institutionalism take for granted.

For Marxism the attention to the state's self-interest in either an anarchical or a hierarchical system overlooks the fundamental factor that propels state-to-state relations: the dynamics of global class relations. For Marxists, the only way to understand how states relate to each other is to explain how societies are organized to work and produce—the relations of production, both locally and globally. Only by understanding the class struggle and, consequently, the behavior of global capital can we make sense of state behavior.[23]

Marxism, together with Structuralism and World System theories, assumes that the position states have within the global capitalist system is what determines world politics; that system is where power is really exercised. Second, the world economy is what ultimately restrains and defines the freedom states have to maneuver, so national interests are ultimately economic concerns. Third, since power is exercised in the economy, it is social classes, not states, that are the important actors in world affairs. Fourth, class conflicts emerge not only nationally but also at a global level, so the key feature of the international economic system is the division of labor between the core states who set the rules and the states of the periphery, which have no choice but to follow.

Latin American states have traditionally formed part of the rule-takers' club and, as such, their role has been to follow the instructions of their more developed counterparts in order to catch up.

For these schools of thought, a clear need emerged to respond to the growing gap between industrialized and underdeveloped countries. As offshoots of these traditions, alternatives began to emerge in Latin America to help address the problems unique to the region.[24]

Underdevelopment and Dependency Theory: Made in Latin America

The Economic Commission for Latin America and the Caribbean (ECLAC), under the direction of Raúl Prébisch, sought to explain the underdevelopment of LAC from a uniquely Latin American point of view.

ECLAC intended to show how the expansion of capitalism, the international division of labor, and, most importantly, the insertion of the Latin American economies into the global economic system, produced asymmetrical relations of production. They intended to prove that the underdevelopment of LAC was part of the development process—basically, that developed economies needed the underdeveloped nations to stay underdeveloped.

The main contribution of these theoretical tendencies is the understanding that underdevelopment was the core problem for Latin America and that this underdevelopment was fueled by an economy built on commodity and primary goods exports, which left them unequal in terms of trade. Consequently it was impossible for underdeveloped countries to simply adopt a method and catch up with other nations. First and foremost,

Latin American economic and political leaders needed their economies to become less vulnerable to shifts in the global market.

Viewing the situation through this lens, government authorities began to search for a solution made in and for Latin America. They sought ways to produce manufactured goods by redirecting and protecting the production process. Thus, the role of the state in the economy became a subject of debate.

Eventually, the development of strong entrepreneurial state institutions that could actively intervene and participate in the economy, together with the transformation of longstanding institutions, became the basis for a new LAC strategy. Even considering the crises of the early stages, the imports substitution industrialization (ISI) strategies implemented in many countries, such as Mexico and Brazil in the 1950s and 1960s, did yield remarkable results.[25]

With all its shortcomings, the ECLAC view of how Latin America was affected by its place in the global economic system changed the way Latin Americans thought about themselves. Whatever the weaknesses of the *dependencia* point of view, from then on, underdevelopment and development were to be considered as one in Latin America. They were in fact two sides of the same coin and, as such, needed to be dealt with from an internal perspective.

Dependency became the big issue of the day, which began to be explained from different perspectives. From a clearly Marxist vantage point, Adre Gunder Frank, for example, fell into a "stagnation trap" by assuming that in a context of dependency, capitalism loses its historically progressive character and can only generate underdevelopment.[26] By assuming that revolution was the only way out, Frank and others failed to understand that history always changes—and more often than not in surprising ways.[27]

This theoretical model could explain what was happening in many countries in the region, especially in the Southern Cone. Authoritarian regimes in South America between the 1960s and the 1980s (such as Brazil from 1964 to 1985, Argentina from 1966 to 1973 and later from 1976 to 1983, Chile from 1973 to 1990, and Uruguay from 1973 to 1985) yielded impressive levels of economic growth, even though wealth and economic dynamism were concentrated amongst the privileged few in small pockets of development.

Latin American societies needed to address dependency and underdevelopment—without the idealist Marxist perspective—because as Cardoso and Falleto (1979) pointed out, dependency and underdevelopment were a direct result of the expansion of the capitalist system and not of Marxist revolution.[28]

Using Theoretical Tools to Understand the Americas

Given that LAC was integrated into the international system as a rule-taker, these theoretical frameworks help us understand the environment in which

LAC states need to interact, not only with each other but also with very powerful actors such as the U.S.

Nevertheless, when using these frameworks throughout this book, it is important to remember that no social theory is capable of explaining everything. Because our social reality is complex, each theoretical tool is designed to tackle just one aspect, problem, or set of problems affecting the societies and timeframes that may be their focus of attention.

When looking at the Western Hemisphere, and specifically at LAC, these IR approaches allow students to focus either on the use of power (be it coercive, economic, or political) or on institutions—be they local such as individual governmental organizations, or international such as IOs or international laws, treaties, and institutions—and see how they affect the role and importance of LAC in world affairs.

Alternatively, students of IR can focus on the knowledge and under-standings of culture and ideological beliefs; on the importance of a shared history; on how the different classes interact, locally and internationally—all of the above are used to inform the decision-making processes of political and economic elites.

Either way it's important to be mindful that these tools serve as windows that allow world affairs to be viewed from very specific standpoints—and this informs the conclusions reached.

Classical Liberalism, for example, is best at explaining the position of LAC during the first era of globalization as it crossed the threshold of the twentieth century as part of a mercantilist international system. The Realist tradition offers an explanation of how and why the U.S. expanded its dominance over the region, using economic power and military intervention to test foreign policy initiatives that would then be utilized elsewhere. Moreover, Realism is useful in understanding the reaction of U.S. authorities in Washington after the events of September 11, 2001—namely, the linking of the War on Drugs and the Global War on Terrorism (GWOT).

Institutionalism on the other hand, helps identify the importance of the institutional framework that has been developing as part of the Inter-American System, a system that has a well-established historical trajectory (English School) during the twentieth century. The Inter-American System has succeeded in identifying common areas where states can find more effective alternatives to war and act cooperatively (Institutionalism). This was the case during the 1990s when democracy became legally binding through institutional means. Liberalism helps explain the importance of Western normative principles—such as the defense of free markets and democracy—that allow for different nations to find common ground and build consensus.

Of course, nations are ultimately made out of societies that are organized to produce. As a result of this division of labor, the social classes that emerge tend to have conflicting interests. Consequently, the Marxist traditions with their class conflict view of the world provide an alternative perspective and a real challenge to the rational choice theoretical traditions. They proved to be particularly powerful during the 1960s and 1970s when they offered Latin Americans an alternative view of their circumstances and their place in their society and in the international system. They are still relevant today with regard to the acute inequality still plaguing the region, as well as the unequal position of LAC societies in the economic international system.

In contrast to other approaches, Constructivism helps in understanding the growing importance and internalization of democratic rules and norms in the Americas. Together with Liberalism, it explains how Latin Americans have come to accept democracy as the best form of government and see capitalism as inevitable.

Last but not least, by framing this volume in a historical perspective, the English School will prove to be particularly helpful in understanding where the American nations came from and where they might be heading. A historical view reveals how the Inter-American System came about, why its rules and norms serve as the foundation of its hierarchical institutional structure, and how it matters to the international system of today. On the other hand, the history of LAC nations exposes the serious obstacles LAC confront (such as the pernicious predisposition toward authoritarianism) that needs to be kept in check if democracy is to prevail.

The world is constantly changing and one single theoretical approach will prove insufficient to understand it.

The U.S.'s wars in Iraq and Afghanistan showed that military might has limits; power can often be exercised more efficiently in other ways. The great games among states today revolve around another dimension of power, one in which geopolitics is making way to geoeconomics. Aiming to contain China, for example, Washington is forging new trade pacts with East Asia and the EU, pacts in which Latin Americans have an important role.

Because economic power has been, and continues to be, the clearest manifestation of the use of force in the Americas, the following section will continue with an explanation of the global economic system.

The role LAC has played in the past, and could play in the future, is of crucial importance to determining whether the West in general (and the U.S. in particular) will be able to retain its hold on the economic system.

Most importantly, this geoeconomics game will determine whether the norms and values underlining the multilateral system, steadily developed since 1945, will survive.[29]

Table 3.1 Theories in brief

Theories	Main concepts	Examples of key thinkers	Instances in LAC
Realism	• State is the key actor • First priority of decision-makers is their survival in an anarchical international system • Actors driven by the endless struggle for power through the use of force • No state can know the real intention of neighboring states • Order is imposed only when a hegemon is able to impose its will	Thucydides (c. 430–400 BC) Machiavelli (1532) Carr (1939) Morgenthau (1948)	• After the Spanish-American War (1898), U.S. imposing its will on LAC—for example, by building the Panama Canal • Response of the U.S. to the Soviet threat in LAC • U.S. ousts President Jacobo Arbenz Guzmán in Guatemala in 1950
Liberalism	• Individuals and private groups not states are the main actors in the international system • States represent the interests of the dominant segment of society, thus it should be limited in scope • Pursue individual goals through economic freedom • States should consider survival and also commercial interests and ideological beliefs	John Locke (1689) Adam Smith (1776) Thomas Jefferson (1776) Simón Bolívar (1821) Andrew Movarsick John Ikenberry	• Republican aspirations of Latin American *criollos* in the 1820s and 1830s • Oligarchic republics at the beginning of the twentieth century imposing *orden y progreso* to take advantage of a mercantilist international economy

Theories	Main concepts	Examples of key thinkers	Instances in LAC
Constructivism	• Important variable for IR is the meaning we adjudicate to power, security, and political and economic interests • International relations occur in a social context where issues of social and international norms, identity and belief, and the subjective perception of friends and foes become key determinants of state behavior • Attention to belief and normative consensus	Wendt (1998) Buzan, Waever, de Wilde (1998)	• The acceptance by LAC political and economic elites of democracy as the best form of government • The acceptance of the normative principle of democracy as binding to be part of the OAS
English School	• International system has developed throughout history • States have linked themselves to one another through international norms and international law • The international system, a result of history and law, is hierarchical • Democracies tend to be mostly peaceful	Hendey Bull (1977) The Copenhagen School	• Identifying the nature of the threat of organized crime to LAC as an existential threat: securitization

Theories	Main concepts	Examples of key thinkers	Instances in LAC
Marxism, Structuralism and World System Theory	• Economic concerns, not power, drives the capitalist international system • The different social classes are the main actors in the international economic system that first emerged in Europe in the sixteenth century • Instead of only focusing on the pursuit of power, coordination or cooperation, thinkers need to look at how the social classes are organized to produce, both domestically and globally • Economic power drives politics and war • The international capitalist system is a relationship between a core of developed countries and the semi-peripheral and peripheral poorer countries they depend on	Marx (1867) Immanuel Wallerstein (1974) Christopher Chase-Dunn (1989)	• View of how the Americas have been inserted into the international capitalist system as a commodity and primary goods exporter • View of many Latin Americans, especially after WW II when the U.S. helped Europe more that LAC • LAC begins to see the region as exploited or abandoned by the U.S.

A THEORETICAL FRAMEWORK

Notes

1 In Chris Brown, Terry Nardin, and Nicholas Rengger, *International Relations in Political Thought; Texts from the Ancient Greeks to the First World War* (Cambridge: Cambridge University Press, 2008), 174–175.
2 For more see John Baylis, Steve Smith, and Patricia Owens, *The Globalization of World Politics: An Introduction to International Relations* (Oxford and New York: Oxford University Press, 2011).
3 For more see Anne-Marie Slaughter, "International Relations: Principal Theories," in *Max Planck Encyclopedia of Public International Law*, ed. R. Wolfrum (Oxford: Oxford University Press, 2011). Available at www.princeton.edu/~sla ughtr/722_IntlRelPrincipalTheories_Slaughter_20110509zG.pdf.
4 Kenneth N. Waltz, *The State and War: A Theoretical Analysis* (New York: Columbia University Press, 1954).
5 For more see Kenneth N. Waltz, *Theory of International Politics* (New York: McGraw-Hill, 1979); John J. Mersheimer *Conventional Deterence* (New York: Cornell Studies in Security Affairs, 1985); John J. Mersheimer, *The Tragedy of Great Power Politics* (New York: W. W. Norton & Company, 2001).
6 Slaughter, "International Relations."
7 Realists are sometimes known as structural Realists or Neorealists, as opposed to earlier classical Realists. They are all part of the same theoretical tradition involving the nature of power and the use of negotiation as a tool. Slaughter, "International Relations."
8 For more see Jennifer Burrell and Michael Shifter, "Estados Unidos, La OEA y la Promoción de la Democracia en las Américas," in *Sistema Interamericano y Democracia, Antecedentes Históricos y Tendencias Futuras*, ed. Arlene B. Tickner Bogotá: Ediciones Uniandes, 2000), 27–49; Brian Loveman, *No Higher Law: American Foreign Policy and the Western Hemisphere since 1776* (Chapel Hill, NC: University of North Carolina Press, 2010).
9 Ibid.
10 Ibid.
11 For more on Institutionalism see Robert O. Keohane, *After Hegemony: Cooperation and Conflict in World Political Economy* (Princeton, NJ: Princeton University Press, 1984); Robert O. Keohane, "Theory of World Politics: Structural Realism and Beyond," in *Neorealism and its Critics*, ed. Robert O. Keohane (New York: Columbia University Press, 1986), 158–203; Robert O. Keohane and Lisa L. Martin, "The Promise of Institutionalist Theory," *International Security*, vol. 20, no. 1 (1995), 39–51; and Robert O. Keohane and Lisa L. Martin, "Institutional Theory as a Research Program," in *Progress in International Relations Theory, Appraising the Field*, ed. Colin Elman, Miriam Fendius Elman (Cambridge, MA and London: MIT Press, 2003), 71–107. For a more complete account of the Washington Consensus in Latin America and the process of democratization as a result of the "third wave," see Rosemary Thorp, *Progress, Poverty and Exclusion, an Economic History of Latin America in the 20th Century* (Baltimore, MD: Johns Hopkins University Press, 1998); Judith A. Teichman, *The Politics of Freeing Markets in Latin America, Chile, Argentina and Mexico* (Chapell Hill, NC and London: University of North Carolina Press, 2011); Anne Krueger, *Crisis Prevention and Resolution: Lessons from Argentina* (Conference on The Argentinian Crisis: Cambridge, International Monetary Fund, National Bureau of Economic Research (NBER), July 17, 2002); Anne Krueger, *Argentina: Remaining Economic Challenges* (Washington, DC: International Monetary Fund, American Enterprise Institute, 2004); and Colin Leys, *The Rise and Fall of Development Theory* (Bloomington, IN: Indiana University Press, 1977).

12 Slaughter, "International Relations."
13 Immanuel Kant, "Perpetual Peace," in *Kant: Political Writings,* ed. Hans Reiss (Cambridge: Cambridge University Press, 1991); Michael W. Doyle, *Liberal Peace, Selected Essays* (New York: Routledge, 2012).
14 For more see Andrew Movarsick, "Liberal Intergovernmentalism," in *European Integration Theory,* ed. Antje Wiener and Thomas Diez, with Frank Schimmelfennig (Oxford: Oxford University Press, 2009); "Liberal Theories of International Law," in *Interdisciplinary Perspectives on International Law and International Relations: The State of the Art,* ed. Jeffrey L. Dunoff and Mark A. Pollack (2012) (wwws.princeton.edu/system/files/research/documents/moravcsik_liberal_theories_of_international_law.pdf). In addition, Thomas Picketty on the other hand, uses a Marxist approach to better understand the dynamics of capital accumulation, unequal concentration of wealth and increasing global inequality. He does so assuming that, over time, new social actors such as multinational corporations and global financial institutions, among others, affect the way in which global social classes interact. Thomas Piketty, *Capital in the Twenty First Century,* trans. by Arthur Goldhammer (Cambridge, MA and London: Belkhap Press/Harvard University Press, 2014).
15 Slaughter, "International Relations."
16 For more information see Thomas M. Franck, "The Emerging Right to Democratic Governance," *American Journal of International Law,* vol. 86, no. 1 (1992), 48–91; Ronald L. Jepperson, Alexander Wendt, and Peter J. Katzenstein, "Norms, Identity and Culture in National Security," in *The Culture of National Security; Norms and Identity in World Politics,* ed. Peter J. Katzenstein (New York: Columbia University Press, 1996), 32–75; Jorge I. Domínguez, "Constructing Democratic Governance in Latin America, Taking Stock of the 1990s," in *Constructing Democratic Governance in Latin America,* ed. J. I. Domínguez and Michael Shifter (Baltimore, MD: Johns Hopkins University Press, 1996), 353–381. Jorge I. Domínguez, "Technopols; Ideas and Leaders in Freeing Politics and Markets in Latin America in the 1990s," in *Technopols; Freeing Politics and Markets in Latin America in the 1990s,* ed. Jorge I. Domínguez (Philadelphia, PA: Penn State University Press, 1997), 1–48; Leonardo Avritzer, *Democracy and the Public Space in Latin America* (Princeton, NJ and Oxford: Princeton University Press, 2002); Carolyn M. Shaw, *Cooperation, Conflict and Consensus in the Organization of American States* (New York and London: Palgrave Macmillan, 2004), 165; John G. Ikenberry, ed., *Power Order and Change in World Politics* (Cambridge: Cambridge University Press, 2014).
17 Alexander Wendt, "Power is What the States Make of It: The Construction of Power Politics," *International Organization,* vol. 46, no. 2 (1992), 391–425 (http://ic.ucsc.edu/~rlipsch/Pol272/Wendt.Anarch.pdf).
18 Slaughter, "International Relations"; also John G. Ikenberry, *Institutions, Strategic Restraint, and the Rebuilding of Order After Major Wars* (Princeton, NJ: Princeton University Press, 2001). John G. Ikenberry, *Liberal Leviathan: The Origins, Crisis, and Transformation of the American World Order* (Princeton, NJ: Princeton University Press, 2011).
19 For a complete look at the concept of securitization see Barry Buzan, Ole Waever, and Jaap De Wilde, *Security: A New Framework for Analysis* (Boulder, CO: Lynne Reinner Publishers, 1998).
20 For more see Andrew Linklater and Hidemi Suganami, *The English School of International Relations: A Contemporary Reassessment* (Cambridge: Cambridge University Press, 2006).
21 Slaughter, "International Relations."

A THEORETICAL FRAMEWORK

22 Linklater and Suganami, *The English School.*

23 Slaughter, "International Relations."

24 Communism presented underdeveloped countries with an alternative path to the well-established notion of modernization. This is why President John F. Kennedy initiated the Alliance for Progress in 1961, calling for programs to relieve the region's poverty and social inequities, programs that included military and police assistance to counter communist subversion. Latin American countries (excluding Cuba) pledged a capital investment of $80 billion over 10 years. As opposed to aid as in Europe, the United States agreed to supply or guarantee $20 billion in loans (Alliance for Progress).

25 Tickner (2003: 7) points out that in addition to an active role of a strong *dirigisme* state in the economy, the ECLAC proposal included fundamental policies that needed to be implemented in order to break the underdevelopment and dependency cycles, such as the elimination of large landholding (*latifundio*) interests, the creation of enlarged internal markets, and the incorporation of marginalized rural populations.

26 For more information on Gunder Frank, see http://rrojasdatabank.info/agfrank/underdev.html.

27 Sing Chew and Robert Denemark, eds, *The Underdevelopment of Development: Essays in Honour of Andre Gunder Frank* (Thousand Oaks, CA: Sage Publications, 1996).

28 Cardoso and others argued that multinational corporate activity concentrated itself in countries that exhibited high levels of economic and technological growth, given their greater potential for establishing monopolistic control over the production, distribution, consumption, and capitalization aspects of industrialization. And although fueling economic growth, this mode of transnational capitalism ended up distorting the political, economic, and social structures of the host countries. Why? The interests that originated in the core countries largely coincided with the interests of the dominant Latin American classes but not with the rest of society. So in order to attract foreign capital, Latin American elites needed to find a way to maintain order and stability. Consequently, Latin American governments opted to impose what Guillermo O'Donnell calls "bureaucratic authoritarianism" regimes, whereby the national ruling and economic elites and the military, along with multinational corporations, imposed repressive governments to control the rising demands of the popular classes during transitions to industrialization. Democracy and equality would be sacrificed in the short term so that their societies could eventually reap benefits in the shape of democracy and equity, by a process of associated dependent development. For more see David Collier, "Bureaucratic Authoritarianism," in *The Oxford Companion to Politics of the World,* 2nd edition, ed. Joel Krieger (Oxford: Oxford University Press, 2001), 93–95. Also Guillermo O'Donell, "Modernization and Bureaucratic-Authoritarianism: Studies in South American Politics," in *Politics of Modernization Series No. 9,* Institute of International Studies, University of California (Berkeley, CA, 1973 and 1998 editions); Ruth Berins Collier and David Collier, *Shaping the Political Arena: Critical Junctures, the Labor Movement, and Regime Change in Latin America* (Princeton, NJ: Princeton University Press, 1991).

29 For more see Stephens, Phillip, "Trade Trumps Missiles in Today's Global Power Plays," *Financial Times,* Comment and Analysis, November 22, 2013.

Part II

LATIN AMERICA AND THE CARIBBEAN: POWER AND POLITICAL ECONOMY

Under a system of perfectly free commerce, each country naturally devotes its capital and labour to such employments as are most beneficial to each. This pursuit of individual advantage is admirably connected with the universal good of the whole.

David Ricardo, "Principles of Political Economy and Taxation" in Chris, Brown, Terry Nardin, and Nicholas Rengger, *International Relations in Political Thought; Texts from the Ancient Greeks to the First World War* (Cambridge: Cambridge University Press, 2008 [1817]), 535.

4

ECONOMIC POWER

Commodity Lottery Booms and Busts

Introduction

Much has been said about the increasing demand for commodities world-wide, especially in nations that are rapidly gaining importance on the international economic stage. Countries endowed with commodities necessary for the new economy, such as China, are enjoying the benefits of the increase (as well as the costs of the unavoidable cyclical decrease) in the demand for their minerals and foodstuffs.

Whether the demand for commodities and primary goods goes up or down, there's no denying that in today's international system more and more nation-states seem to be sharing power with individuals and corporations. That's not to suggest that geopolitics have ceased to matter, but the nature of world affairs is definitely changing.

The exercise of economic power and influence seems to be more important than ever, and Latin America is exceptionally well placed to take advantage of this trend since its commodities can be used to further economic development and political interests. This phenomenon is not new, and now is not the first time that Latin America has excelled in its role as commodity exporter.

All through the nineteenth century, the Americas, including the U.S. and Canada, aimed to establish political stability in order to foster economic growth. By the second half of the nineteenth century, the economic structures of these nations enabled them to achieve a modicum of political stability and economic prosperity.

On the other hand, Latin America was incapable of leaving behind the institutional legacy of colonialism. LAC was organized to work and produce by means of economic and social structures based largely on the monopolization of land ownership and control over a coerced labor force.

What's more, unlike the U.S. and Canada, LAC states established neo-colonial republics with weak authorities rather than representative governments with strong institutions. To maintain order, these republics needed a strong man or *caudillo* at the helm, who would depend on the support of landed elites to stay in power. In turn, these elites, influenced by the thinking of Classic Liberalism,[1] asserted their authority over their governments and societies by expanding their economic power.

As a result, instead of a process of relatively steady economic development and industrialization, the new LAC nations experienced unstable economic growth coupled with blatant inequality and a lack of national security.

By the end of the nineteenth century most LAC states were participating in the global economy as providers of commodities and primary products to emerging industries in other nations. These young LAC states—characterized by colonial structures and weak governments—crossed the threshold of the twentieth century following the laissez-faire strategies of an unfettered free market.

To be able to export their primary goods, Latin American entrepreneurs imported capital goods and finished products from other nations. They also aimed to attract massive inflows of capital, and in the case of Argentina, European immigrants.

Commodities and capital flowed freely to the international system while finished products were brought in mostly for the benefit of the wealthy minorities. All the while, internal politics remained under the purview of dominant groups which drew their leadership almost exclusively from the upper reaches of society and were represented by two main political parties: one liberal and the other conservative.[2]

Growth and Inequality, Dependent Development, and *Orden y Progreso*

Latin American elites pursued their vision of progress through an export-oriented economic growth approach. This entailed the modernization of infrastructure, including railroads, telegraph lines, port facilities, and some degree of urbanization, as well as the welcoming of foreign investment and, in some cases, European immigration, all of which were important to the export process.

In social terms, however, this liberal vision of economic progress was not meant for everyone. True to their neo-colonial mindset, Latin American elites in Mexico, Central America, the Caribbean, the Andes, and the Southern Cone neglected the welfare of the impoverished masses. Instead, the liberal policies implemented by both liberal and conservative-leaning parties translated into support for dictatorships that brutally repressed the majority of citizens. This was true even in countries like Costa Rica, Chile, Argentina, and Uruguay, where electoral politics allowed for some representation of the repressed sectors of society.

In Mexico, the technocratic policies implemented by Porfirio Díaz successfully promoted foreign investment in infrastructure (railways, especially), a strategy that promoted dramatic economic growth. These policies lacked an important social component, however, failing to allow for any of the export-led wealth to trickle down.

Just like the Mexican economic elites, the Díaz administration was uninterested in finding ways to address the needs of the poor majority, deeply undervaluing their contribution to society. Imbued with the classical liberal tradition of the time, they adopted the model of outward-oriented growth without giving a second thought to the benefits that could come from some modicum of economic equity and broad political consensus.

Argentinean leaders took more extreme measures. They believed it was in their best interest to destroy native cultures and replace them with European immigrants. Here (just as in Costa Rica, Chile, and Uruguay, where some modicum of political consensus was successfully established), small landed elites continued to exercise dominant political and economic influence.[3]

The Commodity Lottery

Latin America had adopted the economic model of outward-oriented growth, which relied on the exports of primary products to the U.S. and Europe and the imports of their capital and manufactured goods. In this system, power was exercised and measured mainly in terms of economic achievement.

Victor Bulmer-Thomas (2003) argues[4] that Latin American countries consistently adopted these policies in response to the phenomenon known as the "commodity lottery." This means that the success or failure of any economic strategy was essentially a matter of pure chance, dependent upon the type, number, location, and assortment of commodities a country possessed and was able to extract, process, and, finally, efficiently export.

Regardless of what other factors were involved, LAC societies were at the mercy of the commodity lottery. Courtesy of Mother Nature, the winners of this lottery were endowed with primary goods that were conducive to achieving sustainable economic growth and political stability. Conversely, the losers possessed commodities that made them vulnerable to the volatile cycles of booms and busts, producing glaring inequality and political upheaval.

The winners were able to take advantage of their privileged positions. Argentina with its cattle—and to some degree Chile with its copper—were required to develop some processing or manufacturing capabilities in order to process their primary products for export. The need to produce these primary goods encouraged economic elites to develop an incipient industrial capability, which in turn fostered positive linkages between the extraction sectors and the rest of their economies.

These positive linkages translated into more extensive transportation, infrastructure, and communications networks, connecting the extraction centers to the processing and manufacturing urban centers. More importantly, these processing and manufacturing sectors fomented the development of a better-educated workforce with enough income to support an increasing demand for domestic products, as well as growing political participation.[5] This workforce ended up challenging Latin American elites, demanding access to power.

Consequently in Chile, Argentina and Uruguay, during the first decades of the twentieth century, the remarkable efforts of leadership extended the benefits of economic growth to the general population, creating social and political changes.[6] These commodity lottery winners stood in sharp contrast to Paraguay and Bolivia, which were landlocked and isolated, making transportation of their agricultural products and minerals difficult and consequently more expensive.

In addition to geographical location, winning or losing the commodity lottery depended upon several variables. Some countries, such as Mexico, could rely on more than one commodity to expand their economies. Most Latin American countries were not so lucky, however, and had no choice but to become deeply dependent on a single product (monoculture).

Consequently, the economy in countries like Honduras dramatically rose and fell with the fluctuating demand and prices of its dominant agricultural export.

Leadership was another very important variable. Economic growth depended upon whether decision-makers could foresee the changes in global demand for particular industries, which affected the value of their commodities. While value and demand was (temporarily) high, Peru's leaders, for example, missed the narrow window of opportunity to use guano to diversify the Peruvian economy.

More to the point, the export-led model adopted by Latin America needed to be something it wasn't: extremely dynamic. By following export-led strategies, most Latin Americans found that they were unable to quickly adapt to the demand for raw materials in the industrialized economies that constantly produced technological advances.[7]

Furthermore, Latin American elites felt that they had more in common with their counterparts in the industrialized world than with their own poor countrymen. Influenced by their unique brand of liberalism, they disregarded the need for social policies and instead imposed authoritarian republics. Consequently, LAC crossed the threshold of the twentieth century as a relatively poor region on the periphery of the world economy (see Figure 4.1).

Latin America in the Twentieth Century

After the Great War, the world was changed. The Austria-Hungarian and Ottoman empires were dismantled, the British Empire was weakened, and the Russian empire was diminished and transformed.

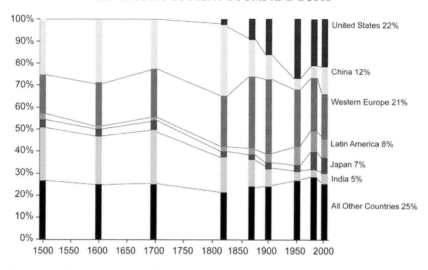

Figure 4.1 Percentage of World GDP (last 500 years)
Source: Angus Maddison, *Visualizing Economics: Making the Invisible Hand Visible*, January 2008 (www.visualizingeconomics.com).

In Europe, territorial and compensation disputes among countries left many conflicts unresolved, while burdensome reparations left other nations—particularly Germany—humiliated, poor, and angry.

In addition and of importance to the Americas, the liberal, free-market foundations of the time were disrupted. The gold standard and the insurance of a continuous and unabated flow of goods and capital ceased to stand as the pillars of the global economic system and Great Britain, the economic frontrunner of the Industrial Revolution, was no longer the main exporter of technology and manufactured goods.

In response, Latin Americans turned to the U.S., already the undisputed hegemonic power in the region. This new maneuvering adjudicated a repositioning in the commodity lottery.

In this new world order, the lottery yielded many losers (Brazil and coffee), some favorites (Central America and the Caribbean with a proximity to U.S. markets and a glut of fruits and sugar; Bolivia with its tin; Peru with its cooper), and some frontrunners (Chile with its nitrates; Venezuela and Mexico with their oil). More importantly, this new world order rendered one big regional winner: the U.S.

With no serious existential threat or military contender in the region, it started to flex its muscles by means of "dollar diplomacy."[8] Besides its uncontested economic influence, with full control of the Panama Canal, the U.S. penetrated markets in South America—such as Argentina and Brazil—which had previously been dominated by Europe.

In addition, with the ability to stay neutral during World War I until 1917, Washington took the opportunity to sharply increase its share of foreign direct investments in Latin America as soon as the flow of capital coming from Europe dried up. Through what was dubbed "the dance of millions," by 1929 Washington had become the most important foreign investor in every Latin American country except Argentina, Brazil, Paraguay, and Uruguay.[9]

This state of affairs should, in theory, have helped countries blessed with strategic resources necessary to the war effort. Far from the actual military conflict, the increase in the income among the war commodity lottery winners should have attracted foreign investment to help develop their incipient industries.

The U.S. and Europe, however, began to impose protectionist policies during the war, measures that were not lifted once the conflict ended. Consequently, Latin Americans found themselves significantly challenged by the temporary protectionist measures that became permanent.

Moreover, the volatility of the suspension of the gold standard and the disruption to shipping routes as a result of the war began to undermine the Latin American export-led model even further. In addition, the tax revenues of governments were undermined, forcing them to incur deficit spending, which caused inflation.

During the 1920/1 depression, the accumulation of inventories and lack of financing contributed to a significant fall in agricultural and raw material prices, adding to the build-up of debt. Consequently, instead of helping, the commodity lottery game ended up adversely affecting not only the countries that were producers of commodities but also those that produced foodstuffs. As a result, both Latin American commodity lottery winners and losers ended up as rule-takers on the periphery of the international economic system.[10]

By the end of the decade, even the countries that had developed some incipient industrial output became mostly dependent on home markets, where the domestic demand was still closely linked to the export sectors.[11] As a result, in tandem with the economic recovery and an emerging industrial base, some Latin American countries (such as Argentina) experienced greater democratic participation that brought an upsurge of strikes, demonstrations, and violent clashes.[12]

The active participation of workers and labor organizations was widely perceived by local elites as part of the worldwide phenomenon that had elsewhere resulted in dangerous uprisings, such as the revolution that had decimated Mexico and the rise of a communist regime in Russia.

Confronting dissatisfied union workers and peasants, Latin American governments changed tactics at the expense of broader representation. As the 1920s rolled along and the Great Depression and initial democratic wave came, the liberal vision of Latin American republics vanished.

Responding to the upsurge of labor unrest during the 1930s and with the support of the more conservative factions, governments reacted to the constant interruption of power and coups by imposing repressive dictatorships—for example, the autocratic regimes of Rafael Trujillo in the Dominican Republic and Juan Vicente Gómez in Venezuela.

Similarly to Europe, totalitarian regimes based on corporatist nationalism were established, such as Mexico's *Partido Nacional Revolucionario*, later renamed *Partido de la Revolucion Mexicana* with President Lázaro Cárdenas, and years later *Partido Revolucionario Institutional* or PRI. In the Southern Cone, fascist regimes became popular, under such figures as Brazil's Getúlio Vargas and Argentina's José Félix Uriuru and, later, Juán Domingo Perón.[13]

Latin American economic and political elites responded to the barriers being lifted in the international system by looking for ways to depart from economic orthodoxy.

With the important exception of Central America, by 1933 Latin American economies had mostly abandoned the gold exchange standard and started implementing protectionist measures such as devaluations and foreign exchange controls.

After the Great Depression, the commodity lottery (still the basis for Latin American economies) adjusted to the new rules of increasing protectionism. In these new circumstances, Latin American leadership played an important role.

The new winners of the commodity lottery were those countries where, in tandem with free-market policies, decision-makers relied on the new mechanisms of import-substituting industrialization (ISI). Conversely, countries with leaders that relied solely on export-led strategies came out as losers.[14]

The ISI strategies contributed to the incipient industrialization that began in Mexico, Brazil, and Chile during the 1930s and Argentina even before that. Investment in the construction industry and the expansion of communications through road and air transport systems positioned these countries ahead of the rest and on the threshold of industrialization. The foundations of the ISI model would reach its peak in the 1950s and 1960s.

World War II, Import Substitution (IS), Economic Growth and Protectionism

World War II was the third external shock to impact on Latin America in the twentieth century, coming at a time when Latin Americans were changing their assumptions of their role in world affairs.

The conservative parties in power presided over autocratic governments with strong figures that stimulated a growing sense of nationalism. This patriotism came hand in hand with a gradual implementation of tariffs and a proactive interventionist state that played a pivotal role in determining the path of industrial growth.[15] U.S. financial support only served to stimulate the role of these entrepreneurial Latin American states, as they became important investors in the commodities and infrastructure sectors.

Consequently, once the U.S. entered the war in 1941, the vast majority of Latin American republics joined the effort against the Axis powers. The Roosevelt government was aware of the importance of protecting markets for U.S. manufactures and securing strategic supplies of raw materials and commodities during wartime. He was also well aware of the appeal of fascism to Latin American conservative elites. It could easily be blended with the Latin American nationalistic sentiment, especially in a time of economic upheaval. That is why the Roosevelt administration implemented the "Good Neighbor Policy" and participated in the Pan-American Conference in Panama in 1930.[16]

The Latin American entrepreneurial state supported the development of its industrial base at the expense of its agricultural base. The domestic demand for agricultural products remained constrained by the slow growth of real domestic consumption, expanding only to fulfill Allied wartime needs.

As a result, when the war was over and developed countries continued to protect their agribusiness, the prices of agricultural products remained artificially depressed and dependent on government subsidies. These problems in the Latin American agricultural sectors came at a time when inflation was accelerating and the rate of population growth increasing. These inward-looking policies—together with population growth and rapid industrialization—triggered the phenomenon of massive rural-urban migration that is characteristic of these economies.

This uncontrolled growth of cities, exacerbated by the lack of investment in agribusinesses, further aggravated the income gap and made Latin America the most unequal region in the world.[17]

The Cold War and a Realist World Order

The outstanding characteristic of the post-war environment was the predominance of the U.S. as a world power. Its preferences and priorities were clearly reflected in the new economic order erected during the 1944 Bretton Woods Conference in New Hampshire.[18]

Operating under the auspices of the United Nations (UN) but based in Washington, DC, the new international economic leadership began to set rules through the International Monetary Fund (IMF) and the International Bank for Reconstruction and Development (IBDR) (later the World Bank).[19] Latin America had adapted to wartime conditions by giving priority to the strategic economic needs of the U.S.—with the hope of some reciprocity in the long run. But once the threat of war was over, the U.S. returned to its practice of acquiring primary products from Asia and turned its attention to the rebuilding of Europe, relegating the economic concerns of Latin America to second place.

Even when the danger of Soviet intervention in the Americas began to emerge, the U.S. prioritized the issues affected by this threat very differently to its Latin American counterparts. Instead of addressing communism from the standpoint of Latin Americans (by improving the area's economy to help impoverished local populations), the U.S. mainly focused on issues of security.[20] In 1948, the U.S. attempted to respond to what Latin American elites rightly perceived as U.S. neglect. Unfortunately, with Europe in shambles, Washington had too much on its plate.

From 1948 to the early 1950s, the U.S promoted hemispheric cooperation in matters of democratic consolidation and security through the OAS. Yet when it came to economic development, the U.S—in contrast to its behavior in Europe—was only ready to provide Latin American nations with loan guarantees.

With these circumstances in place, the 1950s saw the Cold War arrive in Latin America. At that point the U.S. started completely abandoning its— albeit weak—cooperative stance to concentrate on confronting the communist threat.[21]

The Soviet expansion in the Americas was a real concern. The events in Guatemala and the 1959 Cuban Revolution dramatically changed circumstances and led the U.S. to resort to direct intervention in Latin American affairs, sometimes using military force. Most of the time, however, the U.S. flexed its muscle through economic means.

Washington acted through the Inter-American Bank (BID), which was established in 1960. Within it, the Social Progress Fund was specifically designed to lend to neglected Latin American sectors such as education, health, and agriculture. This fund was soon followed by a more ambitious initiative, the Alliance for Progress (AFP), which came formally into existence under the leadership of President Kennedy in 1961.

These inter-American institutions, backed by the U.S. and engaging in economic aid, became interlinked with the already established post-war patterns of state intervention in the economy. The BID facilitated the flow and increase of outside funds directed to the neglected Latin American sectors, if and when LAC state and economic elites agreed to support U.S. foreign policy priorities. Much more modest than the Marshal Plan, however, the Alliance for Progress could not neutralize the effects of U.S. unilateralism during the Cold War, and its conditionality of aid became a source of significant friction among American states.

The U.S. continued to intervene in Latin American domestic affairs as it had many times before, but now it did so with the communist threat in mind. Washington provided financial support to corrupt governments that agreed to support the U.S. unconditionally, and when this failed, resorted to military intervention.

LAC was a region where the Soviet threat could be neither underestimated nor tolerated—an area where the Cold War was fought close to home. The Soviet Union did represent a menace for the U.S. in different ways, especially after Cuba aligned itself with the Soviet Union. Once the missile crisis concluded in 1962, LAC was the main arena for the Soviets to continually threaten Washington, using different counterinsurgency and propaganda strategies.

As a result, it was in Latin America that Washington learned to confront the Soviet threat by trying out new strategies before implementing them elsewhere. In so doing, the U.S. fomented an environment of acute distrust as to the true intentions of its foreign policy initiatives.

In addition to conditional financial aid and military interventions, the U.S. also used the existing Inter-American System as a tool against the Soviet threat. Latin America was an area where the U.S. systematically obstructed any efforts by governments to develop not only strong democratic institutions but also a regional cooperative approach.[22]

With the Soviet threat and Realist shift in U.S. policies, Latin Americans had been relegated once again to the role of rule-takers through the use of military force. Against this backdrop and in a new round of the commodity lottery, the Bretton Woods rules ended up primarily benefiting countries that had achieved a certain level of manufacturing capacity, such as Brazil and Mexico.

Excluding those exceptions, as the world was about to embark on a remarkable 25-year (1948–1973) economic expansion, most LAC republics remained stuck, producing primary goods.

Some countries, including Venezuela, Bolivia, Paraguay, and Peru, continued with the export-led model, making for growth at a rate of 6 percent a year. Generally though, the countries that achieved better results were those with a clear and protected manufacturing export capacity.

The ISI strategies adopted by the new entrepreneurial Latin American states faced important obstacles, such as evaporating foreign reserves and an avalanche of cheaper manufactured imports, mainly from the U.S., for which most Latin American countries began to impose strict trade restrictions and exchange controls. Partly by design and partly in reaction to the international environment, the third stage of industrialization was finally realized.

The Golden Era of Import Substitution

In most medium or large economies, the classic stage of inward-looking development took place between the late 1940s and the early 1960s. The so-called import substitution industrialization (ISI) model was based on tariffs on imports and the protection of domestic industries and some agricultural activities.

To achieve these goals, political elites established capital controls, courted development banks for the investment to fund these activities, and supported strong public sectors and investment in infrastructure and protected strategic sectors.

As a general rule, the industrial gains during this time occurred at the expense of primary production, so LAC nations mostly continued to be providers of commodities and foodstuffs to the international economic system. Yet some economic growth and development did begin to take place, and while not uniform, the financial performance of many Latin American societies over these three decades provoked a widespread transformation of society. Latin America's modern-day state institutions, in both the economic and social areas, are largely a product of this stage of development.[23]

Latin American decision-making elites exhibited a clear bias toward manufacturing, even when agricultural production managed to grow 3.5 percent per annum between 1950 and 1975. In spite of their clear potential and in sharp contrast to Asia, there was a prejudice against agricultural industries in Latin American that resulted in a lack of long-term public or private investment. As a result, Latin American agricultural sectors failed to experience a "green revolution."[24]

LAC focus was on the manufacturing sector, and while elites expected it to produce a significant increase in living standards, the neglected Latin American countryside remained poor. Moreover for all its policy prominence, the role of agrarian reform, including land redistribution, was minor and indirect. The agrarian reforms, including those in Mexico (1910–1917), Bolivia (1952), Cuba (1959), and Nicaragua (1979), resulted only in the modernization of large estates.

A more active Latin American state was important not only for its involvement in society as an economic entrepreneur but also for its role as arbiter between the social classes during democratic transitions. Fernando Henrique Cardoso and Enzo Faletto (1979) examined precisely this area, looking at the dilemma faced by nations such as Venezuela and Bolivia as they attempted to build manufacturing capacity and a domestic market while controlling the hardship, unrest, and upheaval these policies caused.

Latin American governments needed to control the gradual economic and political liberalization so that liberalization, when achieved, would be followed by electoral institutions. This was how Latin American countries such as Brazil and Argentina ended up being presided over by strong men such as Getulio Vargas or Juán Domingo Perón.[25]

A state that wishes to assume a more active and interventionist role needs access to adequate resources, and this was impossible for governments that had never been effective tax collectors. Instead of implementing tax reform during the post-war era, Latin American states expanded through income from public enterprises. Governments started assuming direct control over productive sectors that were considered strategic and required a high level of investment.[26] In underdeveloped economies, an interventionist state can prove useful this way.

At the same time, however, it can also create inflexible and uncompetitive industries and markets. Apart from being incapable of raising funds for public needs through taxes, the major problem of the ISI development model adopted by LAC governments was its lack of flexibility.[27] Eventually, import protection deters the need for innovation and adaptation to new circumstances, so eventually the Latin American entrepreneurial state ceased to play a positive role in the economy.

As time went by, the ISI strategies began to distort the economic environment necessary to induce the creation of new industries in new sectors of the economy. Quantitative restrictions or outright prohibition of competitive imports were left as the only strategies to promote economic growth. After three decades of impressive growth, these systems of protection ended up being self-defeating.

Rather than reduce Latin American dependency on exports of commodities and primary goods, the ISI strategy actually helped increase it. All told, by the 1970s, Latin American nations ended up with cumbersome systems of protection, rendering their industries poorly diversified and their products uncompetitive, all while the fixed exchange rates fostered domestic inflation.

Overall, Latin America started to experience slower rates of growth, particularly compared to Asian economies like Japan or Korea. The end result was that the 1960s trend of Latin American GDP growing faster than Asia's was dramatically reversed—in fact, since the 1970s, Asia has grown faster than LAC, even though initially Latin America had better economic performance.

Debt-led Growth and Globalization

By adopting some or all of the rules of the ISI model, most Latin American countries had diminished incentives to develop their export sectors, leading to a decline in their share of world trade. They had adopted an inward-looking model based on the premise that the protection of local industries and the development of local markets would lower their vulnerability to external shocks. Ironically, as the events after 1970 clearly demonstrated, Latin American economies remained acutely vulnerable to these shocks.

In addition, the collapse of the Bretton Woods system in 1971 and the adoption by the major industrialized countries of floating currencies made it difficult for Latin American states to sustain stable exchange rates. This was true even for countries that benefited from the commodity price boom.

What's more, the first 1973 oil shock served as a bitter reminder to Latin American nations that exported oil (excepting Bolivia, Colombia, Ecuador, and Venezuela) of the limitations that could be placed on economic development by balance of payments constraints.

By the early 1970s a number of changes had already started to take place in the world economy. To start, as critical theorists observed, a number of multinational corporations (MNCs), influenced by the high wages in developed nations, were encouraged to lower costs by looking for a cheaper workforce in developing countries, thus establishing a new international division of labor. This benefited newly industrialized countries (NICs), particularly those in East Asia, which quickly adapted to this new reality.

Latin America stayed on the sidelines watching the spectacular successes of the "Asian Tigers": Japan, Singapore, Taiwan, South Korea, Hong Kong, as well as Indonesia, Malaysia, and Thailand, whose elites chose an export-led model on the basis of meeting the capital requirements of MNCs, which proved to be particularly resilient to external shocks.

In an increasingly interconnected world, the Asian Tigers were better prepared to respond to the effects of the collapse of the Bretton Woods system. The U.S. in particular took advantage of these changes and boosted the budget deficits that had soared due to financing the Vietnam War.

Trying to catch up, Latin American decision-makers responded in three different ways: export promotion (EP), which attempted to add manufactured exports to the inward-looking model; export substitution (ES), which aimed at shifting resources out of protected sectors; and primary export development (PED), which sought to exploit the rise in world commodity prices.

The EP model, mainly adopted by Argentina, Brazil, Colombia, Mexico, and Haiti, was a brave attempt to rescue the inward-looking model of development without sacrificing the safety net of protectionism. Yet even considering such successes as the Mexican *maquiladoras*, the EP strategies were constantly blown off course by their failures to stop currency overvaluation, which made their legal local exports expensive and uncompetitive. In addition, the long-term exchange rate policies demanded by an EP strategy often conflicted with the short-term policies needed to defend local economies from inflationary pressures.[28]

Export substitution (ES) was a more radical alternative that imposed a shift toward a less protected environment in order to offer incentives to exporters. Trade liberalization was successful at first and—in Chile and Uruguay at least—agricultural and industrial products were able to compete in world markets.

To combat persistent inflation, these countries needed to reduce the money supply.[29] With real wages falling, however, the general public started to increase their savings, which had the opposite effect. Unwittingly, the rise in savings—along with financial liberalization measures—ended up fueling the inflationary tendencies that governments were trying to avoid, and both the exchange-rate policy and the experiment in financial liberalization in the Southern Cone proved disastrous. Even when inflation tended to fall, it didn't do so fast enough to keep export products competitive.

Furthermore, despite the inflows of capital, domestic interest rates remained high, which stifled productive investment. The assumption that inflation could be controlled by a monetary approach to the balance of payments and overvalued exchange rate proved to be false, particularly in Argentina. The EP strategy failed to achieve its targets in regimes where the military was in power, undermining their authority and, ironically, allowing democracy to surface.

The remaining republics in South America—Bolivia, Ecuador, Paraguay, and Venezuela—and the five Central American countries plus Panama and Cuba stayed out of the ES strategy and were still too weak to support EP strategies. Instead, they followed the basic export-led model with ISI grafted on as a subsidiary activity, in hope that they could reap some benefit from regional integration.

The surge in prices of primary goods created unique opportunities for these countries, and some emerged as winners in the commodity lottery due to the price boom of the 1970s. Hence, the primary export development model (PED) strategies adopted by these countries emphasized foreign exchange earnings from primary products and some services (Panama) while giving little importance to manufactured exports.

Winning could come as a result of large-scale exports of commodities such as cotton from Central America, or from higher prices, as in the case of oil in Venezuela and oil and tin in Bolivia. Winning could also come from a combination of larger quantities and higher prices, which allowed the income of those economies to grow even as inequality remained.

Not all exports were recorded. In Central America and the Andean region, a huge underground economic sector started to emerge as an important source of unrecorded income. Colombia, Bolivia, and Ecuador began to depend on important inflows of narco-dollars, while Paraguay allowed contraband to flourish.

All in all, the PED strategies were able to improve the fortunes of many within the export sectors, yet the vulnerability of these economies to external shocks was greater than ever before. Only Venezuela and Ecuador, both oil exporters, increased their share of world exports between 1970 and 1980, and even in these countries the inflationary pressures caused by uncontrolled monetary expansion and higher dollar prices for imports contributed to deterioration in the general distribution of income. The failure of the PED strategy was a particular disappointment for Venezuela, Ecuador, and Bolivia, which had most to gain from their oil income, particularly after 1973.

Central American countries depended upon primary products (coffee, bananas, cotton, beef, and sugar) for which they mostly faced unfavorable terms of trade in the world market. Plus, as net oil importers, they stood to lose from the 1970s oil shocks. Still, thanks to the commodity boom, Central

America experienced an increase in foreign exchange earnings, leading to an overall increase in revenues despite continually rising inequalities.

Though the Central American economies appeared to be booming during the 1970s, the fall in real wages fueled social tensions. Furthermore, the lack of political representation and absence of institutional safety nets ended up exploding during the 1980s. In El Salvador, Guatemala, and Nicaragua in particular, fierce civil wars were fought until 1994, when elections were held with the participation of the Farabundo Martí National Liberation Front (FMLN).[30]

The second oil crisis fostered an import boom. Within the space of a few years, imports to Latin America more than doubled. Despite the rise in value of oil exports, the current account deficit had widened by 1981 to $40 billion. Even more alarming was the acceleration of (legal and illegal) capital flights as private businesses lost confidence in the policies adopted by Latin American officials to stop currency devaluation.

Latin America became more and more dependent on foreign borrowing to fuel economic growth. Even after the second oil crisis, Latin American nations failed to heed the warnings and continued to borrow to keep up with the payment of interest. In 1982, the debt ratio jumped to 59 percent.

When the world recession drove down commodity prices, Latin Americans could not generate enough revenue to service their obligations. By August of 1982, with a debt crisis already brewing in Argentina, Brazil, Venezuela, Chile, and even Cuba, the largest oil producer in Latin America, Mexico, threatened to default. During the 1981–1990 decade, Latin America had the worst economic growth for over 50 years.[31]

The "Lost Decade" of Economic Growth

After Mexico's threat of default in August 1982 resulted in a debt crisis that threatened to spread worldwide, Latin America's decision-makers were left with few alternatives. Bank lending to LAC ground to a halt and the net transfer of resources suddenly turned negative, adversely affecting financial institutions even in countries like Colombia, which had remained prudent about accumulating debt.

The decline in bank lending set in motion a chain of events that led Latin America into a decade of stagnation. Country after country would be forced to re-evaluate the ISI model and adopt programs that mirrored the export-led model of the beginning of the twentieth century.

In the eyes of Latin American political elites, the adoption of the ISI model should have provided an opportunity to catch up with more developed economies. Yet while successful at the beginning, the inconsistencies within the model failed to generate the accumulation of capital and product diversification required for sustained economic growth.

In addition, the overburdened and underfunded states were unable to control inflation and mounting public debt. From the mid-1980s and into the 1990s, both the two-term administration of Ronald Reagan in the U.S. and three-term government of Margaret Thatcher in the U.K. championed and successfully enforced an economic model based on deregularization, trade liberalization, privatization, and a smaller role for the state.

Latin America was faced with a fast-changing, interconnected world that favored dismantling the trade barriers and protectionist policies that had framed the international economic system for so long. Increasingly, the new winners of the commodity lottery and the development game seemed to be countries such as the Asian Tigers and China that followed the lead of the U.K. and the U.S. in adopting neoliberal economic policies.

The new economic paradigm championed by the U.S. and U.K. had emerged as a pragmatic response to a series of adjustments and stabilization programs that reflected an unprecedented convergence worldwide. This leaner state/export-led model reflected a new agreement between international financial institutions such as the IMF, the IDB, and the World Bank; among academics such as Milton Friedman's "Chicago Boys"; and among Latin American governments such as Pinochet's Chile.

This economic orthodoxy, also known as the Washington Consensus, ended up drowning out the Latin American voices that saw the need to preserve some inward-looking policies and a bigger role for the state to tackle specific issues such as lack of education and widespread inequality.

In this way, following Chile's example, Latin American governments that came to power during the 1980s and 1990s, such as Carlos Salinas de Gortari in Mexico and Raúl Ricardo Alfonsín in Argentina, opened their markets and shrunk the role and boundaries of their states. Some countries were better prepared than others to take advantage of this new economic game. Yet ultimately the end of the twentieth century saw all the Latin American republics dramatically reduce the role of the state and adopt widespread neoliberal economic reforms.[32]

Eventually, heterodox stabilization programs (which combined fiscal discipline with orthodox measures)[33] began to be implemented. Multilateral institutions encouraged Latin American governments to adopt reforms based on trade liberalization and privatization of public companies in exchange for debt relief. The persistence of economic difficulties in the region gave growing legitimacy to market reformers and highly educated technocrats such as Domingo Felipe Cavallo in Argentina, Pedro Aspe in Mexico, and Alejandro Foxley in Chile, all of whom championed these new policy ideas.

Following the prescriptions of these technocrats, by the mid- to late 1990s, Latin American countries began to adopt what has become known as "second stage reforms." These measures included the privatization of the remaining state companies, the reformation of regulatory policy, changes in labor legislation, and the implementation of measures to combat poverty and improve governance. Some, as in the case of Fernando Henrique Cardoso in Brazil, Carlos Menem in Argentina, and Patricio Aylwin in Chile, were also designed to establish a path to democracy.

As a result of these measures, and in contrast to the 1980s, Latin America began to experience a rise in living standards during the 1990s. Even when fiscal discipline was starting to bear fruit, however, many of the same problems continued to hold Latin America back.

To start with, Latin America remained first and foremost a region that exported commodities, making it—yet again—vulnerable to global economic shocks. More importantly, even if Latin America was experiencing economic growth and development, the notion that LAC could emulate the astounding development of Asia's emerging markets was becoming less likely.[34]

The rate of growth of GDP since 1981 has been less than impressive, even if analysis is confined to the 1990s when neoliberal reforms and regional integration started to bear fruit. Out of all the Latin American republics, only Chile was able to exceed its performance during the ISI phase of development. Yet during the adjustments of the 1980s and the recovery of the 1990s, certain patterns emerged with clarity.

As the economies of Canada, Mexico, Central America, and the Caribbean became increasingly entwined, their futures grew more interdependent. With NAFTA, Mexico was the first to embark on a path towards greater dependence on the U.S.—a path that Central America and the Caribbean would soon follow.

During the first decade after NAFTA, these three economies experienced significant economic growth. Between 1994 and 2003 the average growth of real GDP for Canada was 3.6 percent, for the U.S. 3.3 percent, and for Mexico 2.7 percent. While all three countries grew faster than the OECD average, Mexico's progress was insufficient to address its long-term development challenges.

For Mexico, NAFTA represented a way to lock in the reforms of President Miguel de la Madrid who looked to transform the nation in the wake of a devastating debt crisis and a series of poor decisions. Although NAFTA ended up benefiting many economic sectors, it did not initially fulfill its promise to prompt strong economic growth for Mexico.[35]

Central America and the Caribbean faced even steeper challenges. After a decade of stagnation and when its civil wars had concluded, Central America did adopt neoliberal policies and saw average real regional GDP rise to almost 4 percent, with per capita output increasing at an average 1.2 percent. Yet even when economic growth was impressive, significant differences among countries remained. The economies of Costa Rica, El Salvador, and Guatemala grew twice as fast as those of Honduras and Nicaragua.

To catch up with the rest of the Americas and reduce poverty, Central America needed to achieve a higher rate of economic growth. The rate of growth of GDP per capita in the Caribbean was limited by weak institutional structures and domestic economies. In the 1970s it was 3.0 percent, declining to 2.2 percent in the 1980s, and 1.9 percent in the 1990s. Their dependence on export markets have made these economies particularly vulnerable and reliant on tourism and regional integration schemes such as CARICOM, the 1994 Association of Caribbean States (ACS), and commercial agreements such as the Caribbean Basin Initiative (CBI).[36]

Governance and instability problems have constantly affected the Andean countries of Bolivia, Ecuador, Colombia, Peru, and Venezuela. During the 1990s, the average rate of economic growth for these nations was lower than the average growth of Latin America as a whole.[37]

Argentina's performance has been a case study of the danger of inconsistent policies. By the 1990s, Argentina possessed one of the most neoliberal economies. Yet the exchange rate policy, under which the local currency was pegged to the U.S. dollar, imposed fiscal obligations on the government that were never fully respected. The result was a lack of fiscal discipline that led to a massive increase in external debt. This debt could be overlooked, but only as long as the economy grew rapidly.

After 1998 however, when growth stopped and authorities had no instruments to stimulate the economy or evaluate currency, the Argentinean economy started to suffer. By 2002, it collapsed and the government defaulted on its external obligations.[38]

As Victor Bulmer-Thomas (2003) points out, the economic development of Latin America post-independence is a tale of unfulfilled promise. Despite two centuries of independence, a prime location, an abundance of natural resources, and a favorable ratio of land and labor, not one country has achieved the status of a developed nation (although Brazil and Mexico appear to be well on their way).[39]

Furthermore, the gap between living standards in Latin America and those in the developed world has steadily widened. This is despite the fact that Argentina, for instance, seemed on its way to becoming one of the most prosperous in the world at the beginning of the twentieth century.

The commodity lottery, as well as external restraints imposed by more powerful nations, has offered both great opportunities and formidable obstacles for LAC. As rule-takers in the international economic system, Latin Americans often missed opportunities available to them—three of which were analyzed here—to overcome the obstacles of underdevelopment and become important players in world affairs.

World events certainly helped to determine these circumstances, but that's not the whole story; as demonstrated time and time again, lawmakers and entrepreneurs wasted opportunities offered by the international economic climate to break the mold of commodity booms and busts. Thus, LAC has entered the twenty-first century as the most unequal region in the world.

Main points:

- Latin Americans enter the twentieth century adopting an economic model that relied on exporting commodities and primary goods.
- LAC countries victims of a commodity lottery courtesy of Mother Nature. LAC societies become vulnerable to booms and busts of commodity cycles, with growing inequality and political upheaval.
- Political order achieved through strong men and authoritarian republics.
- As a consequence of two world wars, during second half of twentieth century the IS model is developed to achieve industrial capacity.
- When IS runs its course, debt crisis exacerbates inequality and further weakens state capacity.
- A weaker state allows a void of authority to emerge, opening a space for both democratic expression and organized crime.

Table 4.1 Summary of theories and events

Dates	Theoretical approaches	Issues of the day (Political Economy)	Institutional arrangements
1886–1929 First era of capitalist globalization, World War I, the Great Depression	Classic Liberalism	Export-oriented economies of commodities and primary goods. Gold standard. Free-markets. Booms and busts of commodity values.	Authoritarian republics dominated by conservative and liberal elite parties. As the economy develops, democratic pressure from social groups grows. Elites worry.
1930–1945 U.S. established as the regional power World War II	Liberalism Marxism Class Conflict	Trade barriers, foreign exchange controls begin to emerge in Europe and the U.S. War continues to disrupt shipping routes. Export-led model disrupted. U.S. begins to implement "dollar diplomacy" supporting authoritarianism in the region.	Authoritarian regimes are established to combat social unrest, using a combination of nationalism, populism, and, sometimes, fascism.
1945–1950	Liberalism Marxism Realism	Inward-looking policies begin to develop in response to the protectionism of developed economies. Incipient industrialization and neglect of the agricultural sector begin to trigger massive urban migrations. Soviet threat begins to loom large.	Dictators and military regimes. Weak institutional frameworks allows governments to be replaced violently, often through coups.
1950–1970	Realism Dependency theories Structuralism	Cold War in full force. U.S. constantly intervening. Import substitution (IS) policies are implemented and are useful until they fail to adapt to new circumstances. "Asian Tigers" begin to grow while LAC lags behind.	Authoritarian entrepreneurial state. Development of modern-day LAC institutions.

Dates	Theoretical approaches	Issues of the day (Political Economy)	Institutional arrangements
1970–1989 Debt crises and the "lost decade"	Institutionalism Washington Consensus World System theories	Deterioration of economic development. Abandonment of gold standard. Protectionism and cumbersome regulations begin to be dropped. Weak state institutions allow drug cartels to establish power bases in the region.	The state fails as entrepreneur. Weakening of government institutions accelerate democratic transitions.

Notes

1 The Liberal thinkers who were imagining a future path for their nations emulated the modernizing authoritarian philosophy of positivism spearheaded by Auguste Comte and Herbert Spencer, both of whom helped support these thinkers' dictatorial preferences. Spencer believed that some human races were inferior to others, and Comte believed that science would ultimately resolve all the world's problems. Already imbued with the belief in European superiority, Latin American elites evoked reason and science to understand, place, blend, absorb, or destroy the non-European majorities in their society. The problem, in their eyes, was figuring out how to bring on modernity at any price.

2 Latin America's institutional arrangement played a role in curtailing modernization, forcing governments to support their armed forces with limited capabilities. This was in sharp contrast to the U.S. and Canada, which achieved a modicum of political stability and economic prosperity through an economic structure based on agricultural ranching and industrial diversification. Latin America's dependence upon the large-scale production of staples by a coerced labor force contributed to its failure to foster the necessary conditions to develop successful alternative enterprises, which could have stimulated the creation of basic industries and, eventually, a sizable middle class, crucial to the emergence of a true democracy. Stanley J. Stein and Barbara H. Stein, *The Colonial Heritage of Latin America* (New York: Oxford University Press, 1970).

3 Even when small landed elites continued to exercise the most influence in the political system, by the 1920s the rise of Liberalism did succeed in extending participation and producing electoral politics that strongly resembled that of Western Europe. For more see Marshal C. Eakin, *The History of Latin America: Collision of Cultures* (New York: Palgrave Macmillan, 2007), 219–220. Some political leaders, like Argentinean president Domingo Faustino Sarmiento, saw the need to destroy "barbaric" native cultures. Others, such as the Uruguayan thinker José Enrique Rodó, proposed their absorption, aiming to develop an enlightened and more spiritual Spanish American identity that might be able to oppose the crude and materialistic U.S. The value, role, place, and mere existence of the non-European cultures in the Americas was now being posited by these Latin American Liberals as a problem or obstacle for the development of a new "enlightened" Latin America. Argentina saw little value in its native cultures and peoples and opted for their annihilation. Mexico, on the other hand, after a bloody revolution at the outset of the twentieth century, tried a different approach. Influenced by Darwin, the then secretary of education José Vasconcelos implemented policies to realize his vision of a modern Mexican identity in which the native's aesthetic sensibilities were guided by European rationalism. In his book *La Raza Cósmica*, Vasconcelos defended the *mestizaje* or mixing of races as the basis for a superior mestizo race with Europeanized liberals at the helm. Imbued by "knowledge, rationalism and science," all over Latin America elites imposed authoritarian republics to bring their nations into the modern age, implementing their vision of progress, industrialization, and economic growth—*Ordem e Progresso*, as framed for posterity on the flag of Brazil's New Republic. For more see Domingo Faustino Sarmiento, *Facundo: Civilización y Barbarie en las Pampas Argentinas* (Buenos Aires: Stockcero, 2003); José Enrique Rodó, *Ariel* (Barcelona: Linkgua Ediciones, 1900); José Calderón Vasconcelos, *La Raza Cósmica* (Mexico City: Editorial Porrùa, Colección Sepan Cuantos no. 719, 2007); Enrique Krauze, "Looking at Them: A Mexican Perspective on the Gap with the United States," in *Falling Behind; Explaining the Development Gap*

COMMODITY LOTTERY BOOMS AND BUSTS

between Latin America and the United States, ed. Francis Fukuyama (Oxford and New York: Oxford University Press, 2008), 49–71; Tulio Donghi Halperin, "Two Centuries of South American Reflections on the Development Gap between the United States and Latin America," in *Falling Behind; Explaining the Development Gap between Latin America and the United States*, ed. Francis Fukuyama (Oxford and New York: Oxford University Press, 2008), 11–47; Luis Williamson and Jeffrey G. Bértola, "Globalization in Latin America Before 1940," in *The Cambridge Economic History of Latin America, Volume II: The Long Twentieth Century*, ed. Victor Bulmer-Thomas, John H. Coastworth, and Roberto Cortés Conde (Cambridge and New York: Cambridge University Press, 2006); Victor Bulmer-Thomas, *The Economic History of Latin America since Independence*, 2nd edition (Royal Institute of International Affairs, London: Cambridge University Press, 2003).

4 Bulmer-Thomas, *The Economic History of Latin America since Independence*.

5 The generation of forward linkages happened first by injecting a measure of modernity through the pay of workforces in the emerging factories; second, through the need for domestically produced inputs for the emerging manufactures; and third, through the demand for domestically produced consumer goods to satisfy the newly salaried workforce. These policies also benefited local governments by providing new sources of income in the shape of tax revenues that allowed them to develop some level of sophistication in relation to (and even degree of independence from) their landed elites. In other words, these positive linkages between the export and non-export sectors generated real income growth and political inclusion. Bulmer-Thomas, *The Economic History of Latin America since Independence*, 46–57.

6 By the early 1920s, Chile's president Arturo Alessandri Palma, Uruguay's president José Serrato and Argentina's president Hipólito Yrigoyen, introduced modest economic and social reforms and extended their electoral systems in response to the pressures of their emerging urban workforces. Juan J. Linz and Alfred Stepan, *Problems of Democratic Transition and Consolidation; Southern Europe, South America and Post Communist Europe* (Baltimore, MD and London: Johns Hopkins University Press, 1996).

7 For more see Luis Williamson and Jeffrey G. Bértola, "Globalization in Latin America Before 1940," in *The Victor*, ed. John H. Coastworth, and Roberto Cortés Conde (Cambridge and New York: Cambridge University Press, 2006); Christopher Blattman, Jason Hwang, and Jeffrey G. Williamson, "Winners and Losers in the Commodity Lottery: The Impact of Terms of Trade Growth and Volatility in the Periphery 1879–1939," *Journal of Development Economics*, vol. 82, no. 1 (2007), 156–179.

8 Germany, for example, was denied strategic raw materials (namely, Mexico's oil). In addition, the burden imposed on its economy coupled with rampant inflation in Europe in the 1920s caused spiraling hyperinflation. Combined with the effects of the 1929 Great Depression, Germany's economic and political stability was seriously undermined and so, by extension, was the rest of Europe's. The various crises would adversely affect even the winners of the commodity lottery, who otherwise might have had a chance to catch up. The collapse of the gold standard, and of the British economy in particular, affected Latin American republics in the Southern Cone, including Argentina and Brazil. By this time the U.S. was well under way to becoming the most important market for Mexico, Central America, and the Caribbean. Alan M. Taylor, *Latin America and Foreign Capital in the Twentieth Century: Economics, Politics and Institutional Change*, Working Paper no. E-98–1, Hoover Institutions, April 1998.

LATIN AMERICA AND THE CARIBBEAN: POWER AND POLITICAL ECONOMY

9 This inflow of capital from the U.S. to Latin America far exceeded both the needs and capacities of Latin American governments which, by accepting these monies, saw their judgment and ability to implement fiscal reform (and more importantly, their will to stay honest) negatively affected. Known as the "dance of the millions," these excessive U.S. loans only served to foment the graft and corruption of the autocratic Latin American governments, a habit that would prove difficult to break. Rosemary Thorp, *Progress, Poverty and Exclusion: An Economic History of Latin America in the 20th Century* (Baltimore, MD: Johns Hopkins University Press, 1998); Bulmer-Thomas, *The Economic History of Latin America since Independence*.

10 All told, the combination of imported inflation, internally financed budget deficits, and currency instability fluctuations/lack of credit caused by the suspension of the gold standard (or in some cases such as the Caribbean Basin and Central America, the tying of currencies to the U.S. dollar) produced great social tensions. Factory workers and sectors of the middle class, particularly in countries such as Argentina or Mexico, were less able to defend the value of their wages, while their already weakened governments failed in their appeals for confidence, patience, or patriotic sacrifice. Social unrest ensued, which was often met with violence. The 1916 confrontation in Mexico between Carranza's government and the combative railroads, tram and electricians' unions or the 1919 *Semana trágica* in Argentina stand out as notable examples of the political instability that pervaded the region by the end of the war. For more see Bulmer-Thomas, *The Economic History of Latin America since Independence*, 153–173; Héctor Aguilar Camín and Lorenzo Meyer, *In the Shadow of the Mexican Revolution: Contemporary Mexican History, 1910–1989*, trans. Luis Alberto Fierro (Austin, TX: University of Texas Press, 1993), 64–67; Roberto Cortés Conde, "Fiscal and Monetary Regimes," in *The Cambridge Economic History of Latin America, Volume II: The Long Twentieth Century*, ed. Victor Bulmer-Thomas, John H. Coatsworth, and Roberto Cortés Conde (Cambridge and New York: Cambridge University Press, 2006), 216.

11 Argentina, the richest Latin American republic with manufacturing accounting for nearly 20 percent of its GDP, remained in a class of its own. For this reason, it presented an interesting example of opportunity lost. Nascent Argentinean industries like textiles were not able to acquire capital and durable goods and consequently had to make do with less adequate technologies than those that could be expected in a country of Argentina's wealth. While economic and income growth was combined with demand for industrial goods, offering Argentina the chance to cross the threshold of underdevelopment and become part of the core economies, tariff protections, a monopoly of industrial capabilities, a social infrastructure geared to agro-exports, its close ties with Great Britain with its protected textile industries, and more importantly, a powerful rural elite, obstructed the dissemination of the potential benefits from a successful export sector to the rest of its economy. Bulmer-Thomas et al., *The Cambridge Economic History of Latin America, Volume II*, 188.

12 This included labor conflicts such as the 1917 general strike in Sao Paulo, the wave of strikes known as the "period of renewed trade-union euphoria" that began in Uruguay in 1917 and lasted until 1919, the 1918 and 1919 strikes in Argentina (both in Buenos Aires and several provinces), the labor unrest that began in 1917 in Chile with an explosion of strikes, and so on. Some political leaders used the social unrest to justify their calls for more effective governance and participation. Indeed, the years immediately following the wave of labor unrest were marked by a concerted effort by new political elites such as Chilean president Arturo Alessandri to enhance state intervention in capital–labor

COMMODITY LOTTERY BOOMS AND BUSTS

relations as a response to the potential threat of socialist revolution. Roberto Patricio Korzeniewicz, "Democracy and Dictatorship in Continental Latin America during the Interwar Period," *Studies in Comparative International Development*, vol. 35, no. 1 (2000), 41–72.

13 The price of agricultural and commodity products had started to decline, putting pressure on their already dependent economies and only Venezuela, protected by its oil, and Honduras, helped by the decision of the fruit companies to concentrate global production on their low-cost Honduran plantations, escaped its impact. The fall in imports and export prices affected the burden of debt as well—as the volume of imports fell, the already weakened Latin American governments had to come to terms with the loss of their most important source of fiscal revenue, the tariff duties on imports. Significant barriers to Latin American exports—including the 1930 Smoot-Hawley tariff in the U.S., the imperial preferences imposed by Great Britain during the 1933 Ottawa Conference, and the use of the inconvertible currency imposed by Adolf Hitler in Germany—blocked the re-establishment of a true market system. For more see Bulmer-Thomas et al., *The Cambridge Economic History of Latin America, Volume II* and Korzeniewicz, Roberto Patricio, "Democracy and Dictatorship in Continental Latin America during the Interwar Period," *Studies in Comparative International Development*, vol. 35, no. 1 (2000), 41–72.

14 Within the fastest recovering countries, such as Brazil, Mexico, Chile, Peru, and Costa Rica, where real GDP rose by more than 50 percent, ISI policies played a greater role. Other countries in this group enjoyed an economic recovery due to the increasing value of their commodities: Cuba thanks to the higher price for sugar, Venezuela thanks to the growth of oil production, and Guatemala thanks to its U.S. exports. Within the countries that enjoyed a medium recovery—real GDP rising by more than 20 percent—the increase in the volume of exports played a greater role. This group included Argentina, Colombia, and El Salvador with certainty and, potentially, Bolivia, Ecuador, the Dominican Republic, and Haiti. Still, within this group, ISI was important as a recovery mechanism only in Argentina and Colombia. The countries that had the least successful economic performances were the losers in the commodity lottery game. These countries had little or no chance to offset their weak export performance through an increase in the price of their commodities or in import substitution activities. Within this group, Uruguay did experience a rise in industrial output and ISI was important, but it was not sufficient to compensate for the stagnation of its crucial livestock industry. Overall, republics such as Honduras, Nicaragua, Paraguay, Panama, Bolivia, and also Uruguay suffered terrible losses as the value of their exports continued to fall up to the 1940s. Bulmer-Thomas et al., *The Cambridge Economic History of Latin America, Volume II*, 204–211.

15 Examples of the import substitution process involving strategic sectors of the economy are the significant merger of cement producer CEMEX in Mexico in 1931 and the expropriation of foreign oil interests in Bolivia in 1937 and Mexico in 1938, not to mention the commitment to local industry indicated by the creation of new institutions such as the *Corporación de Fomento de la Producción* (CORFO) in Chile in 1939—all showing how proactive interventionist states played a pivotal role in industrial growth. To do this, Latin American governments received a lot of help from the U.S. through "dollar diplomacy" and the "dance of the millions." Bulmer-Thomas et al., *The Cambridge Economic History of Latin America, Volume II*, 215–227.

16 With the support of the U.S. (in order to secure access to strategic materials), the American republics founded the Inter-American Development Commission

LATIN AMERICA AND THE CARIBBEAN: POWER AND POLITICAL ECONOMY

(IADC), charged with stimulating trade in non-competitive goods between the U.S. and Latin America through subsidies. The Office of Coordination of Commercial and Cultural Relations between American Republics was charged with fending off the spread of fascism in the region. These efforts linked states all over the Americas with strategic industrial structures, providing stimulus for grand infrastructure projects such as the Pan American Highway. U.S. foreign investment in Latin America soared, benefiting the growth of manufacturing in countries such as Argentina, Brazil, Chile, and Mexico. This support for local industries helped increase local demand and also served to develop an intra-American market, which benefited other incipient industries such as Brazil's textile exports. Bulmer-Thomas, *The Economic History of Latin America since Independence*.

17 In Mexico, for instance, Lázaro Cárdenas had implemented land reform in the 1930s. After the war, these reforms started to bear fruit. But in most Latin American countries, because their economies depended mostly on agriculture, these protectionist policies put them at a disadvantage, resulting in only a modest expansion of GDP in, for example, Cuba and Central America.

18 By 1945, while Europe had suffered unprecedented destruction, the productive capacity of the U.S. had grown 50 percent. By the war's end, the U.S. was producing more than half the total worldwide manufactured goods. More significantly, after the war the U.S. owned half the world's shipping and was responsible for one third of world exports while receiving only one tenth of world imports. Enrique Cárdenas, José Antonio Ocampo, and Rosemary Thorp, *An Economic History of Twentieth Century Latin America, Volume 3: Industrialization and the State in Latin America: The Postwar Years* (in association with St. Anthony's College, Oxford: Palgrave, 2000), 4.

19 The IMF was charged with the maintenance of a system of fixed exchange rates centered on the U.S. dollar and gold. The IMF also provided short-term financial assistance to countries experiencing temporary deficits in their balance of payments that could not be addressed through devaluation of their currencies. The IBRD was responsible for providing financial assistance for the reconstruction of war-ravaged nations and the economic development of less advanced countries.

20 With the threat of a complete European collapse looming large, the IMF and IBRD gave priority to Europe over Latin America. But in 1947, when it became clear that the actions of the "heavenly twins" were not enough, the U.S. conceived a more radical approach, offering direct economic assistance for Europe's recovery through the Marshal Plan, spending almost $12,500,000,000 between 1948 and 1951. In the meantime, Latin American political elites realized that the U.S. government's financial support would have to mainly come from other sources since the General Agreements on Tariffs and Trade (GATT) treaty had failed to tackle the problem of the distortions in primary products and commodities. William, Ashworth, *A Short History of the International Economy since 1850*, 4th edition (London: Longman, 1987); Enrique Cárdenas, José Antonio Ocampo, Rosemary Thorp, *An Economic History of Twentieth Century Latin America*.

21 Hollis Chenery classifies the different stages of industrialization by putting the emphasis on production for domestic market vs. exports (a country's inward vs. outward orientation) and on when specific industries appear in the industrialization process (early vs. late). Hollis Chenery, Sherman Robinson, and Moshe Syrkin (eds), *Industrialization and Growth: A Comparative Study* (Washington, DC: World Bank, 1987). Based on Chenery's classification, Enrique Cárdenas, José Antonio Ocampo, and Rosemary Thorp (*An Economic*

History of Twentieth-Century Latin America) find four stages in the evolution of industrialization in Latin America. The first stage came during the export-led phase of globalization at the beginning of the twentieth century, the natural byproduct of export expansion. The second stage—the "empirical" stage of state-led industrialization of the 1930s, the Great War, and World War II—was a response to the volatile conditions derived from the collapse of commodity prices and capital flows. Policy-makers started creating the appropriate price structure to stimulate domestic rather than external demand. This trend accelerated at the conclusion of World War II when, as a byproduct of U.S. policies, Latin American republics that had been able to achieve some industrial capacity gradually opted for exchange controls, protectionism, and a proliferation of bilateral agreements, which led them to develop direct import controls. Countries including Argentina, Mexico, Brazil, Colombia, and Chile began to adopt protectionism, tariff discrimination, direct trade controls, and import substitution in manufacturing to encourage their own essential industries.

22 For more see Brian Loveman, *No Higher Law; American Foreign Policy and the Western Hemisphere since 1776* (Chapel Hill, NC: University of North Carolina Press, 2010).

23 For example, the four success stories of the export age, Argentina, Chile, Uruguay, and Cuba, continued to grow but at a slower rate. Concurrently, countries with incipient industries such as Brazil, which started with a low initial GDP per capita, and Mexico and Venezuela, which both started with a medium-level GDP per capita, experienced very fast growth. In sharp contrast, Bolivia, Honduras, Paraguay, and particularly Haiti, lagged behind and grew at very slow rates. In addition, the shift in the industrial structure toward consumer durables and intermediate and capital goods increased the minimum size of investment needed and required access to technology that could not be purchased on the open market. Hence the ISI republics, including Argentina and Mexico, were reluctantly obliged to adapt their legislation on direct foreign investment to attract multinational corporations (MNCs). The high tariff walls may have kept out imports, but once inside the walls, foreign investors were protected from outside competition. Hence, offering the needed technologies but mostly attracted by captive local markets, MNCs, mainly from the U.S., entered Latin America, often competing with local industries, government directives, and state enterprises. Between 1945 and 1974, continental GDP grew at 5.6 percent per year or 2.7 per capita, a growth that was not uniform. For more information see Jose Antonio Ocampo, "Latin America and the World Economy in the Long Twentieth Century," in *The Long Twentieth Century, The Great Divergence: Hegemony, Uneven Development and Global Inequality*, ed. K. S. Jomo (New Delhi: Oxford University Press, 2006), 39–93.

24 The golden age of import-substituting industrialization (ISI) began in the 1950s. The work of the Economic Commission for Latin America and the Caribbean (ECLAC), based on the assumption of a decline in the external terms of trade of primary products, provided the theoretical justification for the policies Latin American governments had already started to adopt. Under the leadership of Raul Prébisch, this organization concerned itself with Latin American problems deriving from its peripheral position in the world economic structure. Particularly after the Korean War, ECLAC posited that the appropriate response to dependency and the lack of foreign exchange was the promotion of an inward-looking development model, with greater barriers to exports to protect the growth of incipient industries. Bulmer-Thomas, *The Economic History of Latin America since Independence*, 259–273. See also Cárdenas et al., *An Economic History of Twentieth-Century Latin America*, 1–35.

25 According to O'Donnell and Schmitter, the state needed to assume the role of ultimate controller and negotiator in order for these societies to be able to achieve democracy peacefully. O'Donnell in particular advocated for a state able to act as a coercive guarantor to establish the bourgeoisie as the dominant class in a capitalist bureaucratic authoritarian state. Put simply, the main function of the government was to maintain order during economic transitions by articulating and buffering the relations between classes to help the nation first break out of dependency and then achieve modernization and democracy, in that order. Most importantly, state authorities needed to control the military while defending the interests of the bourgeoisie, which was in turn charged with propelling their countries toward modernity. Guillermo O'Donnell, Philippe C. Schmitter, and Laurence Whitehead, eds, *Transitions from Authoritarian Rule: Comparative Perspectives* (Baltimore, MD and London: Johns Hopkins University Press, 1986); Guillermo O'Donnell and Philippe C. Schmitter, *Transitions from Authoritarian Rule: Tentative Conclusions about Uncertain Democracies* (Baltimore, MD: Johns Hopkins University Press, 1986, 2013). See also Fernando Henrique Cardoso and Enzo Faletto, *Dependency and Development in Latin America* (Los Angeles: University of California Press, 1979).

26 For instance, the Mexican entrepreneurial state expropriated national oil reserves and subsoil resources in 1938, invested in the development of oil with *Petroleos Mexicanos*, in railroads with the *Ferrocarriles Nacionales de México* (N de M), and in electricity with the *Comisión Federal de Electricidad* (CFE). Brazil formed Petrobras in 1953 to control the oil industry and complement existing public investments. In Argentina, Perón took charge of fiscal and monetary instruments that increased the government's income from about 20 percent of GDP in 1945 to 30 percent in 1955, allowing the Argentinean government to invest in infrastructure construction and purchase government companies that stimulated the wages of the public sector. Governments also began to promote development through direct intervention. For example, in Brazil, during the presidency of Juscelino Kubithschek, the state started to directly promote economic development through the *Plan de Metas*, aimed at Brazil making in five years the advances that would otherwise have taken 50. Between 1950 and 1961, the Brazilian economy grew from 14.6 percent to 18.9 percent of GDP, with the share of the federal government being about 50 percent, paid via direct investments through credit allocations to foster new industries. During this time, CORFO created public utilities such as *Empresa Nacional de Electricidad* (ENDESA) and the *Compañía de Acero del Pacífico* (CAP). Bulmer-Thomas, *The Economic History of Latin America since Independence*.

27 The success or failure of ISI policies depended not only on the commodity lottery, which determined the level of industrialization each country was able to achieve, but also on how and when import substitution policies were adopted. The inward-looking model was successful in countries that had completed the first stages of industrialization and adopted these policies right away—for example, Argentina, Brazil, Chile, Colombia, Mexico, and Uruguay. Other countries that adopted ISI, such as Peru or the Caribbean nations, which had only modest (or no) manufacturing capacity, fared less well because they decided to preserve their export-led models. Peru is probably the best example of a lost opportunity, as it opted for the ISI model late in the 1960s, against regional and international trends and without backing. Thorp, *Progress, Poverty and Exclusion*; Bulmer-Thomas, *The Economic History of Latin America since Independence*.

28 The main reason for the failure of this model was the fluctuations in the real effective exchange rate (REER)—i.e. the fluctuations in the weighted average

COMMODITY LOTTERY BOOMS AND BUSTS

of any given Latin American currency relative to an index of major currencies adjusted for the effects of inflation. The weights are determined by comparing relative trade balances to determine what a consumer will end up paying for an imported good. In order to keep local export products competitive in the global market, the REER index of any given Latin American currency should have been able to remain constant and even drop, but this wasn't always the case, as seen during the Colombian coffee boom and the inflow of foreign exchange from the drug trade, or the efforts of Mexico and the Dominican Republic to defend their fixed exchange rates.

29 ES was adopted in the 1970s in the Southern Cone by military dictatorships in Argentina, Chile, and Uruguay, and more modestly by the only non-military dictatorship, Peru. Chile was the first to adopt the program after the overthrow of Allende in 1973, during the dictatorship of Augusto Pinochet. After the collapse of its democracy in 1973, Uruguay followed Chile's example, and Argentina came next in 1976. This strategy was implemented against a background of economic dislocation that demanded drastic measures aimed at trade liberalization through political repression.

30 Bulmer-Thomas, *The Economic History of Latin America since Independence*, 313–336.

31 Thorp, *Progress, Poverty and Exclusion*, 251; Bulmer-Thomas, *The Economic History of Latin America since Independence*, 350–352.

32 The IMF blamed government authorities for the lack of fiscal and monetary discipline, but as time went on it became clear that the problem was more deeply rooted. Of the 14 countries that suffered from internal disequilibrium and inflation before the debt crisis, only Costa Rica had made real progress on stabilization by the mid-1980s. Even the Dominican Republic, Guatemala, and Honduras, which had all avoided severe disequilibrium before 1982, were unsuccessful in carrying out the necessary adjustments. For more see Thorp, *Progress, Poverty and Exclusion*, 272–281.

33 Bolivia, for example, succeeded in achieving economic growth after 1985 with the adoption of a program that froze money wages, reformed the fiscal system completely, and liberalized the market for foreign exchange. The Mexican program launched in 1987 as a tripartite agreement between businesses, unions, and government helped bring inflation under control by helping to service the debt. By contrast, the heterodox Austral Plan launched by Argentina in 1985 and Brazil's Cruzado Plan of 1986 lacked tight fiscal policies. That's why, although the rate of inflation in Argentina and Brazil fell initially, it ultimately exploded in response to the freeze on prices and the fixing of the exchange rate, as nominal aggregate demand continued to outstrip supply. Bulmer-Thomas, *The Economic History of Latin America since Independence*, 376–379.

34 Javier Corrales, "Why Argentines Followed Cavallo: A Technopol between Democracy and Economic Reform," in *Technopols; Freeing Politics and Markets in Latin America in the 1990*, ed. Jorge I. Domínguez (Philadelphia, PA: Penn State University Press, 1997), 49–93; Jeanne Kinney Giraldo, "Development and Democracy in Chile," in *Technopols; Freeing Politics and Markets in Latin America in the 1990*, ed. Domínguez, 229–271; Stephanie R. Golob, "'Making Possible What is Necessary': Pedro Aspe, the Salinas Team and the next 'Mexican Miracle'," in *Technopols: Freeing Politics and Markets in Latin America in the 1990s*, ed. Domínguez, 94–143; João Resende Santos," "Fernando Henrique Cardoso: Social and Institutional Building in Brazil," in *Technopols; Freeing Politics and Markets in Latin America in the 1990s*, ed. Domínguez, 145–196; Judith A. Teichman, *The Politics of Freeing Markets in Latin America: Chile, Argentina and Mexico* (Chapel Hill and London: University of North Carolina Press, 2001);

Alan M. Taylor, "Latin America and Foreign Capital in the Twentieth Century: Economics, Politics and Institutional Change," Working Paper no. E-98–1, Hoover Institution, April 1998.

35 Gary Clyde Hufbauer and Jeffrey J. Schott, *NAFTA Revisited: Achievements and Challenges* (Washington, DC: Peterson Institute for International Economics, 2005.

36 Leonardo Cardemil, Juan Carlos Di Tata, and Florencia Frantischek, *Central America, Adjustments and Reforms in the 1990s*, IMF, Western Hemisphere Department, March 2000 (www.imf.org/external/pubs/ft/fandd/2000/03/pdf/cardemil.pdf); José Zaragoza, *The Future of the Caribbean Economy*, Policy Paper for FOCAL, Ontario, 2000 (www.focal.ca/pdf/caribbean.pdf).

37 The countries that experienced a lower rate of deceleration were Colombia and Ecuador. Andrés Solimano,*Governance Crises and the Andean Region: A Political Economy Analysis*, Santiago de Chile, ECLAC, Economic Development Division, February 2003 (www.eclac.org/publicaciones/xml/2/12092/lcl1860i.pdf).

38 Bulmer-Thomas, *The Economic History of Latin America since Independence*, 380–384.

39 Brazil seems poised to become an exceptional success story within Latin America. Fernando Henrique Cardoso was appointed finance minister in 1994 and, together with his team, formulated a complex strategy to fight inflation with cheaper imports, preventing the runaway consumer boom that occurred under the Cruzado Plan. First, they ruled out any shock treatment like wage freezes. Second, they drew up a 1994 balanced budget that was approved by Congress. Third, they created a two-stage transition to a new currency, the Unit of Real Value (URV), into which all previous values were converted. This way, the public would stop thinking in terms of the constantly eroding values of the Brazilian currency, the *cruzado*. Eventually, the *real* was introduced to demonstrate the government's commitment to controlling inflation. The *Plano Real* began to work and inflation dropped from 913 percent in 1994 to 19 percent in 1995. Then the Finance Ministry worked to stabilize the balance of payments by reinstating tariffs and maintaining an overvalued exchange rate to prevent domestic products from becoming more expensive. Eventually, together with a large food harvest that kept prices down, this plan gave Cardoso ample exchange reserves, allowing him to start cutting tariffs. By 1998, Cardoso, now head of government, succeeded in reforming the pension system, privatizing many of the state enterprises, reducing federal deficits, and confronting Brazil's abject poverty. In the wake of the twenty-first century, Brazil became part of a group of emerging giants (China, India, and Russia – BRIC), ahead of the rest of the countries of Latin America. Thomas Skidmore, Peter, H. Smith, and James Green, *Modern Latin America*, 7th edition (New York and Oxford: Oxford University Press, 2009).

5

LATIN AMERICAN AND CARIBBEAN

Political Economy in the Twenty-First Century

> Social scientists, like all intellectuals and all citizens ought to participate in public debate. They cannot be content to invoke grand abstract principles such as justice, democracy, and world peace. They must make choices and take stands in regard to specific institutions and policies, whether it be the social state, the tax system, or the public debt.
>
> Thomas Piketty, *Capital in the Twenty-First Century* [1]

Introduction

As stated in the previous chapter, a history of LAC's political economy helps explain why and how these nations have never managed to truly seize the moment.

Even during periods of global economic expansion, Latin Americans have tended to remain stuck in the middle. The hotly anticipated "economic miracles" in countries such as Brazil and Mexico never fully materialized, and the prospects for development in resource-rich countries such as Argentina and Venezuela have proved disappointing.

Victims of foreign interventions, failed economic experiments, and poor decision-making, LAC nations remain a smaller than expected part of the world economy. In sharp contrast to their counterparts in East Asia, Latin Americans have yet to experience a consistent rate of sustained economic growth (more than 7 percent a year) over at least three decades.[2]

A comparison with the Asian Tigers isn't entirely fair, however, because the economic growth experienced by East Asia is a unique achievement. In fact, for economies to struggle out of poverty and achieve middle-income levels, decision-makers and economic elites must find a way to implement economic strategies that can bring about five decades of the aforementioned 7 percent growth per year (with incomes then doubling every decade)—a time period that's a lot longer than the duration of a normal business cycle (five years at most). China's average rate of growth from 1978 through the first decade of the twenty-first century was 9.8 percent, for example, an impressive performance that is very difficult to duplicate.

Courtesy of the commodity lottery and poor choices, LAC's experience has been one of short periods of small growth spurts followed by stagnation, creating a low average of long-term growth. To confront this problem, decision-makers have implemented different strategies—such as export-led laissez-faire in the beginning of the twentieth century and import substitution during the 1950s and 1960s—with the intention of providing the necessary push to generate half a century of uninterrupted 7 percent growth. This kind of long-term performance was unfeasible, however.

As a consequence, LAC crossed the threshold of the twenty-first century closely linked to the global economic system and still primarily a commodity exporter, which—if history is any indication—should have relegated them to the lower-income economies.

Nevertheless, by the dawn of the twenty-first century, some LAC economies had succeeded in joining the middle-income club. Counting all the independent small Caribbean nations independently, of the 33 LAC nations, 17 countries had achieved a GDP per capita of roughly around $10,000. With this average income level, LAC could be counted as part of the global middle class,[3] but gross income doesn't tell the whole story.

LAC's problem is rampant inequality among states and within the populations. In the mid-2000s, the region's Gini coefficient—a ranking system that runs from 0 (where everyone has the same income) to 1 (where one person has all the income)[4]—was 0.53, meaning LAC continued to have one of the highest levels of inequality in the world. The richest tenth of the population earned 48 percent of the total income, while the bottom tenth earned only 1.6 percent of the same.

Furthermore, even after benefiting from the latest period of global economic expansion, by the end of 2000 Latin America still was 18 percent more unequal than Sub-Saharan Africa, 36 percent more unequal than East Asia and the Pacific, and 65 percent more unequal than high-income countries. In short, acute inequality seems to be ingrained in these societies, severely undermining the development of the region.

At first glance, Latin American countries seem to be a group that is neither strong enough to have a say in setting the economic terms that rule the international system nor weak enough to be failed states that threaten the international order.

Not even the organized crime that threatens Guatemala or Honduras commands the urgent attention of world powers, compelling them to intervene as they have in Libya, Syria, or Ukraine. There is no question that in Washington or Germany's eyes, the Mara Salvatruchas gang does not compare to ISIS, and President Maduro is no Putin.

For better or worse, LAC has earned a reputation as the land that has failed to live up to its potential.[5]

Today, however, most of the region looks as though it has better prospects, and the future might bring a change in circumstances. With the massive demand for commodities from developing countries such as China, Latin America's natural resources—such as Chile's copper or Brazil's agricultural products—have become more important than ever.

And notably, decision-makers are for the most part taking this opportunity to spend their incomes more wisely. In contrast to their East-Asian counterparts, it's very possible that most LAC states and populations will achieve middle-income status by finally learning from past mistakes.[6]

Latin America and the Caribbean Enter the Twenty-First Century

Natural resources, as Latin Americans know all too well, are both a blessing and a curse. This proved to be true once again when the neoliberal reforms of the Washington Consensus changed the way international business was conducted.

During the 1990s, an agreement was reached on the need to roll back the power of the entrepreneurial and dirigisme state and instead emulate the laissez-faire environment of the fin de siècle era. By the end of the twentieth century, Latin Americans found that they had no choice but to open up their economies and compete in an environment that afforded them with very few protections in the form of trade barriers.

Over the last two decades, LAC economies have become increasingly exposed to a more globalized world through ever-larger trade and remittance flows and also by diversifying both the composition and customer base of their export markets, focusing on other rapidly developing economies. The rise of China as a major economic power, in particular, has had consequences not only for world trade but also for Latin American national accounts, with China well on its way to becoming the second trade partner of the region, overtaking the EU's current position.[7]

A similar trend has been observed in the financial realm. While financial openness and exposure are greater than during the crises of the 1980s and early 1990s, most Latin American economies have developed more resilience by running more sustainable deficits, extending the maturity profile of their public debt, and building foreign reserves against potential liquidity shortages.

Additionally, most banking systems have increased their level of provision for non-performing loans and have kept out of speculative games that have proved damaging in other countries, including the U.S.[8]

Latin America's economies gained fiscal space to confront the financial crisis and reduce poverty, but still remain vulnerable to new risks.

Traditionally, when faced with hard choices, Latin American elites had been reluctant or unable to adopt effective strategies. The crises of the

1980s, for instance, prompted the adoption of fiscal and monetary policies that ultimately led to unsustainable burdens of debt, inflation, and an overall loss of institutional credibility. Latin American governments felt they had to respond to their predicament by boosting the size of their stimulus packages in order to improve their short-term performance, which led inevitably to economic problems.

In contrast, however, during the early 1990s, both political and economic authorities in most Latin American countries concluded that they needed to move away from the false sense of security that the IS protectionist policies had provided—policies that had allowed them to become complacent and stagnant. Their goal was to find the best way to create politically viable and sustainable economic policies.

Learning the hard lessons of the debt crises, they opted for the implementation of policies that would facilitate trade and financial openness coupled with resilience mechanisms that bolstered their ability to withstand negative shocks.[9] As a result, most of the region was able to take advantage of the impressive global growth between 2000 and 2008.

Economic Growth and the 2008 Global Downturn

With an average economic growth of around 5 percent a year and inflation in the single digits, the five years that led up to 2008 were the most successful in Latin America since 1960. Latin America's solid economic performance, starting in 2003 in Chile, Uruguay, Brazil, Mexico, Colombia and Peru, opened up the possibility for the implementation of ambitious public policies that locked in prospects of long-term development while mitigating short-term risks.

Despite important differences in economic conditions within the region (with South America outperforming Central America, Mexico, and the Caribbean), strong external demand (especially from emerging economies like China and India) combined with vigorous internal demand resulted in an average annual GDP growth rate of approximately 5 percent.

Furthermore, beginning in 2000 and up to 2007, public debt in the region shrank on average by 15 percentage points of GDP, while fiscal balances moved from an overall deficit of 2.4 percent of GDP to a surplus of 0.4 percent of GDP.

Most of LAC crossed the threshold of the twenty-first century ready to take advantage of the global expansion, thanks to the combination of higher primary export prices; sound macroeconomic policies and proper resource management; some provision for social stability through the implementation of anti-poverty programs; and an increase in access to basic public services. Thus, when the sub-prime crisis hit in 2008, most of Latin America suffered less serious recessions than OECD economies and experienced swifter recovery.[10]

In effect, Latin America, a region that according to *The Economist* (2010)[11] had become a byword for financial instability, mostly sailed through the recent recession. After a brief downturn in 2008 and early 2009, LAC not only recovered but forecast a 5 percent growth rate.

More importantly, between 2002 and 2008, the income distribution became less unequal almost everywhere in the region; some 40 million out of 580 million Latin Americans were lifted out of poverty. This was surprising, especially considering that poverty increased in 2009 due to the recession (but resumed its decline again in 2010).

Latin America weathered this period partly thanks to the good fortune of having an abundance of natural resources needed by other nations across the globe but also due to the sound pragmatic policies introduced between 1998 and 2002, especially in important economies such as Mexico, Brazil, and Chile. These policies played a fundamental role in preventing the recurrence of economic busts.[12]

The test of this last recession proved that stronger institutions, transparency, and good governance are strategies that should be widely developed and followed across the LAC. To date, however, these strategies have not been uniformly adopted, so some nations have not fared as well as they could have, as the case of Honduras clearly shows.

Today, Honduras has the highest murder rate in the world, one that's well past the standard minimum for a homicide epidemic. With a population of approximately eight million, the nation's rate is 85 (and nearly 130 in some parts of the country) murders per 100,000. In addition, thousands of police are engaged in criminal activity. Honduras is also close to becoming a narco-state, with debt forecast to reach 49.4 percent of GDP in 2015 and

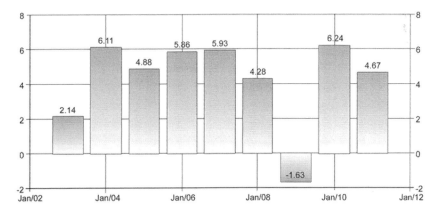

Figure 5.1 GDP growth for Latin America and the Caribbean, 2002–2012
Source: Trading Economics and the World Bank, "GDP Growth (Annual %) in Latin America and Caribbean" (www.tradingeconomics.com/latin-america-and-caribbean/gdp-growth-annual-percent-wb-data.html).

growth forecast to fall below 3 percent in 2015.[13] Lastly, the state's $200 million deal with the IMF expired in 2012 with no new deal in sight.[14]

In 2009, Honduran president Manuel Zelaya was ousted by the military as part of a constitutional crisis, on the order of the Supreme Court, but not even the ascension of Porfirio Lobo in 2010 allowed Honduras to fully return to stability and government institutions and political parties have yet to regain the trust of the population.[15]

Honduras' example underlines the importance of developing a strong institutional framework to create the sound policies that can help a nation take advantage of changes in the global economy. Clearly, not all Latin American and Caribbean countries have been able to achieve this goal.

Nevertheless, even taking into account serious trouble spots such as Honduras, Guatemala, and Haiti or distressed economies such as Venezuela and Argentina, it is important to note that LAC as a whole is sparking the interest of many important economic actors worldwide; developing economies are beginning to care about what happens in LAC, with good reason.

Interestingly, as multinationals face mounting difficulties in China and instability in the Middle East, many businessmen have begun to take a close look at Latin America as an alternative prospect for investment. The area has 15 percent of the world's oil reserves, a quarter of its arable land (much of it unused), 30 percent of its fresh water, and a large stock of minerals—and all of it in a prime location, particularly with regard to the U.S. and Canada.

In addition, it's in a relatively peaceful corner of the world. Mexico suffered a deeper recession in 2009 and is struggling to deal with violent drug cartels (as is Brazil), and while the violence that comes with organized crime should not be taken lightly, it's notable that both countries have maintained sound macroeconomic policies, continued to strengthen their institutional frameworks, and preserved political stability.

In addition to Mexico and Brazil, Chile, Colombia, Panama, and Peru have acquired investment-grade credit rankings and all four are still growing rapidly. Ironically, governments, households, and companies in all these countries are today less indebted than their peers in developed countries.

This newfound economic stability and social progress owes much to the fact that over the last 30 years electoral democracy has become established in a majority of countries, especially the larger ones. The chief exceptions are Cuba and Venezuela, and now some smaller countries—such as Honduras, Haiti, Guatemala, Nicaragua, Paraguay, and El Salvador—are on a slippery slope, both economically and politically.

Broadly speaking however, Latin America is more democratic than ever before, though a lot of work remains to be done. Whether this trend continues, however, is an open question.

It's also important to note that electoral democracy doesn't necessarily mean good government. Hugo Chávez initiated a failed coup in 1992 and was then elected to power in 1999. Clearly, even when elections are involved, societies can make bad choices. Once in power, Chávez opted to govern through populist and plebiscite measures, undermining the capacity of the state to govern democratically. Venezuela under Maduro is becoming more authoritarian and suffering for it, while the economy deteriorates. Not only that, but elected leaders can also choose to rule in fundamentally antidemocratic or authoritarian fashions, such as Cristina Kirchner in Argentina.

Some countries may have found a new path towards economic development, but LAC will face plenty of obstacles in the future. Since 1960, Latin America has had the lowest growth in productivity of any region in the world, largely because a great deal of its economic activity takes place in the informal sector. Second, in spite of some improvement, its income distribution is still the most unequal in the world. Third, Latin America is suffering a widespread epidemic of crime and violence (with Honduras' murder rates as an example), much of it perpetrated by organized drug gangs. Income per person varies widely among countries, which can translate into ideological differences. Venezuela's Hugo Chávez and Nicolas Maduro and Cuba's Castro brothers rejected integration when it wasn't through the Bolivarian Alternative (ALBA), for example, and Nicaragua, Ecuador, and Bolivia stood behind them. Their economies have suffered as a result of this decision.[16]

The production of commodities can earn large amounts of money when combined with low production costs, and if used wisely these temporary windfalls can be used to develop a country more quickly than would otherwise be the case, a lesson that Chile seems to have taken to heart. Most Latin American countries do not follow this path, however; Venezuela is a prime example.

As of 2015, the economic downturn has caused a huge decline in commodity processing, surprising producers, especially in Brazil, and creating a glut of raw materials around the world. At the time of writing (mid-2015), from crude oil to copper to cotton, prices have fallen an average of 9 percent since February 2015, based on the Dow Jones-UBS Commodity Index. The decline marks a sharp turnaround from just a few months ago when economists were optimistic of recovery prospects worldwide, based on U.S. and China. Lower commodity prices are not good news for Latin America, and it remains to be seen whether this downturn will end up adversely affecting the region.[17]

Made in China or *Hecho en Mexico*, or Brazil, Chile, Peru, or Colombia

Since the age of discovery, Latin America has occupied the position of rule-taker in the international system. But taking advantage of the latest 2000–2009 global cycle of economic expansion, the most important economies in Latin America (with Mexico, Brazil, Colombia, Peru, and Chile among them) have been putting fiscal and macroeconomic policies in place that are allowing them to take advantage of the growing demand for their commodities.

As a result, these countries have started turning the tide, experiencing economic growth and developing a more substantial middle class. Mexico's manufacturing sector, for example, is undercutting China, India, and Vietnam's capacity to produce and export cars. It seems that "Made in China" may slowly be replaced by "*Hecho en Mexico*."[18]

With regional trade agreements such as NAFTA in place and bilateral agreements such as the one between the U.S. and Colombia, Latin America is no longer just a simple rule-taker. Rather, it's becoming an attractive trade partner for the U.S.

In a region where geoeconomics matters more than geopolitics, Latin America, with its relative peace dividend (especially when compared to other regions in the world), is becoming an attractive alternative not only for trade and manufacturing but also for transportation and energy supply chains.

In fact, LAC may become the perfect example of how to use power—U.S. power in particular—more efficiently. For example, LAC is perfectly positioned to benefit from the new pacts with East Asia and the EU that are aiming to contain China.

More to the point, Latin American countries with Pacific coasts are starting to look to the East for new trade partners. For instance, Chile, Peru, Colombia, and Mexico signed an accord on June 6, 2012, creating the Pacific Alliance and more deeply integrating their economies to develop new trade links with the Asia-Pacific region. The close linkage between LAC, the U.S., and Canada can be to the advantage of all parties, especially considering the growing presence of China on the global stage.[19]

This idea lay behind the founding in 1991 of MERCOSUR, a group originally comprising Argentina, Brazil, Paraguay, and Uruguay, which was thwarted by leftist regimes.[20]

In sharp contrast to MERCOSUR or ALBA, the Pacific Alliance is a hard-nosed business deal based on affinity rather than proximity, a far cry from the lofty agreements so prevalent in the Americas, such as those proposed during summits. The goal of this alliance is to solve the problem of a "spaghetti bowl" of regional agreements and return to the 1990s principles of "open regionalism," opening up world trade alongside the advantage of a combined, deeper regional market to reap economies of scale.

The last wave of globalization has created an environment where not only the economies but also the populations of the continent are intimately linked. In July 2011, the U.S. Hispanic population reached 52 million, constituting the nation's largest minority at 16.7 percent of the total population.[21] Latin America has now a voice in the domestic issues of the most powerful country in the world. In the last race for the U.S. presidency, for example, the Hispanic vote greatly influenced the outcome of the election, helping Obama win a second term.

So where is LAC now? According to ECLAC and the Organization for Economic Cooperation and Development (OECD), after a decade of continuous expansion (which was interrupted only in 2009), the projections indicated a 3.2 percent growth in 2012 and 4.0 percent in 2013. According to the World Bank, LAC growth slowed markedly to 0.8 percent in 2014, the lowest for 13 years, due to declining commodity prices and the cooling of China's economy, with some countries (such as Mexico) doing much better than others (for example, Venezuela).

These numbers affected each part of the region differently: growth in South America slowed sharply, while it remained robust in North and Central America (led by Mexico) thanks to the strength of the U.S. economy. Meanwhile, at the time of writing, in the Southern Cone, Brazil is expected to remain weak and Argentina's credit downgrade to selective default is likely to hinder access to international capital markets, adding risk to its outlook.[22]

Figure 5.2 indicates an economic slowdown relative to recent performance, accompanied by a decline in inflation. Still, in the short term this means that the economy is likely to perform well compared to the rest of the world, providing continued stability in the region (as long as the strategies implemented follow the lines of the Pacific Alliance, at least as far as economic power is concerned).

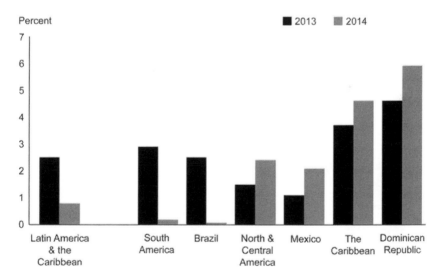

Figure 5.2 GDP growth, 2013 and 2014
Source: World Bank Group, *Global Economic Prospects, January 2015: Having Fiscal Space and Using It* (Washington, DC: World Bank, 2015). doi: 10.1596/978-1-4648-0444-1. License: Creative Commons Attribution CC BY 3.0 IGO.

According to the World Bank, the recovery taking hold in advanced economies could strengthen export demand in the future, offsetting the impact of China's adjustment to a longer-term rate of growth.

Nevertheless, the future of the global economic system is fraught with uncertainty and it is important to remember that human agency plays an important role in every outcome, as the latest (2015) Petrobras political scandal affecting Dilma Rousseff shows.[23]

The global economy experienced sluggish growth in 2012 and 2013 due to fiscal problems, financial fragility, and high unemployment in Europe, but in the U.S., political brinkmanship has proven an important obstacle to full economic recovery. Although the U.S. economy is seeing higher growth than the European area, Washington's political quagmire has allowed the risk of sharp global contraction to remain a threat. Moreover, most developed countries, as well as the Chinese and Indian economies (both key drivers of economic growth, especially in Latin America), are likely to continue to experience a slowdown.

Yet all is not said and done. In the end, the impact on trade will vary from country to country, depending on how diversified its export products and destinations are and the size and dynamism of its domestic market.

A decline in the international price of certain raw materials will affect many countries in the region that export these materials, damaging their trade

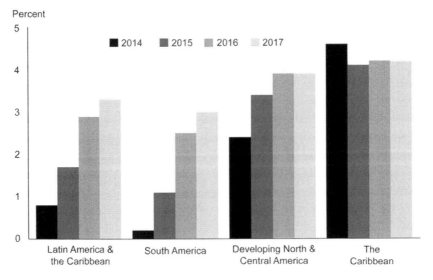

Figure 5.3 Growth is expected to gradually accelerate in all subregions except the Caribbean
Source: World Bank Group *Global Economic Prospects, January 2015: Having Fiscal Space and Using It* (Washington, DC: World Bank, 2015). doi: 10.1596/978-1-4648-0444-1. License: Creative Commons Attribution CC BY 3.0 IGO.

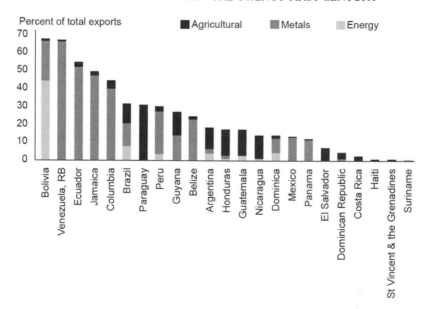

Figure 5.4 Countries with large shares of commodity exports will be more sensitive to commodity price declines
Source: World Bank Group, *Global Economic Prospects, January 2015: Having Fiscal Space and Using It* (Washington, DC: World Bank, 2015). doi: 10.1596/978-1-4648-0444-1. License: Creative Commons Attribution CC BY 3.0 IGO.

balances and lowering their fiscal revenues. For net importers of food and fuel, however, especially Central American and Caribbean countries, it will provide relief.

While there is risk that a reversal in capital inflows might hurt the financial sector, the region has substantially increased its international reserves, which account for 16 percent of gross domestic product (GDP) on average.

Many Latin American countries have relatively low external debt, relatively low-risk debt (short-term external debt made up around 15 percent of the region's total debt), and have access to contingent lines of international liquidity. These factors should allow most countries to prevent any contraction in external financing from contributing to an economic downturn. Moreover, good macroeconomic performance and prudent management of macroeconomic policies in recent years have put the region in a strong position.[24]

For 2015, ECLAC has projected a moderate uptick of 3.1 percent in global growth, with China's growth forecast to reach 7 percent. Commodity prices remain on a downtrend. In the financial sphere, despite the uncertainty of the withdrawal of Washington's monetary stimulus, no major changes or turmoil are expected in the U.S., and the European Central Bank is still expected to maintain or expand its quantitative easing program in the Eurozone.

In this context, regional integration processes can help boost aggregate demand through trade integration, which increases productivity, competitiveness, and cooperation, bulwarks against external shocks.[25]

Latin America Looks to the East

Clouds are gathering on the economic horizon due to declining trade, moderation of commodity prices, and increasing uncertainty surrounding external conditions. As mentioned before, this comes as a consequence of the Euro's weak performance, the slowdown of China's economy, and uncertainty over U.S. monetary policy.

Latin America's position as a provider of commodities highlights the structural challenges facing the region. In 2011, commodities accounted for 60 percent of the region's exports, up from 40 percent in 2000. The value of these exports rose over the past decade, but half the increase was based on price increases and not, as in the 1990s, by rising volumes.

Furthermore, the rise in commodity exports has led Latin Americans to substitute locally made goods with imports. The rise of the middle class poses a number of challenges for policymakers struggling to provide efficient, high-quality services, more and better jobs, the adoption of policies to improve productivity, and greater political rights. Elected governments will need to meet these challenges, funded by more, better, and appropriately managed tax collections.

By December of 2013, Brazil's economy (which among the BRIC countries grew the most during the second quarter) had suffered its worst quarterly performance since early 2009. The government of Dilma Rouseff has been struggling to generate a consistent increase in investment.[26]

With the growing importance of geoeconomics in world affairs, Latin America finds itself in a very interesting position: it no longer needs to fear coercive interventions from Washington but still faces competition from many countries in East Asia. The Asian Tigers, however, seem to be moving away from industrial fields where Latin America can thrive. Furthermore, when it comes to cutting costs, the proximity of Latin America (or at the very least, Mexico, Central America, and the Caribbean) to the U.S. and Canada has given these countries a clear advantage.

It's true that the dynamism of Asia's emerging economies still pose a challenge, as they did in the past, for the competitiveness of manufacturing in Latin America. As Mexico has shown, however, it brings new business opportunities as the Asian production structure continues to shift. For Latin Americans to benefit from these new opportunities, they must continue to diversify exports and add more value.[27]

There are many reasons to believe most of Latin America will seize these openings and make improvements. Bob Zellick, the former World Bank president, pointed out recently that the legacy and future of NAFTA is a global economic strategy worthy of Bismarck—a strategy glued together by regional trade deals, with greater ambition and more strategic impact.[28]

At the top of its agenda, Washington has two potential regional trade deals in which Latin America would have an important role to play: the 12-country Trans-Pacific Partnership (TPP), which includes the three members of NAFTA plus Chile and Peru; and an even bigger E.U.-U.S. deal, the Transatlantic Trade and Investment Partnership (TTIP).

Zellick points out that the NAFTA partners need to work more closely to advance a unified position in global diplomatic and economic debates. They could also co-operate more on security and help each other improve the efficacy of their governments. He also points out that the NAFTA partners need to update and link their energy and border infrastructure, do more to manage human capital, and address the prickly subject of immigration, as well as look after environmental resources.

Already included in the TPP discussions, Canada and Mexico should also have a role in E.U.-U.S. negotiations in the future, Zellick argued, for obvious strategic reasons. The "global weight of three democracies of almost 500 million people"—self-sufficient in energy and possessing an integrated infrastructure as well as interlinked manufacturing and services industries and a common foreign policy outlook—would be substantial. With those assets, North America would be well positioned to contend with 1.3 billion Chinese.[29]

So if the question, "Is Latin America important to the contemporary international system?" is asked again, the answer is clearly yes. Latin America has become far more significant in the twenty-first century, due particularly to its position in the great economic games.

The role and importance of LAC in world affairs can best be understood via a historical overview, specifically through the lens of the use of economic power. The region's strategic position in the international system and main role as provider of commodities, together with its proximity to the most powerful economy in the world, explain its traditional rule-taker role in world affairs.

A history of LAC political economy reveals how and why LAC nations have remained the most unequal in the world, and also how these states could change their fates.

The Economist, [30] for example, points out that between 2002 and 2013, 60 million people in the region moved out of poverty—no small accomplishment. Yet this progress has stopped and for the past three years the poverty rate has stayed at a stubborn 28 percent of the population. According to ECLAC, the proportion that is extremely poor, with a daily income of less than $2.50, has edged up to 12 percent.

One reason progress has stalled is that economic growth has slowed due to the end of the commodity boom. In addition, the labor market has not been able to produce more jobs at higher wages, and many people lack the skills, contacts, or access to education or social programs that could help them improve their chances to get a better job. Also, the lack of strong, astute politics and policies remain a huge obstacle that LAC democracies need to overcome.

If not addressed by the elected decision-makers, the lack of strong institutional frameworks could derail all the progress made and LAC, now considered part of the upper-middle-income club (with an income per person equivalent to $13,500 a year), could once again fall behind.

The next chapters will examine the use of LAC's power, not in terms of political economy, but in terms of the development of political participation, democratic institutions, and security.

Main points:

- LAC as commodity and primary goods producer has remained the eternal land of promise.
- LAC natural resources may finally have been a blessing and not a curse in the last global commodities "super-cycle."
- During the last two decades of the twenty-first century, most Latin American societies have been able to run sustainable deficits and more responsible fiscal policies. Fared better than many others in the world after 2008 financial crisis.
- Latin Americans have been able to reduce poverty and begin to take advantage of their economic capacity and place in the world.
- But still vulnerable. Weak government capabilities and acute inequality remain a problem.

LAC POLITICAL ECONOMY IN THE TWENTY-FIRST CENTURY

Table 5.1 Summary of theories and events

Dates	Theoretical approaches	Issues of the day (Political Economy)	Institutional arrangements
1990–2001 U.S. hegemony	Neoliberal Institutionalism Realism Washington Consensus Constructivism Critical Theory The English School	Fall of the Soviet Union and U.S. emerges as the sole world hegemon. Globalization. Trade liberalization and cooperation. Democratic consolidation. Multilateralism.	Electoral democracies. Inter-American institutions. Trade agreements.
2001–2015	Rational approaches (Institutionalism-Realism) Constructivism Critical Theory The English School	Globalization. China as a global economic power. The "rise of the rest." The emergence of non-state actors (legal and illegal) as important players in word affairs. Terrorism in the Western Hemisphere and terrorism coming from other parts of the globe.	Electoral democracies that allow for legality to cohabit with illegality. Two American lefts, one economically pragmatic, the other populist. Pragmatic governments vying to implement economic policies that allows for trade with the U.S., Europe, and East Asia.

Notes

1 Thomas Piketty, *Capital in the Twenty First Century*, trans. Arthur Goldhammer (Cambridge, MA and London: Belkhap Press of Harvard University Press, 2014), 574–577.

2 Throughout the history of modern Latin America, new strategies have been adopted to fuel economic growth, but time and again the same cycle repeats itself: the business cycle peaks, economic growth decelerates then reverses, and recession sets in. With dire consequences for their populations, growth in Latin American economies always fizzles out, rendering disappointing results and leaving LAC economies stuck in the lower income tiers. The World Bank divides the economies of the world roughly between low, middle, and high-income economies, using as main indicators Gross Domestic Product (GDP), which represents the yearly output of all final goods and services produced in any given economy, and GDP per capita, which is GDP divided by the population. Javier A. Reyes, and Charles W. Sawyer, *Latin American Economic Development* (New York: Routledge, 2011). According to the World Bank, economies are grouped as low income, $1,005 or less; lower-middle income, $1,006–$3,795; upper-middle income, $3,796–$12,275; high income, $12,276 and above (http://data.worldbank.org/about/country-classifications).

LATIN AMERICA AND THE CARIBBEAN: POWER AND POLITICAL ECONOMY

3 This income may seem low compared to that of affluent and developed U.S. and Canada, but it was high compared to $1,163 to $6,793 for the rest of Latin America, where living standards continued to be low, services such as health and educations scarce, and poverty rampant. ECLAC, "Preliminary Overview of the Economies of Latin American and the Caribbean" (UN/ECLAC, 2014) (http://repositorio.cepal.org/bitstream/handle/11362/37345/S1420977_en.pdf?sequence=31), 13.

4 Most countries have a Gini coefficient of between 0.25 and 0.6. In contrast with LAC, the top tenth in industrialized countries earns 29.1 percent, while the bottom tenth earns 2.5 percent. Researchers at the World Bank (2003) found that from the 1970s through the 1990s, Latin America and the Caribbean measured nearly 10 points more unequal than Asia, 17.5 points more unequal than the 30 countries in the Organization for Economic Cooperation and Development, and 20.4 points more unequal than Eastern Europe. Guillermo E. Perry and Norbert Fiess, "Turmoil in Latin America and the Caribbean," World Bank Working Paper no. 3, (Washington, DC: World Bank, 2003) (www-wds.worldbank.org/external/default/WDSContentServer/WDSP/IB/2004/03/23/000090341_20040323143924/Rendered/PDF/281320Turmoil0in0LAC0WBWP0no.03.pdf); Luis F. López Calva and Nora Lustig, eds, *Declining Inequality in Latin America: A Decade of Progress?* (New York: Brookings Institutions and the United Nations Development Programme, 2010)

5 Reyes and Sawyer, *Latin American Economic Development.*

6 Michael Spence points out the rule of 72 (used by statisticians and economists), which shows the number of years it takes for income to double in size, calculated by dividing the specific annual growth rate into the number 72. So at 1 percent growth, for example, income doubles in 72 years. At 7 percent growth, which is about the highest sustained level ever achieved (until recently), the figure for doubling income is a decade. Since 1978, China has averaged a growth rate of 9.8 percent. In sharp contrast with other regions of the world, China and South Korea have been able to sustain a more than 7 percent growth rate for at least the last three decades, an unprecedented and so far unique achievement. This is how they made their unparalleled fast jumps out of poverty to become middle and upper-middle-income countries, and in the case of South Korea, a high-income country. This means that in order to achieve an income of between $8,000 and $16,000 per capita a year, a Latin American state is required to experience half a century of uninterrupted 7 percent growth, far longer than any typical economic growth cycle duration. Michael Spence, *The Next Convergence: The Future of Economic Growth in a Multispeed World* (New York: Farrar, Straus and Giroux, 2012).

7 For more see ECLAC, "Latin America and the Caribbean in the World Economy: The Region in the Decade of the Emerging Economies", United Nations/ECLAC, 2011 (http://repositorio.cepal.org/bitstream/handle/11362/1182/S2011521_en.pdf?sequence=1), 92.

8 Since the 1990s, responsible policymaking has created substantially more headroom for effective and sustainable fiscal and monetary stimuli than was the case during the 1980s. Chile, for example, wisely chose to accumulate significant fiscal resources during the copper boom. This example was followed closely by Peru and Mexico, with Brazil and Colombia trailing behind. In fact, with the notable exceptions of populist regimes like Nicaragua, Venezuela, and Argentina, most of Latin America has worked hard to build credibility and, as a result, has begun to be rewarded with a more robust monetary policy tool kit. Central bank authorities are increasingly anchored in responsible policymaking rather

LAC POLITICAL ECONOMY IN THE TWENTY-FIRST CENTURY

than strict exchange-rate regimes or price controls. Rather than helplessly watching reserves hemorrhage in vain attempts to protect the value of the local currency, policymakers have been able to mobilize them to address liquidity shortages. Institutional strength and inflation targeting in countries such as Brazil, Chile, Colombia, Mexico, and Peru has proven particularly successful. For more see OECD, *Latin American Economic Outlook* 2010 (www.oecd-ilibrary.org/development/latin-american-economic-outlook-2010_leo-2010-en).

9　For more see Jorge I. Dominguez, *Technopols: Freeing Politics and Markets in Latin America in the 1990s* (Philadelphia, PA: Penn State University Press, 1997).

10　For more see OECD, *Latin American Economic Outlook 2012: Transforming the State for Development* (overview: www.oecd.org/dev/americas/48965859.pdf).

11　Michael Reid, "So Near and Yet So Far," *The Economist*, Special Report: Latin America, September 9, 2010 (www.economist.com/node/16964114).

12　For more see ECLAC, *Preliminary Overview of the Economies of Latin America and the Caribbean*, 2014 (Santiago, Chile: ECLAC, 2014).

13　See Mejía, Thelma, "Honduras Worried About becoming a Narco-State," Inter Press Service (IPS), October 22, 2010 (www.ipsnews.net/2010/10/honduras-worried-about-becoming-narco-state/); Stephen Sackur, "Honduras Counts the Human Rights Cost of America's War on Drugs," *The Guardian*, July 15, 2012 (www.theguardian.com/world/2012/jul/15/honduras-human-rights-war-drugs); Jude Webber, "Honduras Claims: Worst is Yet to Come," *Financial Times*, Beyond BRICS, January 10, 2014 (http://blogs.ft.com/beyond-brics/2014/01/10/honduras-claims-worst-is-yet-to-come/); Human Rights Watch: World Report 2015: Honduras (www.hrw.org/world-report/2015/country-chapters/honduras).

14　2015 CIA World Factbook and Other Sources, *Honduras Economy, 2015* (www.theodora.com/wfbcurrent/honduras/honduras_economy.html); Global Finance, *Honduras GDP and Economic Data*, September 29, 2015 (www.gfmag.com/global-data/country-data/honduras-gdp-country-report).

15　Jude Webber, "Rival Contenders for Honduras Presidency Claim Poll Victory," *Financial Times*, November 25, 2013 (www.ft.com/cms/s/0/82a7fbc8-558b-11e3-a321-00144feabdc0.html#axzz3n7rToY3Z).

16　Michael Reid, "So Near and Yet So Far: A Richer, Fairer Latin America is Within Reach, But a lot of Things Have to be Put Right First," *The Economist*, Special Report: Latin America, September 9, 2010 (www.economist.com/node/16964114).

17　Carolyn Cui, "Prices of Raw Goods Plunge on Slowdown," *Wall Street Journal*, July 2, 2012, A1.

18　"Señores Start Your Engines," *The Economist*, Special Report, Mexico, November 24, 2012, 5–7.

19　Hong Kong and Chile officially signed a free trade agreement at the Asia-Pacific Economic Cooperation Leaders Summit, September 7/8, 2012 (reported *Stratfor*, August 15). For Chile and India's negotiations see *Global Tax News*, November 13, 2012 (http://taxnews.com/news/Chile_Seeks_South_Americas_First_FTA_With_India____58128.html).

20　With the Pacific Alliance, Chile, Colombia, Mexico, and Peru signed an agreement removing tariffs on 90 percent of their merchandise trade and agreed a timetable to remove the remaining 10 percent. They've already removed visa requirements for each other's citizens and are setting up a common market. Brazil's two main regional partners, Argentina and Venezuela, have slow-growing, state-controlled economies and their policies flirt with autarky, which makes them captive markets for Brazilian construction companies and exporters of otherwise uncompetitive capital goods. Brazil had a trade surplus of $4 billion with Venezuela last year. MERCOSUR has only signed regional trade agreements with Israel, Egypt, and the Palestinian Authority. Argentina has stalled a proposed trade deal with the European Union, for which talks began in 1999. Brazil's bet has been on the Doha round of world trade talks, and was cheered when Roberto Azevêdo, a Brazilian diplomat, was chosen this month to head the World Trade Organization (WTO). However, many trade specialists consider the Doha round all but dead and the WTO increasingly irrelevant. In practice, trade policy is "not a priority" for Ms Rousseff's government, which is "very focused on the domestic market," says Welber Barral, a former trade official. For more see "Latin American Geoeconomics, A Continental Divide," *The Economist*, May 18, 2013 (www.economist.com/news/americas/21578056-region-falling-behind-two-alternative-blocks-market-led-pacific-alliance-and?zid=305&ah=417bd5664dc76da5d98af4f7a640fd8a).

21 www.census.gov/newsroom/releases/archives/facts_for_features_special_editions/cb12-ff19.html.

22 For more see World Bank, *Global Economic Prospects: Having Fiscal Space and Using It* (Washington, DC: World Bank Group, January 2015), Ch. 2.

23 See, for instance, the article by Simon Romero, "Brazil's Power Dynamics Shifting Amid Political Scandals," *New York Times*, Americas, April, 26, 2015 (www.nytimes.com/2015/04/27/world/americas/brazils-power-dynamics-shifting-amid-legislative-scandals.html).

24 For instance, if aggregate demand falls there is scope for fiscal stimulus thanks to relatively low government debt (39 percent of GDP on average) and generally well-balanced budgets (-1.8 percent of GDP on average). For more see OECD/ECLAC, "Latin American Economic Outlook 2013: SME Policies for Structural Change" (ECLAC and OECD, 2012: www.eclac.org/publicaciones/xml/5/48385/LEO2013_ing.pdf).

25 For more see ECLAC, "Preliminary Overview of the Economies of Latin American and the Caribbean" (UN/ECLAC, 2014) (http://repositorio.cepal.org/bitstream/handle/11362/37345/S1420977_en.pdf?sequence=31), 13.

26 Joe Leahy, "Brazil's Economy Turns in Worst Quarter in Five Years", *Financial Times,* Global Economy, December 3, 2013 (www.ft.com/intl/cms/s/0/95c2ef90-5c3b-11e3-b4f3-00144feabdc0.html#axzz2mVrxlwRx).

27 For more see OECD, "Latin American Economic Outlook 2014: Logistics and Competitiveness for Development" (OECD, ECLAC, and CNF, 2014) (www.keepeek.com/Digital-Asset-Management/oecd/development/latin-american-economic-outlook-2014_leo-2014-en#page1).

28 Shawn Donnan, "The Future of NAFTA," *Financial Times*, December 2, 2013 (www.ft.com/intl/cms/s/0/b4371e1e-4c51-11e3-923d-00144feabdc0.html#axzz2mVrxlwRx).

29 Ibid.

30 For more see Bello, "The Poverty Alert: Latin America's Social Progress Has Stopped. What is to be Done?" *The Economist*, The Americas, February 21, 2015.

Part III

SECURITY AND DEMOCRACY

And we ask you on your side not to imagine that you will influence us by saying that you, a colony of Sparta, have not joined in the war, or that you have never done us any harm. Instead we recommend that you should try to get what is possible to get, taking into consideration what we both really do think; since you know as well as we do that, when these matters are discussed by practical people, the standard of justice depends on the equality of power to compel and that in fact the strong do what they have the power to do and the weak accept what they have to accept.

Thucydides, *The Melian Dialogue*, Book 5, taken from Chris Brown, Terry Nardin, and Nicholas Rengger, *International Relations in Political Thought: Texts from the Ancient Greeks to the First World War* (Cambridge and New York: Cambridge University Press, 2002), 54.

6

POWER

Political Institutions and Democracy

Introduction

The role and importance of Latin America in world affairs is better understood by first examining this region's place in the international economic system, including how economic advantage, dominance, and influence have been exercised in the Americas by both state and non-state actors.

Power, of course, is complicated. The truth is that the exercise of power—or the lack thereof—is not limited to the economic dimension. This is true even on the American continent, which is considered to have had rather a peaceful trajectory compared to Europe or the Middle East.

To get a fuller picture of the dynamics of world affairs and the Western Hemisphere's role, it's important to dig deeper. This chapter goes beyond the realm of political economy to study how power is (to paraphrase Carl Von Clausewitz) a continuation of war exercised by other means.

In the Americas, states and non-state actors have both used military capacity to exercise dominance. The War of 1812 (Canada and the U.S.), the Mexican-American War (U.S. and Mexico in 1846–1848), the War of the Triple Alliance (Brazil, Argentina, and Uruguay against Paraguay in 1865–1870), the Bay of Pigs invasion (U.S. in Cuba in 1961) or President Reagan's 1983 invasion of Grenada in the Caribbean illustrate how—although American states have mostly exercised power through economic might and influence—they are no strangers to war.

As Thucydides would say, Latin Americans have been consistently compelled "to accept what they had to accept."[1]

The history of the Americas has had its share of violence, and the use or threat of force has clearly been an important factor.

Power is exercised in many ways, however, especially in a world that has developed institutional frameworks that make negotiation a viable and efficient alternative to conflict. The price of military interventions has become so steep (as Colin Powell famously said, "You break it, you own it") that states tend to try and change the behavior of others by means of economic pressures; sanctions through institutions; treaties and laws; or even

105

persuasion through rules and norms.[2] These different methods do not necessarily reflect a fair international system but rather a hierarchical structure that creates rule-makers and rule-takers.[3]

This chapter goes beyond economics to explain how, over time, the internal structures of LAC societies have put them at a disadvantage in terms of their ability to achieve stability, security, economic development, tolerable levels of equality, and strong institutional frameworks.

Although inhabiting the same neighborhood as the U.S., LAC nations have constantly lagged behind and become the quintessential rule-takers. As rule-takers, however, they have also learned to navigate the international system.

This chapter also examines how LAC states have learned to adapt and respond to the growing complexity of an international system where power is exercised in more effective and profitable ways than through the use of military force.

The aim is to gain a better understanding of not only where LAC currently stands but also how these societies have learned to manipulate the international system to achieve at least some of their goals.

To better understand the political realm, this chapter begins with a historical overview of how LAC state actors and decision-makers have organized their societies domestically in an attempt to either overcome or take advantage of their status as rule-takers in the international system.[4]

How *Caudillismo* Helped Establish a State

In the 1820s, at the cusp of the Industrial Revolution, the Latin American traditional societies established independent states based mostly on agriculture or mining. The leaders of Latin American independence movements[5] sought to benefit from their participation in the world economy by achieving economic and political autonomy, only to face a monumental obstacle: their new republics still depended on the large-scale production of staples by a coerced labor force.

As commodity exporters par excellence, they soon realized that their traditional colonial structures made them susceptible to external economic shocks and constant foreign interventions. While the wars of independence proved to be worthwhile for those who owned land or mines and had Spanish ancestry, they were far less so for everyone else.[6]

To gain their independence, these new leaders had forged political alliances with economically and politically underprivileged *mestizos* and impoverished *criollos* looking for opportunities to prosper. Because of these relationships, once the goal of independence was achieved, the new republics ended up with a peculiar social structure: propertied *criollos* in charge, with the majority of peasants still a poor and coerced labor force.

The less fortunate *criollos* and *mestizos* stayed in the army or continued serving in government with the understanding that these two options remained their only way to advance in their new countries.

The owners of *latifundios* and mines had a big advantage: they presided over self-sufficient units that didn't depend on government support to survive. Because of their financial independence, the elites in these new American republics had no interest in getting involved with everyday government affairs or fostering strong, independent, long-lasting government institutions. Those tasks were left to the *mestizos* and impoverished *criollos* who were allowed to stay in power—as long as they maintained order.

As a rule, landowners supported incoming government officials in times of chaos and then removed them once they ceased to be of use. When the conflict ended, the elites retreated to their domains, and the menial task of everyday governing was left to Latin American *mestizo* and poor *criollo* leaders: *caudillos* or *caciques*, strong men of a dictatorial caste. This only lasted until these men became too strong for their own good (in the opinion of the elites) and consequently needed to be deposed. Elites then recruited new strong men to do their bidding, and the cycle began all over again.

As a result, instead of supporting a gradual process of institutionalization of government, *criollo* landowners continued backing the strong men of their choice. Interestingly, the fighting forces led by these *caudillos* were kept on a retainer and retained their pillaging privileges. While this arrangement enabled elites to keep the loyalty of the impoverished *mestizos* and *criollos* and made sure their estates were safe, it actually meant they were sacrificing any chance they might have had to acquire a full monopoly of power.

Through this system, elites, *criollos*, and *mestizos* entered into an unholy alliance that rested on mutual dependency, thus establishing the basis for a political structure that permeates Latin American societies even today. This type of social structure prioritizes personal ties over strong institutions.[7]

The beneficiaries of this distorted arrangement were the new breeds of leaders, the *caudillos*, who successfully established a sui generis—or completely unique—political system in which the lawful resolution of disputes as a function of government was nonexistent.[8]

The upper classes decided to forgo the opportunity to gradually build strong functioning state institutions or write constitutions that would reflect their social realities. They failed to understand the value of developing a tradition of good governance.

Consequently, over time, Latin America oscillated between liberalism and conservatism, centralism and federalism, or presidentialism and dictatorship. The *caudillaje* system supported unstable and inexperienced governments, unable to establish effective rule of law or collect taxes to pay public debt in economies overwhelmingly based on agriculture and mining.

Throughout the nineteenth century, efforts to strengthen the role of the state through strong men or *caudillos* like Diego Portales in Chile or Juan Manuel de Rosas in Argentina unleashed conflict and disorder.

By the 1870s, the social structure of *caudillismo* (based primarily on plunder) started to give way to a new political system: the authoritarian republic, a regime that created a centralized government to transform the countries' infrastructure and national currencies while retaining some of the *caudillo* features.

Weak government institutions made for weak states, vulnerable not only to internal and inter-state conflict but also to outside interventions. The European powers, and later on the U.S., saw Latin American nations as easy prey.

Moreover, these invasions and interventions served to exacerbate the already existing breach between conservatives and liberals within the embryonic Latin American political party systems, a gap that not only became a permanent feature during the nineteenth century but also helped define the Latin American landscape during the twentieth century.

As a result, these new nations with weak government structures were linked to the world economy through the export of primary goods. They adopted a passive stance towards modernization, and any sign of dynamism was forced from outside.[9]

An economy like Argentina's greatly benefited from the ability to produce cash crops and maintain some light industry, primarily in urban areas. More importantly, the transformations that were taking place in certain sections of production triggered the demand for new commodities, boosting huge investments in different areas.

The shift from investment in guano to nitrates is a case in point. In this instance, Peru, exporter of guano, lost to Chile once new technologies allowed for nitrates to be transformed into fertilizers. No other structure was more affected that the *hacienda*, which was forced to change its labor-intensive structure and become a mechanized and capital-intensive plantation, complete with railroad spurs leading to the nearest port.

Through these measures, the authoritarian republics embraced modernity, capitalism, and progress at the dawn of the twentieth century, while allowing representation and inclusion to fall by the wayside. As the executive offices became more stable, legitimate, and reliable, *caudillos* were replaced by authoritarian presidents who came to power through a restricted form of electoral competition.

As a result, Latin American republics became "competitive oligarchies"[10] through alliances between foreign corporations, native *criollo* oligarchies of landowners and miners, and merchants. These stable environments were guaranteed by the use of armed forces, supported by foreign powers and typically under the direction of a new and improved dictator, usually a former *caudillo*.

Thus, the great concentration of political power by one person became the most important authoritarian legacy of *caudillismo*.[11]

POLITICAL INSTITUTIONS AND DEMOCRACY

The *Caudillo* Tradition and Presidentialism in Latin America

By no means did the "oligarchic republics" seek to include everyone in the political process. The leaders of these regimes considered the democratic process complete once the constitutional procedure of electing a government was followed. Electoral competition was restricted to certain factions of the ruling elite, so it was hardly a consolidated democratic system.[12]

From 1900 to approximately 1939, elections took place in more than half the countries of Latin America, including important countries such as Argentina, Chile, Peru, and Colombia. These essentially fair-but-not-free electoral competitions undermined the *caudillos* or military dictators' hold on power. At the same time, however, the restriction of the electoral process ensured the victory of a privileged few in their stead.

Divided mostly between Conservatives and Liberals, these privileged factions became accustomed to showing little respect for compromise or the rule of law. If and when elections failed to meet their expectations, the polarized Liberal-Conservative camps shunned negotiated solutions and resorted to violence—mostly through military coups.

The electoral processes were thus reduced to a tool by which elites could compete for power by exploiting the votes of the general public for the sole purpose of achieving legitimacy.

As a result, military coups became common, and by 1940 the process of democratization that had begun to take place in Latin America by means of a restricted electoral process came to a halt.[13]

The elected governments governed using different strategies. For example, after a bloody revolution in Mexico, political power ended up concentrated in one political party. Through a corporatist strategy, the 1929 *Partido Nacional Revolucionario* (PNR) (renamed the *Partido de la Revolución Mexicana* in 1938, and finally in 1946, the *Partido Revolucionario Institucional* (PRI), established processes of competition and negotiation among the different social groups representing Mexican society, all under one umbrella. That is not to say that the PRI was the only political party; elections for congress and the office of the president took place regularly, with *Partido de Acción Nacional* (PAN) representing the minority opposition, especially in Congress.

When it came to the presidency, however, there was never any doubt that the PRI's candidate would always win. Endowed with the absolute power to act as a deal-breaker and, more importantly, to rename the next PRI presidential candidate (who would become his unquestioned successor), the Mexican president acted like the head of a perfect dictatorship until 2000.

South America achieved the concentration of executive power through a different route. To establish a modicum of social stability and suppress dissent while fostering economic development, countries such as Argentina and Brazil developed a unique partnership between the upper bourgeoisie and the armed forces: the "bureaucratic-authoritarian" (BA) state.[14]

The argument in favor of the BA state was that foreign investment would bring economic development, which would eventually lift people out of poverty. In other words, the need to foster economic growth superseded the need to develop political representation—only after the huge problem of economic inequality was addressed could democratic consolidation proceed.

Both the corporatist (Mexico) and the BA (Brazil, Argentina) options were successful in establishing order, fostering economic growth, and creating an environment favorable to foreign investment. More importantly, during the Cold War these options established powerful executive branches, something Washington deemed necessary to confront the Soviet threat in the Americas.

These options, however, left out negotiations with other social actors.

Mexico may have succeeded in designing a state in which negotiation and civilian control successfully took place under the PRI umbrella, but in South America the coercion needed to maintain order constantly compromised the institutional framework of the state by demanding a larger and more active role for the armed forces.

Subsequently, especially during the 1960s and 1970s, Central and South America experienced escalating patterns of increasingly brutal military intervention, most notably in Brazil (1964), Argentina (1966 and 1976), and Chile and Uruguay (both in 1973).

By the mid 1970s there were only four democracies in the region: Colombia, Costa Rica, Venezuela, and the Dominican Republic.[15] With the overthrow of Salazar in Portugal in 1974, however, an unprecedented wave of democratization began to sweep the world. With the election of a civilian leadership in the Dominican Republic in 1978, the "Third Wave" of democratization arrived in the Americas. This wave reached its peak in the 1990s when Chile inaugurated an elected civilian government under Patricio Aylwin and Mexican president Ernesto Zedillo recognized the electoral victory of the opposition PAN leader Vicente Fox. In contrast to the 1970s, by 2000 nearly 90 percent of the people of Latin America lived under an electoral democracy.

The Importance of the "Third Wave" of Democratization in LAC

Author Mark F. Plattner observes that the modern-day protests labeled as the "Arab Awakening" or "Arab Spring" clearly disprove that the Arab world is a global region impervious to the spread of democracy.[16]

The different Arab protests and revolts (which broke at a moment when the "Third Wave" of democratization seemed mired in stagnation) are invoking the universal principles of human dignity, freedom, citizenship, and democracy.

POLITICAL INSTITUTIONS AND DEMOCRACY

Whether democracy will come to all or some of the Arab societies involved in these protests or civil wars remains to be seen. Nevertheless, these protests do echo a time in the late 1970s when issues such as human rights, governance, and even democracy widely came to the fore in Europe and then the Western Hemisphere—a time when a general consensus also existed that democracy was impossible in Latin America.

Before the phenomenon of the "Third Wave," democracy was considered a privilege of the developed West. From the 1950s to the 1970s, common wisdom dictated that due to its Spanish colonial past, Latin America could only be led by emblematic strong men.

Based on this belief, Washington constantly interfered in Latin American domestic affairs, especially during the Cold War, backing dictators and perpetuating the notion of LAC's inescapable undemocratic fate.

According to this argument, Latin America's Spanish heritage gave these nations no choice but to accept the imposition of repressive regimes that alternated between violent interruptions and military coups. Cases in point include the 1954 coup against President Arbenz in Guatemala, the 1964 coups against President Goulart in Brazil, or the 1976 coup against Isabel Perón in Argentina.

In Washington's view, these authoritarian governments were needed and tolerated in order to oppose Soviet expansion. What's more, this approach to Latin American governance—which included a one dominant party regime in Mexico—supported the traditional claim by most Latin American elites that nothing but authoritarianism would work in their countries.

Consequently, economic and political elites were able for years to avoid making the hard choices needed to confront political and economic inequality, opting instead to govern by fostering patron-client networks and authoritarian policies.[17]

In the long run, this perception contributed to the curbing of the development and continuity of state capabilities (i.e. better government, better services, stronger rule of law) and private organizations (i.e. free press, advocacy groups, small businesses), rendering LAC states with limited institutional structures necessary for the development of democratic channels to ensure peaceful resolution of disputes.[18]

Fundamentally, Latin Americans were considered incapable of understanding how democracy works. The Western Hemisphere was the region where fate unquestionably established that advanced democracies such as the U.S. (and to a lesser extent, Canada) needed to lead the way on behalf of the less fortunate, underdeveloped authoritarian LAC states. History, however, often disproves what was once considered obvious and absolute, and when the Soviet threat disappeared, U.S. support for these authoritarian regimes began to crumble. As the 1980s drew to a close, Latin American societies realized that authoritarian dictators were not only no longer desired, they were no longer needed.

111

SECURITY AND DEMOCRACY

Table 6.1 Military coups, autogolpes, and illegal interruptions to democracy (including failed elections) in Latin America, 1900–2009

Country	Year
Argentina	1930, 1943, 1951, 1955, 1962, 1966, 1976, 1982, 1989, 2001
Bolivia	1930, 1934, 1936, 1943, 1946, 1951, 1964, 1969, 1970, 1971, 1978, 1979, 1980, 1981, 1982, 1989, 2003, 2005
Brazil	1930, 1937, 1945, 1954, 1955, 1964, 1992
Chile	1924, 1925, 1927, 1931, 1932, 1973
Colombia	1900, 1909, 1921, 1948, 1953, 1957
Costa Rica	1917, 1919
Dominican Republic	1902, 1903, 1906, 1911, 1914, 1916, 1930–1961, 1963, 1964–1965, 1994
Ecuador	1906, 1911, 1912, 1925, 1931, 1935, 1937, 1944, 1947, 1961, 1963, 1970, 1972, 2000, 1997, 2004–2005
El Salvador	1913, 1931, 1944, 1948, 1960, 1961, 1970–1979
Guatemala	1921, 1922, 1926, 1930, 1931, 1954, 1957, 1963, 1982, 1983, 1993
Haiti	1902, 1908, 1911, 1912, 1913, 1914, 1915, 1946, 1950, 1956, 1986, 1988, 1990, 1991, 1994, 2000–2003, 2004
Honduras	1903, 1907, 1911, 1919, 1924, 1956, 1957, 1963, 1972, 1975, 1978, 2009
Mexico	1913, 1914, 1920
Nicaragua	1909, 1910, 1911, 1912, 1926, 1936, 1947, 2001–2005
Panama	1931, 1941, 1949, 1951, 1968, 1983, 1990
Paraguay	1902, 1904, 1905, 1908, 1911, 1912, 1921, 1936, 1948, 1949, 1954, 1989, 1996, 1999–2000
Peru	1914, 1919, 1930, 1931, 1933, 1948, 1962, 1963, 1968, 1975, 1992
Uruguay	1933, 1951, 1973, 1984
Venezuela	1908, 1936, 1945, 1947, 1948, 1952, 1958, 1992, 1999, 2002

Horwitz, Betty, *The Transformation of the Organization of American States: A Multilateral Framework for Regional Governance* (London: Anthem Press, 2011).

Consequently, once the Cold War ended, Latin America began to address past human rights abuses with the support of Washington. This growing support for human rights in the Americas helped boost the spread of the "Third Wave" of democratization during the 1990s. The seeds for this were planted during the 1980s when U.S. unilateralism in the fight against communism began to yield negative results. Washington's support for the anti-communist government in El Salvador; its funding for the anti-Sandinista

POLITICAL INSTITUTIONS AND DEMOCRACY

rebels in Nicaragua; and its deposing and subsequent support of the drug-trafficking indictment of General Manuel Antonio Noriega, for example, began to seriously affect U.S. standing both at home and abroad.

The approach started to be perceived as outdated and counterproductive, and Latin American states began to seek alternative ways of addressing the problems plaguing the region. One success was the Contadora and Esquipulas multilateral accord, which negotiated a resolution to the Central American conflict without active U.S. participation. Efforts such as these contributed to changing the international environment at a time when communism was no longer a threat. More importantly, these efforts helped fuel the change in attitude among decision-makers, who began to accept democracy as the best form of political organization.[19]

The shift toward democratization in the Western Hemisphere had begun during the 1980s when political authorities began to realize that complying with international instruments, treaties, and organizations worked to their advantage.[20] This was true for both rule-makers and rule-takers in the Americas.

The first sign of political change in the practices of Latin American states was the OAS resolution condemning the human rights record of the Somoza regime in Nicaragua.[21] This commitment helped establish an important precedent regarding the advancement of collective obligation for the defense of human rights and the advancement of democracy.

Subsequently, in 1985 the Protocol of Cartagena de Indias made the defense of human rights and democracy an explicit purpose. This constituted an important step in changing the international political environment as well as the political behavior of state and non-state actors worldwide.

Despite these facts, it is important to keep in mind that the advance of democracy was not only spurred on by a change in ideas and attitudes. During the 1980s, the neoliberal policies and market reforms that came into play took for granted an affinity between freer markets and freer politics.

In other words, the line of thinking widely accepted among high-ranking policymakers in Latin America was that government corruption and ineffectiveness needed to be dealt with through neoliberal policies and democratic measures applied simultaneously.[22]

With the collapse of the Soviet Union, worldwide acceptance of the need for orthodox economic reforms and a change of culture in the international arena, democracy was no longer just a lofty goal. Gradually, it became a requirement in order for states to be able to participate in international decisions.

Policymakers and academics needed to define what, other than the free and fair election of government officials, needed to be included for an elected regime to be considered democratic. Eventually a general consensus materialized around a standard model for democracy. Focused mainly on procedure, it was called polyarchy.[23]

This basic formula allowed countries to consider different "democratic recipes." Nations explored ways of using the basic ingredients of a polyarchy to develop democratic modalities that were tailored to their own realities, histories, and places in the world.[24]

Different theoretical perspectives began to focus on the process of democratic achievement and consolidation, seeking explanations for why some countries achieved democratic governance while others failed.

A "How To" Guide to Democracy for Latin America and the Caribbean

The main goal of theorists and politicians was to find the combination of elements that would work for their unique countries, ultimately providing a general "how to" guide for democratic consolidation.

Looking at Latin American elites, Guillermo O'Donnell and Phillipe Schmitter focused on the problems and possible choices facing political leaders, either "soft liners" or "hard liners", during periods of authoritarian transitions. In their view, the success or failure of the process of democratization depended upon the choices made by political elites when gradually liberalizing their societies and extending political rights to previously excluded persons and organizations.

Fernando Henrique Cardoso and Enzo Falettto, on the other hand, examined the decisions made by Latin American authorities, seeking to establish the right conditions to achieve democratic consolidation while breaking the cycle of dependent development.

Thinking about the role of the armed forces in the history of Latin America, Felipe Agüero, David Pion-Berlin, and Harold Trinkunas looked at the role and extensive influence of the military over decision-makers during democratic transitions.

Pion-Berlin and Trinkunas were particularly concerned with the deterioration of defense capabilities during democratic transitions. They were worried about "ministerial frailty" in the executive and legislative centers of government, foreseeing (rightly as it turned out) situations in which the erosion of military power would reveal the incompetence of civilian institutions and their inability to guarantee and maintain order.[25]

Democracy in LAC owes much to changes in normative attitudes worldwide, but it was truly made possible by economic shifts. By the end of the 1980s, democracy had slowly begun to take root in Latin America and this was due, in part, to the so-called "lost decade" of economic growth that helped loosen the grip of authoritarian states over their societies.

In many ways, democratic forces in LAC are not new. There have been efforts (all of them short-lived) to establish some manner of popular representation before—for instance, during the nineteenth century with the influence of the Enlightenment on Latin American elites, or in 1944 and

POLITICAL INSTITUTIONS AND DEMOCRACY

1945 following the defeat of fascism, when discussions of democracy and justice emerged in Latin America. Political elites always found reasons to stop their development. This time round, however, they were beginning to change the patterns of the past. Economic crises (such as the ones suffered during the 1980s) eroded the capacity of state bureaucracies to support elected officials. Once in power, decision-makers all over Latin America found that they could not back their promises with immediate action.

Trying to maintain the status quo, Latin American authorities tended to avoid taking the steps necessary to tackle the lack of institutional capacity to make democracy work. In short, they overlooked the importance of working through streamlined, efficient, and competitive state systems.[26]

The rapid rate of globalization was not helping matters. By the beginning of the 1990s, Latin Americans, still primary commodity exporters with stagnant economies, again assumed the role of rule-takers in an increasingly interconnected world.

This time, however, Latin Americans expected more accountability from their elected officials. This was reflected not only in their economic outlook but also by a change in perspective as a result of how different theories fine-tuned concepts to improve the "democratic recipe." Policymakers in many LAC countries realized market reforms were necessary, but also that they required fiscal discipline and strategies to develop functioning state institutions.

In other words, it became evident that electoral choice, though critical to democracy, was not enough. Beyond the issue of the quality of democratic procedure, the accountability of elected officials became increasingly important, and this began to have positive consequences for the economy.[27]

Main points:

- Latin American societies structured around land ownership, making for weak government structures.
- Need of strong men (*caudillos*) to keep the peace. Depose them if they get too strong.
- *Caudillos* in government positions create authoritarian republics.
- Governments reflect inequality and exclusion.
- IS model makes for entrepreneurial state that fails to adapt to globalizing forces.
- Debt crises eventually weaken government structures and "Third Wave" of democratization arrives in LAC.
- LAC countries develop electoral democracies with strong reliance on executive branch: *presidencialismo*.

Notes

1 Von Carl Clausewitz, *On War* (indexed edition, ed. and trans. by Michael Howard and Peter Paret (Princeton, NJ: Princeton University Press, 1984). For more see Anne-Marie Slaughter, "International Relations: Principal Theories," in *Max Planck Encyclopedia of Public International Law*, ed. R. Wolfrum (Oxford: Oxford University Press, 2011). Available at www.princeton.edu/-slaughtr/722_IntlRelPrincipalTheories_Slaughter_20110509zG.pdf.

2 Institutions are established, recurrent and valued patterns of behavior that structure, govern, and constrain human interaction. Institutions include formal rules, written laws, formal social conventions, and informal norms of behavior. Institutions also include the means by which rules and norms are enforced. North, Wallis, and Weingast worry about the negative means that institutions create and use in mature natural states, and are particularly concerned with how institutions such as elections, representative legislative bodies, corporations, and political parties operate differently in the presence of open or limited entry and access and are often misused by elected officials in societies where a significant part of the population is not treated equally. Douglas C. North, John J. Wallis, and Barry B. Weingast, *Violence and Social Order: A Conceptual Framework to Interpret History* (Cambridge: Cambridge University Press, 2009), 15 and 259; Douglas C. North, John J. Wallis, and Barry B. Weingast, "Violence and the Rise of Open Access Orders," *Journal of Democracy*, vol. 22, no. 1 (2009), 55–68.

3 The English School discusses the development of a society of states over time. In this society, not all states are equal, and some matter more than others. Nevertheless, the development of an international structure bound by rules and norms imposes limits on the legitimate uses of war and explains in great part the decline of its use over time. For more see Barry Buzan, *From International to World Society?* (Cambridge: Cambridge University Press, 2004), 192–193.

4 For more see Tim Dunne and Brian C. Schmidt, "Realism," in *The Globalization of World Politics: An Introduction to International Relations*, ed. John Baylis, Steve Smith, and Patricia Owens, 4th edition (Oxford: Oxford University Press, 2008), 90–103.

5 For the most part, the heroes of Latin American independence movements proved utterly unprepared to assume the responsibilities of good government. Antonio José de Sucre, for example, excelled at assisting Bolívar during military campaigns aimed at creating a unified republic of Gran Colombia. Nevertheless, neither of them was able to prevent the dissolution of Gran Colombia at a later date. Sucre and Bolívar are just two examples of the kind of Latin American leadership— aristocrats and *criollos*—that came with independence.

6 Stanley J. Stein and Barbara H. Stein, *The Colonial Heritage of Latin America* (New York: Oxford University Press, 1970).

7 Eric R. Wolf and Edward C. Hansen, "Caudillo Politics: A Structural Analysis,"*Comparative Studies in Society and History*, vol. 9, no. 2 (1967), 168–179.

8 The *caudillaje* system was defined by four salient characteristics: 1) the repeated emergence of armed patron-client sets, cemented by personal ties of dominance and submission and by a common desire to obtain wealth by force of arms; 2) the lack of institutionalized means for succession of offices; 3) the use of violence in political competition; and 4) the repeated failure of incumbent leaders to guarantee their tenures as chieftains. For a detailed description, see Eric R. Wolf and Edward C. Hansen, "Caudillo Politics: A Structural Analysis," *Comparative Studies in Society and History*, vol. 9, no. 2 (1967); Thomas E. Skidmore and Peter E. Smith, *Modern Latin America* (New York and Oxford: Oxford University Press, 2005), 20–41.

POLITICAL INSTITUTIONS AND DEMOCRACY

9 The cycle of change from *caudillaje* to dictatorship was triggered by the great European depression of 1873–1886. This marked the onset of protectionism at home and imperialist expansionism abroad. In addition to mechanization and modern transportation, this transformation required the development of credit unions and national currencies. Even more importantly, it required an end to the system of anarchic pillage and the establishment of a degree of political stability to make possible the transformation of the haciendas and mines through the use of force, combined with state bureaucracies that maintained *caudillaje* traits. For more see Skidmore and Smith, *Modern Latin America*, 20–41.

10 Porfirio Díaz in Mexico, for example, typified the kind of head of state that brought Latin America into the twentieth century. Yet even when they were allowed or obliged to vote, the mostly poor and uneducated Latin American public was never given a real political voice. As in the case of the aristocratic "generation of 1880" in Argentina from 1880 to 1915 or the "parliamentary republic" of Chile from 1891 to 1923, the right to compete for political office was directed by economic and political elites and restricted to the upper classes, which exhibited a winner-takes-all mentality. Because there was no other effective channel to mediate conflicts, the competition for the executive branch became the only way to achieve political goals. Eric R. Wolf and Edward C. Hansen, "Caudillo Politics: A Structural Analysis," *Comparative Studies in Society and History*, vol. 9, no 2 (1967), 178.

11 Paola Cesarini and Katherine Hite, *Authoritarian Legacies and Democracy in Latin America and Southern Europe* (Stanford, CA: Hellen Kellog Institute for International Studies, 2004), 4–6, define authoritarian legacies as those rules, procedures, norms, practices, dispositions, relationships, and memories originating in a well-defined authoritarian experience of the past that survives democratic transitions and intervenes in the quality and practice of post-authoritarian democracies by restraining the spaces where political discourse occurs.

12 For more see Brian Loveman, *The Constitution of Tyranny: Regimes of Exception in Spanish America* (Pittsburg, PA: University of Pittsburg Press, 1993); Brian Loveman, *No Higher Law: American Foreign Policy and the Western Hemisphere since 1776* (Chapel Hill, NC: University of North Carolina Press, 2010), and Peter Smith, *Democracy in Latin America, Political Change in Comparative Perspective* (New York and Oxford: Oxford University Press, 2005).

13 According to Peter H. Smith, *The Talons of the Eagle: Dynamics of U.S.-Latin American Relations* (New York, Oxford: Oxford University Press, 2005), 27–31, during this time the democratic curve took the shape of an M. Coinciding with the end of World War II, Latin America experienced a sharp upturn in democratic politics in Guatemala (1945), Peru (1945), Argentina (1946), Brazil (1946), Venezuela (1946), and Ecuador (1948), alongside the pre-existing democracies of Chile, Uruguay and Colombia that dated back to 1942. Because of the power bestowed on the executive branch and the weakness of the other branches of government, compounded by the onset of the Cold War, Latin America suffered a democratic downturn in the early 1950s (largely as a result of military coups), followed by a fairly swift recovery.

14 The BA state was viewed by economic and political elites as a necessary tool to impose social order and create an environment conducive to foreign investment, even if this meant the economic and political exclusion of the popular sectors. Guillermo O'Donnell, "Tensions in the Bureaucratic-Authoritarian State and the Question of Democracy," in *Counterpoints, Selected Essays in Authoritarianism and Democratization*, ed. Guillermo O'Donnell (Notre Dame, IN: Notre Dame University Press, 1999), 35–62.

SECURITY AND DEMOCRACY

15 Ibid.

16 Mark F. Plattner, "Comparing the Arab Revolts: The Global Context," *Journal of Democracy*, vol. 22, no. 4 (2011), 5–12.

17 For instance, still in a Cold War frame of mind, Washington felt compelled to unilaterally invade Panama. Time and again, Washington failed to support the advance of democracy in Latin America. U.S. leaders halted the ascendancy of the left in Chile, and failed to pressure countries such as Brazil and Argentina to face their authoritarian legacies. All the while, Latin American authorities kept state institutions weak, relying on clientelism as the main instrument for governance. Elected officials in countries like Colombia came to power facing internal governability obstacles that could not be addressed through the rule of law or state institutions alone. Heraldo Muñoz, "Chile: The Limits of Success," in *Exporting Democracy: The United States and Latin America*, ed. A. L. Lowenthal (Baltimore, MD and London: Johns Hopkins University Press, 1991), 39–52. OAS, "Protocol of Cartagena de Indias", O.S.P.A.d. (XIV-E/85), Organization of American States, Washington, DC (1986).

18 Wallis, North, and Weingast, *Violence and Social Order*, 32–49

19 These negotiations, together with the rising importance of the defense of human rights worldwide, contributed to the change in attitudes among LAC authorities, compelling them to act cooperatively. For more see Carolyn M. Shaw, *Cooperation and Consensus in the Organization of American States* (New York and London: Palgrave McMillan, 2004), 156–157.

20 Constructivism focuses on the importance of norms and ideas in the functioning of the international system. For more see Michael Barnett and Martha Finnemore, *Rules for the World: International Organizations in Global Politics* (Ithaca, NY and London: Cornell University Press, 2004).

21 These multilateral efforts failed to appropriately respond to the actions of General Anastasio Somoza or Manuel Antonio Noriega. For more see Andrew F. Cooper, and Thomas Legler, "The OAS Democratic Solidarity Paradigm: Questions of Collective and National Leadership," in *Latin American Politics and Society*, vol. 43, no. 1 (2001), 103–126; OAS, "17th Meeting of Consultation of Ministers of Foreign Affairs of the OAS" (June 23), Res/2,Ser/F II.17, Doc 49/79.Rev 2 (Washington, DC: OAS, 1979).

22 The thinking behind neoliberal reforms was that by harmonizing a wide range of fiscal, monetary, industrial, labor, and commercial policies among multiple nations, vast zones of the former Third and Second Worlds could be reintegrated into global capitalism and find a way to catch up to the First World, both economically and politically. Consequently democratic authorities began to rely on highly educated technocrats who would design a competent state and foster relationships with business and labor to create and maintain stability. A leaner and more competent state would invest in education and health both because it was the right thing to do and because it contributed to market efficiency. The competent state would address market failures and channel resources to enable the poor to overcome their conditions. Consequently, the logic of democracy would work for its own sake and for the consolidation of market economies. This was the basic strategy followed by Alejandro Foxley in Chile, Domingo Cavallo in Argentina, Fernando Henrique Cardoso in Brazil and Pedro Carlos Aspe Armella in Mexico among others. Jorge I. Dominguez, "Technopols: Ideas and Leaders in Freeing Politics and Markets in Latin America in the 1990s," in *Technopols: Freeing Politics and Market Reforms in Latin America in the 1990s*, ed. Jorge I. Dominguez (Philadelphia, PA: Penn State University Press, 1996), 1–48; William I. Robinson, "Promoting Poliarchy in Latin America: The Oxymoron

POLITICAL INSTITUTIONS AND DEMOCRACY

of "Market Democracy," in *Latin America After Neoliberalism: Turning the Tide in the 21st Century?*, ed. Eric Hershberg and Fred Rosen (New York and London: The New Press, North American Congress on Latin America (NCLA), 2006), 96–119.

23 Robert A. Dahl argued that a large country aiming to become democratic in modern times needed to acquire very specific institutions or "ingredients" that could turn any regime into a polyarchy (rule of the many). These ingredients established the minimal requirements for a regime to be considered a democracy. The main ingredients of a polyarchy were:(1) Elected representatives (2) Free, fair and frequent elections (3) Freedom of expression (4) Alternative information (5) Associational autonomy (6) Inclusive citizenship. Robert Dahl, *On Democracy* (New Haven, CT and London: Yale University Press, 1998), 83–99. The definition of democracy as a polyarchy is part of a tradition that defined democracy in procedural terms. Daniel H. Levine and José E. Molina (page 5 of "The Quality of Democracy: Strengths and Weaknesses in Latin America," in *The Quality of Democracy in Latin America*, ed. Daniel H. Levine, and José E. Molina (Boulder, CO and London: Lynne Rienner Publishers, 2011), point out those procedural definitions of democracy, conceived as a system of representation with universal adult participation according to equal rules, rest on a liberal and pluralist understanding of politics and the political process. They correctly imply that procedural definitions of democracy have the attraction of clear and analytical boundaries and portability across cases. They can also easily run into difficulties if the motivations and institutional channels specified in the definition are not linked explicitly with the surrounding social context.

24 For examples of these explanations see Juan J. Linz and Alfred Stepan, *Problems of Democratic Transition and Consolidation: Southern Europe, South America and Post-Communist Europe* (Baltimore, MD and London: Johns Hopkins University Press, 1996); Scott Mainwaring, and Matthew Soberg Shugart, eds, *Presidentialism and Democracy in Latin America* (Cambridge and New York: Cambridge University Press, 1997); Felipe Agüero and Jeffrey Stark, eds, *Fault Lines of Democracy in Post-Transition Latin America* (Miami, FL: North-South Center Press, University of Miami, 1998).

25 For more on dependency and authoritarianism during democratic transitions, see Fernando H. Cardoso and Enzo Faletto, *Dependency and Development in Latin America* (Berkeley, CA and London: University of California Press, 1979); Guillermo O'Donnel and Philippe Schmitter, *Transitions from Authoritarian Rule: Tentative Conclusions about Uncertain democracies* (Baltimore, MD: Johns Hopkins University Press, 1986, 2013). For the role of the armed forces in the history of Latin America during democratic transitions, Felipe Agüero, David Pion-Berlin, and Harold Trinkunas, for example, were concerned with democratizing elites in Latin America effectively taking control of their new governments. Looking at the Spanish transition for comparison, Agüero argued that the position the military occupied in the outgoing authoritarian regime and the specific nature of the transition path would impact the structure of authority patterns in the new regime. These patterns would necessarily extend beyond the transition, determining the impunity, position, and power of the military authorities within the new civilian governments. If, as in Chile, the military emerged in a position of power, it could affect civilian supremacy by overpowering the civilian authorities and unduly influencing the shape of their new constitutional orders. Conversely, when looking at Argentina, Pion-Berlin argued that the deterioration of defense capabilities during democratic transitions impacted the "ministerial frailty" of the executive and legislative centers of government. He foresaw a

situation in which the erosion of military power would reveal the incompetence of civilian institutions and their inability to guarantee and maintain order. Felipe Agüero and Jeffrey Stark, *Fault Lines of Democracy in Post-Transition Latin America* (Miami, FL: North-South Center Press, University of Miami, 1998); David Pion-Berlin and Harold Trinkunas, "Attention Deficits: Why Politicians Ignore Defense Policies in Latin America," *Latin American Research Review: The Journal of the Latin American Studies Association*, vol. 42, no. 3 (2007), 78–100.

26 Margaret D. Hayes, "Building Consensus on Security: Toward a New Framework," in *Governing the Americas: Assessing Multilateral Institutions*," ed. Mace Gordon, Thérien, Jean-Phillipe. and Haslam Paul (Boulder, CO and London: Lynne-Reinner Publisher, 2007), 71–96.

27 Jonathan Hartlyn, Jennifer McCoy, and Thomas M. Mustillo, "La Importancia de la gobernanza electoral y la calidad de las elecciones en América Latina Contemporánea," *América Latina Hoy*, no. 51, April, 2009, 15–40. Daniel H. Levine and José E. Molina, "Evaluating the Quality of Democracy in Latin America," in *The Quality of Democracy in Latin America*. ed. Daniel H. Levine and José E Molina (Boulder, CO and London: Lynne Rieneer Publishers, 2011), 245–60.

7

ELECTORAL DEMOCRACIES IN LATIN AMERICA AND THE CARIBBEAN

A democracy, in our view, is any political regime in which 1) free and fair elections choose the lawmakers and the head of government; 2) there is nearly universal adult suffrage except among immigrant noncitizens; 3) the state protects civil liberties and political rights; 4) armed actors, including the military, criminal organizations, and paramilitary groups do not significantly influence government policies.

Scott Mainwaring and Aníbal Pérez-Liñán[1]

Introduction

In an often-cited article published in 1990, John Williamson coined the term "Washington Consensus" to refer to the minimum requirements of policy advice being offered to Latin American countries by Washington-based institutions.[2]

The list summarized ten propositions that many U.S. policy-makers argued would help Latin Americans embark on a process of market-oriented economic reforms. These reforms were considered the central component of a strategy that would allow Latin American economies to become more efficient, follow the example of the Asian Tigers, and benefit from an increasing globalized world. This was seen as the only way to re-establish economic growth and make the region's transition to democracy sustainable.

Ironically, market reform and liberalization policies pushed Latin American countries closer to democracy by loosening the grip of state bureaucracies and giving the general public the right to choose, but the failure to adequately pair this push towards democratization with solid, sustainable growth during the 1990s resulted in increasing difficulties in the consolidation and institutionalization of democratic regimes, especially in Venezuela, Bolivia, Ecuador, and Argentina.[3]

Latin Americans became accustomed to electing their governments, but once the electoral processes were successfully completed, political authorities were faced with rising expectation from their electorates.

In sharp contrast to previous decades, newly elected Latin American elites found that they were being held accountable. Unfortunately, they were incapable of responding to the changing social and political conditions—both internally and in the international arena—with the swiftness required by their citizens. This made the fragility of these democracies very apparent during the 1990s.

In effect, Latin American states were well on their way to becoming consolidated electoral democracies, but their leadership often failed to respond to the general plight of the citizenry through existing institutionalized channels, organizations, institutions, or rule of law. This was the case during the presidential terms of Gonzalo Sánchez de Lozada (2002/3) and Carlos Mesa (2003–2005) in Bolivia.[4]

Instead of making the tough choices needed to develop the institutions required by a modern state, these leaders opted for populist measures to respond to immediate crises while remaining in power. Sadly, they also failed to use the new regional environment that was developing around them to their advantage, choosing not to seek the support of other state and international organizations (IOs) that offered legal constraints protecting their elected regimes.

The choices elected officials made during this period determined how their countries would enter the twenty-first century. Their decisions determined whether the electorate would be satisfied with their governments or have a say in what their country's role in world affairs should be, especially with regard to economic development and integration.[5]

Electoral Democracies

Democratic consolidation was an important goal as part of the market reform process. At the same time, however, elected officials all over the region were confronted with the task of modernizing their economies and political structures.

A freer political arena coupled with a freer economy was considered a split strategy for achieving economic growth while diminishing underdevelopment and inequality. These strategies ended up falling short, however, especially in any comparison with China, Singapore, or South Korea, where democratic consolidation was not a high priority.

It became increasingly clear that the quality of governance was the problem—and one that elected officials needed to confront sooner rather than later if they wished to establish internal legitimacy and external credibility.

If it was to be done by democratic means, elected officials needed to find a way of fostering the kind of widespread economic and political participation that involved impersonal delivery of public goods and services (rather than a focus on personal ties and clientelism).

ELECTORAL DEMOCRACIES IN LAC

Impersonality means being able to rely on established and independent institutions and laws, and in these circumstances, elites and other social actors are both obliged and able to settle their differences via compromise through constitutional arrangements. These established "rules of the game" protect the rights of all members of society (including those at a disadvantage) by limiting and defining the powers of government and also guaranteeing an unbiased application of the rule of law.[6]

In this way, internally, elected political elites can secure their own rights and the rights of other elite groups by making citizens feel less threatened by their own governments. Externally, as part of an inter-American state system, if and when internal forces threaten it, a democratically elected government can face dissent by exercising legitimacy through broadening the scope of their foreign policies.

In this system, elected officials who find themselves under threat can appeal to the inter-American instruments established for the defense of democracy. The idea behind this is that an elected government (one that's also functioning and trustworthy) can project influence internationally or seek support or cooperation from other states through a reputation for stability and competence.[7]

Chile and Uruguay are cases in point. After years of fiscal discipline and democratic consolidation, Chile has been an active participant on the world stage as part of the Pacific Alliance and Trans-Pacific Partnership (TPP). Chile is hoping to link its economy to other countries such as Singapore, South Korea, and Malaysia, and can aspire to do so because of its internal environment of good governance and stability.[8]

This path toward an increased international profile is in sharp contrast to nations like Venezuela, Argentina, Nicaragua, Ecuador, and Bolivia, which continue to avoid the difficult task of changing their social structures and rely on tools such as decrees, plebiscites, and referenda, thus perpetuating the general economic and political exclusion that has become a permanent Latin American feature.[9]

There is no doubt that the free market model of the "Washington Consensus" succeeded in controlling inflation and developing responsible fiscal policies to control public debt. Yet in much of the region it failed to alleviate the suffering inflicted on many through weak growth, periodic financial crises, and deepening social and economic inequalities.

At the same time, it did create new opportunities for mobilizing the opposition, some channeled through the electoral arena and some fueling the mass protest movements that toppled governments in Ecuador, Bolivia, and Argentina. Leftist leaders took advantage of this popular backlash against the market reforms that failed to fulfill their promise of enhancing prosperity and exacerbated long-standing problems such as precarious employment.

Essentially, it became clear that the advance of democracy and market reforms were not necessarily two sides of the same coin, and that the left

SECURITY AND DEMOCRACY

remained a factor in post–Cold War America (albeit no longer in the Soviet or even Marxist tradition).

By the beginning of the twenty-first century, an unprecedented number of leftist presidential candidates achieved victory all over Latin America. Instead of aiming to gain power by assuming the mantle of revolution (as they had done from the 1960s through the 1980s), leftist leaders proved that it was possible to achieve office through the electoral process.

The wave of electoral victories began with the 1998 Venezuelan presidential victory of former paratrooper Hugo Chávez (who had ironically led a failed coup six years earlier). Chávez was followed by the Socialist candidate Ricardo Lagos in Chile (2000); ex-metal-worker and Workers' Party (PT) leader Ignácio Lula da Silva in Brazil (2002); left-of-center Peronist Néstor Kirchner in Argentina (2003); Tabaré Vásquez of the Leftist Broad Front (FA) in Uruguay (2004); the coca growers' union leader Evo Morales of the Movement toward Socialism (MAS) in Bolivia (2005); ex-revolutionary leader of the Sandinista National Liberation Front (FSLN) Daniel Ortega in Nicaragua (2006); Rafael Correa in Ecuador (2006) and Ollanta Humalla in Peru (2011).

By 2009, nearly two-thirds of Latin Americans lived under some form of left-leaning national government. By the end of the decade, leftist candidates won in Paraguay (ex-Catholic bishop Fernando Lugo) and El Salvador (Mauricio Funes of the Farabundo Martí National Front (FMLN)). Incumbent leftist presidents or parties were subsequently re-elected in Venezuela (2000, 2006), Chile (2006), Brazil (2006, 2010), Argentina (2007), Ecuador (2009), Bolivia (2009), and Uruguay (2009).[10]

With market reforms already in place and the scope, depth, and speed of Latin American nations' integration into the global economy increasing, a frontal attack on the capitalist system had become prohibitively costly. Leftist leaders needed to confront the new reality that without the Soviet alternative there was no longer any real competitor for capitalism.

More importantly, the experience of brutal authoritarianism (such as the atrocities committed against civilians during the Central American conflicts of the 1980s) was still fresh in the memories of many Latin Americans and leftist leaders needed to be sensitive to this. At the very least they needed to be perceived as committed to upholding democratic principles.[11]

Interestingly, leftist leaders started winning elections by promising to put pressure on economic elites and work toward reorienting the economy to foster prosperity for the majority, thus creating the omnipresent dilemma of modern Latin American authority: once in power, governments have the obligation to maintain order while gradually effecting change in order to fulfill the promises to their electorates.

These elected governments thus found themselves in the same bind that faced the officials who preceded them: any effort in the direction of change faced difficult internal obstacles and tight external constraints.

Latin American democracies seemed unable to move beyond their previous fates as victims of the commodity lottery; yet again they were inserted into the global economic system mainly as commodity exporters, but now with elected officials working through inefficient bureaucracies and states.

These constraints precluded any reform strategy by political authorities that could immediately and profoundly alter the distribution of socioeconomic benefits in their societies. Ironically, Latin American leftist governments could neither break the existing constraints through a revolution nor evade these constraints through social-democratic synergies between economic growth and social justice.

As Weyland (2010) aptly describes,[12] they faced the classic dilemma of leftism in an especially straightforward fashion: how to bring about change despite significant obstacles. Although the boundaries of feasibility had tightened and their range of options had narrowed (if they wanted to stay in power), leftist political authorities still had to decide whether to put activism or realism first.[13]

Latin America's Two Lefts

In his 2006 article, "Latin America's Left Turn,"[14] Jorge G. Castañeda pointed out that as the twenty-first century began, Latin America continued to face many of its traditional problems. Even when 2007 marked the fourth consecutive year of economic growth, high levels of corruption, violence, crime, and political gridlock persisted, and the benefits of foreign investment and free-trade agreements with the U.S. had yet to trickle down to the general population.

In these circumstances, Castañeda argued, a strong ideological and policy reaction against the pro-market "Washington Consensus" was not surprising.

Yet these left-leaning governments were confronted by the same dilemma that today's leaders face—the inter-American legal framework and macroeconomic orthodoxy puts clear constraints on any government, regardless of its platform.

After campaign promises had been made, Latin American leaders from the right, center, or left of the political spectrum needed to make strategic choices vis-à-vis their own populations.

When it comes to the new wave of leftist leaders in the region, it is the response to macroeconomic constraints while aiming to achieve the promised goals of social equity and justice that differentiates the moderate from the populist wing of the Latin American left. In fact, Latin American electorates have been choosing between not one but two lefts.

On the one hand there were parties, leaders, and movements that had authentic socialist and progressive roots. Ricardo Lagos from the Socialist Party in Chile, Luiz Inácio Lula da Silva and Dilma Rouseff from the Worker's Party (PT) in Brazil, Tabaré Vázques and José Mujica in Uruguay,

Chile's Michelle Bachelet: these leaders followed pragmatic paths, with policies remarkably similar to those of their predecessors. They demonstrated a full-fledged and genuine respect for democracy.

Castañeda makes the important point that revolutionary zeal and old-school anti-Americanism was tempered by experience of the authoritarianism of the left and years of exile and resignation, engendering greater realism.

The moderate left has accepted the basic framework of Latin America's new market model, with some modifications. They advocate for industrial policy initiatives, new public investment policies, and better and firmer regulation for business activities alongside attempts to boost human capital and improve worker training.

For example, Chile's government needed to deal with the inherited political constrains of the Pinochet-era constitution that had obliged the Lagos (2000–2006) and Bachelet (2006–2010) administrations to form coalition governments. Both Lagos and Bachelet had to manage the business of government while maintaining the support of both the left-of-center coalition of political parties, the *Concertación*, and (when possible) the right-wing parties of the *Alianza*.

The main goals of the *Concertación* governments have been to protect macroeconomic stability, generate economic growth and employment, invest in human capital, and alleviate poverty. Taking a gradual approach, they've maintained the orthodox economic policies of their predecessors while pursuing a distinct form of social policy that moves toward a more universal system of social protection, inspired by leftist commitments to social equity, justice, and solidarity.[15]

The Lula administration for example, maintained Cardoso's economic policies. It embraced a generally market-oriented economy and the traditional clientelistic rules of operating within Brazil's legislature (*fisiologismo*),

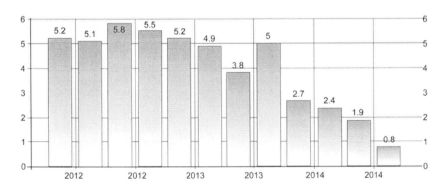

Figure 7.1 Chile GDP annual growth rate
Source: Trading Economics, www.tradingeconomics.com/chile/gdp-growth-annual.

helping the nation achieve stability and modest growth and displaying a steady commitment to addressing historic injustices.

Interestingly, over time, despite the difficulties of political reform, the levels of poverty in Brazil have consistently declined. Even though a large sector of the left voiced their disappointment with Lula's choices, around 29 million people were lifted out of poverty between 2003 and 2009, without disruption to the economic or political structure.[16]

On the other hand, the region also saw leftist leaders from a populist, purely nationalist background, with few ideological underpinnings. Officials such as Venezuela's Hugo Chávez and Nicolas Maduro or Nicaragua's Daniel Ortega, all with military backgrounds; the Kirchners with their Peronist roots; even some leaders within the Mexican political PRI establishment such as Iguala's mayor, José Abarca Velázquez, and his wife María—who allegedly masterminded the abduction of protesting students[17]—have proven much less responsive to modernizing influences.

For them, power has always been the key factor, and the despair of the poor and constituencies willing to "work the system" (rather than demand accountability) can be manipulated in order to win elections or criticize the U.S.

At the end of the day, however, even leaders holding to traditional clientelistic patterns cannot avoid the reality of the capitalist global economy that surrounds them. When they do, as the examples of Venezuela or Argentina have shown, their economies and most vulnerable citizens suffer.

Whether an elected government comes from the moderate left, the populist left, or the right, the issue of good governance needs to be confronted. For example, for much of the decade Brazil has grown at a very fast

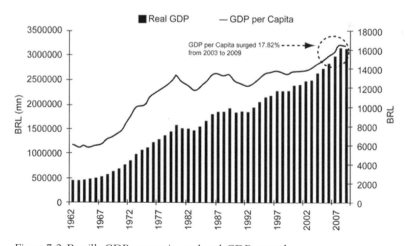

Figure 7.2 Brazil's GDP per capita and real GDP growth
Source: CEIC Data Blog, http://blog.securities.com/2010/12/will-brazil's-gdp-per-capita-continue-to-boom/.

rate. In 2010, growth jumped to 7.5 percent thanks to China's insatiable appetite for its commodities and credit-driven consumption:

Nevertheless, the progress of the commodity cycle exposed the limits of Brazil's economic model, overly dependent on primary goods and commodities. The trouble with the Brazilian economy is its chronic lack of infrastructure. At 19 percent of national income, investment is well below the typical level for an emerging market.

Since domestic savings are low, Brazil must rely on external capital to finance the roads and bridges it needs, but foreign investors have become increasingly wary because of the country's high taxes and excessive red tape.

Since her election in 2010, President Dilma Rousseff has done little to make the economy more competitive. Instead, she has opted for an array of Chinese-style infrastructure programs, financed by BNDES, Brazil's development bank. This spending spree has failed to re-energize growth and has also cast a shadow over the sustainability of public finances.[18]

The end of the commodities boom cycle is also affecting Brazil. Its GDP is forecast to grow by only 0.5 percent in 2015, following an estimated 0.15 percent expansion in 2014. Finance minister Joaquim Levy remarked that for 2015, Brazil's economic growth is expected to be "almost flat" amid a series of tax increases and spending cuts. And even downplaying the impact China's recent slower growth has had on Brazil, there is no denying that Brazil's economy has been gravely affected by the corruption probe of the oil giant, *Petroleo Brasileiro* (PETROBRAS).[19]

Brazil may want to take a closer look at countries that have remained overly dependent on commodities. Invoking the slogans and symbols of the revolutionary tradition (and putting ambition ahead of prudence), the contestatory left has rejected Brazil and Chile's gradualist approach, deeming it too slow in helping the poor and excluded sectors, and instead advocates for increasing pressure on business, especially foreign investors.

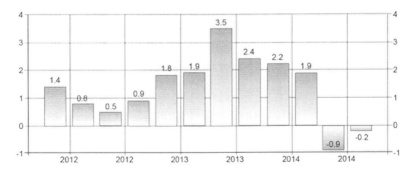

Figure 7.3 Brazil's DP annual growth rate
Source: Trading Economics, www.tradingeconomics.com/brazil/gdp-growth.

With a poor and discontented majority, they can fend off any challenge to their authority from below. They can opt for higher taxes and royalty payments and decree more strident controls, especially through forced government participation—even nationalization. To be successful, contestatory leftist governments tend to rely heavily on oil and gas exports, often mismanaging these resources, producing an overheating of the economy and inflation, and becoming (sooner rather than later) victims of the booms and busts.[20]

Since Hugo Chávez, Venezuela has switched from a system of political coexistence (in which established political parties compete in elections and share access to the spoils of office) to one in which a single party reserves the right to claim political victory and monopolize all the spoils of office.

Chávez expanded the system's presidential powers through the approval of the 1999 constitution, as well as via informal mechanisms, including mobilizing the poor and urban dwellers with a new brand of nationalist populism and direct funding.

Moreover, he expanded military expenditures, curtailed the freedom of the press, and undermined the institutional framework of Venezuela by targeting the opposition's elected officials and staging what amounted to inside coups (for example, pushing mayors such as Maracaibo's Manuel Rosales and Caracas's Antonio Ledezma out of office).

In other words, before his passing, Chávez expanded presidential powers to the detriment of the check-and-balance institutions. He systematically gutted Venezuela's democratic structure by undermining the Venezuelan judiciary; increasing the obstacles for the opposition and disregarding their victories; curtailing the operations and content of the private media; and granting more power to the military.

Economically, Chávez's Venezuela seems to have returned to the ISI development model and oil boom mismanagement that characterized the

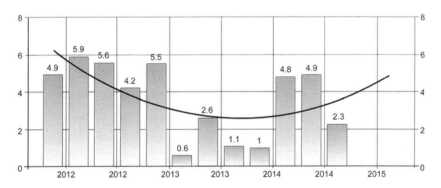

Figure 7.4 Venezuela's GDP annual growth rate
Source: Trading Economics, www.tradingeconomics.com/venezuela/gdp-growth-annual.

nation prior to the 1990s. His heir, President Nicolas Maduro, has failed not only to win over the opposition but also to stabilize national finances.

With oil prices around $60.00 a barrel, Venezuela's economy, almost entirely reliant on oil exports, is in decline, and the president is facing a serious political and economic crisis.[21]

In Bolivia, Evo Morales faced the impossible challenge of responding to the immense inequity that has characterized the nation's society for centuries. Once elected, he needed to show immediate, tangible results while fulfilling his international obligations, thus avoiding the fate of his predecessors.

Bolivia's hydrocarbon nationalization processes coupled with the 2007 negotiations signed with multilateral corporations (on a contract-to-contract basis) need to be understood in this light. The key objective was to suppress the factors that had always caused inequality and social exclusion by changing the pattern of export-driven development and the foundations of colonialism and neoliberalism that sustained it, all while improving Bolivia's place in the global economic system. Bolivia is an interesting case because Morales has not been able to govern in the exact same manner as Chávez—he doesn't have the same popular support or amount of resources to disperse so has not enjoyed the power and free rein of his Venezuelan neighbor.

Consequently, Morales' strong popularity helped boost support for democracy as Bolivia's system of government. As this experience suggests, there are no quick technical or political fixes to long-term developmental challenges. It has taken policy activism over three decades to deliver significant improvements in human development and empower the poor and excluded Bolivian majority in the political sphere.

Morales was not able to deliver on all his promises, however. LAC governments still face the old choice between voluntaristic activism and prudent realism.[22] Relations between the U.S. and Bolivia may soon start to

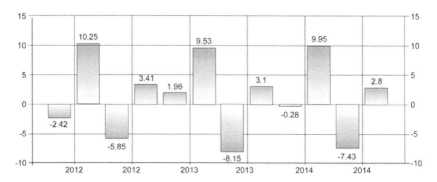

Figure 7.5 Bolivia's GDP growth rate
Source: *Trading Economics,*www.tradingeconomics.com/bolivia/gdp-growth.

improve, given that the growing Bolivian economy could benefit from a better U.S. relationship connected to exports of its silver, tin, and gas.[23]

In a nutshell, the moderate left strategy of modifying established constraints rather than challenging them (as the contestatory wing has been doing) has achieved better and more solid economic results. It has also charted a more promising course for the long run. Conversely, the achievements of the contestatory left in the social and economic spheres seem so far to rest on quicksand. In sharp contrast to their moderate counterparts, they seem to be failing in their goal of producing substantial, lasting social progress.

Today, Latin America faces real constraints that governments ignore at their peril.[24] This does not mean that the "democratic recipe" for Latin America cannot or should not be improved, but the region needs to heed the lessons of the early twentieth-century commodity lottery.

Specifically, left-leaning governments need to maintain the basic outline of the market model—namely, concern for the macroeconomic equilibrium (low budget imbalance, low inflation, protection of private property, etc.) and openness to the global economy, especially in trade and investment. At the same time, however, these governments need to search for a way to spread the benefits of this market model more broadly.

Elected governments should move away from the dogmatic, extreme version of this model embodied by neoliberalism, which accepts only minimal state action and a hands-off approach when it comes to the states providing for social protection networks.

The moderate left in Brazil, Chile, and Uruguay, for example, abandoned neoliberalism but remained inside the market model. These leaders have gradually found ways to alleviate poverty through government intervention. Radical contestatory left governments however—Venezuela specifically—have not only abandoned neoliberalism but have also infringed fundamental market principles through price and exchange controls, skyrocketing and wasteful public spending, and nationalization and other threats to property rights.

The commodity boom of 2003–2008 provided a windfall that allowed leftist regimes an extension of political agency. Not for the first time, however, the enormity of this sudden windfall prompted a good deal of inefficient and imprudent usage, limiting economic and social payoffs and running up against the limits of sustainability. Argentina comes to mind in this context.

The commodity boom fueled export growth in Argentina and brought massive amounts of dollars into the country. A large proportion of the export proceeds were used to further stimulate the economy and fund popular social programs and policies that contributed to the re-election of President Cristina Kirchner.

Argentina is again falling victim to the busts of the commodity lottery, as uneasiness and investor uncertainty are bringing about rampant inflation and

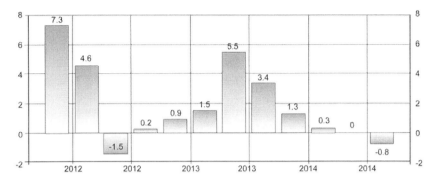

Figure 7.6 Argentina's GDP annual growth rate
Source: Trading Economics, www.tradingeconomics.com/argentina/gdp-growth.

political instability.[25] Contestatory left or right-leaning principles have been of little use to Cristina Fernández de Kirchner's government, which is now accountable to its electorate while facing international constraints. The bind in which the Argentinean government finds itself vis-à-vis the Elliot Management Corporation, the management affiliate of U.S. hedge funds Elliot Associates and Elliot International founded by Paul Singer's claim in the U.S. Supreme Court, is a clear example of how far populism can go in today's international environment.[26]

More than leftist ideology, the quality of democracy seems to be on the minds of most Latin Americans. Generally satisfied with democratic procedure, they remain deeply dissatisfied with democratic performance and the ability of their leaders to address persistent social and economic problems.

If the rise of the left (called the "pink tide" by Ross and Samuels[27]) is primarily a function of retrospective voting, then it will ebb as soon as the region's economies enter a period of stagnation and the leftist states fail in their efforts to govern by means of clientelistic methods. Moreover, if the pink tide is driven by economic performance, it's unlikely to leave an enduring impression, and there is also little likelihood of it making a sustained new policy orientation following the neoliberal reform era.

Finally, if incumbent performance is the driving force behind Latin America's "left turn," there is really no strong social basis for "leftism" (unless it is narrowly and vaguely defined as a desire for growth and equity—hardly the basis for a new political juncture in Latin America).[28]

The Pragmatic Center and the Ghost of *Caudillismo*'s Past

At times, the rhetoric Latin American political leaders employ can obscure the centrist trend, giving the impression that ideology is more salient than it actually is. Although ideology may dominate the political discourse and environment in some countries, a careful examination of the approach taken by most LAC nations reveals that the ideological range has narrowed considerably. Even Ollanta Humala in Peru, for example, displayed a greater measure of predictability and pragmatism once elected to office.

At the same time, however, despite a growing focus on developing practical and realistic solutions to economic problems (an approach that tends to coincide with embracing the rules of the democratic game), a democratic deficit still looms large.

Weak political institutions, inadequate judicial systems, stubbornly high levels of inequality, and rampant organized crime and insecurity trouble too many countries. There are also clear signs, especially among young people, of discontent with "politics as usual" regarding cronyism and corruption.

Latin America's move to the pragmatic center is largely a product of fundamental changes that include, first of all, the region's recent prosperity. Between 2003 and 2008 most Latin American countries (excluding Mexico, whose economy is more interlinked with the U.S.) have experienced a solid period of economic growth and have weathered the 2008/9 economic crisis reasonably well.

The region's sound performance reflects improved macroeconomic policymaking and a growing sense of the importance of government investments in social programs and human capital, as well as deepening ties with the rest of the world, especially China. Brazil especially stood out in this respect, its approach to poverty reduction resulting in a growing middle class.

Second, Latin America's experience of economic development and democratic consolidation is not uniform. Although certain important recent elections in South America (namely those in Brazil, Argentina, Chile, Uruguay, and Mexico) have received the world's attention, it is essential to examine developments elsewhere in Central America and the Caribbean, Latin American subregions that are falling behind.

Third, because of the value of and demand for their commodities, South American countries are becoming more independent from the U.S. and expanding their economies by cultivating ties with other powers such as China.

On the other hand, Mexico and Central American and Caribbean countries are increasing their integration with the U.S. through a series of trade agreements, while at the same time competing with China in the area of light manufacturing.

All of this has contributed to the decline in ideological fervor traditionally associated with both the right and left. Despite the occasional heated rhetoric, most government leaders in the area (such as the Dominican Republic's president Leonel Fernández) seem to understand the value of a moderate-leaning government with a problem-solving bent.

This is a lesson that apparently been learned by the Institutional Revolutionary Party (PRI) in Mexico with the election of Enrique Peña Nieto. The PRI is counting on his ability to tackle the grave problems of drug-related violence, organized crime, and corruption.[29]

Nevertheless, the current authoritarian trends in countries such as Brazil, Chile, Mexico, and now Colombia cannot be ignored. Argentina, with its tragic history, is again being lured by "the siren song of personalistic plebiscitarianism."[30]

Unfortunately, populism and the logic of personalism still enjoy considerable influence all over LAC, undermining institutional protections against the abuse of power as they seek political hegemony. Once these populist leaders—from the left but also from the right—establish pre-eminence, they use their unfettered control over all branches of government to limit debate, strike opponents, and drastically tilt the electoral playing field. These maneuvers dismantle democratic accountability and eliminate the safeguards of democracy. Lately—as in the cases of Rafael Correa in Ecuador and Daniel Ortega in Nicaragua—populist leaders damage democracy by staying in power and knocking down institutional safeguards, squeezing opponents, and skewering competition.

Using this methodology, these leaders have entrenched their rule and wielded far too many tools designed to extend it, aided by the latest commodity boom. In Argentina, Bolivia, Nicaragua, Venezuela, and even Colombia, neither domestic opposition nor the international community has found a way to stop the method of discriminatory legalism these leaders use.[31]

Despite the persistence of personalistic politics, however, populist discrimination against the rule of law, and the recent economic slowdown, most Latin Americans support democracy and, increasingly, accountability. Nevertheless, *Latinobarómetro* data reveal that democracy goes hand in hand with economic development. The 2015 *Latinobarómetro* poll, for example, shows that Latin Americans are fed up with the performance of their institutions and leaders. Government approval ratings across the 17 countries polled have fallen from 60 percent in 2009 to 47 percent in 2015. *The Economist* points out that Latin Americans are losing faith in civic institutions (34 percent of the public polled said they don't trust the state, down from 42 percent in 2013).[32] The arms of the state (the courts, the legislature, political parties, the police, etc.) are consistently ranked at the bottom of the list of the institutions they trust, while interpersonal ties rank at the top.[33] Satisfaction with democracy varies strikingly across the region, depending less upon economic growth and more upon the quality of institutions.

Successful democratic consolidation is the product of a combination of, first, effective institutional frameworks; second, representative democracies with state institutions able to respond adequately to the demands of citizens (especially when it comes to the persistent Latin American social and economic inequities); and third, the normative consensus that has been growing around democracy as the best form of government in the Western Hemisphere. The latter is important because the democratic principle has been legally binding among the American states since the 1990s. Even considering its significant recent setbacks, the Americas have a reputation as a region comprising a community of democracies and the period since 1991 has been the most democratic by far.

Nevertheless, as Scott Mainwaring and Aníbal Pérez-Liñán[34] explain, democratization trends across Latin America have been mixed. Democracy has been eroded in three Andean countries (Venezuela, Ecuador, and Bolivia) and Nicaragua. Honduras experienced a coup and democratic breakdown in 2009. In other countries—including Guatemala, Haiti, and Paraguay—democracy is weak; Cristina Fernández de Kirchner (in office since 2007) has sometimes demonstrated the illiberalism seen in hegemonic populist regimes like those of Venezuela, Bolivia, Ecuador, and Nicaragua. Yet, as the endless drama around the latest scandal, the assassination of Prosecutor Alberto Nisman, shows, she has met relatively stiff resistance not only from the courts, civil society and the international community but also from critics within her own party.

On the bright side, democracy has become more solid in Brazil (with a population of around two hundred million people) and remains robust in Chile, Costa Rica, and Uruguay. In Mexico, in spite of its shortcomings, the democratic shift achieved in 2000 remains intact. Additionally, Peruvian democracy is in its best shape ever, with little chance of breakdown, and Colombian democracy has survived a large spike in violence that began in 1980 and ran through the early 2000s. Cuba remains the only openly authoritarian regime in LAC, which is a stunning contrast to the situation before the start of the "third wave of democratization" in the 1970s.

As Mainwaring and Pérez-Liñán point out, one cannot broadly claim that democracy in LAC is being eroded, but there is cause for concern that democratic advances have not been more widespread and that the quality of democracy is still poor in many countries.

Four variables can make sense of the LAC mosaic of erosion, stagnation, and advances in democracy. First, countries with higher levels of socioeconomic development such as Uruguay and Costa Rica have been more likely to make the transition to robust democracy. Second, the party system needs to be institutionalized and support high-quality democracy (such as Chile's). Third, the commitment of leadership to democracy (such as Mexican president Ernesto Zedillo) cannot be underestimated. Once elected, an administrator's role in democratic transition or consolidation is vital. Fourth, solid states underpin robust democracies. Building democracy in weak states remains a task of excruciating difficulty—something that is important to keep in mind for the next chapter.

Several indicators reveal the relationship between state capacity and democratic quality. Even when top political leaders are committed to the task, building effective states requires time and resources, as well as strong will. Inevitably, some corporations, wealthy individuals, criminal organizations, politicians, police and military officers, judges, and others gain from clientelism, corruption, complicity with organized law-breaking, failure to enforce rights, and failure to protect the public by tighter regulation.

Contemporary LAC is a patchwork of democratic erosion, stagnation, and progress. Even accepting that the region is in the middle of a long-term democratic trajectory (its longest ever), there's still cause for concern.

The lack of economic growth, political representation, weak state institutional frameworks, and strong leadership can continue to encourage rougher state (and more importantly, non-state) actors, such as drug cartels, to take the place of elected officials.

The important democratic gains and the potential for greater economic growth in Latin America keep being marred by the widespread existence of poverty, social inequity, and exclusion; the reliance of their economies on the export of commodities; and, as discussed in this chapter, the new face of authoritarian populism.

Elected officials that return to power and work through institutional arrangements based on personal ties undermine not only the future prospects of their own countries but also their standing in the international political arena, where their competence and influence is questioned.

As the next chapter addresses, this institutional deficit has also impacted on the security of some LAC societies, with drug traffickers, and organized crime groups proliferating.

Main points:

- *Caudillismo* tradition in LAC creates strong presidential structures.
- Latin American societies develop electoral democracies. Legitimacy is attached to a regime coming to power as a result of an election; the rest of the institutional framework remains weak.
- Two lefts emerge: a populist left with the strong authoritarian tendencies of the past and a pragmatic left that aims to address the inequality and exclusion of their societies while participating in a globalized world.

Notes

1 Scott Mainwaring and Aníbal Pérez-Liñán, "Cross-Currents in Latin America," *Journal of Democracy*, vol. 26, no. 1 (2015), 115.
2 The list consisted of fiscal discipline; a redirection of public expenditure toward fields offering high economic returns and the potential to improve income distribution; tax reform; interest rate liberalization; a competitive exchange rate; trade liberalization; liberalization of inflows of foreign direct investment; privatization; deregulation; and secure property rights. John Williamson, "What

Washington Means by Policy Reform," in John Williamson (ed.), *Latin American Adjustment: How Much Has Happened* (Washington, DC: Institute for International Economics, April 1990). Available at: www.iie.com/publications/papers/paper.cfm?ResearchID=486.

3 Francisco Rodríguez, "Does One Size Fit All in Policy Reform? Cross-National Evidence and its Implications for Latin-America," in *Democratic Governance in Latin America*, ed. Scott Mainwaring and Timothy R. Scully (Stanford, CA: Stanford University Press, 2010), 88–128.

4 Both terms were curtailed by citizen groups representing the indigenous majority who acted against the three largest traditional political parties: Revolutionary Nationalist Movement (MNR), Nationalist Democratic Action (AND), and Revolutionary Left Movement (MIR). In December 2005, Evo Morales Ayma, sustained by his Movement Toward Socialism (MAS) party majority, won the election. Martín Mendoza-Botehlo, "Bolivia: The Growth of Grassroots Participation," in *The Quality of Democracy in Latin America*, ed. Daniel H. Levine and José E Molina (Boulder, CO and London: Lynne Rienner Publishers, 2011), 137–172.

5 Scott Mainwaring, Guillermo O'Donnell, and Samuel J. Valenzuela, "Introduction," in *Issues in Democratic Consolidation: The New South American Democracies in Comparative Perspective*, ed. Scott Mainwaring, Guillermno O'Donnell and Samuel J. Valenzuela (Notre Dame, IN: University of Notre Dame Press, 1992), 1–16; Scott Mainwaring and Matthew Soberg Shugart, eds, *Presidentialism and Democracy in Latin America* (Cambridge and New York: Cambridge University Press, 1997).

6 Douglas C. North, John J. Wallis, and Barry B. Weingast, *Violence and Social Orders: A Conceptual Framework to Interpret History* (Cambridge: Cambridge University Press, 2009), 25–27 and 112–115.

7 See chapter 8 for a detailed explanation of the inter-American system.

8 Banyan, "Trade, Partnership and Politics: With Negotiations Secret, Optimism about a Path Breaking Trade Deal is Hard to Share," *The Economist*, August 22, 2013.

9 Miguel Angel Centeno, *Blood and Debt: War and the Nation-State in Latin America*, (Philadelphia, PA: Penn University Press, 2002), 261–280; North, Wallis, and Weingast, *Violence and Social Orders*, 25–27 and 112–115.

10 All in all, between 2000 and 2005 Latin America experienced some of its best years in terms of economic growth. But even after two decades of structural reform, the economic performance delivered disappointing results for the great majority. For more see Steven Levitsky and Kenneth M. Roberts, "Democracy, Development and the Left," in *The Resurgence of the Latin American Left*, ed. Steven Levitsky and Kenneth M. Roberts (Baltimore, MD: Johns Hopkins University Press, 2011), 1–30; and Steven Levitsky and Kenneth M. Roberts, "Introduction, Latin America's 'Left Turn': A Framework for Analysis," in *The Resurgence of the Latin American Left*, ed. Steven Levitsky and Kenneth M. Roberts (Baltimore, MD: Johns Hopkins University Press, 2011, 1–30). For the rise of the left see Kurt Weyland, "The Left: Destroyer or Savior of the Market Model?" in *The Resurgence of the Latin American Left*, ed. Steven Levitsky and Kenneth M. Roberts (Baltimore, MD: Johns Hopkins University Press, 2011), 71–92.

11 Ibid. See also the paper by Kenneth M. Roberts, "Latin America's Populist Revival," 2011 (www.einaudi.cornell.edu/LatinAmerica/conference/leftturn/pdf/Roberts.pdf).

12 Kurt Weyland, "The Left: Destroyer or Savior," 71–92.

13 Raúl L. Madrid, Wendy Hunter, and Kurt Weyland, "The Policies and Performance of the Contestatory and Moderate Left," in Kurt Weyland, Raúl Madrid, and Wendy Hunter (eds), *Leftist Governments in Latin America; Successes and Shortcomings* (Cambridge, New York: Cambridge University Press, 2010), 140–180.

14 Jorge G. Castañeda, "Latin America's Left Turn," *Foreign Affairs*, vol. 85, no. 3 (2006). See also Jorge G. Castañeda, "Latin America's Two Lefts" (http://jor gecastaneda.org/notas/2009/06/02/latin-america-s-left-turn). According to the World Bank, Latin America and the Caribbean's growth rate was 5 percent. World Bank, "Year in Review" (http://siteresources.worldbank.org/EXTANN REP2K8/Resources/YR00_Year_in_Review_English.pdf).

15 Steven Levitsky and Kenneth M. Roberts, "Introduction, Latin America's 'Left Turn': A Framework for Analysis," in *The Resurgence of the Latin American Left*, ed. Steven Levitsky and Kenneth M. Roberts (Baltimore, MD: Johns Hopkins University Press, 2011), 49–56; Steven Levitsky and Kenneth M. Roberts, "Democracy, Development and the Left," in *The Resurgence of the Latin American Left* ed. Levitsky and Roberts, 399–427; Evelyne Huber, Jennifer Pribble, and John D. Tephens, "The Chilean Left in Power: Achievements, Failures, and Omissions," in *Leftist Governments in Latin America; Successes and Shortcomings*, ed. Kurt Weyland, Raúl L. Madrid, and Wendy Hunter (Cambridge and New York: Cambridge University Press, 2010), 77–97.

16 The reduction of poverty rates seem to be caused not only by the economic growth experienced between 2003 and 2008 but also by the implementation of programs such as Bolsa Família, which gives cash transfers to poor families to keep children in school, and the Fome Zero (Zero Hunger) program. Evelyne Huber, Jennifer Pribble, and John D. Tephens, "The Chilean Left in Power: Achievements, Failures, and Omissions," in *Leftist Governments in Latin America: Successes and Shortcomings*, ed. Kurt Weyland, Raúl L. Madrid, and Wendy Hunter (Cambridge and New York; Cambridge University Press, 2010), 77–97.

17 The students had been protesting rejecting cuts to their state-financed school. The police confronted them and the students went missing. Although the Peña Nieto administration has tried to catapult Mexico into the twenty-first century through significant reforms, the traditional issues of police corruption and complicit political authorities have come to cast a shadow on the PRI establishment. For more see Randal C. Archibold, "43 Missing Students, A Mass Grave and a Suspect: Mexico's Police," *New York Times*, October 6, 2014.

18 "Brazil Slows Down: The Time Has Come for Dilma Rouseff to Change Track," *Financial Times*, Editorial, December 4, 2013 (www.ft.com/intl/cms/s/ 0/fe25491c-5cdf-11e3-a558-00144feabdc0.html#axzz2nMaJwNSe) and Joe Leahy and Samantha Pearson, "Brazil Economy Turns in Worst Quarter for Five Years," *Financial Times*, December 3, 2013 (www.ft.com/intl/cms/s/0/95c2ef90-5c3 b-11e3-b4f3-00144feabdc0.html?siteedition=intl#axzz2nMaJwNSe).

19 Matt Murray, "Brazil's 2015 Economic Growth Will Be 'Almost Flat,' Says Finance Minister," *Wall Street Journal*, World, January 23, 2015.

20 Weyland, "The Left: Destroyer or Savior."

21 For more see Javier Corrales, "The Repeating Revolution: Chávez's New politics and Old Economics," in Kurt Weyland, Raúl L. Madrid, and Wendy Hunter, eds, *Leftist Governments in Latin America; Successes and Shortcomings* (Cambridge and New York: Cambridge University Press, 2010), 28–56; BBC News, "Venezuela's Leader Nicolas Maduro Divides Opinion," January 21, 2015 (www.bbc.com/news/world-latin-america-20664349).

22 George Gray Molina, "The Challenge of Progressive Change under Evo Morales," in *Leftist Governments in Latin America: Successes and Shortcomings*, ed. Kurt

ELECTORAL DEMOCRACIES IN LAC

Weyland, Raúl L. Madrid, and Wendy Hunter (Cambridge and New York: Cambridge University Press, 2010), 57–76; Government of Bolivia, *Plan Nacional de Desarrollo* (La Paz, Bolivia: Ministry of Development and Planning, 2006).

23 *Stratfor*, "U.S., Bolivia: The Pieces Are in Place for Improved Relations," January 15, 2015.

24 Weyland, "The Left: Destroyer or Savior."

25 Weyland, "The Left: Destroyer or Savior" and Ken Parks and Matt Moffett, "Argentina Can't Slow Drain on Dollar Reserves," *Wall Street Journal,* Latin American News, November 11, 2011 (http://online.wsj.com/article/SB100014 240529702042246045770306934382711117.html?keywords+argentina+canperce nt27t+slow+the+drain+of+reserves).

26 Augustino Fontevecchia, "The Real Story of How a Hedge Fund Detained a Vessel in Ghana and Even Went for Argentina's 'Air Force One,'" *Forbes.com* (https://caneid.miami.edu/cas/login);Peter Davis, "Hedge Funds Win Ruling in Argentina Bond Case, *New York Times*, DealBook, August 24, 2013 (http://dea lbook.nytimes.com/2013/08/23/hedge-funds-win-ruling-in-argentina-bond-ca se/?_r=0).

27 Christopher Chase-Dunn, Mathew Kaneshiro, James Love, Kirk Lawrence and Edwin Elias, "Neoliberalism and the Pink Tide in Latin America," Department of Sociology and the Research Group on Transnational Movements at the Institute for Research of World-Systems (IROWS), Preliminary Draft v. 4-21/ 10, April 2010 (http://irows.ucr.edu/papers/irows58/irows58.htm); and Tom Chodor, *Neoliberal Hegemony and the Pink Tide in Latin America; Breaking with TINA?* (London: Palgrave Macmillan, 2015).

28 More than any particular ideology, change is being fueled by the impact growth and sound social policies are having on Latin America's middle class. A study by the United Nations Economic Commission for Latin America and the Caribbean (ECLAC) concluded that Latin America has been benefiting from a strong period of economic growth fueled by high commodity prices in many countries. Tens of millions of the region's inhabitants have risen into the middle class over the past two decades, and millions of Latin Americans have punched their ticket into the consumer class in the last decade, helped not only by economic performance but also by aggressive social programs with a decided focus on education. For example, with the Maoists now mostly out of the picture and the country enjoying a mining boom, Peru's poverty rate has fallen to 31 percent from 55 percent over the past decade. The middle of the spectrum grew to 33.1 percent of the population this year from 28.7 percent in 2004, according to Lima's *Apoyo* consultancy. In Brazil, largely as a result of the *Bolsa Familia* program, the percentage of children between the ages of seven and 14 who are out of school has fallen to 2 percent, from 16 percent in 1990, and the work force's improved education level has helped foster upward mobility and greater equality. In Chile, the middle class's income share edged up to 11.7 percent in 2009 from 10.9 percent in 2000, and the share of the richest 10 percent slipped to 42.7 percent from 45.3 percent. These advances are still tenuous, however, and the possibility of a global recession still threatens these prospects. For more see A. Ross, Jason Arnold, and David L. Samuels, "Evidence from Public Opinion," in *The Resurgence of the Latin American Left*, ed. Steven Levitsky and Kenneth M. Roberts (Baltimore, MD: Johns Hopkins University Press, 2011), 31–51; Matt Moffet, "A Rags-to-Riches Career Highlights Latin American Resurgence," *Wall Street Journal*, November 15, 2011 (http://online.wsj.com/ news/articles/SB10001424052970204422404576595211776435404?mod=ITP_ pageone_0); International Monetary Fund, "World Economic and Financial

Surveys, Regional Economic Outlook. Western Hemisphere: Time to Rebuild Policy Space," IMF, Washington, DC, 2013 (www.imf.org/external/pubs/ft/reo/2013/whd/eng/pdf/wroe0513.pdf).

29 Michael Shifter, "Latin America; A Surge to the Center," *Journal of Democracy*, vol, 22, no.1 (2011), 107–121.

30 A plebiscitary vote is that in which the entire electorate is invited to vote directly by accepting or refusing a proposal, bypassing the institutional framework based mainly on political parties. The quote comes from Kurt Weyland, "Latin America's Authoritarian Left," *Journal of Democracy*, vol. 24, no. 3 (2013), 18–32.

31 For more see ibid.

32 *The Economist*, "The Latinobarómetro Poll: When the Tide Goes Out," *The Economist*, The Americas, September 26–October 2, 2015.

33 See also *Latinobarómetro*, "Informe 1995–2015: Latinobarómetro, opinion pública Latinoamericana" (www.latinobarometro.org/INFORME_LB_2015.pdf).

34 Scott Mainwaring and Aníbal Pérez-Liñán, "Cross-Currents in Latin America," *Journal of Democracy*, vol. 26, no. 1 (2015), 115–127.

8

CHALLENGES TO DEMOCRACY
Drug Trafficking, Organized Crime and Terrorist Networks in LAC

Good laws lead to the making of better ones; bad ones bring about worse. As soon as any man says of the affairs of the State, what does it matter to me? The State may be given up for lost.
Jean-Jacques Rousseau, *The Social Contract* [1]

Introduction

In today's international environment, most of the great games between state and non-state actors revolve around economic power, which is the clearest manifestation of the use of force in the Americas. As mentioned before, the role LAC plays in the present and future will determine whether the West in general (and the U.S. in particular) retains its hold on the international economic system and, ultimately, its influence in world affairs. Finally and more importantly, this geoeconomics game will determine whether or not the norms and values underlining the multilateral system that has been developing since 1945 will survive.

As explored in the previous sections, the geoeconomics game can take place through legally institutionalized channels backed by consensual normative principles—or through illegal means, producing terrible violence. Among the significant threats to the inter-American multilateral system are the proliferation of illegal drugs, groups, and organized crime networks, all of which are undermining the fabric of Latin American societies.[2]

What are the major trends that have characterized the evolution of illicit drug trafficking, organized crime (organized criminal networks), and terrorist activities in the Americas over the last quarter of a century? What principal transformations or adaptations (economic, political, and organizational) have taken place within the region's vast illegal drug economy during the first decade of the twenty-first century? What if any connections to terrorism exist? What challenges or obstacles do criminal and terrorist networks in the hemisphere represent for national security and the continued consolidation of democratic forms of governance in the region?

This chapter identifies nine key trends or patterns that typify the ongoing transformation of the drug trade and the organized criminal groups it has spawned as of mid-2011—as well as the terrorist groups that have sought to profit from the lucrative illicit drug trade in the region.

These trends are: 1) the increasing globalization of drug consumption in the Western Hemisphere and beyond; 2) the limited or "partial victories" and unintended, destructive consequences of the U.S.-led "War on Drugs," especially in the Andes; 3) the proliferation of areas of drug cultivation and of drug-smuggling routes throughout the hemisphere (so-called "balloon effect"); 4) the dispersion and fragmentation of organized criminal groups or networks within countries and across subregions ("cockroach effect"); 5) The formation of linkages between criminal drug-trafficking organizations and terrorist groups both inside and outside the Western Hemisphere; 6) the concomitant negative impacts on democratic political reforms and state-building efforts (deinstitutionalization effects) in the region; 7) the inadequacies or failures of U.S. domestic drug and crime control policies (demand control failures); 8) the ineffectiveness of regional and international drug control policies (regulatory failures); and 9) the apparent growing support for harm reduction, decriminalization, and legalization policy alternatives (legalization debate) to the U.S.-led "War on Drugs" in many countries and regions in LAC over the first decade of the twenty-first century.

The Globalization of Drug Consumption

Many Latin American political leaders have long argued that if the U.S. population did not consume such large quantities of illegal drugs like marijuana, cocaine, and heroin, Latin American and Caribbean countries would not be producing these drugs for export and the region would not be plagued by the powerful and well-financed drug trafficking organizations— often called cartels—that have sprung up throughout the hemisphere over the last several decades.[3]

It is certainly accurate to say that the United States is the largest single consumer market for illicit drugs on the planet. Although there is no definitive estimate, the value of all illicit drugs sold annually in the United States may be as much as US $150 billion, with perhaps $37 billion per year spent on cocaine alone.[4]

Nonetheless, illegal drug use (and/or addiction) is not a uniquely "American" disease, despite the title of David Musto's pioneering book on the origins of drug control in the United States.[5] Over the last decade in the now 27 countries of the European Union, cocaine users have increased from 4.3 to 4.75 million, and the region's consumption represents 30 percent of worldwide cocaine use.

Europeans are almost catching up with the approximately five million regular cocaine users found in the United States.[6] Indeed, levels of cocaine use in the United States have dropped steadily since the early 1990s, while cocaine consumption in Europe exploded exponentially during the first decade of the twenty-first century.[7]

Moreover, the Europeans pay more than twice as much per gram, ounce, kilo, or metric ton (mt) of cocaine as do American consumers. The UNODC 2011 report estimated that Americans consumed 63 percent of the 440 mt of cocaine available, while the European population consumed 29 percent of the world supply. Cocaine consumption in the U.S., however, has decreased by 40 percent between 1999 and 2009.[8]

In terms of the supply chain, the global heroin market is quite complicated. Afghanistan leads the world in heroin production, producing 380 mt or 83 percent. It's been estimated that Afghanistan produced 6,900 mt of opium in 2009 alone. With the exception of Latin America, the heroin produced in Afghanistan is trafficked to every major region in the world.

Next, Mexico produces 9 percent of the heroin supply, which is trafficked to the U.S. market. Myanmar produces 5 percent. Colombia, on the other hand, only accounts for 1 mt, which is less than 1 percent of the world production of heroin.

In terms of consumption, the UNODC 2011 report estimates that Central and West Europe consumed 70 mt of heroin in 2009 alone. People residing in East Europe consumed even more, approximately 73 mt in 2009. Over the last decade or more, the bulk of the heroin consumed in Europe has come from Afghanistan, whereas most of the heroin consumed in the United States has come from either Colombia (roughly 2 percent of world supply) or Mexico (roughly 1.5 percent of world supply).[9]

Cocaine, by contrast, is produced in only three countries of the Western Hemisphere: Colombia (45 percent), Peru (35–40 percent), and Bolivia (15–20 percent). It's trafficked from these three Andean countries to 174 countries around the globe.[10]

Cocaine consumption is not limited to advanced capitalist markets such as the United States and Europe.[11] Cocaine use in Latin America has also skyrocketed over the last decade. Indeed, Latin American consumers were estimated to use some 200 mt of cocaine in 2010.

Until 2009, Argentina was considered to be the world's second largest market for cocaine.[12] Then, in the 2011 World Drug report, the United Nations reported that Brazil had replaced Argentina in this position. The report estimated that Brazil had 900,000 cocaine users, which made it the number one consumer in South America. Cocaine use in Argentina is reported to be 2.6 percent; in Chile, 2.4 percent.[13]

Cocaine consumption rates are also quite high in other regions of the world. In 2009, Africa had between 940,000 and 4.42 million cocaine users. In the same year, Asia had between 400,000 and 2.3 million users. Eastern and South-Eastern Europe had fewer cocaine users in 2009 (between 310,000 and 660,000).[14]

The dramatic rises in European and South American cocaine consumption over the past decade have greatly expanded world market demand for this illicit Andean product. As a consequence, this region has seen the creation of new global trafficking routes and increased involvement of criminal trafficking networks originating outside the Andean subregion.

Partial Victories Against Drugs

From the middle of the nineteenth century through the mid-1980s, Peru and Bolivia were the two principal suppliers of both coca leaf and refined cocaine to the U.S., Europe, and other world markets.[15] As of 1985, Peru produced roughly 65 percent of the world's supply of coca leaf, while Bolivia grew approximately 25 percent and Colombia 10 percent or less.[16]

With the "partial victories" achieved by the U.S.-led war on drugs in the southern Andes during the late 1980s and early 1990s specifically— U.S.-financed crop eradication programs in Bolivia's Chapare under President Victor Paz Estensoro after 1986 (Operation Blast Furnace) and presidents Hugo Banzer/Jorge Quiroga from 1998 to 2002 (Plan Dignidad), along with Peruvian president Alberto Fujimori's interruption of the "air bridge" between the Alto Huallaga coca region in Peru and the clandestine cocaine laboratories located in Colombia in the mid-1990s—coca cultivation in the Andes rapidly shifted to Colombia in the mid- and late 1990s.[17] By 2000, Colombia cultivated an estimated 90 percent of the world's coca leaf, while production in Peru and Bolivia dwindled to historic lows.[18]

In the early 1990s, Colombia's U.S.-backed war against drug lord Pablo Escobar and the Medellin cartel (during the César Gaviria administration) led to Escobar's death on December 2, 1993, and the rapid dissolution of the Medellin cartel.[19] The subsequent plea bargaining of 1994/5 (during the Ernesto Samper administration) with the major drug lords of the Cali cartel, specifically the Rodríguez Orejuela brothers, catalyzed the dismantling of the cartel.[20]

While some large criminal trafficking networks (e.g. the Cartel del Norte del Valle), continued to operate in Colombia in the late 1990s and early 2000s, some 300+ smaller drug trafficking organizations (known as *cartelitos*) surfaced to fill the vacuum left by the dismantling of the two major cartels.

By the late 1990s, essentially as an unanticipated and unintended consequence of the demise of the country's major cartels, Colombia's left-wing *Fuerzas Armadas Revolucionarias de Colombia* (Revolutionary Armed Forces of Colombia, or FARC) guerrillas and right-wing *Autodefensas Unidas de Colombia* (United Self-Defense Forces of Colombia, or AUC) paramilitary militias took control of coca cultivation and processing throughout rural Colombia. This precipitated more drug-related violence between these two groups of armed illegal actors, each seeking to eliminate the other and consolidate their own territorial control over drug cultivation regions and peasant growers across the Colombian countryside.[21]

As a direct result, levels of drug-fueled violence in Colombia spiraled out of control in the late 1990s and early 2000s. Indeed, during much of the first decade of the 2000s, Colombia was one of the most dangerous and violent countries in the world.

In July 2000, President Clinton and the U.S. government responded by backing the Andrés Pastrana administration in its war against runaway drug production and trafficking in Colombia via the adoption of Plan Colombia. In August 2002, the newly inaugurated government of Álvaro Uribe received additional drug war assistance from Washington and the George W. Bush administration in the wake of the 9/11 terrorist attacks on the United States.

Supported by almost $8 billion in U.S. aid under Plan Colombia over the course of a decade, by 2010 Colombian president Uribe and his program of "democratic security" had managed to beat back the FARC guerrillas, demobilize many—if not all—of the country's paramilitary bands, and substantially reduce the country's astronomically high levels of drug-related violence.[22]

Despite the substantial achievements of Plan Colombia and the Uribe administration's "democratic security" policies, however, Colombia remained a principal source of coca leaf and refined cocaine in the Andes. Drug-related violence and criminality appeared to be once again on the rise after 2010.

The 2011 UN Drug Report stated that Colombia's land area used for coca cultivation decreased by an estimated 15 percent in 2010, leaving it just slightly ahead of Peru as the world's largest coca leaf producer. Currently, the area under cultivation in Colombia is estimated at 62,000 hectares (ha). In comparison, 2009 statistics report 73,000 ha in terms of area under cultivation.[23]

As an unintended consequence of the (partially) successful U.S.-backed war on drugs through Plan Colombia, the locus of organized criminal involvement in cocaine trafficking gradually shifted northwards to Mexico. As a result, drug-related violence and criminality shifted northwards into Mexican territory as various trafficking organizations vied for control over the highly lucrative smuggling trade from Colombia and the southern Andes into the large and profitable U.S. market.[24] Thus, Mexico's current drug-related bloodbath is, in part, directly attributable to the partial victory in the war on drugs achieved in Colombia in recent years via Plan Colombia.

If the U.S.-backed Mérida Initiative presently under implementation in Mexico achieves results similar to those of Plan Colombia, it unfortunately won't halt drug trafficking or end organized crime in Mexico or the region. Most likely, it will drive both further underground while pushing some smuggling activities and criminal network operations into neighboring countries such as Guatemala and Honduras and back to Colombia and the

Andes. Indeed, there is abundant evidence that some Mexican drug trafficking operations (Sinaloa, Zetas) are already moving from Mexico into Central America.[25]

Proliferation of Areas of Cultivation and Smuggling Routes (the Balloon Effect)

The 2010 World Drug report indicates that Colombia successfully reduced its total number of hectares under coca cultivation in the second half of the 2000s, although production still hasn't sunk beneath pre-2000 levels.

How large the reductions in Colombian coca cultivation over the past three years have actually been is a controversial topic plagued by inadequate data, methodological problems, and major uncertainties regarding the actual extent of cultivation and yield levels.

With similar caveats, coca cultivation in both Peru and Bolivia appears to have expanded once again, following almost two decades of decline.[26] Most observers believe that overall coca leaf production and cocaine availability in the Andean region remain roughly on par with 2000 levels and well above those of 1990 or 1995.

Evidently, the balloon effect that allowed coca cultivation to shift north from Bolivia and Peru to Colombia in the 1990s continued to operate as cultivation moved back into Peru and Bolivia from Colombia at the end of the first decade of the 2000s.

Various observers have speculated that the tropical variety of coca—known in Portuguese as *epadu*—might shift cultivation from the traditional growing areas on the eastern slopes of the Andes into Brazil and elsewhere in the Amazon basin if eradication efforts prove successful in Colombia, Peru, and Bolivia.

The 2010 UN report registered a 10–20 percent decline in coca production in Colombia between 2008 and 2009. Enthusiasm regarding such statistics should be tempered by realism, however.[27] First, it is important to note that year-to-year variations are commonplace due to climate factors and short-term disruptions. Declines over several years are required to identify enduring trends. Second, the UN statistics are approximations rather than firm data points; it is entirely possible that the 2010 UN report underestimated the real levels of production. Third, innovations in more productive hybrid plants, yields per hectare, and processing can produce higher levels of refined cocaine production than anticipated by the UN analysts. Finally, the ongoing decentralization and dispersion of cultivation in Colombia makes accurate mapping of the total numbers of hectares under cultivation a very problematic endeavor.[28]

Such caveats aside, the key reason that Colombia appears to have experienced a significant decline in production is that the Uribe government moved away from a (U.S.-backed) reliance on aerial spraying to a more effective mixture of spraying and manual eradication linked to comprehensive alternative development programs in key coca growing areas such as La Macarena.

As a consequence of the weakening of FARC control in vast stretches of rural Colombia and the partial demobilization of the paramilitary bands engaged in drug trafficking from 2002–2007, 2008/9 marked the beginning of an important decline after at least three years of steady increases in total production. To sustain this decline will certainly require that Colombia continue its manual eradication efforts and provide additional funds for well-designed and executed alternative development programs in coca growing areas throughout the country.[29] Meanwhile, recent increases in coca cultivation in both Peru and Bolivia suggest that the focus of U.S. attention and resources on Colombia has led to the resurgence of coca cultivation in traditional coca-growing countries in the central Andes.

To forestall a recurrence of the balloon effect (pushing cultivation out of one country only to have it reappear in others), the Obama administration will have to seek to re-establish a workable relationship with the government of President Evo Morales in Bolivia, as well as find effective ways to combat the renewal of *Sendero Luminoso* (Shining Path) and coca cultivation in Peru. Failure to achieve more effective drug control policies in both countries will likely result in a continuing shift of coca production back to Peru and Bolivia, thereby nullifying any real progress made in reducing coca cultivation in Colombia.[30]

In the 1980s, largely as a result of the formation of the U.S. government's South Florida Task Force in 1982 (headed by then-Vice President George H. W. Bush), established Caribbean routes used by the Medellin and Cali cartels in the 1970s and early 1980s were essentially closed down by American law enforcement and military operations. They were quickly replaced in the mid- to late 1980s and early 1990s with new routes that used Panama and Central America, the Gulf of Mexico, and the Pacific Corridor to reach Mexico and cross into United States.[31] When the Mexican cartels took over from Medellin and Cali in the late 1990s, the Pacific Corridor became the principal smuggling route north from Colombia to the United States, though the Gulf route also remained active.[32]

From December 1, 2006, onward, Mexican president Felipe Calderón (with Washington's active assistance since 2008 via the Mérida Initiative) has waged an intense military campaign against Mexico's major drug cartels.[33] Though not successful in eliminating Mexico's key drug trafficking groups (as of 2010), Calderón's militarization of the drug war has unquestionably made smuggling across the U.S.-Mexican border from Mexico more dangerous and expensive than it was previously. As a result, some of the Mexican trafficking organizations have begun to move their smuggling operations into weaker states in Central America—especially Guatemala and Honduras.[34]

There is also abundant evidence that Colombian traffickers are using Venezuelan and Ecuadoran territory to replace the increasingly problematic Mexico routes. Venezuela serves as a jumping-off point for smuggling through the Caribbean to the east coast of the United States, or across the Atlantic, through West Africa and into Europe. Venezuela is also used for drug flights into Honduras or Guatemala, with shipments then transferred to trucks and transported by land across the Guatemalan-Mexican border, then northwards to the United States.[35]

The balloon effects produced by the partial victories in the war on drugs in the Andes are visible in both drug cultivation patterns and drug smuggling routes. Over the past 25+ years, the war on drugs has succeeded in repeatedly shifting coca cultivation from one area in the Andes to another and forcing frequent changes in smuggling routes. It's proven unable to seriously disrupt (much less permanently stop) either production or trafficking in the hemisphere. The traffickers' constant, successful adaptations to law enforcement measures have led to criminality and violence in more and more countries.[36]

Dispersion and Fragmentations of Criminal Drug Trafficking Organizations (the Cockroach Effect)

The differential insertion of individual countries into the political economy of drug trafficking in the hemisphere has produced a variety of intermediaries between peasant growers of illicit crops and consumers.

In Bolivia, the presence of peasant cooperatives in the countryside since the *Movimiento Nacional Revolucionario* (National Revolutionary Movement, or MNR) revolution of 1952 produced coca grower associations and generally inhibited the rise of either criminal organizations or guerrilla movements as intermediaries, although the Bolivian military itself has (on various occasions) fulfilled this role.[37]

In Peru, the absence of strong grassroots associations among peasant growers opened the way for both elements of the country's military apparatus (led by intelligence chief Vladimiro Montesinos) and guerrilla organizations (*Sendero Luminoso*) to perform the role of intermediaries or traffickers.[38]

In Colombia, the absence of both peasant organizations and military intermediaries paved the way for the rise of major criminal organizations such as the Medellin and Cali cartels. The demise of the major cartels opened the way for illegal armed actors such as the FARC and the paramilitaries.[39]

In Mexico and Central America, elements of the military and/or police have sometimes functioned as intermediaries in previous decades, but in the 1990s and 2000s these countries have followed in Colombia's footsteps, owing to the absence of strong grower associations.[40]

In terms of criminal organizations and/or criminal trafficking networks, Colombia and Mexico provide the two most important examples in recent history. In Colombia, the rise and fall of Medellin and Cali (and subsequently the Norte del Valle cartel) vividly illustrate the perils and vulnerabilities of large, hierarchical criminal trafficking organizations, especially when they attempt to openly confront the state.

Both major cartels in Colombia were hierarchically structured and proved to be vulnerable targets for both Colombian and international law enforcement agencies. In the wake of Medellin and Cali, Colombia witnessed a rapid fragmentation and dispersion of criminal networks that have proven far more difficult for law enforcement authorities to track down and dismantle than their larger and more notorious predecessors.[41]

Although there may be counter-tendencies leading to re-concentration among criminal trafficking organizations in Colombia today (e.g. *Los Rastrojos*, *Las Águilas Negras*), the basic lesson to emerge from the state's history appears to be that smaller criminal networks are less vulnerable to law enforcement and state repression.

Colombia's emergent *Bandas Criminales* (BACRIM), the descendants of the now formally demobilized paramilitary groups that made up the Colombian Self-Defense Forces (*Auto Defensas Unidas de Colombia*—AUC) represent a new generation of drug traffickers in Colombia. They differ from the "paras" in several important respects: 1) they tend to be more politically deft and subtle in seeking political alliances inside the Colombian economic and political establishment, often hiding their political linkages through indirect contacts and "clean" candidates without records of paramilitary affiliations or ties in the past; 2) they focus on establishing political influence at the municipal and departmental (provincial) levels rather than the national level; 3) the locus of their activities includes not only Colombia's Caribbean coast but also the Pacific southwest; and 4) they have expanded their economic interests beyond drug trafficking to include other illegal activities (land piracy, gold mining, timber) as well as legal enterprises. From the Colombian state's perspective, such organizations are, at least to date, far less threatening because they don't have the capacity to directly threaten state security.[42]

In Mexico, as in Colombia in the 1980s and early 1990s, cocaine profits appear to have energized the country's major criminal networks and unleashed a wave of violence among criminal organizations seeking to strengthen and consolidate their control of key smuggling routes. As of 2011, this struggle was still playing itself out in a brutal and bloody fashion. Nonetheless, Mexico's criminal trafficking groups appear to be following the Colombian pattern of dispersion and fragmentation, although the evidence is not yet conclusive.

In 2000, the Tijuana cartel (Arrellano Félix family) and the Juárez cartel (Carrillo Fuentes family) were the two largest and most dominant drug-trafficking organizations in Mexico. Since 2000, after the Vicente Fox administration went after Tijuana and then Juárez, Mexico has seen the rise of at least five new major trafficking organizations and a host of smaller, lesser-known groups: the Sinaloa, Gulf, *Familia Michocana*, Beltrán-Leyva, and Zetas.[43] See Table 8.1.

This dispersion of criminal networks in Mexico may well represent the beginning of the kind of fragmentation observed in Colombia in the 1990s. If it does, the trend would be warmly welcomed by Mexico's authorities, as it would lead to a considerable reduction in the capacity of organized criminal networks to directly challenge state authority and national security.

A key reason some analysts do not accept the concept of organized crime fragmentation in contemporary Mexico relates directly to the emergence of a new criminal network model—the Sinaloa cartel. Unlike its predecessors and current rivals in Mexico, the Sinaloa cartel is less hierarchical and more federative (hub and spokes) in its organizational structure. Its principal leader, Joaquín "El Chapo" Guzmán Loera has forged a new type of "federation" that gives greater autonomy (and profits) to affiliated groups. To date, Sinaloa, also known as the Federation, seems to be winning the war against its rivals, although its fight against the Zetas (a paramilitary-style organization) is proving to be prolonged, costly, and bloody. It is likely that the Sinaloa model will prove more sustainable and better for business than other criminal trafficking organizational models in Mexico, but the jury is still out.[44]

The escalating urban gang wars in Colombia's *Comuna 13* Medellin neighborhood, exemplify the kinds of violent internecine conflicts taking

Table 8.1 Proliferation of Mexican cartels, 2006–2010

2006	2007–2009	2010
Pacífico cartel	Pacífico cartel	Pacífico cartel
	Beltrán Leyva cartel	Pacífico Sur cartel
		Acapulco Independent cartel
		"La Barbie" cartel
Juárez cartel	Juárez cartel	Juárez cartel
Tijuana cartel	Tijuana cartel	Tijuana cartel
	"El Teo" faction	"El Teo" faction
Golfo cartel	Golfo cartel	Golfo cartel
		Zetas cartel
La Familia Michoacana	La Familia Michoacana	La Familia Michoacana
Milenio cartel	Milenio cartel	La Resistencia
		Jalisco Cartel-Nueva Generación
6 organizations	**8 organizations**	**12 organizations**

Source: Table created by the author based on personal interviews in Mexico in 2011.

CHALLENGES TO DEMOCRACY

place across contested drug trafficking areas and routes throughout the entire Latin American region (e.g. the states of Nuevo Leon, Chihuahua, Michoacán, and Tamaulipas in Mexico, the Pacific coast of Guatemala, the Valle de Cauca Department near Cali, Colombia, the municipality of Caucasia in Colombia, and the favelas of Rio de Janeiro in Brazil).

In Medellin, scores of relatively small competing drug gangs have generated a pattern of "disorganized" crime; rather than doing what's best for business (keeping murder rates low and police attention to a minimum), the criminal world is in turmoil and in need of an arbitrator to re-establish authority.[45]

Like Mexico, where the splintering of authority has led to the creation of smaller (but no less violent) groups such as the *Cartel de Acapulco* and *Mano con Ojos*, Colombia's drug gangs are fighting to establish their place in the new criminal hierarchy in Medellin's poor and marginalized barrios, long ignored by both the central Colombian state in Bogotá and Medellin's municipal government.

Under former mayor Sergio Fajardo, Medellin did see a significant decline in violence—especially homicide rates—for several years via informal negotiations with the gangs, new mayoral initiatives to reduce gang violence (e.g. increased social services, expanded educational opportunities, job programs, new public recreational spaces for youth), and the demobilization of the nation's paramilitary groups in 2005 and beyond.

The relative peace achieved in Medellin by the Fajardo administration and the successive mayoral administration of Alonso Salazar eventually gave way to renewed violence in Medellin's *Comuna 13* and other urban neighborhoods, as drug trafficking and BACRIM activity resurged in 2010 and 2011.

Medellin's *Comuna 13* or Ciudad Juarez's Rivera del Bravo slums are perfect launching platforms for gang warfare. In such neighborhoods, drug traffickers have found readily accessible pools of new gang members and potential drug consumers, as well as efficient corridors for smuggling drugs and arms.

In *Comuna 13*, the violence mainly revolves around controlling the San Juan highway, which leads out of the city to northern Antioquia and Urabá on Colombia's northern Caribbean coast. The gangs that control the highway decide who and what enters and leaves Medellin: drugs, guns, money.

The armed group established by former Medellin capo Pablo Escobar, now known as "the Office," remains the largest and most powerful criminal network in Medellin, even though it's splintered into rival factions and neither side has managed to achieve control over Comuna 13 and the San Juan transit route.[46]

The *maras* (youth gangs) in Central American countries such as Honduras and Guatemala; the *Barrio Azteca* prison gang in El Paso, Texas, and Juárez, Mexico; and the Comando Vermelho in Rio de Janeiro provide further examples of the proliferation of gangs or *pandillas* (which often work and fight in close association with major cartels) that have appeared along with the phenomenon of fragmentation and dispersal.

151

In 2004, for example, the armed wing of the Juárez cartel—*La Línea*—started to openly attack the local police while employing the *cobro de piso* (right-of-way tax) to transit drug shipments through Chihuahua. This was possible due to the incorporation of former police officials from Juárez into the ranks of the Juárez cartel.

Following the introduction of the Sinaloa cartel into Juárez in the mid-2000s, rising levels of violence and murder involving *Los Aztecas* (a gang affiliated with *La Línea*) against opposition gangs such as the Mexicles, the *Artistas Asesinos* (Artistic Assassins), and the *Gente Nueva* (literally, new youth) have become the order of the day in what is now the murder capital of Mexico.[47]

By October 2005 there was also an estimated 17,000 gang members operating in Ciudad Juárez belonging to Mara Salvatrucha or MS-13 and 18th Street.[48] While no recent statistics are available, anecdotal evidence indicates that the number of *maras* active in Juarez and Mexico has increased to more than 25,000.

As in Colombia during the 1980s and 1990s, paramilitary groups have also surfaced in recent years in Juárez, Monterrey, and other parts of Mexico in response to the cartels and associated gang violence. The appearance of these paramilitary bands highlights the weak law enforcement capacity of the Mexican government and its perceived inability to effectively confront and defeat the country's powerful drug trafficking organizations.[49]

Under pressure from Mexican and U.S. law enforcement, Mexican trafficking organizations have (since the mid-2000s if not before) sought to move at least part of their smuggling operations from Mexico into neighboring countries. Guatemala and Honduras are currently targets for both the Sinaloa cartel and the Zetas.[50] The upsurge in drug-related violence in both of these Central American nations is closely related to these shifts in operational base.

This trend, observable throughout the hemisphere, is sometimes labeled the "cockroach effect" due to its similarity to the scurrying of cockroaches once a light switch is flicked. Closely linked to the "balloon effect," the "cockroach effect" refers specifically to the displacement of criminal networks from one city/state/region to another within a given country (or from one country to another) in search of safer havens and more pliable state authorities.

Transnational Criminal Organizations and Terrorism in LAC and Beyond

Although the U.S. has been engaged in a "Global War on Terrorism" (GWOT) for over a decade, the U.S. government has yet to agree on a standardized definition of terrorism itself. All definitions of the term agree, however, that terrorism involves the use of politically motivated violence against noncombatants.[51]

Terrorism is a tactic employed by a variety of inherently weak actors, individuals, or groups from various backgrounds. These actors resort to terrorism because they lack the power to impose their political will through ordinary political or military means. The elements of any act of terror are typically related to a larger political goal. No matter what issue—be it religion, ideology, or social injustice, etc.—a terrorist act intends to attract the world's attention.

Because terrorism is a tactic used by the weak, it generally focuses on "soft" civilian targets rather than more difficult military targets. Terrorist attacks are relatively easy to conduct if they are directed against civilians, especially if the assailant is not concerned with escaping after the attack (as was the case in the Mumbai attacks of 2008). As Scott Steward points out, while authorities in many countries have been quite successful in foiling attacks over the past couple of years, no government has the resources to guard all targets, so, particularly given the open nature of societies of the West, some terrorist attacks will inevitably succeed.[52]

When it comes to terrorism in LAC, the U.S. has certainly been concerned about threats from various insurgent groups that have attempted to influence or overthrow elected governments, but LAC hasn't been the focal point of the GWOT. Nevertheless, LAC nations have struggled with domestic terrorism for decades, and international terrorist groups have at times used the region as a battleground to advance their cause (as in Buenos Aires at the Jewish Cultural Center in 1994).

The 2011 Department of State annual report, issued in July of 2012, maintained that terrorist attacks in the Western Hemisphere rose 40 percent between 2010 and 2011, with 343 attacks in 2010 and 480 attacks in 2011.

The majority of terrorist attacks in the region were perpetrated by organizations in Colombia such as the Revolutionary Armed Forces of Colombia (*Fuerzas Armadas Revolucionarias de Colombia*, FARC), the National Liberation Army (*Ejército de Liberación Nacional*, ELN), and other radical leftist Andean groups such as the Shining Path in Peru.

Despite the rise in attacks, the report maintained that the threat of transnational terrorist attack in the hemisphere remained low. Nevertheless, U.S. policymakers have expressed concerns over the past several years about possible penetration by Iran in several countries, especially Venezuela. The 2011 Country Report on Terrorism issued by the U.S. Department of Defense reflected these concerns, and cited the 2011 foiled assassination attempt on the Saudi Ambassador to the U.S. in Washington by an Iranian operative. This operative (who was actually a DEA informant) was working undercover as a member of a Mexican drug trafficking organization.[53]

Nevertheless, in Mexico, where the proliferation of drug-trafficking organizations has brought increasingly brutal violence, the U.S. Department of State asserted in its 2010 and 2011 terrorism reports that there is no evidence (so far) of ties between these drug-trafficking organizations and terrorist groups. Nor is there evidence that these criminal groups aim to gain either political or territorial control, aside from seeking to protect and expand their ability to perpetrate criminal activity.[54]

In contrast to Mexico, drug-trafficking activities in Colombia have been linked to political motivations for years. The U.S. Secretary of State has designated three groups as foreign terrorist organizations (FTOs): the remaining elements of the right-wing paramilitary United Self-Defense Forces of Colombia (*Autodefensas Unidas de Colombia*, AUC), the leftist Revolutionary Armed Forces of Colombia (FARC), and *Ejército de Liberación Nacional* (ELN).

The U.S. state department contends that the FARC and ELN were responsible for the majority of attacks in the hemisphere. The FARC alone perpetrated 79 percent, or 377 attacks. The AUC, on the other hand, has been inactive and not carried out terrorist attacks, though some former AUC paramilitaries have continued to engage in illegal activities, mostly with the new criminal organizations known as BACRIM (*bandas criminales emergentes*).[55]

In 2013, General John Kelly, leader of the Southern Command, stated that hundreds of millions of dollars in drug revenue that the FARC receives enables them to purchase surface-to-surface missiles and fund the construction of "Narco-subs" (although the Colombian defense minister disputed this report).[56] Over the years the FARC has been considerably weakened, and has even been engaged in peace negotiations with the Colombian government. Nevertheless, the U.S. state department has expressed concern regarding continued FARC activities in neighboring countries including Panama, Peru and Venezuela.

According to the Department of State, the FARC also has training and logistical supply camps along Ecuador's northern border with Colombia. In Panama, a small number of FARC members from the group's 57th Front have operated in the country's Darien province for a number of years, using the area as a safe haven. In recent years, Panama's government has stepped up its efforts to confront this presence by patrolling the province and conducting raids against the FARC camps.

In Peru, the FARC uses remote areas along the Colombian-Peruvian border to rest, regroup, and make arms purchases, according to the state department's terrorism report. The FARC reportedly also funds coca cultivation and cocaine production among the Peruvian population in border areas.

With regard to Venezuela, both the FARC and ELN have long been reported to have a presence in its territory, and the U.S. has imposed sanctions on several current and former Venezuelan government and military officials for providing support to the FARC. As described in the Department of State's 2010 terrorism report, the Colombian government of President Álvaro Uribe had publicly accused the Venezuelan government of harboring members of the FARC and ELN in the country several times.

In July 2010, the Uribe government presented evidence at the Organization of American States (OAS) of FARC training camps in Venezuela. In response, Venezuela suspended diplomatic relations on July 22, 2010, yet less than three weeks later the new Colombian president Santos met with Venezuelan president Chávez, and the two leaders agreed to re-establish diplomatic relations and improve military patrols along their common border.

Since then, Venezuelan-Colombian relations on border security have improved. Venezuela has captured several members of the FARC and ELN and returned them to Colombia. In the aftermath of President Chávez's death in early March 2013, most observers expressed the belief that Venezuelan cooperation with Colombia on border security issues will continue.[57]

In Peru in the 1990s, the brutal Shining Path (*Sendero Luminoso*, SL) Maoist insurgency was significantly weakened with the capture of its leader, Abimael Guzman, who was sentenced to life in prison after a new trial in 2006. According to the 2011 Department of State terrorism report, there are two remaining SL factions in Peru, one operating in the Apurimac and Ene River Valley (VRAE) and the other in the Upper Huallaga River Valley (UHV). Both factions have engaged in drug trafficking and in 2011 were reported to have carried out a total of 74 terrorist acts, including the killing of 19 people.[58]

The "Terrorist Issues Report" mentions that Cuba has been playing a role by hosting talks between the FARC and Colombian government of President Juan Manuel Santos since 2012, but the nation continues to permit fugitives from the U.S. to reside in Cuba.

Some observers who argue that the U.S. should concentrate on serious threats elsewhere have questioned Cuba's continued presence on the terrorism list. In February 2013, a press report claimed that high-ranking state department officials concluded that Cuba should not be on the state sponsors of terrorism list, but state department officials responded by saying that the report was incorrect and there are no current plans to remove Cuba from the list.[59]

In Mexico, violence (such as murders and kidnappings) perpetrated by drug-trafficking organizations (DTOs) has spiked in recent years, reaching a new level of brutality many analysts have characterized as unprecedented. In the six-year term of Mexico's former president Felipe Calderón (2006–2012), homicides related to organized crime increased, numbering between 47,000 and 65,000 (depending on the source). In 2012 (the Calderon government's final year in office), some analysts estimated that the high level of homicides had leveled off or declined, while others recorded a slight increase.

Mexico is a major transit point for the lucrative cocaine trade and a major source and trafficking base for marijuana, methamphetamine, and heroin. The U.S. government estimates that the annual profits that flow back to Mexico from the U.S. from drug trafficking range between $8 and $29

SECURITY AND DEMOCRACY

billion. This highly lucrative market has generated fierce competition within and between the DTOs to control trafficking routes into the United States and for a share of the growing drug market inside Mexico.[60]

According to the "Latin America: Terrorist Issues" report, the Calderón administration made combating the drug-trafficking organizations its central focus, and the government's aggressive counterdrug strategy was violently resisted. The government operations that targeted the DTOs removed top leaders or "kingpins" through arrest or death-in-arrest efforts, causing fragmentation, with a handful of the larger DTOs that were dominant at the start of the Calderón administration splintering, while two organizations became dominant. The two polarized rivals—the Sinaloa DTO in the western part of the country and the Zetas in the east—remain the largest drug-trafficking organizations in Mexico and have both moved aggressively into Central America.

Furthermore, the Mexican syndicates that traffic illegal drugs have diversified into other illegal activities including kidnapping, human trafficking, robbery, extortion, resource theft, and product piracy. Many authorities now refer to the DTOs as "transnational criminal organizations (TCOs)" in recognition of their widespread extension into other types of crime.

The government of President Enrique Peña Nieto, which took over in Mexico in December 2012, has proposed a new security strategy that builds on many of the programs that the Calderón government initiated.

To combat the DTOs, the Mexican government under President Calderón had sought and received assistance from the U.S. government. U.S.-Mexico security cooperation has been structured upon the Mérida Initiative, a bilateral and anti-crime assistance package that began in 2008. The Mérida Initiative has significantly deepened U.S.-Mexico security cooperation based on a principle of joint responsibility, with Mexico's government committed to reforming its judicial and police sectors as top priorities.

Exactly how the Mérida Initiative will be reshaped under the new Peña Nieto government remains to be seen. During his electoral campaign and in his first 100 days in office, President Nieto pledged to focus on reducing violent crime in order to improve citizen security in Mexico and advocated for the strengthening of crime prevention efforts. More importantly, he has tried to shift the national conversation to a more positive message about economic growth rather than remaining focused on the DTOs, the U.S.-led "War on Drugs," and the violence and mayhem they have caused.[61]

Iran's Activities in Latin America

Hezbollah (the radical, Lebanon-based Islamic Shiite terrorist group) appears to have an increasing number of ties in the region, leading to greater concern about Iran's involvement in South America. While the state department asserted in its "Latin America: Terrorist Issues" report that there were no known operational Hezbollah or Al Qaeda cells in the hemisphere, ideological sympathizers in South America and the Caribbean continue to provide financial and moral support in Venezuela.[62]

Apart from its ties to Venezuela, Hezbollah was widely reported to have been linked to two bombings against Jewish targets in Argentina in the early 1990s: the 1992 bombing of the Israeli embassy in Buenos Aires that killed 30 people and the 1994 bombing of the Argentine-Israeli Mutual Association (AMIA) in Buenos Aires, which killed 85 people.

Over the past several years, U.S. officials have expressed concern about Venezuela's lack of cooperation with anti-terrorism efforts, especially after President Hugo Chávez's sympathetic statements about Colombian terrorist groups and Venezuela's relations with Iran. As a result, the United States imposed an arms embargo on Venezuela in 2006, which ended all U.S. commercial arms sales and retransfers to the country. (This isn't to be confused with the "state sponsors of terrorism" list; other countries currently on the same list as Venezuela include Cuba, Eritrea, Iran, North Korea, and Syria.)

In June 2011 congressional testimony, Department of State officials again expressed concern about "Venezuela's relations with Iran, its support for the FARC, [and] its lackluster cooperation on Counterterrorism."[63] The state department also testified that "Colombian-Venezuelan cooperation on terrorism and security matters is clearly increasing and being systematized, yielding notable results."[64] The state department noted Venezuela's deportation of several FARC and ELN members to Colombia, including key operatives and high-profile political actors, and its 2011 report maintained that Venezuela and Colombia continued the dialogue on security and border issues that was initiated in 2010.[65]

The report mentions that with regard to Venezuela's relations with Iran, "Venezuela maintained its economic, financial, and diplomatic cooperation with Iran as well as limited military-related agreements," adding that Iranian President Mahmoud Ahmadinejad had visited Latin America several times since 2006. Ahmadinejad mainly traveled to Venezuela, but had also visited Bolivia, Brazil, Ecuador, Nicaragua, and Cuba. For example, in 2012, Ahmadinejad undertook two trips to the region: a visit in January to Cuba, Ecuador, Nicaragua, and Venezuela; and a June trip to Brazil to attend the U.N. Conference on Sustainable Development in Rio de Janeiro, along with side trips to Bolivia and Venezuela. In 2013, he attended the funeral of President Chávez, who died in early March after battling cancer.

Nevertheless, Iran's trade with Latin America is miniscule, and for most countries in the region, non-existent. The trade that does exist consists largely of Latin American exports to Iran.[66]

The report also mentions that credible sources suggest that Hezbollah sympathizers may be engaged in fundraising efforts in Venezuela. Moreover, past comments by Venezuela about potential Iranian support for the

SECURITY AND DEMOCRACY

development of nuclear energy in Venezuela raised concerns among U.S. officials and other observers. For example, comments in September 2009 by Venezuelan officials offered conflicting information about Iran's support for Venezuela's search for uranium deposits. Subsequently, however, Venezuela's then minister of science, technology, and intermediary industry Jesse Chacon denied that Iran was helping Venezuela seek uranium, while Venezuela's minister of energy Rafael Ramirez maintained that Venezuela has yet to develop a plan to explore or exploit its uranium deposits.

So far, there is no real evidence to support the claims of cooperation between Iran and Venezuela to invest in the exploration of uranium mining. More importantly, in the aftermath of Hugo Chávez's death in March of 2013 and with the new interim agreement between Iran and the West, it is possible that Venezuela's relations with Iran could begin to wane.[67]

The terrorism report includes SOUTHCOM commander General John Kelly's assertion that although Iran maintains embassies in many Latin American countries, it is struggling to maintain influence in the region. According to General Kelly, while "the Iranian regime has increased its diplomatic and economic outreach across the region with nations like Venezuela, Bolivia, Ecuador, and Argentina," the "outreach has only been marginally successful ... and the region as a whole has not been receptive to Iranian efforts."

No matter the scope of Iran's involvement in Latin America, Iran's key foreign policy focus remains closer to home. Iran perceives that threats to its survival may emanate from the Middle East and South and Central Asia, and this is where the Iranian state—be it for ideological, religious or political reasons—has long tried to alter strategic outcomes.[68]

Nevertheless, it is always possible that Iran will choose to meddle in Latin American affairs. In October 2011, the Department of Justice filed criminal charges against a dual Iranian-American citizen from Texas, Manssor Arbabsiar, and a member of Iran's Qods Force in Iran, Gholam Shakuri, for their alleged participation in a bizarre plot to kill the Saudi ambassador in Washington, DC. The indictment alleged that Arbabsiar met several times with an informant of the U.S. Drug Enforcement Administration (DEA) in Mexico City, posing as a member of Mexico's most violent drug-trafficking organization, *Los Zetas*. Arbabsiar then reportedly arranged to hire the informant to murder the ambassador with the financial support of Shakuri. Other alleged plans included plots to pay *Los Zetas* to bomb the Israeli embassy in Washington, DC, and the Saudi and Israeli embassies in Buenos Aires.[69]

In recent years, U.S. concerns regarding Hezbollah in Latin America have focused on its fundraising activities among sympathizers in the region, particularly the tri-border area (TBA) of Argentina, Brazil, and Paraguay (but also in other parts of the region).

In March 2011 congressional testimony, General Douglas Fraser (then leader of the U.S. Southern Command) maintained that he had not witnessed the growth of Hezbollah or Hamas in the region, and reiterated that "primarily any support that they are giving is financial support, principally back to parent organizations in the Middle East."[70]

In December 2011, a documentary featured on the Spanish-language network Univisión alleged that Iranian and Venezuelan diplomats in Mexico tried to recruit Mexican students for possible cyber attacks against the United States. Although there is no indication that U.S. officials have been able to corroborate the allegations in the documentary, the Department of State subsequently declared the Venezuelan consul general in Miami, Livia Acosta (who had been based in Mexico at the time of the documentary), persona non grata.[71]

As of late, the assassination of Prosecutor Alberto Nisman and the subsequent allegations of a cover-up have only served to fan the rumors of conspiracy and collusion between President Cristina Fernández de Kirchner and the government of Iran.[72]

Beyond its fundraising in the TBA, U.S. officials have expressed concern that Hezbollah has the ability to tap into the large Lebanese diaspora in Venezuela and elsewhere in Latin America. These fears were especially pronounced after the Department of the Treasury discovered that the Lebanon-based Lebanese Canadian Bank (LCB) was facilitating the money-laundering activities of an international narcotics trafficking and money-laundering network with ties to Hezbollah. Officials then imposed sanctions that effectively prohibited the bank from operating in the United States. The treasury department maintained that the network was involved in moving illegal drugs from South America to Europe and the Middle East via West Africa.[73]

Following the U.S. investigation of the LCB, the Department of Justice announced the federal criminal indictment of Lebanese citizen Ayman Joumaa in November 2011 for conspiring to coordinate shipments of cocaine from Colombia through Central America for sale to *Los Zetas*, one of Mexico's most violent drug-trafficking organizations. The treasury department had already designated Joumaa a narcotics trafficker and money launderer in January that year.

The indictment alleged that Joumaa laundered hundreds of millions of dollars in drug trafficking proceeds from Europe, Mexico, the United States, and West Africa for cocaine suppliers based in Colombia and Venezuela. A civil indictment filed by the Department of Justice in December 2011 alleged that Joumaa's drug-trafficking organization operated in Lebanon, West Africa, Panama, and Colombia, laundering proceeds through various channels (including bulk cash smuggling operations and Lebanese exchange houses), then paying fees to Hezbollah to facilitate the transportation and laundering of these proceeds.[74]

Thanks to its underlying conditions, Latin America and the Caribbean are seen as fertile soil for terrorist groups and recruitment; though poverty has dropped in the region since the 1980s, the number of people living in absolute poverty has increased.[75] The United States has consequently bolstered its efforts to develop innovative policies, economic and political, and cooperative networks to counter these security threats.

It has also provided assistance for Latin American countries to improve their capacity to confront terrorist groups that are working against their governments or fundraising to act against other states in the international system. The United States has also flexed its military muscle by sending military vessels loaded with munitions as well as medical and health supplies.[76]

Reaction to Terrorism and Regional Cooperation

The United States and many countries within Latin America have reacted to terrorism in a similar way: militarily.

In 1986, the U.S. began to "certify" countries in order to determine which ones could receive aid for the funding of anti-drug policies. This marked the beginning of a collaborative effort, led by the United States, which has focused almost exclusively on the sources of supply. To combat subversive groups and drug traffickers, the U.S. committed itself to take whatever steps were necessary to protect American lives, property and interests, and help countries in the hemisphere work together to eliminate terrorist sanctuaries, counter state-supported terrorism and employ all available means to punish terrorists.[77] U.S. unilateralism against local sources of supply, however, failed to consider the immediate benefits that the illegal drug industry brought to local economies, while the U.S.-imposed policies created great burdens on local and federal governments.

From the Latin American states' perspective, a comprehensive solution depended upon a U.S. government policy that offered significant resource allocation for reforming law enforcement and judicial institutions, confronting poverty, and expanding and diversifying economies in the region.[78] This suggests that the U.S. needs to find ways to encourage the institutionalization of democratic norms within defense establishments and engage in cooperative security initiatives to include combating transnational crime.[79]

Both the U.S. and LAC need to reassess their views on terrorism, how they relate to drug-traffickers, and what threat they represent (together and individually) to the Western Hemisphere. Since the 9/11 attacks, Washington's perception is that even though traditional threats to the military have not diminished, new and even more dangerous threats have emerged.

The history of U.S.-Latin American relations demonstrates unequivocally that multilateral cooperation provides the only reliable formula for

CHALLENGES TO DEMOCRACY

institutionalizing effective collective security arrangements in the Western Hemisphere in the long run. The current "security gap" dividing the U.S. and Latin America may well represent the region's most serious threat. Latin America can no longer be considered a single region that is unequivocally veering towards integration and acquiescence to U.S. hegemonic management. On the contrary, due to Washington's lack of attention to the region, the American continent may well be set on a path of subregional fragmentation.

While Canada, Mexico, Central America, and the Caribbean are clearly heading towards greater economic integration with the U.S., the Southern Cone is increasingly resisting Washington's authority.[80] More importantly, the Andean region is openly rejecting U.S. supremacy and may be regressing to the authoritarianism of yesteryear.[81]

The U.S. must use its political influence, diplomacy, and bilateral, regional and multilateral mechanisms to counter any benefits that illegality has brought to many of the forgotten areas in LAC. Washington must work through new and currently existing treaties such as the ones created at the UN Convention against Transnational Organized Crime, the International Convention against the Taking of Hostages, the International Convention for the Suppression of Acts for Nuclear Terrorism, etc.[82]

Financial actions are also an important impetus, including blocking and freezing the assets of terrorists and criminals and strengthening financial systems and infrastructures to block money laundering, cash smuggling, and informal value transfer systems through pre-paid cards, mobile banking systems and the internet. Together with cooperative military actions, intelligence gathering is also crucial in order to detect, influence, and target networks.

All of these actions are integral for the protection of United States' interests both domestic and abroad; partnerships with domestic actors and governments and within regional institutions are essential for success.

Failure of Political Reform or State Building (the Deinstitutionalization Effect)

State structure is what ultimately determines the form or type of organized crime that can operate and flourish within any given national territory. Criminal organizations, in contrast, do not determine the type of state they operate in, although they can certainly deter or inhibit political reform efforts at all levels of a political system, from local to national.

Advanced capitalist democracies—from the United States to the countries of Europe to Japan—exhibit wide variation in the types of organized crime they generate and/or tolerate.

The United States, for example, has virtually eliminated the Italian mafia model and seen it replaced by fragmented and widely dispersed domestic criminal organizations, many of which are affiliated with immigrant communities. Europe is characterized by a similar evolution of organized crime groups affiliated with immigrant populations. Japan, by contrast, has coexisted with the Yakuza, a more corporate-style criminal network. In China, state capitalism coexists with the Chinese triads and other criminal organizations. In Russia, the Putin government in effect subordinated and incorporated various elements of the Russian mafia as para-state organizations.[83]

In Colombia, the paramilitary organizations, heavily involved in drug trafficking, were linked directly to both state institutions and specific political parties. In Mexico, the formerly dominant PRI party developed almost tributary relations with organized crime groups. When the PRI's almost 71-year monopoly over political power was broken at the national level in 2000 by the victory of PAN presidential candidate Vicente Fox, the old lines of tribute/bribery broke down and unleashed a wave of internecine violence among trafficking organizations as they struggled for control of cocaine transit through the country.[84]

Transitions from authoritarian regimes to more open and democratic forms of governance in Latin America (as in Russia and Eastern Europe) are particularly problematic. In these cases, the old, authoritarian institutional controls often collapse or are swept away but cannot be easily or quickly replaced by new, democratic forms of control.

Mexico is currently experiencing just such a transition. The old institutions—police, courts, prisons, intelligence agencies, parties, and elections—no longer work. Indeed, they are inherently corrupt and dysfunctional. Nevertheless, few new institutional mechanisms have arisen to replace them.

Moreover, reform efforts can be and often have been stymied or derailed entirely by institutional corruption and criminal violence intended to limit or undermine state authority and the rule of law. There were certainly significant institutional reforms proposed or underway in México at the end of the Felipe Calderon *sexenio* (2006–2012), but such reforms have not come fast enough nor have they been deep enough (to date) to contain drug-trafficking criminal organizations and related violence and corruption throughout the nation.

Such observations do not constitute arguments against democratization. Rather, they highlight challenges and obstacles within the democratic process that are frequently overlooked or ignored. Democratic theorists have only recently begun to seriously examine the problems that stem from entrenched criminal networks.

In the countries of Latin America and the Caribbean, such neglect of institutional reform may well imperil both political stability and democracy itself. Rather than democratic consolidation, the consequence of ignoring organized crime and its corrosive effects may include institutional decay or democratic de-institutionalization.

Countries emerging from internal armed conflicts are significantly more vulnerable, although such conflicts are not the only source of institutional weakness. Transitions from authoritarian to democratic political systems may also engender institutional deficits even in the absence of prior prolonged internal conflict.

The Inflexibility and Ineffectiveness of Regional and International Drug Control Policies

Reflecting the hegemonic influence of the United States over international drug policy during the post-World War II period, the United Nations (UN) Organization of Drug Control (UNODC) and the Organization of American States (OAS) both faithfully reproduced the U.S. prohibitionist regime at the multilateral level.

The UN's approach to drug control (like that of the OAS) has severely limited the flexibility of responses by member states because it effectively rules out any possible experimenting with legalization and/or decriminalization. Both the UN and the OAS operate on the assumption that all illicit drugs are "evil" and must be prohibited and suppressed. The UN-OAS-U.S. unwavering prohibitionist strategy has dominated international discourse on drug control and prevented individual countries from experimenting with alternative approaches (or forced them to ignore or defy their UN treaty obligations regarding narcotics control).[85]

For example, the UN, the OAS and the U.S. have all, in effect, systematically rejected Bolivian president Evo Morales' declared policy of fostering traditional and commercial uses of legally grown coca leaf while preventing the processing of coca leaf into cocaine. (It must be noted, however, that coca cultivation in Bolivia did rise significantly, beyond the amount that was necessary to supply traditional or ceremonial purposes and "legal" non-cocaine uses.)

In practice, the UN prohibitionist inclination has meant that there is little or no international backing for options other than the current "War on Drugs," no matter what collateral damage is incurred in the process. The ten-year UN review of international drug control policies (1998–2008) predictably concluded that the current prohibitionist policies in place were the best and only real strategic option available moving forward. It recommended no significant alterations in international drug control policies and practices, despite growing doubts and questions among some member states and many independent analysts.[86]

The Failure of U.S. Drug Policies

Despite its efforts, the U.S. certainly hasn't eliminated American demand for illicit drugs or the drive for profits associated with supplying the huge U.S. market. Washington has routinely underfunded demand control, while primary emphasis has almost always been on expensive (but ultimately ineffective) supply-side control strategies. Although there have been efforts by the Obama administration and "drug czar" Gil Kerlikowske to redress this long-standing imbalance in U.S. drug policy, prevention and treatment remain woefully under-resourced. Analysis of the reasons behind the U.S. insistence on supply versus demand control strategies lies beyond the scope of this book.

The consequences of Washington's strategic choices are obvious, however. Washington has demanded that the countries of LAC follow its lead in the War on Drugs and uphold a formal "certification" process that has often led to the sanctioning of nations that did not "fully cooperate." U.S. insistence on such a policy approach has not only led to overall failure in the war on drugs over the last 25+ years, it has been counterproductive for the interests of both the U.S. and individual Latin American countries.

Colombia has paid a high price (in both blood and money) for its role in the war on drugs. The price that Mexico is being asked to pay today is as high or higher. These massive costs have generated a new debate about alternatives to American prohibitionist approaches such as harm reduction, decriminalization, and legalization.[87]

The Search for Alternatives: The Debate over Legalization, Decriminalization, and Harm Reduction

Some Latin American analysts anticipated that the possible passage of California's Proposition 19, which sought to legalize the cultivation, distribution and possession of marijuana in the state, would signal the beginning of the end of the U.S.-led war on drugs and allow Mexico and other countries in the region to move away from the "prohibitionist" strategy that has generated so much drug-related violence throughout Latin America and the Caribbean in recent years.

It is entirely possible that, had the state's voters approved the Proposition 19 initiative on marijuana, it would have run foul of both U.S. federal statutes and America's UN treaty obligations. Many Latin American political leaders, however, openly oppose the legalization of marijuana in California and continue to argue against the legalization or decriminalization of harder drugs in the U.S. and around the globe.

In the end, Proposition 19 was defeated at the polls by a majority (52 percent against versus almost 48 percent in favor) of California voters. Undeterred, and since voters in Oregon, Washington state, and Colorado are in favor of the legalized use and sale of the drug, proponents of marijuana legalization in California are likely to place another, similar vote on the ballot at some point.

Regardless of personal opinion about marijuana legalization in California and beyond, there are many reasons to be skeptical about the impact of marijuana legalization on drug trafficking and organized crime.

First, even if such an initiative is ultimately approved in some states, there are likely to be challenges from the U.S. federal government that could delay the implementation of any such new state law for years. Second, legalization of marijuana (if and when it occurs) will not address the issues raised by criminal activity, violence, and corruption spawned by the traffic in harder drugs such as cocaine, heroin, and methamphetamines, among others. Criminal gangs in Mexico and elsewhere in the hemisphere will most likely move away from marijuana to deeper involvement with the drugs that remain illegal, and organized crime and drug-related violence will continue.

In the long run, as the 2011 Global Commission on Drug Policy report argues, some combination of legalization and/or decriminalization of illicit drugs along with serious harm reduction policies and programs worldwide may offer the only realistic formula for reducing the huge profits that drive drug-related crime, violence, and corruption in Latin America and the Caribbean and around the globe—even if addiction rates go up, as they did when alcohol prohibition ended in the U.S. in the 1930s.[88]

In the short- and medium-run, Latin American and Caribbean countries will have to address their own seriously flawed institutions by ending long-standing corrupt practices; undertaking the reform of police, judiciary, prison, and other key institutional reforms; and ensuring greater electoral accountability. Such measures are essential for their own future political stability, democratic consolidation, and national security, and cannot wait for global decriminalization or legalization to take place at some nebulous point in the future.

With all of this in mind, the OAS, through former secretary general José María Insulza, issued a stark review of the realities experienced by the countries in the Americas in relation to production, distribution, trade, and consumption of drugs. These reports aimed to serve as a reality check by LAC leaders—a warning of what will happen if the entire drug phenomenon is not dealt with honestly and in a coordinated manner.[89]

Neither the legalization of marijuana nor the decriminalization of harder drugs (if and when they ever take place) will constitute panaceas for the resolution of the problems created by crime, corruption, and violence throughout the region. They will not do away with the many other types of organized crime that operate with virtual impunity in Latin America and the Caribbean today. Clearly, there are many issues left to address.

It's clear that Latin Americans are full of contradictions. They live in the eternal land of promise, faced with the real possibility of achieving economic development and democratic consolidation; at the same time, however, a lack of state capacity, high levels of inequality, and, as seen in this chapter, violence all contribute to derailing their trajectory.

After examining LAC from the viewpoint of political economy and democracy and security, the last section will explore LAC as part of the international system and why it matters in the context of world affairs.

Looking to the future of Latin America, much is at stake for the U.S., the Americas, and the international capitalist system. How LAC nations manage economic development obstacles, the surge of authoritarian populist regimes through electoral means, the low quality of democracies and governance, and the growing power and influence of illegal actors are all issues that matter greatly to the continuing success and stability of not only a region but also an international system that functions mostly through the use of power in a globally interconnected economy guarded and constrained by Western values.

Main points:

- Weak governmental structures and lack of territorial control allow drug production and trade to flourish in LAC.
- LAC allow legality to coexist with illegality.
- The illegal drug industries adapt, avoid control, and foster economic growth in Latin American societies.
- As of today, there are weak links between global terrorism and the drug trade in the Americas.
- Failure of political reform and state building permits an extremely adaptive drug phenomenon to endure.
- For LAC, the drug phenomenon is an existential threat. For the U.S. it is a health and security problem.
- LAC are searching for new approaches to confront the drug phenomenon.

Notes

1 Jean Jacques Rosseau, "The Social Contract," in *Democracy: A Reader*, ed. Ricardo Blaug and John Schwarzmantel (New York: Columbia University Press, 1983), 147–149.
2 For more see Phillip Stephens, "Trade Trumps Missiles in Today's Global Power Plays," *Financial Times*, Comment and Analysis, November 22, 2013.
3 The ex-presidents of Brazil, Colombia and Mexico, Fernando Henrique Cardoso, César Gaviria, and Ernesto Zedillo, respectively, highlight the fact that it's necessary for the United States and Europe to "design and implement policies leading to an effective reduction in their levels of drug consumption and, as a consequence, in the overall scope of the narcotics criminal activities," *Latin American Commission on Drugs and Democracy, Drugs and Democracy: Toward a Paradigm Shift* (New York: Open Society Institute, 2008), 7.
4 United Nations Office on Drugs and Crime (UNODC), *The Globalization of Crime: A Transnational Organized Crime Threat Assessment* (New York: UNODC, 2010), 5–6; United Nations Office on Drugs and Crime (UNODC), *World Drug Report, 2011* (New York: UNODC, 2011), 8.
5 David F. Musto, *The American Disease: Origins of Narcotic Control*, 3rd edition (New York: Oxford University Press, 1999).
6 UNODC, *World Drug Report, 2011*, 87. Note that the five million users of cocaine in the U.S. are between the ages of 15 and 64.

CHALLENGES TO DEMOCRACY

7 Cocaine demand has been decreasing steadily in the U.S. since 1982, from an estimated 10.5 million users in 1982 to some 5.3 in 2008. Cocaine users in the 27 European Union countries have more than doubled in the past decade, however, increasing from 2 million in 1998 to 4.1 million in 2008 (4.5 million in all of Europe). UNODC, *World Drug Report, 2010* (New York: UNODC, 2010), 16; also UNODC, *The Globalization of Crime*, v–vi and 82. The consumption of cocaine has decreased in the U.S. to 1.9 percent in 2009 from 2.5 percent in 2006. UNDOC, *World Drug Report, 2011*, 93.

8 Despite declines in the overall total area of coca leaf cultivation in the Andes, cocaine production remained essentially stable from the mid-1990s through 2008 at approximately 800–1,100 metric tons. North America, including Canada, accounted for some 40 percent of worldwide cocaine consumption. The EU and the EFTA (European Free Trade Area) countries consumed more than 25 percent of the world total. Together, these two regions accounted for more than 80 percent of the global cocaine market, estimated at US$ 88 billion in 2008. UNODC, *The Globalization of Crime*, 82. In 2008, the total value of worldwide cocaine and heroin markets combined was estimated at $US 153 billion. UNODC, *World Drug Report, 2010*, 19; UNODC, *World Drug Report, 2011*, 119.

9 UNODC, *World Drug Report, 2011*, 71–73.

10 UNODC, *The Globalization of Crime*, 81–82.

11 Some 4.3–4.75 million people have used cocaine in Europe as of 2009. UNODC, *World Drug Report, 2011*, 86.

12 South America was the third largest consumer market for cocaine in the world in 2008 with some 2.4 million users. The bulk of South American consumption was concentrated in two countries of the Southern Cone, although there was evidence of rising cocaine use in virtually every country in the hemisphere. Given its population of nearly 200 million, Brazil had the largest number of users at roughly 1 million. Use was most intense in Argentina, however, where an estimated 2.6 percent of the adult population used cocaine in 2006—a statistic roughly similar to that of the United States. UNODC, *The Globalization of Crime*, 82.

13 UNODC, *World Drug Report, 2011*, 91

14 UNODC, *World Drug Report, 2011*. 86.

15 Paul Gootenberg, *Andean Cocaine: The Making of a Global Drug* (Chapel Hill, NC: University of North Carolina Press, 2008), 1–14 and passim.

16 Bruce Bagley, "La Conexión Colombia-México-Estados Unidos," in *Atlas de la Seguridad y la Defensa de México 2009*, ed. Raúl Benítez Manaut, Abelardo Rodríguez Sumano, and Armando Rodríguez Luna (México City: CASADE, 2009), 25; Patrick L. Clawson and Rensselaer W. Lee III, *The Andean Cocaine Industry* (New York: St. Martin's Griffin, 1998), 12–16.

17 After the Peru-Colombia "air bridge" that transported paste or base from Peru's Alto Huallaga to Colombia by small airplanes was disrupted by Peruvian president's Fujimori's shoot-down policy in 1993/4, the subsequent termination of the cocaine flights out of Peru during the Fujimori dictatorship in the mid-late 1990s and the launching of Plan Dignidad in 1998 (with U.S. government funding) by the newly installed Banzer government in Bolivia led the epicenter of illegal coca cultivation to shift from Eastern Peru and Bolivia to southeastern Colombia. Gootenberg, *Andean Cocaine*, 291–324; Clawson and Lee, *The Andean Cocaine Industry*, 16–21; Francisco E. Thoumi, *Illegal Drugs, Economy and Society in the Andes* (Baltimore, MD: Johns Hopkins University Press, 2003), 7 and passim.

18 Bruce Bagley, "La Conexión", 29; UNODC, *Coca Cultivation in the Andean Region: Survey of Bolivia, Colombia and Peru* (New York: UNODC, June 2006).

167

19 Steven Dudley, *Walking Ghosts: Murder and Guerrilla Politics in Colombia* (New York: Routledge, 2004), 195–198; Virginia Vallejo, *The Andean Cocaine Industry*), 352–385.

20 By September 1996, after allegations surfaced in 1994 that the Cali cartel financed Ernesto Samper's presidential campaign, the Rodriguez Orejuela brothers and other major the Cali cartel leaders were imprisoned in Colombia. See Maria Clemencia Ramirez Lemus, Kimberly Stanton, and John Walsh, "Colombia: A Vicious Circle of Drugs and War," in *Drugs and Democracy in Latin America: The Impact of U.S. Policy*, ed. Coletta A. Youngers and Eileen Rosen (Boulder, CO: Lynne Rienner Publishers, 2005); also Camilo Chaparro, *Historia del Cartel de Cali: El Ajedrecista Mueve sus Fichas* (Bogotá: Intermedio Editores, Círculo de Lectores S.A., 2005), 125–148; Fernando Rodríguez Mondragón y Antonio Sánchez, *El Hijo del "Ajedrecista"* (Bogotá: Editorial Oveja Negra, Quintero Editores, 2007), 169–173.

21 Bruce Bagley, "La Conexión"; Douglas Farah, "Organized Crime in El Salvador: The Homegrown and Transnational Dimensions," in Cynthia J. Arnson and Eric Olson, eds, *Organized Crime in Central America* (Washington, DC: Woodrow Wilson Center for International Scholars, 2011).

22 On the paramilitary demobilization, see Elvira María Restrepo and Bruce Bagley, eds, *La desmovilización de los paramilitares en Colombia: Entre la esperanza y el escepticismo* (Bogotá: Uniandes, 2011). The Uribe government emphasized a counterinsurgency strategy in Plan Colombia, an important difference from the Pastrana government's original "Plan Marshall." During 2002/3 Uribe increased the number of combat troops and pursued constitutional reforms to expand the military activities. Ramírez Lemus et al., "Colombia: A Vicious Circle," 111–112.

23 The 62,000 ha and 73,000 ha includes small fields in the calculations. UNODC, *World Drug Report, 2011*, 100–111; Adam Isacson, *Don't Call it a Model: On Plan Colombia's Tenth Anniversary, Claims of 'Success' Don't Stand Up to Scrutiny* (Washington, DC: Washington Office on Latin America, July 13, 2010).

24 Bruce Bagley, "La Conexión," 31. The U.S. government estimates that the Mexican cartels make $19 or 39 billion annually from the drug trade. Drug policy analyst Dr. Peter Reuter estimates Mexican cartel drug profits at the much lower figure of $7 billion per year for 2010. Even at Reuter's lower estimate level, the profits remain quite substantial and are certainly enough to spur on the intense violence Mexican drug traffickers have exhibited in recent years.

25 The Northern Triangle countries of Central America (Guatemala, Honduras, and El Salvador) have been deeply effected. The intense drug-related violence presents serious challenges to governance. UNODC, *World Drug Report, 2010*, 26.

26 From 2009 to 2010, the area under cultivation increased in Peru by 2 percent. In terms of hectares, the estimates for 2010 are 61,200. Cultivation has varied in Peru based on region. Some smaller regions located in the Amazon Basin saw dramatic increases, as much as 90 percent (in terms of the area under cultivation). It is important to note that cocaine production in Peru has been increasing since 2005, according to the UN report. On the other hand, Colombia saw a decrease in production in 2010; the 2010 estimate for production is 350 mt. For more information, see UNODC, *World Drug Report, 2011*, 101. Between 2000 and 2009 coca cultivation increased by 38 percent and 112 percent in Peru and Bolivia, respectively. UNODC, *World Drug Report, 2010*, 65. Coca cultivation is, in short, returning to countries where eradication policies damaged the reputation of the U.S. and its drug control policies, and incentivized peasant unrest. Gootenberg, *Andean Cocaine*, 315.

CHALLENGES TO DEMOCRACY

27 In 2008 Colombia produced 450 metric tons of cocaine out of a UN-estimated 865 mt produced worldwide. U.S. government estimates of total cocaine production were higher, ranging up to 1,000 mt. Regarding cultivation, there was a decrease in hectares cultivated from around 80,000 to 68,000 in 2008/9 in Colombia according to the UNODC, *World Drug Report, 2010*, 66. Estimates of cocaine production per ha of cultivated coca are quite unreliable.

28 For a discussion in historical perspective of the difficulties of quantifying cocaine production, see Gootenberg, *Andean Cocaine*, 325–336. For a discussion of the difficulties with the UNODC estimates, see Francisco E. Thoumi, "Debates recientes de la Organización de las Naciones Unidas acera del régimen internacional de drogas: Fundamentos, limitaciones e (im)posibles cambios," in *Drogas y Prohibición: Una Vieja Guerra, un Nuevo Debate*, ed. Juan Gabriel Tokatlian (Buenos Aires: Libros del Zorzal, 2010), 27–56; Francisco E. Thoumi and Ernestine Jensema, "Drug Policies and the Funding of the United Nations Office on Drugs and Crime," in *Global Drug Policy: Building a New Framework*, contributions to the Lisbon International Symposium on Global Drug Policy (New York: The Senlis Council, 2003).

29 See Coletta A. Youngers and John M. Walsh, "Development First: A More Humane and Promising Approach to Reducing Cultivation of Crops for Illicit Markets" (Washington, DC: WOLA, March 2010) Also Vanda Felbab-Brown, Joel M. Jutkowitz, Sergio Rivas Ricardo Rocha, James T. Smith, Manuel Supervielle, and Cynthia Watson, "Assessment of the Implementation of the United States Government's Support for Plan Colombia's Illicit Crop Reduction Components," produced for review by the U.S. Agency of International Development (USAID), April 17, 2009; U.S. Government Accountability Office (GAO), "Plan Colombia: Drug Reduction Goals Were Not Fully Met, but Security Has Improved: U.S. Agencies Need More Detailed Plan for Reducing Assistance" (Washington, DC: GAO, October 2008); Adam Isacson and Abigail Poe, *After Plan Colombia: Evaluating "Integrated Action: The Next Phase of U.S. Assistance"* (Washington, DC: Center for International Policy, 2009).

30 United Nations, *Coca Cultivation Survey June 2009* (New York: United Nations, 2010). "If the current trend continues, Peru will soon overtake Colombia as the world's biggest coca producer—a notorious status that it has not had since the mid-1990s," said UNODC Executive Director Antonio Maria Costa. Coca cultivation in Peru increased 6.8 percent in 2009—from 56,100 hectares in 2008 to 59,900 ha. Cultivation of coca in Colombia, however, decreased in 2009 by 16 percent—from 81,000 hectares in 2008 to 68,000 in 2009. Despite Colombia's apparent decline, overall coca cultivation in the Andean region decreased only 5.2 percent in 2009. According to the UNODC data, cultivation of coca in Bolivia barely changed between 2008 and 2009, increasing only by 400 ha (about 1 percent–from 30,500 ha in 2008 to 30,900 in 2009). This UNODC report contradicted the U.S. estimate for Bolivia, which showed a 9.4 percent increase in cultivation between 2008 and 2009 (and a 2009 cultivation estimate that is 4,100 ha higher than the UNODC estimate). See "Just the Facts: A Civilian's Guide to U.S. Defense and Security Assistance to Latin America and the Caribbean," June 23, 2010 (http://justf.org).

31 Bruce Bagley, "La Conexión"; Peter Dale Scott and Jonathan Marshall, *Cocaine Politics: Drugs, Armies and the CIA in Central America* (Berkeley, CA: University of California Press, 1998), 186–192.

32 This displacement is also confirmed by the fact that Mexican criminal organizations have increased their activities in the U.S. By 2008 these organizations had a

169

SECURITY AND DEMOCRACY

presence in 230 U.S. cities. Three years before they were present in only 100 cities. Moreover, the Colombian groups now controlled the illicit cocaine and heroin distribution in only 40 cities, mostly in the northeast. UNODC, *World Drug Report 2010*, 79.

33 For more on Calderon's military strategy and the Mérida Initiative, see Rafael Velázquez Flores and Juan Pablo Prado Lallande, eds, *La Iniciativa Mérida: Nuevo Paradigma de Cooperación entre México y Estados Unidos en Seguridad?* (Mexico City: Universidad Nacional Autónoma de México, 2009); Raul Benitez Manaut (ed.), *Crimen organizado e Iniciativa Mérida en Las Relaciones México-Estados Unidos* (Mexico City: CASADE Colectivo de Análisis de la Seguridad con Democracia, 2010); David A. Shirk, *The Drug War in Mexico: Confronting a Threat*, Special Report no. 60 (New York: Council on Foreign Relations, March 2011).

34 Bruce Bagley, "La Conexión", 28–29; International Crisis Group "Learning to Walk Without a Crutch: An Assessment of The International Commission Against Impunity in Guatemala," Latin America Report no. 36 (Brussels: International Crisis Group, May 31, 2011), 3; Steven S. Dudley, "Drug Trafficking Organizations in Central America: Transportistas, Mexican Cartels and Maras," in *Organized Crime*, Cynthia J. Arnson and Eric Olson, passim.

35 Between 2006 and 2008, over half of the maritime shipments of cocaine to Europe that were detected came from the Bolivarian Republic of Venezuela. Ecuador has also been affected by an increase in transit trafficking, and both countries are experiencing increasing problems with violence. *World Drug Report 2010*, 30.

36 Randall C. Archibold and Damien Cave, "Drug Wars Push Deeper into Central America," *New York Times*, March 2, 2011.

37 In Bolivia, coca-growing peasants joined unions and this helped to keep their struggle for recognition in national politics relatively peaceful. Gootenberg, *Andean Cocaine*, 313.

38 In Peru, the eradication policy caused discontent among the peasants and favored the growth of the Shining Path (the nation's Maoist guerrilla insurgent organization). Thus, the guerrillas took control of particular areas, forcing local authorities to resign and flee while the guerrilla leadership demanded payments for processing and transporting the drugs. Intense eradication efforts without economic alternatives led people to join the guerrillas. Mariano Valderrama and Hugo Cabieses, "Questionable Alliances in the War on Drugs: Peru and the United States," in *The Political Economy of the Drug Industry: Latin America and the International System*, ed. Menno Velling (Gainesville, FL: University Press of Florida, 2004), 60–61.

39 This collapse of Colombia's two major cartels opened the way for new actors to assume expanded roles in the drug industry, particularly paramilitary and guerrilla organizations that use the illegal drugs to fund their activities. Francisco E. Thoumi, "Illegal Drugs in Colombia: From Illegal Economic Boom to Social Crisis," in Menno Vellinga, *The Political Economy*, 76.

40 Ibid., 159–264; Kevin Healy, "Coca, the State and the Peasantry in Bolivia," in *Assessing the America's War on Drugs*, special issue of *Journal of InterAmerican Studies and World Affairs*, vol. 30, no. 2/3 (1988), 105–126; International Crisis Group, "Coca, Drugs and Social Protest in Bolivia and Peru," Latin American Report no. 12 (Brussels: International Crisis Group, March 3, 2005).

41 Juan Carlos Garzón, *Mafia & Co.: The Criminal Networks in Mexico, Brazil and Colombia* (Washington, DC: Woodrow Wilson International Center for Scholars, June 2008); Luis Jorge Garay-Salamanca, Eduardo Salcedo-Albarán, and

CHALLENGES TO DEMOCRACY

Isaac De León-Beltrán, *Illicit Networks Reconfiguring States: Social Network Analysis of Colombian and Mexican Cases* (Bogotá: Método Foundation, 2010).

42 Elyssa Pachico, "The New Political Face of Colombia's Drug Gangs," *InSight* (www.insightcrime.org/insight-latest-news/item/1743-the-new-political-face-of -colombias-drug-gangs).

43 Luis Astorga Almanza, *Seguridad, traficantes, y militares: El Poder y la sombra* (Mexico City: Tusquets, 2007); Luis Astorga Almanza and David A. Shirk, "Drug Trafficking Organizations and Counter-drug Strategies in the U.S.-Mexican Context," in *Shared Responsibility: U.S.-Mexico Policy Options For Confronting Organized Crime*, ed. Eric L. Olson, David A. Shirk, and Andrew D. Selee (Washington, DC: Mexico Institute, Woodrow Wilson International Center for Scholars/San Diego, CA: Trans-Border Institute, 2010). From 1995, several Mexican cartels became progressively more involved in cocaine trafficking out of Colombia. The Tijuana and Juarez cartels started to fight for control of cocaine smuggling routes across Mexico and cross-border plazas into the United States. Only after 2000, however, did Mexico experience the rise and participation of newer cartels such as Sinaloa, the Gulf, and the Zetas. Bruce Bagley and Aline Hernández, "Crimen organizado en México y sus vínculos con Estados Unidos," in *Seguridad regional en América Latina y el Caribe: Anuario 2010*, ed. Hans Mathieu and Catalina Niño Guarnizo (Bogotá: Friedrich Ebert Stiftung, 2010), 332–333.

44 Carlos Antonio Flores Pérez, *El Estado en Crisis: Crimen Organizado y Política. Desafíos para la Consolidación Democrática* (México D.F.: Centro de Investigaciones y Estudios Superiores en Antropología Social (CIESAS), 2009), 137–228; Jorge Chabat, "El Estado y el crimen organizado transnacional: Amenaza global, respuestas nacionales," *ISTOR: Revista de Historia Internacional*, vol. 11, no. 42 (2010), 3–14; Phil Williams, "El crimen organizado y la violencia en México," *ISTOR: Revista de Historia Internacional*, vol. 11, no. 42 (2010), 15–40.

45 Elyssa Pachico, "Investigation: Medellin's Turbulent Comuna 13," *InSight,* May 2011.

46 Ibid.

47 Patricia Dávila, "La Disputa por Ciudad Juárez," in Rafael Rodríguez Catañeda, *El México Narco* (Mexico: Planeta, 2010); Charles Bowden, *Murder City: Ciudad Juarez and the Global Economy's Killing Fields* (New York: Nation Books, 2010).

48 Agnes Gereben Schaefer, Benjamin Bahney, and K. Jack Riley, *Security in Mexico: Implications for U.S. Policy Options* (Santa Monica, CA: RAND Corporation, 2009).

49 See www.elpasotimes.com/newupdated/ci_17627581; also George W. Grayson, *Mexico's Struggle with "Drugs and Thugs,"* Headline Series no. 331 (New York: Foreign Policy Association, 2009); Hal Brands, *Mexico's Narco-Insurgency and U.S. Counterdrug Policy* (Carlisle, PA: The Strategic Studies Institute, U.S. Army War College, May 2009).

50 On March 11, 2011, Honduran officials reported that they had, for the first time, dismantled a cocaine lab that belonged to the Zetas. This highlights the changing location activities of Zetas due to the pressures they're feeling elsewhere. *Stratfor*, March 22, 2010.

51 In fact, the government doesn't have a standardized definition for homeland security either. Shawn Reese, "Defining Homeland Security: Analysis and Congressional Considerations," *Congressional Research Service*, January 8, 2013 (www.fas.org/sgp/crs/homesec/R42462.pdf). Cindy Combs, for example, provides an accurate definition of terrorism as: "A synthesis of war and theatre, a dramatization of the most proscribed kind of violence—that which is perpetrated on innocent victims—played before an audience in the hope of creating a

171

mood of fear, for political purposes." Cindy Combs, "Terrorism in the Twenty-First Century," 3rd edition (Upper Saddle River, NJ: Prentice Hall, 2003), 10.

52 Scott Steward, "The Myth of the End of Terrorism," in *Stratfor*, February, 23, 2013 (www.stratfor.com/weekly/myth-end-terrorism).

53 This report also cited U.S. sanctions against several Venezuelan companies for violating U.S. sanctions against Iran. U.S. Department of State, "Country Reports on Terrorism," July, 31, 2012 (www.state.gov/j/crt/2011/index.htm). For more on U.S. concerns about terrorism in the Western hemisphere, see Mark P. Sullivan and June S. Beittel, "Latin America, Terrorism Issues," Congressional Research Services Report 7-5700, August 15, 2014 (www.fas.org/sgp/crs/terror/RS21049.pdf).

54 Ibid.

55 The ELN, facing diminished resources, has lately begun to cooperate with the FARC to conduct attacks. Peace talks with the Colombian government ended in 2008 but the ELN recently indicated a willingness to join peace talks between the government and the FARC. For more see ibid. See also June S. Beittel, *Colombia: Background, U.S. Relations, and Congressional Interest,* Congressional Research Services Report RL3225, November, 28, 2012 (www.fas.org/sgp/crs/row/RL32250.pdf).

56 General John F. Kelly, Commander, United States Southern Command, Posture Statement, Senate Armed Services Committee, March 19, 2013 (www.south com.mil/newsroom/documents/southcom%202013%20posture%20statement%20final%20sasc.pdf); Jason Sherman, "DOD: Colombian Rebel Group Has Acquired Surface-To-Air Missiles," *Inside Defense*, March 28, 2013; "Colombia's FARC Denies Link to Drug Haul," *LatinNews Daily Report,* March, 18, 2013; Vivian Sequera, "Colombia Officials: No Evidence Rebels Have Surface-to-Air Missiles," *Associated Press*, April 4, 2013. Also Sullivan and Beittel, "Latin America, Terrorism Issues."

57 Ibid.; U.S. Department of State, "Country Reports on Terrorism, 2010," August 18, 2011 (www.state.gov/j/ct/rls/crt/2010/index.htm).

58 Ibid.

59 Ibid. Also Bryan Bender, "Talk Grows of Taking Cuba Off Terror List," *Boston Globe*, February 21, 2013; U.S. Department of State, Daily Press Briefing, February 21, 2013.

60 Ibid. For further background on Mexico, see also the two Congressional Research Service reports, June S. Beittel, "Mexico's Drug Trafficking Organizations: Source and Scope of the Rising Violence," no. R41576, and Clare Ribando Seelke, "Mexico's New Administration: Priorities and Key Issues in U.S.-Mexican Relations," no. R42917; Cory Molzahn, Octavio Rodriguez Ferreira, and David A. Shirk, "Drug Violence in Mexico: Data and Analysis Through 2012," Trans-Border Institute (TBI), February 2013; U.S. Department of State, 2013 International Narcotics Control Strategy Report, March 2013. According to the 2013 INCS report, more than 90 percent of the cocaine seized in the United States transits the Central America/Mexico "corridor."

61 Ibid. Several other U.S. agencies have made estimates in recent years. For example, the U.S. Department of Homeland Security (DHS) estimates that between $19 and $29 billion flows back to Mexico each year generated by illicit drug sales in the United States. See DHS, Immigration and Customs Enforcement (ICE), United States-Mexico Criminal Proceeds Study, June 2010. For more background on the Merida Initiative see Clare Ribando Seelke and Kristin M. Finklea, "U.S.-Mexican Security Cooperation: The Mérida Initiative and Beyond," CRS Report R41349. For more on drug cartels in Mexico see

CHALLENGES TO DEMOCRACY

Patrick Corcoran, "Mexico Has 80 Drug Cartels: Attorney General," *Sight: Organized Crime in the Americas*, December 20, 2012.
62 Ibid.
63 Joint Hearing on "Venezuela's Sanctionable Activities," House Committee on Foreign Affairs, Subcommittee on the Western Hemisphere and Subcommittee on the Middle East and South Asia, and House Committee on Oversight and Government Reform, Subcommittee on National Security, Homeland Defense and Foreign Operations. State department testimony of Ambassador Daniel Benjamin, Coordinator for Counterterrorism; Kevin Whitaker, Acting Deputy Assistant Secretary for Western Hemisphere Affairs; and Thomas Delare, Director of the Terrorist Finance and Economic Sanctions Policy, Bureau of Economic, Energy, and Business Affairs, June 24, 2011 (http://foreignaffairs.house.gov/112/ben062411.pdf).
64 Ibid.
65 Ibid. For additional background on Venezuela, see Mark P. Sullivan, "Venezuela: Issues for Congress," CRS Report R40938, and Mark P. Sullivan, "Hugo Chávez's Death: Implications for Venezuela and U.S. Relations," CRS Report R42989;
66 Ibid. See also Brian Ellsworth, "Iranian Leader Ends Lackluster Latin America Tour," *Reuters News*, January 13, 2012; Douglas Farah and Pamela Philips Lum, "Ecuador's Role in Iran's Latin American Financial Structure," International Assessment and Strategy Center, March 12, 2013 (www.strategycenter.net/resea rch/pubID.304/pub_detail.asp).
67 Ibid. Also "Hugo Chávez Says Venezuela Is Studying Idea of Starting Peaceful Nuclear Energy Program," *AP Newswire*, September 28, 2010; "Russia to Build Nuclear Power Plant in Venezuela," *Reuters News*, October 15, 2010; Diego Ore, "Venezuela Halts Nuclear Program After Japan Disaster," *Reuters News*, March 15, 2011. See the following press reports: "Iran Helps Venezuela Find Uranium Deposits," *BBC Monitoring Caucasus*, September 26, 2009; and "Iran Helps Venezuela Find Uranium Deposits," *Tehran Press TV Online*, September 26, 2009.
68 General John F. Kelly, Commander, United States Southern Command, Posture Statement, Senate Armed Services Committee, March 19, 2013 (www.armedser vices.senate.gov/statemnt/2013/03percent20March/Kellypercent2003-19-13.pdf).
69 Ibid. See also Frank Bajak, "Top U.S. General: Venezuela Not a National Security Threat," *Associated Press*, July 31, 2012; U.S. Department of Justice, "Two Men Charged in Alleged Plot to Assassinate Saudi Arabian Ambassador to the United States," Press Release, October 11, 2011 (www.justice.gov/opa/pr/2011/October/11-ag-1339.html); Charles Savage and Scott Shane, "Iranians Accused of a Plot to Kill Saudis' U.S. Envoy," *New York Times*, October 12, 2011; and Siobhan Gorman, Devlin Barrett, and Stephanie Simon, "U.S. News: Accusations Against Iran Fleshed Out," *Wall Street Journal*, October 13, 2011.
70 Jim Garamone, "Fraser Testifies Before Senate, Says SOUTHCOM Focused on Transnational Organized Crime," American Forces Press Service, United States Southern Command, Partnership for the Americas, March 14, 2012 (www.southcom.mil/newsroom/Pages/Fraser-Testifies-Before-Senate,-Says-SO UTHCOM-Focused-on-Transnational-Organized-Crime.aspx).
71 Gorman, Barrett, and Simon, "U.S. News." See also Department of Defense, "Unclassified Report on Military Power of Iran," April 2010 (for the full text of the report, see www.politico.com/static/PPM145_link_042010.html). For background on the Qods Force, see Kenneth Katzman, "Iran: U.S. Concerns and Policy Responses," CRS Report RL32048; Anne Flaherty, "Pentagon Says

173

SECURITY AND DEMOCRACY

Iran's Reach in Latin America Doesn't Pose Military Threat," *AP Newswire*, April 27, 2010. General Fraser reiterated that Iran's focus in Latin America has been "primarily diplomatic and commercial," in testimony before the House Armed Services Committee, March 30, 2011. See "Hearing of the House Armed Services Committee; Subject FY2012 National Defense Authorization Budget Requests for the U.S. Southern Command, U.S. Northern Command, and U.S. European Command," *Federal News Service*, March 30, 2011. U.S. Department of Justice, "Two Men Charged in Alleged Plot to Assassinate Saudi Arabian Ambassador to the United States," Press Release, October 11, 2011 (www.justice.gov/opa/pr/2011/October/11-ag- 1339.html). Charles Savage and Scott Shane, "Iranians Accused of a Plot to Kill Saudis' U.S. Envoy," *New York Times*, October 12, 2011; and Siobhan Gorman, Devlin Barrett, and Stephanie Simon, "U.S. News: Accusations Against Iran Fleshed Out," *Wall Street Journal*, October 13, 2011. Also U.S. Congress, House Committee on Foreign Affairs, Subcommittee on Terrorism, Nonproliferation, and Trade, Narco-terrorism and the Long Reach of U.S. Law Enforcement, Part II, 112th Cong., 1st sess., November 17, 2011, Serial No. 112–81 (Washington, DC: GPO, 2011), written testimony of Derek S. Maltz, Special Agent in charge of the Special Operations Division, Drug Enforcement Administration (http://foreigna ffairs.house.gov/112/mal111711.pdf).

72 Karen Zraick, "The Mysterious Death of Alberto Nisman," *New York Times*, The Americas, February 20, 2015 (www.nytimes.com/interactive/2015/02/07/ world/americas/argentina-alberto-nisman-case.html?_r=0).

73 Ibid. See also U.S. Department of the Treasury, "Treasury Identifies Lebanese Canadian Bank Sal as a Primary Money Laundering Concern," Press Release, February 10, 2011.

74 Karen Zraick, "The Mysterious Death of Alberto Nisman." See also U.S. Department of the Treasury, "Treasury Identifies Lebanese Canadian Bank Sal as a Primary Money Laundering Concern"; U.S. Department of Justice, U.S. Attorney's Office, Eastern District of Virginia, "U.S. Charges Alleged Lebanese Drug Kingpin with Laundering Drug Proceeds for Mexican and Colombian Drug Cartels," Press Release, December 3, 2011; Jo Becker, "Beirut Bank Seen as a Hub of Hezbollah's Financing," *New York Times*, December 14, 2011; U.S. Drug Enforcement Administration, "DEA News: Civil Suit Exposes Lebanese Money Laundering Scheme for Hizballah," News Release, December 15, 2011 (www.justice.gov/dea/pubs/pressrel/pr121511.html); U.S. Department of the Treasury, "Treasury Targets Major Money Laundering Network Linked to Drug Trafficker Ayman Joumaa and a Key Hizballah Supporter in South America," Press Release, June 27, 2012 (www.treasury.gov/press-center/p ress-releases/Pages/tg1624.aspx); U.S. Department of the Treasury, "Notice of Finding," April 20, 2013 (www.fincen.gov/statutes_regs/files/311–ExchHou se-R-NoticeofFinding-Final.pdf); U.S. FBI, "U.S. Government Seized $150 Million in Connection with Hezballah-Related Money Laundering Scheme," Press Release, August 20, 2012, (www.fbi.gov/newyork/press-releases/2012/u. s.-government-seizes-150-million-in-connection-with-hizballah-related-money-laundering-scheme).

75 United Nations Office on Drugs and Crime (UNDOC), "World Drug Report 2011," New York, 2011 (www.unodc.org/documents/data-and-analysis/ WDR2011/World_Drug_Report_2011_ebook.pdf). For more current data, the UNDOC "World Drug Report 2015" indicates little change in the overall global situation regarding the production, use, and health consequences of illegal drugs. UNDOC (United Nations Office on Drugs and Crime, "World Drug

Report 2015," New York, 2015 (www.unodc.org/documents/wdr2015/World_Drug_Report_2015.pdf).

76 J. Stavridis, "Posture Statement of Admiral James G. Stavridis, United States Navy" Senate Armed Services Committee, March 17, 2009, 22.

77 For more information on the history of economics (production, extraction and distribution) of cocaine before the 1980s see Bruce Bagley, "La conexión Colombia-México-Estados Unidos," in *Atlas de la Seguridad y la Defensa de México 2009*, ed. Raúl Benítez Manaut, Abelardo Rodríguez Sumano, and Armando Rodríguez Luna (Mexico City: CASADE, 2009), 25; and Patrick L. Clawson and Rensselaer W. Lee III, *The Andean Cocaine Industry* (New York: St. Martin's Griffin, 1998), 12–16.

78 In 1982, President Ronald Reagan declared a full-scale "War on Drugs", and by 1986, imposed the certification mechanism. Bruce Bagley, *Myths of Militarization: The Role of the Military in the War on Drugs in the Americas* (Miami, FL: North-South Center, University of Miami, 1991); Bruce Bagley, "After San Antonio," in *Drug Trafficking in the Americas*, ed. Bruce Bagley and William O. Walker III (Miami, FL: North South Center, University of Miami, 1996) 61–73; Bruce Bagley and Juan G., "Dope and Dogma: Explaining the Failure of U.S.-Latin American Drug Policies," in *Neighborly Adversaries: Readings in U.S.-Latin American Relations*, ed. Bruce Bagley, M. LaRosa, and Frank O. Walker III (Lanham, MD, Boulder, CO, New York and Oxford: Rowman & Littlefield, 1999), 219–235. Together with the imposition of the 1980 neoliberal market reforms, these unilateral U.S. policies contributed to the diminished capacities of Latin American civilian governments and fostered the corruption of their militaries, charged with controlling their territories during their democratic transitions. See Betty Horwitz, "The Role of the Inter-American Drug Abuse Control Commission (CICAD) Confronting the Problem of Illegal Drugs in the Americas," *Latin American Politics and Society*, vol. 52, no. 2 (2010). Also G. Weeks, *US and Latin American Relations* (New York: Pearson, 2008), 251.

79 Ibid.

80 The Bolivarian Alternative for the Americas (ALBA) (set up by Cuba's leader Fidel Castro and Venezuela's Hugo Chávez) was supposed to represent a "solidarity" pact that rejected the free-trade model of integration espoused by Washington. Mr. Chávez wanted to turn it into a mutual defense pact that would protect its members from attack by the United States and its ally, Colombia. But the other three ALBA members: Bolivia, Nicaragua, and Dominica, met this proposal with derision. Populist leaders in the Andean region such as Nicaragua's Daniel Ortega or Mr. Chávez were merely looking to boost their flagging support at home by manufacturing external threats. James Brooke, "Drug Spotlight Falls on an Unblinking Cali Carte," *New York Times*, World, December 17, 1993 (www.nytimes.com/1993/12/17/world/drug-spotlight-falls-on-an-unblinking-cali-cartel.html?pagewanted=all); *Los Angeles Times*, "Former Drugpin Faces New Charges," March 13, 2003 (http://articles.la times.com/2003/mar/13/world/fg-briefs13.1); and Bruce Bagley, "Drug Trafficking and Organized Crime in the Americas: Major Trends in the Twenty-First Century," Woodrow Wilson Centre, Update on the Americas, August 2012 (www.wilsoncenter.org/sites/default/files/BB%20Final.pdf).

81 This fragmentation and distancing from Washington is exemplified by the establishment of the *Banco del Sur*. The conditionality imposed by Washington and international organizations such as the IMF or the IDB has prompted Venezuela, Argentina, Brazil, Bolivia, Ecuador, Paraguay, Uruguay, and probably Colombia to find alternative ways to promote investment in infrastructure

and stimulate greater regional trade and integration. On November 3, 2007, these countries formed the *Banco del Sur*. It remains to be seen whether this institution, with up to $7 billion in initial capital, can become a real alternative to the current institutional framework favored by Washington. Betty Horwitz, "Cooperation, Security, and the Drug Phenomenon in the Inter-American Context," in *Cooperation and Drug Policies in the Americas: Trends in the Twenty-First Century*, ed. Roberto Zepeda and Jonathan D. Rosen (New York: Lexington Books, 2015), 199–222.

82 Recommended by John Rollins and Liana Sun Wyler in "Terrorism and Transnational Crime: Foreign Policy Issues for Congress" in Congressional Research Service: Report for Congress, October 19, 2012.

83 Bruce Bagley, "Globalization and Transnational Organized Crime: The Russian Mafia in Latin America and the Caribbean," in Vellinga, *The Political Economy*, 261–296.

84 Bruce Bagley and Aline Hernández, "Crimen Organizado en México," 332.

85 Francisco E. Thoumi, "Debates recientes de la Organización de las Naciones Unidas acera del régimen internacional de drogas: Fundamentos, limitaciones e (im) posibles cambios," in Juan Gabriel Tokatlian (ed.), *Drogas y Prohibición*, 27–56; Global Commission on Drug Policy, *War on Drugs: Report of the Global Commission on Drug Policy*, June 2011 (www.globalcommissionondrugs.org/Report).

86 Rafael Pardo, "Introducción: Hacia un nuevo pensamiento sobre drogas. Nueve anomalías sobre el paradigma convencional y dos propuestas de nuevos caminos," in Juan Gabriel Tokatlian (ed.), *Drogas y Prohibición*, 13–26.

87 Bruce Bagley and Juan Gabriel Tokatlian, "Dope and Dogma: Explaining the Failure of U.S.-Latin American Drug Policies," in *Neighborly Adversaries: Readings in U.S.-Latin American Relations*, ed. Michael LaRosa and Frank O. Mora (New York: Rowman & Littlefield, 2007), 219–234. Bruce Bagley, "Políticas de control de drogas ilícitas en Estados Unidos: ¿qué funciona y qué no funciona?," in Juan Gabriel Tokatlian (ed.), *La Guerra Contra las Drogas en el Mudo Andino: Hacia un Cambio de Paradigm* (Buenos Aires: Libros del Zorzal, 2009), 283–296; Bruce Bagley, "The New Hundred Years War? US National Security and the War on Drugs in Latin America," *Journal of InterAmerican Studies and World Affairs*, vol. 30, no. 1 (1988): 161–186.

88 War on Drugs: Report of the Global Commission on Drug Policy, 2011 (www.globalcommissionondrugs.org/Report).

89 For more see Betty Horwitz, "A Change in the Approach to the Drug Problem in the Americas," in *New Approaches to Drug Policies: A Time for Change*, ed. Jonathan D. Rosen and Marten W. Brienen (London and New York: Palgrave-Macmillan, 2015), Ch. 11. See also Organization of American States, *Report of the Drug Problem in the Americas: Terms of Reference, 2012–2013* (Panama City: OAS, 2013). For a link to the report, see www.countthecosts.org/sites/default/files/CICAD-Marketing-Document-ENG.pdf. Organization of American States, *Scenarios for the Drug Problem in the Americas: 2013–2025* (Panama City: OAS, 2013). For a link to the report see www.oas.org/documents/eng/press/Scenarios_Report.pdf).

Part IV

LATIN AMERICA AND THE CARIBBEAN ON THE WORLD STAGE

That a man be willing, when others are too, as far forth, as for peace, and defense of himself he shall think it necessary, to lay down this right to all things; and be contented with so much liberty against other men, as he would allow other men against himself … . Whatsoever you require that others should do to you, that do ye to them.

Thomas Hobbes, "Of the First and Second Natural Laws, and of Contracts", Chapter 14, *Leviathan*, in Chris Brown, Terry Nardin, and Nicholas Rengger, *International Relations in Political Thought: Texts from the Ancient Greeks to the First World War* (Cambridge: Cambridge University Press, 2008 [1651]), 339–340.

9

LATIN AMERICA AND THE CARIBBEAN AND THE DEVELOPMENT OF THE INTER-AMERICAN SYSTEM

Introduction

When it comes to influencing world affairs, the vast majority of students and policymakers have consistently written off the nations of LAC. As this volume has shown, since the dawn of independence Latin American nations have remained heavily dependent on commodity and primary goods exports, thus remaining essentially at the mercy of larger world powers.

LAC nations have never been weighty enough economically to impact the international economic system, strong enough to play an important role in world conflicts, nor disruptive enough to command the world's attention. Until recently, the majority have remained poor, underdeveloped, fragmented, prone to dictatorial or authoritarian regimes, and essentially subordinate to the dominant power of the U.S.

Yet by the second decade of the twenty-first century, Latin America itself, and its role in and importance to the international system, has changed dramatically for the better. Some countries in Latin America today have learned to exploit their strengths and project their influence in the international environment, making them significantly more important (in both global economic and security terms) than at any time in the region's independent history.

Thanks mostly to their ability to take advantage of the latest cycle of increase in demand for commodities worldwide, some of the biggest (Mexico, Brazil) and fastest-growing (Chile, Colombia, Peru) economies in Latin America today are increasingly able to exercise greater influence in international affairs, especially when they do so cooperatively.

Particularly during the commodities "super-cycle" between 2002 and 2009, Latin American countries endowed with sought-after exports enjoyed the benefits of an increase in demand for their minerals and foodstuffs. More importantly, even after the "super-cycle" ran out of steam, most countries in Latin America were still in a better position because they had saved and invested more of their windfall than in the past.[1]

Even taking into consideration the negative impact of the 2008/9 financial crisis on the world economic system and the weakening of demand for commodities as a result of the 2012 sovereign debt crises, as of 2014 the almost 25 percent of GDP investment rate in the region (excepting Brazil, at 18 percent) had at last caught up with that of South East Asia, according to the World Bank's chief economist for Latin America, Augusto de la Torre.[2]

There is still much work to be done, but this marks a clear change in attitudes (either by choice or by necessity) among Latin American elites. While it's true that the economic growth in LAC has been and will continue to be significantly affected by both the world economic slowdown and the end of this commodity boom cycle (with notable exceptions such as Venezuela, Argentina, Nicaragua, Ecuador, Haiti, San Salvador, and Guatemala), the fact remains that Latin American natural resources have become more important than ever, particularly to the U.S. LAC has a particular advantage with energy-related resources (as they're found in a fairly stable environment compared to other regions in the world), as well as the strategic location of the Caribbean Basin.

Most importantly, Latin American decision-makers have taken this opportunity to spend their incomes more wisely. Corruption has not disappeared, but the power and reach of the internet and social media have made LAC politicians vulnerable to exposure. Together with the perceived relative decline in U.S. hegemony both worldwide and in the Western Hemisphere, fiscal discipline has allowed countries such as Mexico, Brazil, Chile, Peru, Panama, and Uruguay to project an image of stability and competence in the international arena, affording them a unique opportunity to assert their influence in the region and in the global economy sphere.

Individually, LAC countries have never really had the capacity to project power in the international arena using coercive force, nor have they been powerful enough economically to assert their presence in the international arena. That's not likely to change anytime soon. Latin Americans seem to be learning from the lessons of history, however—particularly how to make themselves heard through regional and international instruments.

This chapter will explain how LAC states have learned to take advantage of not only their internal capabilities but also their optimal location and relatively peaceful environment. It will cover how Latin Americans have learned to use the international instruments and international organizations (IOs) to pursue their interests.

The main goal of this chapter is to understand how Latin Americans have learned to navigate world affairs cooperatively by means of the Inter-American system, as well as address why the state of affairs in LAC is significant to the world at large.

The Inter-American Context

The Western Hemisphere cannot be accused of lacking in regional and multilateral mechanisms that attempt to strengthen cooperation. On the contrary, if there is anything that characterizes multilateralism in the Americas, it's the plentiful number of institutions and instruments with lofty goals and no specific or objective purpose.

Since they emerged as newly independent states in 1824, LAC nations have longed for some form of multilateral stance and integration. Yet they've been unable to find a reason or cause powerful enough to inspire them to truly unite. In short, LAC cannot agree on the main questions regarding integration: how and for what?

European Union (EU) member states, for example, have been able to drive their integration process by identifying a common purpose: making war not only unthinkable but materially impossible.[3] This is why the institutional structure of the EU can justify the erosion of European sovereignty and the deepening of integration among its members.

Ultimately, to avoid war, the EU's institutional framework allows it to integrate both the economic and political spheres of its members and, more importantly, to transcend the authority of the European states in many ways.

In contrast, the calls for unity in the Americas have always lacked an underlying principle strong enough to propel a major multilateral movement. The idea of a fully integrated American continent has always been present, but it's been overshadowed by inter-state conflicts and the mistrust of foreign policy interests, mainly those of the U.S.[4] The need to defend the principles of national sovereignty and self-determination (particularly against U.S. interference) has again and again limited the reach and authority of any multilateral ideal.

The story of the Inter-American system is one of nation-states seeking collaboration or partnership while always ensuring their rights to complete sovereignty. These goals are pursued through an oversupply of multilateral groups with limited reach and overflows of proposals that often overlap and hinder the development of a common agenda. A shared antagonism (whether unspoken or explicit) against Washington's foreign policies has been typical of these groups.

When the attacks of September 11, 2011, occurred, Washington's attention immediately shifted almost exclusively to the Middle East and it ignored its own neighborhood. Unexpectedly, the story of the Inter-American system (which could until then have been summarized as a love-hate relationship between the U.S. and LAC) became one of U.S. neglect and LAC subsequently searching for alternative paths.

The Inter-American System and LAC Independence

Throughout the nineteenth century, the newly independent Latin American states were continually trying to advance a common agenda while fending off European re-colonization attempts and efforts by the United States to reassert its hegemonic power.

Facing what seemed to be a never-ending dilemma, LAC elites continuously found themselves choosing between two paths: neo-colonialism or industrialization in the economic sphere; and authoritarianism or democracy in the political domain. These choices determined their ability (or lack thereof) to establish states and societies capable of controlling their territories and project their influence in the international arena.[5]

The ideals of cooperation and integration among the newly independent LAC states emerged as a defensive measure to repel external threats. Simón Bolivar's 1812 Cartagena Manifesto, for example, kept the ideal of unity alive through numerous Pan-American congresses and initiatives.[6]

Yet while proclaiming dreams of unification, the *caudillo* leaders of the different national liberation movements (such as Agustín de Iturbide in Mexico or Antonio José de Sucre in Ecuador) defended their autonomy above all else. As a result, as well as Pan-Americanism, Bolivar inspired the famous principle of *uti possidetis juris*, formally adopted during the Angostura Congress in 1919. This principle reaffirmed the integrity of the original colonial borders and the complete sovereignty of the young LAC states.[7]

From the start, conflicting interests and persistent European interventions frustrated Pan-Americanism. More importantly, however, by 1867, the rise of the U.S. (with its belief in Manifest Destiny) as a regional power allowed it to assume a supervisory role in the Western Hemisphere while tripling its size. This supervisory role, enshrined in the 1823 Monroe Doctrine, gave Washington the right to intervene in LAC domestic affairs at any time.

By the end of the nineteenth century, the U.S. was able to establish its uncontested regional hegemony.[8] In the eyes of Latin Americans, however, Washington's actions under the umbrella of the Monroe Doctrine (and the Roosevelt Corollary doctrine of the "Big Stick," referring to his famous quote: "speak softly, and carry a big stick") only proved that cooperation was clearly not a U.S. priority.

The U.S. demonstrated this when it asserted its supremacy in Central America in 1903, recognizing the newly independent government of Panama, and subsequently building and administering the Panama Canal.[9] The constant intervention of the U.S. in local affairs tended to reinforce the longstanding domestic authoritarian tendencies in the region.[10]

Furthermore, the failure by the Wilson administration to ratify the Treaty of Versailles coupled with the regional policy established by the Monroe Doctrine and the Roosevelt Corollary, undermined Washington's Pan-American leadership.

In addition, the negative U.S. involvements in Latin American domestic affairs (during the Mexican Revolution against Francisco Villa and in Nicaragua against the guerrillas of Augusto Cesar Sandino, for example) only deepened the prevalent mistrust against Washington.

This mistrust began to change once the U.S. modified the Monroe Doctrine to include a regional consensus towards common security concerns. Because of this, the 1936 Inter-American Conference for the Maintenance of Peace in Buenos Aires offered the first opportunity for the U.S. and LAC states to adopt a joint effort in preventing war.[11]

World War II, Security and the Birth of the Inter-American System

In 1936 war was looming large over Europe and rapidly becoming a threat for the rest of the world, including the Americas. The possibility of an all-inclusive war and invasion by a common enemy united the governments of the Western Hemisphere, allowing them to pursue a common security purpose and permitting Washington to assume the mantle of leadership in the region.

Because of the circumstances, instead of being just one of many Pan-American conferences with a wide and abstract agenda, the 1936 Inter-American Conference for the Maintenance of Peace in Buenos Aires offered the first real opportunity for a joint effort by the U.S. and LAC states to cooperate on security issues.

The common objective was the creation of an inter-state institutional framework to preserve peace and prevent war from reaching American shores. Two years later, the 1938 Lima declaration refined these ideals, calling for collective action to prepare the Western Hemisphere for the possible outbreak of war in Europe.

Subsequently, during the second meeting of foreign ministers in Havana in 1940, as World War II wreaked havoc in Europe, Asia, and Africa, the U.S. and LAC states were ready to establish a common front against war with Collective Security Resolution XV. This resolution aimed to establish a common security framework through the Declaration of Reciprocal Assistance (*Tratado Interamericano de Asistencia Recíproca*—TIAR).

Subsequently, early in 1942, the Inter-American Defense Board (*Junta Interamericana de Defensa*—JID), an institution led by the United States and designed to coordinate military-to-military cooperation in the hemisphere, was created. Thus, TIAR was given a practical counterpart to implement concrete actions.

Once World War II came to an end, the states in the Americas were ready to promote mutual security cooperation and reciprocal assistance. To confront a common threat, the Act of Chapultepec (which encompassed both the Washington-led JID and the TIAR) formally established the Inter-American Defense System.

Latin American governments greatly hoped that Roosevelt's Good Neighbor Policy was finally becoming a reality, especially after the Eight Conference in Peru, with the Declaration of Lima (reinforced and further articulated in Panama in 1939) calling for collective action to forge a common defense front in the case of global war.

This common goal took concrete form with Collective Security Resolution XV, created during the 1940 second meeting of foreign ministers in Havana. It broadly stated that an attack on any country in the hemisphere was an attack on all. Of course, broadly stated principles tend to be tested by concrete events—such as the attack on Pearl Harbor, when a united response did not materialize.[12]

Yet even considering the Pearl Harbor fiasco, the threat of global war was a compelling incentive to develop a path toward unity among American states. At the end of World War II, during the 1945 Inter-American Conference on Problems of War and Peace in Mexico City, the participating countries agreed on a resolution to establish an International Organization of the American Republics. In contrast to the already existing U.S.-led 1942 Inter-American Defense Board (IADB) or *Junta Interamericana de Defensa* (JID), the new organization would collaborate on issues of reciprocal assistance as well as military-to-military cooperation.

The Act of Chapultepec (1945) committed the states of the Western Hemisphere to negotiating a mutual security treaty through the Inter-American Treaty of Reciprocal Assistance or *Tratado Interamericano de Asistencia Recíproca*: the Rio Treaty (TIAR) (1947). Through the dual mechanisms of U.S. controlled inter-military cooperation (JID), and a mutual security treaty (TIAR), a multilateral security framework began to develop. Interestingly, as part of this security framework, the U.S. and LAC enshrined the principles of democracy, national sovereignty, and self-determination.[13]

In 1948, the Bogotá Ninth Conference of American States consolidated an inter-state organization, the Organization of American States (OAS). It contained the following: the Treaty of Peaceful Resolution of Conflicts, the Pact of Bogotá; the Economic Bogotá Agreement; the Inter-American Convention for Granting Equal Rights to Women; the Inter-American Convention for Civil Rights for Women; the Final Act of the Ninth Conference; and the Preservation and Defense of Democracy in the Americas Act: Resolution 32. The latter was also the first U.S.-Latin American expression of anti-communism.

Through the OAS, the JID and TIAR, the Inter-American system's architecture (which persists today) began to take shape. What's more, from 1948 to the early 1950s, the U.S. seemed willing to foster economic development in LAC, not only through the OAS but also through the economic programs of the newly established Inter-American Development Bank (IADB).

By trying to simultaneously advocate a broad range of principles, it appeared that the U.S. was effectively supporting multilateralism while exercising its leadership in the hemisphere, even if it couldn't create the kind of institutional structure that it wanted.[14]

From 1948 to the early 1950s, the U.S sought to construct a Western Hemisphere-wide regional security institutional framework grounded (at least rhetorically) in the principles of respect for national sovereignty, self-determination, and democratic governance under the OAS umbrella.

This regional framework was intended to confront common problems in the areas of democratic consolidation, economic development, and more importantly, security, and Washington's simultaneous advocacy of democratic consolidation, economic development, and collective hemispheric security was positively received by the key states of Latin America and the Caribbean.

This two-tier arrangement—security under the JID and TIAR; and democratic/economic issues under the OAS and IADB—made it seem as though the U.S. and Latin America would come together to forge common policies, but the rapid intensification of the East-West conflict between the U.S. and the former Soviet Union and the repeated global crises that ensued soon drew U.S. foreign policy attention away from Latin America and refocused it elsewhere, especially on Europe and Asia.

Indeed, intensifying security threats (particularly from Soviet and Chinese activities in the Third World) came to dominate U.S. foreign and security policy attention as the Cold War heated up in the late 1940s and the early 1950s.[15]

Soon after assuming office in 1948, President Harry S. Truman asserted that the destiny of the U.S. was to provide global leadership in order to defend freedom. Through the Truman Doctrine, which was based mainly on the principles of containment, the U.S. assumed the role of global policeman, tasked with restraining and controlling the Soviet Union's ambitions of world domination.

By joining the Truman Doctrine to the Monroe Doctrine, Truman's administration started using the TIAR or Rio Pact, the JID, and the OAS as defenses against communism in the Americas, essentially leading to U.S. acquiescence in military coups and dictatorships across the region for many years to come.[16]

The Cold War and U.S. Supremacy

The Cold War arrived in Latin America during the 1950s. Perceiving the spread of communism in the region as an imminent danger, Washington abandoned its rhetorical embrace of regional cooperation and instead concentrated on the anti-communist fight, often at the expense of democracy and economic development in the region.

In 1950 President Truman approved a National Security Council memorandum on Inter-American Military Collaboration that asserted that the Cold War was a "real" war in which the survival of the free world was at stake, and that the American continent needed to adopt a unified position against the threat of communist aggression in the hemisphere.

As the Cold War intensified, the U.S. treated the new hemispheric institutions such as TIAR and the OAS primarily as mechanisms for the consolidation and maintenance of an anti-communist, U.S.-dominated sphere of influence in the Americas. Washington arrogated to itself the right to intervene in the domestic affairs of any LAC state that faced communist political or military aggression (or even undue influence).

To assure regional security outcomes, Washington consistently opted to support strong, dependable, pro-American dictatorial regimes rather than to accept liberal or progressive regimes that might be (even potentially) susceptible to communist penetration. This U.S. security policy preference was clearly illustrated in the 1954 U.S.-backed overthrow of the leftist leader Jacobo Arbenz in Guatemala and by the 1961 U.S.-supported Bay of Pigs invasion of Cuba by Florida-based Cuban exiles.

Repeated U.S. interventions in Latin American states' domestic affairs during the 1950s, the 1960s, and beyond facilitated the rise of authoritarian regimes. U.S. policies toward authoritarian governments in the hemisphere oscillated between passive acceptance and outright endorsement, especially when these regimes touted their anti-communist credentials.

U.S. military assistance, economic aid, and bilateral loans to repressive regimes (such as that of François "Papa Doc" Duvalier in Haiti, of Anastasio Somoza in Nicaragua, and of Alfredo Stroessner in Paraguay) continued well into the 1970s. If authoritarian rule failed or democratically elected governments leaned too far left for U.S. policymakers, Washington consistently proved willing to directly or indirectly intervene to guarantee that pro-American and anti-communist governments remained in power.

From Washington's perspective, international and regional institutions were created and maintained so that it could retain effective control of its sphere of influence within the bipolar international system. Not even President John F. Kennedy's efforts to encourage regional cooperation through the Alliance for Progress could change U.S. hemispheric policy.[17]

Yet even as the Cold War reigned supreme in the eyes of U.S. leaders, some form of economic cooperation among Latin Americans began to emerge. The UN Economic Commission for LACs (CEPAL) was created with the initial intention of providing international cooperation to an underdeveloped region. Under the leadership of Raúl Prebisch, however, CEPAL became an influential think tank in search of a specific internal development path for LAC.

Prebisch, and also Hans Singer, pointed out that Latin America had always been at a disadvantage because it had been inserted into the global economic system as a commodity exporter. As such, LAC nations had become perennial victims to the downward trend that resulted from the terms of trade between commodities and manufactures.

LAC AND THE INTER-AMERICAN SYSTEM

According to Prebisch and Singer, if Latin America was to break the cycle of poverty and underdevelopment, it had to find a way to stimulate its industrialization process. To do so, the "CEPAL doctrine" suggested that Latin America should pursue a strategy of industrialization based on import substitution (IS) and protectionism to take advantage of economies of scale for which a common market would be desirable.[18]

Based on this, LAC pursued import-substituting industrialization (ISI) at regional level during the 1950s. This "old regionalism" was a way to revive the dynamism of the industrial sector in countries where domestic output was limited by the size of the national markets. It also served as a means to promote modern manufacturing in countries where economies of scale were impossible.

Following CEPAL's recommendations in the 1950s, the creation of a Latin American common market was discussed. After a decade of negotiations, several limited-in-scope multilateral schemes emerged,[19] each of which had a brief life. It was not until after the debt crisis of the 1980s that the push for a new strategy based on an open market, undistorted relative prices, privatization, and deregulation allowed for a "new regionalism" to appear.[20]

As the Reagan administration launched its global crusade against the "Evil Empire" during the 1980s, Latin America was facing its gravest economic and security challenges since the 1930s. On the economic front the Americas were afflicted by surging oil prices, rising interest rates, and a price decline of imports from 1979 through 1981. In 1982 with the "*tequilazo*," Mexico defaulted on its foreign debt and Latin America began to experience a financial crisis that brought misery to the whole region.

Ironically, as the debt crisis weakened Latin America's economic infrastructure, it also undermined the military regimes previously supported by Washington as "necessary evils" to help stop the spread of communism.[21]

The weakening of military and military-supported regimes all over the region accelerated a transition back to civilian government in much of the Southern Cone. Governments in countries like Bolivia (1982), Argentina (1983), Uruguay (1984), Brazil (1985), and Chile (1990) began to experience democratic transitions.

In Central America, however, the weakening of governments intensified insurgencies, and several civil wars were fought in Nicaragua, Guatemala, San Salvador, and Honduras. Long before the unveiling of what became known as the 1985 Reagan Doctrine, decision-makers in the U.S. were intent on "taking back" the Caribbean and Central America from the Soviets through covert operations.

To roll back Soviet-Cuban influence in the region, material support was provided for opposing groups such as the "*Contras*" in Nicaragua, while militaries were shored up to support cooperating governments. Between 1984 and 1987 with U.S. backing, the Salvadorian military fought the guerrillas to a stalemate, undermining the institutional framework. The war continued for five more years without resolution until the Cold War ended and a peace accord was signed in the Castle of Chapultepec, Mexico, in 1992. The societies in Honduras, Nicaragua, and El Salvador paid a very high price for U.S. intervention.

During the decades of the Cold War, the authoritarian regimes supported by Washington in an attempt to curtail communism failed to build legitimate and stable political systems capable of effectively governing their national territories. As noted previously, these U.S.-backed regimes repeatedly failed to establish stable and effective governing structures; to forestall the rise of new security threats such as drug trafficking and organized crime; or to prevent the emergence of radical populist and anti-American regimes in many countries in the region, especially during the turbulent 1980s.[22]

The international environment was shifting. The backlash against the Reagan administration's invasion of Grenada in 1983 to oust the radical New Jewel movement (or its remnants) from power and its covert support for the "*Contra*" war against Nicaragua's leftist Sandinista regime during the 1980s; and outrage against the George H. W. Bush administration's invasion of Panama in 1989 to remove Manuel Noriega from office and bring him to trial on drug trafficking charges in the United States, were clear indications of this change. LAC authorities were no longer willing or even able to acquiesce blindly to Washington's wishes. Put simply, the policies that had been in place to control the Soviet threat in the Americas were no longer relevant and Latin Americans were no longer willing to tolerate them.[23]

Security Cooperation

The end of this era of East-West conflict in global politics had profound implications for affairs in the Western Hemisphere. With the final collapse of the former Soviet Union in December 1991, the world witnessed the demise of the bipolar international system and Latin America ceased to be an important theater of military operations. As the actions of Contadora Group countries and the subsequent creation of the Rio Group indicated, however, the international and regional environments had already begun to change.[24]

The emergence of the U.S. as the sole superpower dissipated the uncertainties generated by the Soviet threat, so Washington felt ready and able to shift its foreign policy priorities towards economic development and democratic governance rather than security. Many Latin American states began to perceive new opportunities for expanded cooperation in their relations with the U.S.[25]

For the first time in several decades, U.S. authorities—especially President George H. W. Bush and then President Bill Clinton—felt secure and confident enough to promote a new paradigm meant to dispel the perception of the U.S. as a unilateral power bent on imposing its will.

For the U.S., the post-Cold War era represented a great opportunity in LAC. Once again, the region was the perfect theater to try a new security strategy: the creation of a community of market democracies integrated around the shared values of democratic governance. This community of like-minded countries was to be achieved through foreign policy strategies including U.S. leadership, government downscaling, privatization of public enterprises, and most importantly, the creation of a regional free trade zone.[26]

President George W. Bush recognized the need to begin shifting U.S. foreign priorities by providing debt relief, and in June of 1990 he announced the "Enterprise of the Americas Initiative" (EAI), a necessary first step to establishing a free trade zone from Anchorage to Tierra del Fuego. The EAI meant to expand foreign investment and provide official debt relief administered by the Inter-American Development Bank. Challenging the notions of "old regionalism" that attempted to boost import-substituting industrialization (ISI) policies through government direction and protection from the 1950s to the 1970s, these policies were meant to protect local development and markets and promote limited regional trade cooperation. Conversely, the EAI promoted the privatization of government enterprises as a tool for downsizing government. In lieu of state enterprises and government intervention in the economy, these policies were designed to encourage foreign investment and the opening up of domestic markets to create a hemisphere-wide free trade zone.[27] This "new regionalism" was intended to help LAC enter the new international economic system by developing a free zone in the Western Hemisphere that would encourage integration and thus prepare Latin Americans for the challenges of globalization.

From their point of view, Latin American elites thought that they could use these treaties and agreements to take advantage of their resources while avoiding past mistakes, allowing them to level the playing field between developed and underdeveloped economies.[28] By 1992, all the governments in the Western Hemisphere except Cuba, Haiti, and Suriname had signed "framework agreements" with the U.S. to promote free markets.

For the next 15 years, the push for bilateral and regional free trade agreements together with the privatization of structural reforms took over the public discourse. To pursue a common foreign policy based on economic priorities, the U.S. and many LAC states began to rely upon regional initiatives and regimes such as the 1994 Summit of the Americas and NAFTA. For common security concerns, the U.S., along with many of its regional allies, also sought to better utilize the two-tier regional institutional arrangements established after World War II.

The post-Cold War era environment presented Washington with a dilemma. U.S. politicians needed to make U.S. unilateralism compatible with the new multilateralism heralded by President Clinton. From the U.S. standpoint, even if the threat of communism was no longer an issue, the resistance to U.S. global hegemony that was now emerging from diverse quarters represented a threat to security. At the same time, the Clinton administration felt that the defense of the expanding democratic market communities was a security priority for the U.S. and therefore required special attention.

In Washington's eyes, LAC countries were the ideal theater of operations for trying out this new security strategy based on the promotion and defense of market democracy communities. From that moment on, the mission to expand the "community of free nations" worldwide was seen by the U.S. as requiring the development of a military force able to maintain a global presence that could respond to old and new threats anywhere. The U.S. defense budget continued to increase during Clinton's tenure in order to develop such a force.

To promote its hemispheric agenda, the Clinton administration started to resort to new forums—including the Summit of the Americas and defense ministerial meetings, which started in Williamsburg in 1995—to concentrate on defense. More importantly, in 1996/7, the Department of Defense (DOD) added considerable territory to its Southern Command (SouthCom) jurisdiction, moving the command headquarters to Miami. From then on, the SouthCom's area of responsibility encompassed 32 nations—19 in Central America and 13 in the Caribbean (of which 31 were democracies)—and 14 U.S. and European territories, covering more than 15.6 million square miles in total.

As far as LAC was concerned, this reconfiguration aimed to achieve a regional cooperative strategy between Washington's DOD and Latin American governments and militaries. Interestingly, in this case the Americas' new security strategy actually coincided with Latin American concerns.[29]

As Marx once said, however, "even when men try to make their own history, they do not make it as they please." Exporting market democracy (which included the downscaling, or privatization of public enterprises and public services) also meant the erosion of government institutions. Because of this reality, the promotion of market democracy and free trade had serious consequences in Latin America, especially for the commodity and agricultural sectors. The overreliance of most Latin Americans on commodities and primary products, compounded by their weakened institutional frameworks, gave strength to the anti-liberal, nationalist, and populist discourse of new-era *caudillo* figures like Venezuela's Hugo Chávez.

Nevertheless, Latin American states began to hope that a new era of hemispheric cooperation was beginning to take shape and that free markets and liberalism would prevail. Then the events of September 11, 2001, changed everything.

9/11 and the Global War on Terrorism (GWOT)

The security strategy of the U.S. shifted toward unilateralism once again in the period following 9/11. The Bush administration insisted that the hemispheric security agenda should focus on the immediate threat of global terrorism and closely related security issues, rather than on the broader gamut of regional security concerns that had emerged as part of the collective security agenda during the 1990s.

After the trauma of the September 11 attacks, Washington quickly concluded that regional security, especially as it infringed on U.S. national security, could not be entrusted to any multilateral organism—not even the OAS. Thus, the JID and the TIAR became marginal players. To rally regional solidarity for the U.S.'s new anti-terrorism security priorities (with direct funding and guidance from the U.S. DOD), the administration of President George W. Bush sought to activate and reinforce the 1995 Williamsburg Process by means of the Defense Ministerial of the Americas (DMA).

Washington viewed key aspects of the 1995 Williamsburg accords (including provisions for the promotion of democracy and the building of strong institutions with special emphasis on the police and the military) as adaptable to the post-9/11 environment. From Washington's point of view, the DMA could be trusted to define foreign policy priorities via the role of the armed forces in the region by concentrating on military-to-military cooperation.[30]

In September 2002, the newly released "National Security Strategy of the United States of America" made the country's war against terrorism (and, when necessary, the nations that harbored it) official. As part of the "War on Terror" the U.S. announced a strategy of pre-emptive war and "proactive counter-proliferation" measures against rogue states, terrorist clients, and terrorist groups.

White House authorities were adapting a centuries-old precept of international law and updating the concept of "imminent threat" as a rationale for self-defense and for increasing the offensive capabilities and objectives of the U.S. defense forces. On top of the implementation of the Trade Promotion Authority (TPA), the Bush administration decided to waive the restrictions on U.S. military aid to countries that were previously considered ineligible—as long as those countries agreed to exempt U.S. personnel from the provisions of the International Criminal Court (ICC) (an exemption that became possible thanks to Article 98 of the American Service members Protection Act of 2002).

This essentially implied that the U.S. was justified in pursuing a perpetual war wherever its enemies might be. To this end, the U.S. needed to achieve an asymmetric advantage in order to face nontraditional threats. LAC states were once again the ideal theaters of operation for trying out this new security strategy.[31]

In the face of the 9/11/01 terrorist attacks and the subsequent U.S. invasions of Afghanistan (2001) and Iraq (2003), the U.S. effectively abandoned multilateralism in its approach to Latin America and Western Hemisphere security.

Since the heyday of the Cold War, the U.S. has been gradually reducing bilateral assistance to Latin America. Although U.S. aid was about the same in 2005 as it had been in 1985, when adjusted for inflation it has fallen by a third.

Moreover, almost half of U.S. aid in 2005 went to just five countries on the front line of the drug war: Colombia, Peru, Bolivia, Ecuador, and Mexico. The only other countries receiving aid were Haiti and Central American states. Military assistance was similarly concentrated in the drug war states, which received 85 percent of the total.[32]

Even during the current Obama administration, American backing for multilateral policies in the region has been largely replaced with either unilateral policies or, as in the case of the Pacific Alliance, different strategies based on economics vis-à-vis China.

While this may be more efficient for Washington in the short run, the history of U.S.-Latin American relations indicates that in the long run, multilateral cooperation provides the only reliable formula for institutionalizing effective collective security arrangements in the Western Hemisphere. The current "security gap" dividing the U.S. and Latin America may well represent the region's most serious security challenge.

While the Bush and the Obama administrations focused their attention elsewhere, the American continent continued to change. Latin America can no longer be considered as a single region unequivocally veering towards integration and acquiescence to U.S. hegemonic management. On the contrary, due to Washington's lack of attention to the region, the American continent seems to be set on a path of sub-regional fragmentation. While Canada, Mexico, Central America and the Caribbean are clearly on a path towards greater economic integration with the U.S., the Southern Cone is increasingly resisting Washington's authority.

More importantly, the Andean region is openly rejecting U.S. supremacy and may be regressing to the authoritarianism of yesteryear. For instance, despite the overwhelming U.S. military power so often used during the Cold War when Latin American leaders ran against U.S. political, security, or economic interests, the Bush administration discovered that force was no longer an effective tool. In Mar del Plata in 2005, for example, Venezuela's Hugo Chávez decided to derail the free trade agenda, showing that Latin America has become surprisingly resistant to the assertion of U.S. hegemony. At the same time, Latin American governments expected some sort of interventionist reaction from Washington to the challenges raised by the new populist elected officials such as Chávez. Instead, Latin American governments encountered indifference—the U.S. appears to have simply abandoned not only the FTAA agenda but also their historical response to the initiatives of populist leaders.

The Caribbean, for example, typically considered a sensitive region for the U.S. (it was once called the "third border" by President George W. Bush), is now experiencing a flood of Chinese investment. Chinese investment in the Caribbean increased by more than 500 percent between 2003 and 2012, reaching almost $500 million, according to official Chinese statistics. Since then, several major projects have started, including highways, ports, and hospitals, and more are expected in the years to come. In a prominent $65 million project, the China Harbour Engineering Company has rebuilt the main road to Kingston airport, including better sea defenses for a road that has a history of storm damage.[33]

By no means does this imply that the U.S. is ignoring the region. In addition to heavy spending on the drug war in countries such as Colombia, Washington is helping to fight resurgent cocaine trafficking in the Caribbean and has spent $263 million since 2009 through the Caribbean Basin Initiative. The U.S. Agency for International Development is also active across the region. It is clear, however, that the U.S. is avoiding the kind of grand, symbolic investments and outright budgetary aid that China is ready to lavish on many Caribbean countries at a time when most of the Anglophone countries in the tropical archipelago off the coast of the U.S. are struggling with large government debts.[34] It would seem that, for the time being, Latin America has become a secondary security concern for any U.S. administration, regardless of party affiliation. The greatest new economic opportunities seem to lie in places like China, Turkey, Malaysia, Singapore, or India, and existential threats to the U.S. as well as risks to its hegemony lay in the Middle East and Asia rather than the Western Hemisphere.

This attitude became particularly evident following the arrest of Honduran president Manuel Zelaya by the armed forces in June of 2009. Acting on behalf of the National Congress, the Honduran generals executed a military coup. Initially the administration of President Obama and the OAS presented a unified front. They condemned the coup and encouraged the efforts of Costa Rican President Oscar Arias in negotiating a solution. In the end, however, once the negotiated agreement unraveled and Zelaya's reinstatement was rejected, the Obama administration abandoned its multilateral stance and took no action. Instead, the White House, together with other Latin American governments, decided to recognize the electoral outcome. Incredibly, this happened even though OAS members reminded the U.S. that the recognition of this government directly violated a multilateral process that has been taking place in the Western Hemisphere since 1991.[35]

The protracted history of inter-American cooperation and integration has led to the development of a wide range of regional institutions with diverging interests, unrelated development institutions, inarticulate development priorities, and a chronic lack of funding that has further exacerbated the level of economic and military asymmetry.

The Americas: A Community of Democracies

Because the Soviets possessed terrifying military capacities and undeniable global aspirations, the spread of communism represented a real danger for liberal democracies. The Cuban missile crisis, the Soviet Union's support for

Cuban interventions in Central America, etc., were clear indicators that the East–West confrontation was very real.

In addition to a physical threat, communism represented a different kind of danger to LAC because in the minds of many it represented a viable alternative to liberal capitalism and democracy. Soviet-style regimes were tyrannical to be sure, but for many Latin American revolutionary leaders (particularly those that saw themselves as fighting for the poor and disenfranchised) it represented a real alternative to the leadership of the U.S. The U.S. recognized that Cold War policies needed to open up not just a military front but also an ideological front to limit Soviet and Cuban influence in the hemisphere.

The story of the fight for liberal democracy in the Americas during the Cold War has been examined extensively elsewhere; it suffices to say here that this ideological battle against communism served to bind LAC governments to the U.S. in order to create a united front. And once the Soviet threat disappeared post-1991, the U.S., Canada, and LAC found that democratic rules and norms—together with market reforms—could act as ideological glue. Further, the defense of democracy gradually became a condition for OAS membership. This new attitude, combined with a broader definition of a security threat to include any dangers and risks posed to democratic regimes, opened the door to an increased role for the OAS.

As Carolyn Shaw[36] asserts, the redefinition of regional security has taken place at many levels and in many forums, but the broadening of the concept to include the threat to democracy has contributed greatly to the institutionalization of this type of regime in the Americas. By making the interruption of democracy basically illegal via treaties such as Resolution 1080, through the OAS via the Unit for Promotion of Democracy (UPD), and via mechanisms such as the Electoral Monitoring Process (EOM), electoral democracy has served to bind OAS members together. As a result, electoral democracy has become engrained in Latin American societies and established as a condition of eligibility for all regional integration processes in the Western Hemisphere.[37]

The defense of democracy in the Americas emerged as a result of human rights movements after World War II. It evolved through complex networks formed by NGOs, IGOs and private foundations such as the UN Human Commission on Human Rights (UNHCHR), and the Inter-American Commission on Human Rights (IACHR), the Ford Foundation, the Mothers of the Plaza de Mayo, and America's Watch. These groups started working together and pressuring Latin American autocratic governments with problematic human rights records to change their behavior.

The defense of human rights served to launch the promotion of the democratic doctrine in Latin America. It established a precedent for the scrutiny of the domestic practices of Latin American governments who could not, from then on, avoid the constant inquiries of international institutions.[38]

With the end of the Cold War, the type of regime that presided over a country became increasingly important. Governments in the Americas could no longer count on automatic recognition or international participation if their political systems were not considered democratic. Put simply, democracy began to act as ideological glue. During the 1990s, when democratic consolidation was well underway in Latin America, the member states of the OAS were able to take advantage of the precedent established by the human rights groups and establish a new regime to protect democracy from the threat of authoritarian reversals.

As Thomas Legler points out,[39] propelled by the defense of human rights, the foundation of the democratic regime began to be built atop a set of international legal pillars that included the Protocol of Cartagena de Indias (1985), Resolution 1080 (1990), the Washington Protocol (1992–1997), and the Inter-American Democratic Charter (IADC, 2001). These concrete steps and legal foundations reflected the specific concern of U.S. and LAC governments that democracy should be promoted and protected. At the same time, these norms reflect the ever-present meanings and practices of LAC regarding sovereignty and self-determination, which also affect the way each nation views multilateralism and its implementation.

This duality influenced the growth of the democratic regime in its formative period from 1990 to 2001. The result was a series of many gains and a confusing set of norms and values.[40]

One anti-coup norm was established by Resolution 1080 and the Washington Protocol, with strong responses by the OAS to attempted coups and self-coups in Haiti (1991), Peru (1992), Venezuela (1992), Guatemala (1993), and Paraguay (1996). The Washington Protocol and the IADC included the possibility of membership suspension as the ultimate sanction for any state where democracy was violently interrupted (or even undermined). The Rio Group also reinforced this norm in its own membership requirements and in fact Peru's membership was temporarily suspended in 1992 following President Fujimori's *autogolpe*, or self-coup. Thanks to this Peru event, the Democratic Charter included self-coups as unacceptable practice in the Inter-American System.

The OAS helped establish a new external validation form through their Electoral Observation Mechanisms (EOM). Through this program, the OAS was invited to observe an electoral process and given the authority to validate, criticize, or even invalidate the election. Such was the case for elections in the Dominican Republic (1994), Haiti (2000), Peru (2000), and Venezuela (2005). What's more, rather than adhering to strict legal logic, Latin American political elites and their diplomatic representatives have preferred to address threats to democracy primarily through political negotiation and maneuvering.[41]

Recent events, however, are calling the future of the Inter-American democracy regime into question. Democracy no longer seems to be a membership requirement in a number of new and pre-existing multilateral forums. Cuba, for example, has become a member of the Rio Group, the Latin American and Caribbean Summit (CALC), the Community of Latin American and Caribbean States, and ALBA. In 2009, a number of states in the region pushed for Cuba's reintegration to the OAS and the Summit of the Americas without the necessary precondition of democracy. Furthermore, without first calling for an electoral change, on July 1, 2015, President Barak Obama announced that the U.S. and Cuba will formally re-establish diplomatic ties. The U.S.-Cuban rapprochement stands out because it underlines how the Obama administration's foreign policy values pragmatism over common ideals. Taking advantage of the decline of Venezuela, the U.S. may be using this rapprochement with Havana to once again reassert its influence in LAC over the coming years.[42]

Even though provisions do exist in the Democratic Charter, the OAS has not been able (or perhaps willing) to respond adequately to repeated instances of "authoritarian backsliding" among its members (namely Ecuador, Nicaragua, and Venezuela). In spite of unprecedented international condemnation, isolation, and sanctions, the OAS and the international community failed to confront and overturn the June 28 coup and restore Honduras's president Zelaya to office.

In addition, the vision of representative democracy championed by the OAS and based on the development of institutions such as a functioning political party system, a representative legislature, a transparent and working judiciary, and a clean and professional police force is now being challenged by participatory and plebiscitary alternatives.

The creation of the Inter-American democracy regime under this specific criterion had a lot to do with the post-Cold War environment, in which LAC's newly elected leaders were willing to project their new democratic values— as well as create multilateral safeguards as an additional line of defense against internal authoritarian and populist threats to help them lock-in their new constitutional orders. More importantly, the rise of democracy occurred against a backdrop of dynamic hemispheric regionalism, with growing numbers of cooperative forums that championed free trade and security in tandem with democracy. True to its traditional preference for personalistic ties and populism, a democratic regime in LAC was seen as a representative regime with an elitist slant, making democratic consolidation more difficult.[43]

After 2001, the consensus around Latin American elitist representative democracy began to unravel. Weak institutional structures that tended to tolerate the exclusion of large sectors of Latin American society and turn a blind eye to the persistent problems of corruption and inequality contributed to the general citizenry's diminished support for state institutions.

As a response to the perception of the region's democratic tradition as exclusionary and low functioning, the idea of a plebiscitary and populist democracy (espoused and promoted by Chávez) gained ground. This concept, like Maduro and Ortega's populist alternatives, eliminates or weakens institutional mediation between citizens and the executive. With power centered on one strong man, this regime tries to do away with democratic institutions that may challenge his authority (such as political party systems, legislatures, and judiciaries) and instead creates a more direct link between the voter and elected leader. Sadly, this type of popular representation, which clearly echoes *caudillismo*, seems to have gained ground in Argentina, Venezuela, Ecuador, and Bolivia as horizontal accountability has eroded.[44]

The distinct definition of democracy in the Americas is at a crossroads. Fragmentation of ideology is reflected in the creation of a plethora of sub-regional multilateral and integration initiatives in which democracy is no longer a priority, including the unification of South America through UNASUR or the Andean Community (both of which are weak prospects at best).

Interestingly, instead of support for a free trade area, ideological fragmentation represented by groupings such as ALBA is presenting itself through aggressive social agendas with anti-free trade initiatives. Whether they succeed or not, it is still remarkable that Latin American countries have stopped waiting for Washington's guidance or support and have begun constructing new regional spaces for political *concertación* and integration that intentionally exclude both Canada and the U.S. These efforts are particularly interesting when considering, for example, the nascent Pacific Alliance through which Latin American countries are specifically searching for ways to cooperatively influence the international economic system.

Luckily, the anti-coup norm is still strong. The 2002 coup in Venezuela and the 2009 coup in Honduras clearly indicate that coups, which became almost routine in LAC during the Cold War, have become prohibitively costly and are no longer acceptable. This was proven when, for the first time, the OAS invoked Article 21 of the IADC to suspend Honduras's membership.

Nevertheless, the representative democracy as elaborated in Articles 3 and 4 of the IADC is in trouble. The new acceptance of a populist democracy by plebiscite in Venezuela, Nicaragua, Ecuador, and Bolivia points to a new type of regime that seems to reject an elitist point of view and points to a glaring need for Latin American authorities to concentrate on social issues. It is believed that citizen participation and socioeconomic equality are championed by the plebiscitary democratic variants, but actually they end up undermining the capacity of their states to govern democratically through institutional means. As a result, there is no longer a consensus among American states around what constitutes a legitimate democracy, nor what constitutes a serious threat to democracy.

Countries that have engaged in populist measures leading to authoritarian backsliding, such as Ecuador in 2004/5, Nicaragua since 2008, and Venezuela since 2004, have garnered little reaction from the OAS and the international community. In general, Latin Americans now expect that their leaders come to office as a result of an election, even when they may disagree on what exactly democratic governance means. The different democratic (electoral, plebiscitarian, traditional political institutions, etc.) variants may have divided the region and show that Latin Americans are becoming somewhat disillusioned with their governments. One reason is that Latin Americans in general have become more demanding. More than empty campaign promises, Latin Americans now expect results from their elected officials and state institutions. So, not withstanding the latest 2015 *Latinobarómetro* figures, which seem in the short-term worrisome, over the long-run democratic values in LAC seem to have taken hold. Brazil, Chile, and Uruguay, for example, have found that the defense of the democratic regime is a strong enough reason to compel American states to unite. When it comes to the international environment, though, the Western Hemisphere's community of democracies increasingly considers economic influence as a key factor in the balance of power.

From the economic point of view, the experience with the U.S.-sponsored FTAA points to a willingness by the U.S. and LAC to pursue limited cooperation, preferably at a subregional level. In contrast to the experience of the EU, bilateral and subregional arrangements such as NAFTA, CARICOM, and MERCOSUR seem the preferred path for seeking cooperation in the Western Hemisphere.

The U.S. specifically seems to be opting to act as a hub and working to establish bilateral agreements on a one-to-one basis. These days, however, U.S. leadership is not the only option. Brazil (through UNASUR) and Venezuela (through ALBA, now at a clear disadvantage) are both competing by providing different economic agendas. In addition, other economic giants such as China are competing with the U.S. for a share of South America's commodity market. The future is uncertain, as economic cooperation "á la Western Hemisphere" is still in the very early stages of development.

From the security standpoint, the Western Hemisphere would benefit greatly from a concerted effort, but agreement on what constitutes an existential or tangible security threat remains elusive.

Even more importantly, for different reasons, both the U.S. and LAC authorities have been unable to overcome their traditional mutual distrust. Time and time again, the need to defend the LAC principles of national sovereignty and self-determination (particularly against U.S. interference) have ended up limiting the reach and authority of any regional body that could confront the new intermestic threats that are eroding the capacity of weak democratic states.

Finally, it is important to keep in mind that while new security threats may be global in scope, the implementation of security is always local in nature. The application of any guidelines proposed or imposed by international organizations is ultimately left in the hands of local authorities in incomplete states where a lack of law and order is the norm.

LAC societies have accepted democracy as the institutional arrangement that best allows social actors to peacefully resolve their differences. The *Latinobarómetro*, for example, has shown that economic growth in Latin America has prompted a slow but steady rise in support for democracy and its institutions, even as Latin Americans remain frustrated by the way their political systems work.

A government in the Western Hemisphere, whether right or left, is recognized as legitimate only if it comes to power as a result of an election. During the past decade, however, the consolidation of the democracy promotion regime has been problematic. Changes in the international context as well as differing ideas of how democracy should work have changed and diminished the expectations championed by the OAS and embodied in the IADC. Even though the anti-coup norm is still strong, the weakening of local democratic structures and the undermining of horizontal accountability, particularly in the Andean region, has challenged full democratic consolidation in the hemisphere.

Threats to democracy come in different guises. Up until 2001, an electoral representative democracy was the system that all states in the Americas aspired to adopt. Today, however, alternatives to traditional democratic forms of representation are emerging which have begun to erode democratic institutions from within.

The multilateral context that developed after 2001 presents a serious challenge to any effort, be it related to economics, security, or ideology. Instead of using existing organizations and forums to act cooperatively, American governments are opting to engage with a plethora of new political spaces, producing a lack of institutional coordination, mandate duplication and overlap as well as organizational competition for scarce resources.

It is ironic that just as LAC states have finally won autonomy vis-à-vis (first) Europe and (now) the U.S., their chosen course seems to be characterized by the development of numerous multilateral forums with limited scope and little authority for action.

The traditional pillars of the Inter-American system formed by the OAS, the IADB, and the Summit of the Americas (the Rio Treaty, TIAR, the CHS and IADB, and the Williamsburg Process), together with the IADC and the OAS democracy promotion regime, face increasing competition and mandate overlap from a striking proliferation of new subregional and regional integration schemes.

On top of MERCOSUR, CARICOM, and the Central American Integration (SICA) system, the longlist also includes the Rio Group, ALBA, UNASUR, and the Ibero-American Summit. The Rio Treaty has seen some serious challenges, first by Mexico's withdrawal in 2003 and then by the creation of an ALBA military alliance and the new South American Defense Council (*Consejo Suramericano de Defensa*) linked to UNASUR.

For its part, the Summit of the Americas faces a new, albeit very weak challenger: the Summit of LAC (CALC), which held its second meeting in

Mexico City in 2010. Furthermore, the *Banco del Sur* intends (at least in theory) to eventually compete with the IADB. Multilateral cooperation mechanisms such as ALBA are becoming alternative forums for confronting any efforts that involve U.S. leadership or participation, but ALBA has yet to put forth a shared vision and concrete focus for its members and as a result has become irrelevant.

Overall as in the case of ALBA, when searching for alternative paths that exclude the U.S. and Canada, LAC authorities seem to prefer multilateral forums with limited scope, narrow obligations, and vague goals. In essence, when looking for ways to act multilaterally, LAC states seem to prefer a wide range of instruments that require no real commitment or follow-up.

LAC states have a powerful tradition of "defensive multilateralism"[45] (Legler) whereby, instead of searching for convergence, they tend to use multilateral forums to balance and resist U.S. attempts to dominate the agenda and in this way assert their autonomy.[46] This is why the forums and organizations that constitute part of the Inter-American system today do work, just not very well, and it is doubtful whether this assortment of integration schemes has successfully deepened the interdependence among American states or provided a strong sense of purpose.

By design, the Inter-American system tends to be unruly. When it comes to multilateralism in the Americas, efficiency and concrete outcomes are not highly valued. Performance is often a secondary consideration to the posturing of a particular stance. Basically, multilateralism in the Western Hemisphere is not intended (as was the case of the EU) to seek a powerful impetus for unity because deep integration is not what sovereign states in the Americas are really looking for.

As a final point, any multilateral effort requires funding. The current phenomenon of multilateral proliferation, mission creep, summit fatigue, and autonomous regional governance means that Latin America and Caribbean governments (not the U.S.) are the ones who'll have to foot the bills. Yet many of the region's pressing issues, such as combating narco-trafficking and organized transnational crime, require considerable resources and therefore come with a hefty price tag.

The success of these efforts will depend upon the interest or goodwill of larger countries such as Brazil, which need to see the value in supporting multilateral forums. LAC authorities prefer a kind of "light multilateralism" in which regional and subregional organizations keep a limited reach and authority over their respected sovereignties.

Reimagining Hemispheric Regionalism: The Economy

For the first time since 1948, in the 1990s a historic opportunity emerged in Latin America. Far-reaching transformations in the international arena such as the arrival of the "Third Wave" of democratization during the 1980s, the crumbling of the Berlin Wall in 1989, and the reunification of Germany and liberation of much of Eastern Europe from Soviet domination in 1990 were major signs of the impending end of the Cold War and beginning of a new international environment.

The end of the East–West confrontation gave way to the triumph of representative democracy and liberal economic order in a unique "unipolar moment." It was then that LAC had a great opportunity (as well as no other choice) to harmonize state strategies with those of the U.S. The administrations of President George H. W. Bush and Bill Clinton felt secure and confident enough to promote regional economic integration and democratic consolidation together with common defense and security policies.[47]

In response to the domino effect of Latin America's economic crises, the first Bush administration paid almost frenetic attention to the Brady Plan and the Enterprise for the Americas Initiative (EAI). These approaches complemented the existing Caribbean Basin Initiative (CBI) as welcome, albeit insufficient, acknowledgement by Washington of the importance of debt relief to the economies of the region. In addition, on the trade front, in August of 1992 the first Bush administration began to press for the completion of the North American Free Trade Agreement (NAFTA). This foreign policy shift by the U.S. was welcomed by LAC states, which in turn began to show a willingness to trust the U.S.

From Latin America's point of view, it was now in its best interest to rely upon regional initiatives and regimes (such as the 1994 Summit of the Americas process or 1994's NAFTA) to negotiate with each other and the U.S. The U.S., in turn, sought to utilize the already established two-tier regional institutions to greater effect. The IADB and the OAS were called upon to promote economic development and democratic governance in the hemisphere, and the JID and the TIAR were activated for the purpose of forging a more cooperative security agenda.

The First Summit of the Americas, held in Miami in 1994, launched the process towards a Free Trade Area for the Americas (FTAA) that was supposed to become a reality by 2005. The implementation of the FTAA was to take place gradually through several initiatives by means of the summitry process.[48] By 2000, however, it became evident that regional interests were not necessarily converging. During the Third Summit of the Americas in Québec City in 2001, the discussion shifted away from the creation of a free trade zone to the arbitration of conflicting interests and agendas. Thereafter, the summitry process became an instrument to manage the Western Hemisphere's emerging asymmetric regionalism instead of attempting to facilitate a full convergence of interests.

By 2005, economic multilateralism reached an impasse. Latin American political elites and civil society groups proved once again unwilling to completely accept U.S. leadership. In turn, as a result of the September 11 attacks and as was evident during the appearance of U.S. Secretary of State

Condoleezza Rice at the OAS General Assembly meeting in Fort Lauderdale in June 2005, the U.S. government seemed to have adopted a regional policy of indifference, something LAC governments had difficulty grasping.[49]

Moreover, on the streets, President Hugo Chávez used this opportunity to boycott the process and rally support for an alternative to any U.S.-supported institutionalized multilateral effort. From this moment on, the U.S. also abandoned efforts to achieve a Free Trade Area for the Americas (FTAA), opting instead for bilateral agreements. Neither LAC nor the U.S. saw it in their best interest to compel all governments in the hemisphere to create the biggest free trade area in the world.[50]

The Mar del Plata Summit was the last nail in the coffin of the U.S.-backed FTAA, as challengers such as Venezuela's Hugo Chávez and Bolivia's Evo Morales gained momentum. Meanwhile, the U.S. opened multiple negotiating windows, benefiting from an increasingly interconnected economic environment worldwide. In spite of the rhetoric of Chávez and Morales, the globalization trend continued to deepen.

This approach allowed U.S. companies to create a strategy of competition, establishing bilateral free trade agreements with Chile, Peru, Colombia, Panama, and—signatories of the Central American-Dominican Republic Free Trade Agreement, CAFTA-DR—El Salvador, Costa Rica, Guatemala, Honduras, Nicaragua, and Dominican Republic, which launched a race for access to U.S. markets. More importantly, this bilateral strategy allowed the U.S. to keep control of the multilateral agenda, attempt to prevent the emergence of Brazilian leadership in the Southern Cone,[51] and level off the ALBA project led by Venezuela's Maduro.[52]

Against the backdrop of U.S. indifference, Latin Americans searched for ways to pool their resources and act cooperatively to assert influence in the international environment. The advocates of ALBA, for example, shunned full participation in the capitalist economy by promoting a socially oriented trade block, whereas Venezuela could exert its influence in the region through its oil largesse. Now, however, the search for a new social contract in the absence of strong, established state institutions—and without Hugo Chávez as an anti-Washington figure—has called into question the relevance (if not the existence) of ALBA.

A regional integration scheme that would allow all states in the Western Hemisphere to act cooperatively on economic policies thus seems unlikely right now. Yet when it comes to regional cooperative efforts, there seems to be a different perspective of late. The Pacific Alliance differs substantially from regionally focused agreements like the *Unión de Naciones Suramericanas* (Union of South American Nations—UNASUR, 2004), the *Alianza Bolivariana para los Pueblos de Nuestra América* (Bolivarian Alliance for the Peoples of Our America—ALBA, 2004), and the *Comunidad de Estados Latinoamericanos y Caribeños* (Community of Latin American and Caribbean States—CELAC, 2010). Unlike the other groupings, the goal of the Pacific Alliance is to deepen cooperation among members in order to forge closer relations with the Asia-Pacific region. Whereas UNASUR, ALBA and CELAC view regionalism and integration as tools for combating globalization, the Pacific Alliance sees them as critical links to global flows.

To assert their influence in the international arena, Colombia, Peru, Chile, and Mexico have agreed to liberalize 92 percent of their countries' goods and services, with the goal of 99 percent in three to seven years, as part of a nascent regional integration block. The aim is to create a more seamless environment for business that will attract foreign investment.

The Pacific Alliance is perceived as a geopolitical counterweight to ideological and political trends in countries like Brazil and Venezuela. It looks outward, acting in some ways like a free trade zone while promoting greater cooperation and partnership among member countries. Another key objective is facilitating entry into the Asian market and creating greater collective bargaining power when approaching China. At the same time, it seeks a competitive edge for its members when competing against Asian countries for trade with the U.S.

It's too soon to know for sure, but with efforts such as these it seems that Latin Americans are learning to use international instruments to achieve a cooperative stance and assert their influence on the global economy. As the latest efforts of the Trans-Pacific Partnership (TPP) (arguably the most important trade agreement in a generation) seem to show, some LAC nations may be well on their way to re-engaging Washington and becoming relevant actors in the global economy vis-à-vis China.

As the limits of military might have become increasingly evident, some Latin American states are learning to exercise their collective power in different ways. By participating in the new trade pacts with East Asia and the EU, Latin America will help determine whether the West in general (and U.S. in particular) retains its hold on the economic system.[53]

Main points:

- While fending off foreign interventions by (first) Europe and then the U.S., Latin Americans have always aimed at some kind of unified agenda while defending their sovereignty and right to self-determination.
- The Inter-American system develops as an overflow of overlapping proposals, treaties, organizations, etc., with limited authority and reach.
- Inter-American institutions concentrate on different areas where common interests can be identified. American states develop structures based on security, economic, and normative agendas.
- During the Cold War, the U.S. exerts control using the Inter-American structure.

- When the Soviet threat disappears, Latin Americans begin to learn to use the Inter-American structure to act cooperatively with or against the U.S.
- Latin Americans are searching for alternative cooperative paths to achieve a better position on the world stage.

Notes

1 The commodities "super-cycle", which entered full force in 2002, was largely buoyed up by Chinese buying and driven by a combination of strong demand from emerging nations and low supply growth. For more see Eric Ng, "Commodities super-cycle is 'taking a break'," *South China Morning Post,* Wednesday, July 10, 2013 (www.scmp.com/business/commodities/article/1279041/super-cy cle-taking-break).

2 "Latin America's Economies: Life after the Commodity Boom," *The Economist,* March 29, 2014 (www.economist.com/news/americas/21599782-instead-crise s-past-mediocre-growth-big-riskunless-productivity-rises-life).

3 Robert Schuman, "Schuman Declaration and the Birth of Europe," Speech of May 9, 1950 (http://users.belgacombusiness.net/shchuman/9May1950.htm).

4 The contemporary Inter-American security system specifically, is the outcome of the often-contradictory security policy concerns that have emerged between the hegemonic United States and the governments of Latin America and the Caribbean. These contradictions result from the traditional need of Latin American states to guarantee their individual national security while simultaneously bolstering the collective security of the Western Hemisphere. Since its independence (but especially in the aftermath of WWII and its rise to superpower status), Washington's pursuit of regional and international dominance has time and again conflicted with the LAC states' perennial aspirations to preserve their own national sovereignty and right of self-determination. For more see Brian Loveman, *No Higher Law: American Foreign Policy and the Western Hemisphere Since 1776* (Chapel Hill, NC: University of North Carolina Press, 2010).

5 Robert A. Pastor (2011), "Foreword," in (eds), *Inter-American Cooperation at a Crossroads*, ed. Gordon Mace, Andrew F. Cooper, and Timothy M. Shaw (London: Palgrave Macmillan), x–xiii.

6 These Pan-American initiatives were kept alive through the American congresses of 1826 in Panama, 1847 in Lima, 1856 in Santiago and Washington, and 1864 in Lima.

7 Oliver Dabène, *The Politics of Regional Integration in Latin America: Theoretical and Comparative Explorations* (New York: Palgrave Mcmillan, 2009), 12–15. For *uti possidetis juris*—as you possess under law—see Aaron X. Fellmeth and Maurice Horwitz, *Guide to Latin in International Law* (Oxford and New York: Oxford University Press, 2009), 28.

8 Once it established its role as the uncontested regional power, the U.S. assumed a leadership role in promoting the second initiative of Pan-Americanism. As a result, the First International Conference of American States took place in Washington in 1889. At this time, Latin American states accepted the establishment of some of the arrangements proposed by Washington. Nevertheless, LAC representatives managed to unite and block some of the more comprehensive U.S. initiatives, such as the establishment of a customs union and an inter-American monetary union. Still, the U.S. did succeed in rallying support for the establishment of the Commercial Bureau of American Republics (later

renamed the Pan-American Union) and for partial negotiations of reciprocity treaties of an experimental character, such as the adoption of a metric decimal system and treaties in favor of the protection of trademarks and copyrights. For more see Jennifer Burrell and Michael Shifter, "Estados Unidos, La OEA y la Promoción de la Democracia en las Américas," in Arlene B. Tickner (ed.), *Sistema Interamericano y Democracia, Antecedentes Históricos y Tendencias Futuras* (Bogotá: Ediciones Uniandes, 2000), 27–49; Peter H. Smth, *The Talons of the Eagle, Dynamics of U.S.-Latin American Relations* (New York and Oxford: Oxford University Press, 1996); Thomas E. Skidmore and Peter E. Smith, *Modern Latin America*, 6th edition (New York and Oxford: Oxford University Press, 2005); Betty Horwitz, *The Transformation of the Organization of American States: A Multilateral Framework for Regional Governance* (London: Anthem Press, 2010); Loveman, *No Higher Law.*

9 With all its good intentions, Washington could not make Latin Americans forget their past experience of U.S. involvement, including the death of Jose Marti in 1895 during the Cuban struggle for independence and the U.S. invasion of the island during the Spanish American War. The aggressive role played by the U.S. in securing independence for the Philippines and Puerto Rico, as well as Cuba, made it crystal clear to all of Latin America that the U.S. was willing and able to resort to unilateral actions to assert its hemispheric hegemony. This became particularly real when the U.S. asserted its supremacy in Central America in 1903, recognizing the newly independent government of Panama and subsequently building and administering the Panama Canal. Rut Diamint, "Entre el Temor y la Armonía," in *Sistema Interamericano y Democracia: Antecedentes Históricos y Tendencias Futuras*, ed. A. B. Tickner (Bogotá: Ediciones Uniandes, 2000); Rut Diamint, "A More Secure Hemisphere?" in *Inter-American Cooperation at a Crossroads*, ed. Gordon Mace, Andrew F. Cooper and Timothy M. Shaw (London: Palgrave Macmillan, 2011), 131–152.

10 The magnitude of the problem was evident at the Third Conference of the American States in Rio de Janeiro in 1906 when all cooperative and integration efforts were dropped. LAC states decided to instead uphold the defense of the principles of Latin American self-determination and national sovereignty and to condemn conflict that resulted from the compulsory collection of private and public debts. The U.S. took advantage of this opportunity to further expand its authority by supporting the idea of limiting force used for the recovery of contracted debts, private or public, in favor of U.S. arbitration. Consequently, the Latin American initiatives to create a common front against the forced collection of debt through the Drago and Calvo doctrines failed to establish a permanent cooperative presence in the form of an organically grown Latin American arrangement. It was at this point, when U.S. power and influence was no longer in question, that President Woodrow Wilson pledged a policy of promotion of democracy, regional integration, and U.S. economic investment in Latin America. Robert Holden and Eric Zolov, eds, New *Latin America and the United States, A Documentary History* (New York and Oxford: Oxford University Press, 2010).

11 It is not surprising then that neither the Fifth Santiago International Conference in 1923 nor the 1928 Havana Conference succeeded in achieving continental cooperation, even after the proclamation of President Roosevelt's Good Neighbor Policy during the Montevideo Convention in 1933. Andrew Hurrell, "Power, Institutions and the Production of Inequality," in *Power in Global Governance*, Cambridge Studies in International Relations no. 98, ed. Michael Barnett and Ramond Duval (Cambridge: Cambridge University Press, 2005), 33–58.

12 Subsequently, to salvage the initiative put forth in Resolution XV, a more comprehensive proposal was presented at the 1942 Third Meeting of Foreign Ministers in Rio de Janeiro by Colombia, Mexico, and Venezuela, which provided an alternative response to armed retaliation allowing the severing of diplomatic relations with Japan, Germany, and Italy by each individual government. For more see Burrell and Shifter, "Estados Unidos"; Diamint, "Entre el Temor y la Armonía"; and Horwitz, *The Transformation of the Organization of American States*.

13 Blanco, C. Ruiz, "Visiones de Seguridad en las Américas," in *La Seguridad Regional en las Américas: Enfoques Críticos y Conceptos Alternativos*, ed. Wolf Grabendorff (Bogotá: Fondo Editorial Cerec, 2003), 133–160; Ana Covarrubias Velasco, "No Intervención Versus Promoción de la Democracia Representativa en el Sistema Interamericano," in *Sistema Interamericano y Democracia, Antecedentes Históricos y Tendencias Futuras*, ed. Arlene B. Tickner (Bogotá: Ediciones Uniandes, 2000), 51–64.

14 For more see C. G. Fenwick, "The Inter American Regional System," *American Journal of International Law*, vol. 50 (1956), 18; C. G. Fenwick, *The Organizations of American States: The Inter-American Regional System* (Washington, DC: Kaufmann Printing, 1963); Hal Klepak, "Power Multiplied or Power Restrained?" in Rosemary Foot, Neil S. McFarlane, and Michael Mastranduno (eds), *US Hegemony and International Organizations* (Oxford: Oxford University Press, 2003), 239–263.

15 The 1948 Ninth Conference had mixed results for the U.S. On the one hand it reinforced the institutional architecture of hemispheric regionalism with the adoption of the Charter of Bogotá and the OAS as the principal political arm of the Inter-American system. This main structure would be complemented, first, by the already established defensive military alliance of TIAR and a military-to-military channel of cooperation through the JID; second, by an important new development tool implemented through the IADB; and third, by the establishment of institutions in charge of fostering and defending democracy and human rights such as the Inter-American Convention of Human Rights (IACHR), the Inter-American Commission on Human Rights, and the Inter-American Court of Human Rights. On the other hand, the conference fell short of its goal to establish an institutionalized path for the settlement of disputes. Instead, the strategy assumed by Latin American governments was to defend their right to full sovereignty, non-intervention, and self-determination. In addition, the Economic Agreement of Bogotá included so many reservations that even if signed, it would be useless. Nevertheless, the Inter-American system established its basic architecture for a cooperative approach that legally included the U.S., providing LAC states with a shield against unilateral U.S. interventions. Unfortunately, global crises drew U.S. attention away from Latin America to events elsewhere in Europe and Asia while security threats attributed to Soviet and Chinese aggressions came to dominate U.S. foreign policy as the Cold War began.

16 Gordon Mace, Andrew F. Cooper, and Timothy M. Shaw, "Introduction," in *Inter-American Cooperation at a Crossroads*, ed. Gordon Mace, Andrew F. Cooper, and Timothy M. Shaw (London: Palgrave Macmillan, 2011), 1–19.

17 Examples of direct intervention include the Dominican Republic in 1965, Grenada in 1979, and Panama in 1989. Examples of indirect intervention include Guatemala in 1954, Bolivia in 1956, Chile in 1973, and Nicaragua in the 1980s. During the Cold War, an ideological alliance within a bipolar international system remained a primary goal and essential part of the geopolitical

calculations between the rival superpowers. Consequently, in defiance of the spirit of TIAR and with the tacit support of the OAS, several military coups took place in Argentina and Peru in 1962; in Guatemala, the Dominican Republic, Honduras, and Ecuador in 1963; and again in the Dominican Republic in 1965. For more see Robert A. Pastor, *Exiting the Whirpool, U.S. Foreign Policy Toward LAC* (Boulder, CO: Westview Press, 2001); Carolyn M. Shaw, *Cooperation, Conflict and Consensus in the Organization of American States* (New York and London: Palgrave Macmillan, 2004); Bruce Bagley and Betty Horwitz, *Regional Security in the Americas: Past, Present and Future* (www.as.miami. edu/internationalstudies/pdf/Bagleypercent20BHSecuritypercent2815percent29perc ent20February percent204 percent202007.pdf); Loveman, *No Higher Law*.

18 Olivier Dabène, *The Politics of Regional Integration in Latin America*, 16–17.

19 These multilateral schemes—including the 1960 Latin American Free Trade Association (LAFTA), comprising South American countries, Mexico, and the Central American Common Market (CACM); followed by the East Caribbean Common Market (ECCM) in 1967; the Caribbean Free Trade Association (CARIFTA) in 1969; and the Andean Pact in 1969—could not withstand the trend towards an inward-looking market.

20 During the 1980s, under the framework of the Latin American Integration Association (ALADI)—a successor to LAFTA—initial limited agreements for trade preferences were negotiated as Economic Complementary Agreements (ACE). Eventually, in the Southern Cone the ACE agreements between Argentina, Brazil, Paraguay, and Uruguay evolved into the Southern Common Market (MERCOSUR) customs union in 1991. Meanwhile, a presidential initiative in the Andean Group induced the member countries to form a customs union among Colombia, Venezuela and Ecuador in the early 1990s. Eventually, in 1995, the agreement changed its name to the Andean Community. A similar initiative was relaunched in 1990 by the Central American Common Market (CARICOM). All in all, it was not until 1991 that economic integration on a larger scale emerged as a reason that could prove strong enough to drive unification. For more see Victor Bulmer-Thomas, "Introduction," in *Regional Integration in LAC: The Political Economy of open Regionalism*, ed. Victor Bulmer-Thomas (London: Institute of Latin American Studies, University of London, 2001), 1–13; Esteoval R. Devlin, Luis Antony and Jorge Garay, "Some Economic and Strategic Issues in the Face of the Emerging NAFTA," in *The Future of Inter-American Relations*, in J. I. Dominguez (New York and London: Routledge, 2000), 153–196; Antoni Estevadeordal and Kati Suominen, "Economic Integration in the Americas: An Unfinished Agenda," in *Inter-American Cooperation at a Crossroads*, ed. Gordon Mace, Andrew F. Cooper, and Timothy M. Shaw (London: Palgrave Macmillan, 2011), 81–94.

21 Between 1982 and 1989 Latin America sent over 200 billion dollars to its creditors in the U.S., Western Europe, and Asia, a sum far greater than the one received by Europe through the Marshal Plan. During this time Latin America was mired in depression, and more people than ever were trapped in poverty, hence why the 1980s came to be known as Latin America's "lost decade." For more see Loveman, *No Higher Law*, 320–330.

22 In Central America, for example, U.S. interventionist polices in the early 1980s had prompted four Latin American governments—Mexico, Colombia, Venezuela, and Panama—to meet on the island of Contadora, Panama, to broker a peace agreement outside the auspices of the OAS and without U.S. approval or participation. The ultimate success of these initiatives in 1989–1990 clearly indicated that many Latin American countries no longer perceived the threat of

Soviet/Cuban intervention as sufficient justification for their unquestioning support for either U.S. unilateral security policies or for backing undemocratic regional regimes. Thomas E. Skidmore and Peter E. Smith, *Modern Latin America*, 6th edition (New York and Oxford: Oxford University Press, 2005); Peter H. Smith, *The Talons of the Eagle, Dynamics of U.S.-Latin American Relations* (New York and Oxford: Oxford University Press, 1996).

23 After the collapse of the Contadora initiative in 1985, and over initial objections by the U.S., the Esquipulas Accords (a Central American initiative led by Costa Rican President Oscar Arias in 1986) set in motion a process that ultimately succeeded in restoring relative peace and stability in the region. Interestingly enough, the peace initiatives that started with the Contadora group encouraged the Latin American governments of Argentina, Brazil, Colombia, Mexico, Panama, Peru, Uruguay, and Venezuela to meet in Rio de Janeiro in 1986. This group (known as the Rio Group) meant to stand as an alternative to the OAS for establishing common ground in foreign policy issues dealing mostly with security, disarmament, arms control, and non-proliferation. Interestingly, this grouping included Cuba and, more importantly, excluded the U.S. Even today, the Rio Group, currently a security alliance with 23 members, purposefully excludes Canada and the U.S. and stands as an alternative for developing foreign policies on security.

24 For more see Jorge I. Domínguez, "Security, Peace, and Democracy in Latin America and the Caribbean: Challenges of the Post-Cold War Era," in *International Security and Democracy: Latin America and the Caribbean in the Post-Cold war Era*, ed. Jorge I. Domínguez (Pittsburg, PA: University of Pittsburg Press, 1998), 3–38; Jorge I. Domínguez, David Mares, Manuel Orozco, Scott Palmer, David Rojas, Francisco Aravena, and Andres Serbin, "Boundary Disputes in Latin America", in *Peaceworks* no. 50, ed. Jorge I. Dominguez (Washington, DC: United Institute of Peace, 2003).

25 With international communism no longer considered an imminent threat, the U.S. and Latin America began to reassess and redefine their views of regional security. The U.S. Department of Defense (DOD) adopted a new, expanded security agenda for the region that included the following issues: 1) Cold War residuals, particularly in Central America and Cuba; 2) insurgency and terrorism, which at the time were represented by disruptive anti-democratic elements primarily in Peru, Colombia and Mexico; 3) drug-trafficking and organized crime activities; 4) illegal or undocumented immigration and refugee issues; 5) arms control and non-proliferation issues, mainly regarding conventional arms; 6) traditional inter-American security cooperation such as protecting the Panama Canal; 7) conflict resolution and peacekeeping in places such as Haiti; 8) social issues and the environmental problems, including assistance in poverty alleviation, nation-building and democratic consolidation; 9) energy security; and 10) civil–military relations and the role of the armed forces in democratic societies. William Perry and Max Primorac, "The Inter-American Security Agenda," *Journal of Interamerican Studies and World Affairs*, vol. 36, no. 3 (1994), 111–127.

26 Abraham F. Lowenthal, "The United States and Latin American Democracy: Learning From History," in Abraham F. Lowenthal (ed.), *Exporting Democracy: The United States and Latin America, Case Studies*, (Baltimore, MD and London: Johns Hopkins University Press, 1991), 261–283; Robert A. Pastor, *Exiting the Whirlpool: U.S. Foreign Policy Toward Latin America and the Caribbean* (Boulder, CO: Westview Press, 2001); Hal Klepak,"Power Multiplied or Power Restrained?" in *US Hegemony and International Organizations*, ed. R. Foot, Neil S.

LAC AND THE INTER-AMERICAN SYSTEM

McFarlane, and Michael Mastranduno (Oxford: Oxford University Press, 2003), 239–263.

27 The IADB and the OAS were called upon to promote economic development and democratic governance in the hemisphere more than at any time since their creation in the late 1940s. The JID and the TIAR were activated for the purpose of forging a more cooperative security agenda. Lowenthal, "The United States and Latin American Democracy"; Burrell and Shifter, "Estados Unidos"; Pastor, *Exiting the Whirlpool*.

28 This broad security agenda, which included issues that had previously not been defined as security threats, required the construction of a more effective multilateral institutional mechanism at the hemispheric level. In 1991, under the auspices of the OAS, the Hemispheric Commission of Security (renamed in 1994 as the Hemispheric Security Committee (CHS)) was created to forge a hemispheric consensus around an expanded security strategy. President Clinton backed these efforts toward multilateralism; working groups began to revise the role of both the *Junta Interamericana de Defensa* (JID) and *Colegio Interamericano de Defensa* (CID) to achieve the demilitarization of border conflicts (especially in Central America) with the final goal of modifying the hemispheric security doctrine. The inclusion of such a wide range of security concerns including poverty, democracy, and the environment depended upon the willingness of Latin American states to trust and engage with the U.S. within the framework of the CHS and the OAS's umbrella. Thus, success depended heavily on whether or not Washington would be willing to expand its security agenda and adopt a more cooperative approach to hemispheric security problems. For more see Mónica Hirst, "Seguridad regional en las Américas," in *La seguridad regional en las Américas*, ed. Wolf Grabendorff (Bogotá: Friedrich Ebert Stiftung en Colombia-Fescol/Fodo Editorial Cerec, 2003), 25–8; Bruce Bagley and Betty Horwitz, *Regional Security in the Americas*; Betty Horwitz, *The Transformation of the Organization of American States*; Loveman, *No Higher Law*.

29 Loveman, *No Higher Law*, 350–359.

30 This meant improving security-building measures and interestingly enough, giving special attention to drug-trafficking and international terrorism. This became even more pronounced after Washington increased free trade initiatives by tying them more explicitly to economic cooperation in the content of the Trade Promotion Authority (TPA) Act approved by the U.S. Congress in 2002. While it's true that the DMA undoubtedly constituted a step toward greater multilateralism in regional security matters, decision-making and resource allocation processes clearly remained in U.S. military hands. For more see Mónica Hirst, "Seguridad Regional en las Américas," in *La seguridad regional en las Américas*, ed. Wolf Grabendorff (Bogotá: Friedrich Ebert Stiftung en Colombia-Fescol/Fodo Editorial Cerec, 2003), 25–80; Bantz J. Craddock, *Posture Statement of General Bantz J. Craddock, United States Army Commander, United States Southern Command Before the 109th Congress Senate Armed Service Committee* (U.S. S. Command, Department of Defense, 2006), 1–27; Brian Loveman, "Introduction: U.S. Regional Security Policies in the Post Cold War Era," in Brian Loveman, *Strategy for Empire: U.S. Regional Security Policy in the Post Cold War Era* (Oxford: SR Books, 2004), xiii–xxviii.

31 Kathleen T. Rhem, *Rumsfeld in Nicaragua for Talks with Regional Defense Ministers,* American Forces Press Service (www.defenselink.mil/utility/printitem.aspx?/print), 1–2.

32 In October 2003 during the Defense Ministerial of the Americas (DMA) Conference in Mexico City, the threats of terrorism, narco-trafficking, illicit arms

trafficking, and organized crime were linked, once and for all, and subsequently identified as the highest security priority. In contrast with the previous security initiatives of the 1990s, basic security issues important to Latin America such as the maintenance of territorial integrity or strengthening of state institutions were excluded from the final text. In addition, the JID, now part of the OAS, was clearly relegated to a secondary role in hemispheric defense matters. By November of 2004 in the DMS meeting in Quito, U.S. defense secretary Rumsfeld succeeded in linking terrorism, organized crime and drug trafficking (Rehm, "Rumsfeld in Nicaragua for Talks with Regional Defense Ministers," American Forces Press Service, 2006 (www.defenselink.mil/utility/printitem.asp x?/print)). As a result, through a series of bilateral agreements rather than sub-regional or hemispheric accords, by the time of the final 2006 DMA Declaration of Managua, the cooperative security agenda that emerged in 1991 with the CHS was definitively subordinated to terrorism-related issues. Given the recent rise in violence in Latin America, during the 2008 Eighth DMA Conference in Canada, the Declaration of Banff gave particular emphasis to only one of the many regional multilateral conventions aimed at combating the proliferation of small arms and light weapons: the Illicit Trade in Small Arms and Light Weapons in All Its Aspects and the Inter-American Convention Against the Illicit Manufacturing of and Trafficking in Firearms, Ammunitions, Explosives, and Other Related Materials (CIFTA). For more see Rehm, *Rumsfeld in Nicaragua*; William Leogrande, "A Poverty of Imagination: George Bush's Policy in Latin America," *Journal of Latin American Studies*, vol. 38, no. 2 (2007), 355–385.

33 Robin Wigglesworth, "Caribbean in Crisis: Checkbook Diplomacy; With the U.S. becoming an absentee power the Chinese are moving in," *Financial Times*, Analysis, December, 17, 2013 (www.ft.com/intl/cms/s/0/7f7b0d8e-5ea 8-11e3-8621-00144feabdc0.html?siteedition=intl#axzz2nnJ5jXDN).

34 There are 31 Commonwealth states classified as "small", but the Caribbean members are primarily leading the lobbying. One of the options touted is to use the money promised by rich countries to combat climate change for development, or to pay back or offset their government debts. Since 2010, St. Kitts and Nevis, Grenada, Belize, Antigua and Barbuda, and Jamaica (twice) had to restructure their debts and enter IMF programs. Others, including Barbados, are also being forced to impose austerity. This is causing social hardship, exacerbating the already high crime rates and endangering the health of their democracies. For more see Robin Wigglesworth, "Caribbean in Crisis: Checkbook Diplomacy; With the U.S. becoming an absentee power the Chinese are moving in," *Financial Times*, Analysis, December, 17, 2013 (www.ft.com/intl/ cms/s/0/7f7b0d8e-5ea8-11e3-8621-00144feabdc0.html?siteedition=intl#axzz2n nJ5jXDN); Robin Wigglesworth, "Caribbean Blown by Winds of Financial Crisis," *Financial Times*, Latin American and the Caribbean, December 16, 2013 (www.ft.com/intl/cms/s/2/ead62cda-60ec-11e3-b7f1-00144feabdc0.html#axzz 2nnJ5jXDN).

35 Mark J. Ruhl, "Trouble in Central America; Honduras Unravels," *Journal of Democracy*, vol. 21, no. 2 (2010), 93–107.

36 Carolyn Shaw, Cooperation, Conflict and Consensus in the Organization of American States (London and New York: Palgrave Macmillan, 2004), 45.

37 For more see Michael Barnett and Martha Finnemore, *Rules of the World, International Organizations in Global Politics* (Cornell, NY: Cornell University Press, 2004); Carolyn M. Shaw, ed., *Cooperation, Conflict and Consensus in the Organization of American States* (London and New York: Palgrave Macmillan, 2004); Dabène, *The Politics of Regional Integration in Latin America*.

LAC AND THE INTER-AMERICAN SYSTEM

38 Kalevi J. Holsti, *Taming the Sovereigns; Institutional Change in International Politics* (Cambridge: Cambridge University Press, 2004), 317–318.

39 Thomas Legler, "El Perfil del Multilateralismo Latinoamericano," *Foreign Affairs Latinoamerica*, vol. 10, no. 3 (2011).

40 For more see Andrew Cooper and Thomas Legler, "The OAS Democratic Solidarity Paradigm: Questions of Collective and National Leadership," *Latin American Politics and Society*, vol. 43, no. 1 (2001), 103–126; Andrew Cooper and Thomas Legler, *Intervention Without Intervening? The OAS Defense of the Promotion of Democracy in the Americas* (New York: Palgrave Macmillan, 2006); Thomas Legler, "Demise of the Inter-American Democracy Promotion Regime?" in *Inter-American Cooperation at a Crossroads*, ed. Gordon Mace, Andrew F. Cooper, and Timothy M. Shaw (London: Palgrave Macmillan, 2010), 111–130; Thomas Legler and Lesley Burns, "Introduction," in *Latin American Multilateralism: New Directions*, Compilation of Articles (Canada: FOCAL, September 2010), 6–7; Thomas Legler and Thomas Kwasi Tieku, "What Difference Can a Path Make? Regional Democracy Promotion Regimes in the Americas and Africa," *Democratization*, vol. 17, no. 3 (2010), 465–491; Thomas Legler, "El Perfil del Multilateralismo Latinoamericano," 2–5.

41 In 2001, OAS member states reached a consensus on a set of criteria that was to be present in any state considered to be a democracy—elements that were codified in Articles 3 and 4 of the IADC. With the Declaration of Quebec City and the Inter-American Democratic Charter, representative democracy became a requirement for membership and participation in the OAS, the Summit of the Americas, and the Inter-American system. By invitation only, the OAS opted for the *Mesa de Diálogo* (Dialogue Table) model to encourage intra-elite negotiations and avoid a conflict that would have resulted in complete democratic failure. The *Mesa* model made a positive contribution by way of political process, particularly in Venezuela in 2003 when it kept the line of communication open between the hostile *Chavistas* and the opposition. Cooper and Legler, *Intervention Without Intervening?*; Legler, "El Perfil del Multilateralismo Latinoamericano."

42 *Stratfor*, "Improving U.S.-Cuban Ties Create Openings in Colombia and Venezuela," July 1, 2015.

43 By 2001, a specific democratic criterion was finally made obligatory. Under the capable leadership of Secretary-General César Gaviria, the OAS could then be used by its member states in the pursuit of a normative democratic consensus, understood as a representative regime with an elitist slant, centered in the executive. This list of requirements included first, a strict anti-coup norm reflected in Resolution 1080 and the Washington protocol and reflected in the strong responses of the OAS in Guatemala (1993), Haiti (1991), Paraguay (1996), Peru (1992) and Venezuela (1992). The second requirement was the explicit promotion of a representative democracy, specifically defined by a set of criteria codified for the first time in Articles 3 and 4 of the IADC. Thanks to the ten years of deepening authoritarianism during the Fujimory presidency in Peru (1990–2000), the IADC established the third requirement of the democratic regime, protection against not only coups or self-coups, but also backsliding of the type the Peruvians have been victims during the Fujimory years. Article 19 of the IADC specifically identifies coups, self-coups, unconstitutional interruptions of the democratic order and authoritarian regressions by incumbent elected leaders as unacceptable practices. The fourth requirement consisted of the external validation of elections, which became a norm following Article 25 of the IADC. The OAS was invited and had the authority to validate, criticize and

even invalidate elections for example, in the Dominican Republic (1994), Haiti (2000), Peru (2000) and Venezuela (2005). The fifth requirement was the promotion, above all, of conciliation and compromise. Unless the interruption of democracy happened as a result of a coup, the collective defense of democracy in the Americas was to follow a preferred logic of a graduated, flexible, diplomatic response to political crises. Diplomatic representatives, however, preferred to address threats to democracy through negotiation and maneuvering as was the case of the crises in Peru (2000) and Venezuela (2005) through the inter-elite *Mesa* process (see Cooper and Legler, *Intervention Without Intervening?*). The sixth requirement was the defense of self-determination and sovereignty. With the exception of a military coup, the IADC is very clear that the sovereign governments have the final say over most OAS interventions, monitoring and participation. According to Articles 17 and 18 of the IADC, the OAS requires a formal invitation by a member state and cannot act on its own. So last but not least, in conjunction with the "by invitation rule", the seventh requirement of the inter-American democracy promotion regime reinforced a particular elitist style of sovereignty: executive sovereignty, whereby diplomacy and limits of intervention resides on the authority and judgments of the head of government.

44 This lack of horizontal accountability has emerged in conjunction with growing distrust and suspicion against U.S. policies. George W. Bush's "War on Terror" and "War on Drugs" programs have served to undermine the promotion of democracy championed by multilateral institutions such as the OAS. In addition, recent actions such as the Bush administration's tacit support of the Venezuelan coup in 2002, the covert actions of the International Republican Institute criticizing and possibly undermining Aristide's government in Haiti, the electoral intervention by U.S. government officials or Congressmen against left-wing candidates in Bolivia (2003, 2005) and Nicaragua (2006), compounded by selective use of the Millennium Challenge Account, the Annual Congressional drug certification process, the Andean Trade Preferences Act, and even human trafficking reports used to criticize the governments of Cuba, Bolivia and Venezuela, have all damaged the reputation of the U.S. in the region. The Obama administration has tried to improve U.S. credibility, as seen during the 2010 Trinidad and Tobago Summit of the Americas when he signaled a willingness to redefine U.S. relations with Cuba. Nevertheless the U.S. unconditional recognition of the November elections in Honduras/ Porfirio Lobo's administration has called unconditional support for the democracy promotion regime into question (Legler, "El Perfil del Multilateralismo Latinoamericano," 119).

45 Ibid.

46 For more see Michal A. Seligson, "The Rise of Populism and the Left in Latin America," *Journal of Democracy*, vol. 18, no. 3 (2007), 81–95. Andrés Serbin, "Old Factors and New Challenges in Regional Multilateralism: A Latin American Idiosyncrasy?" in *Latin American Multilateralism: New Directions* (Canada: FOCAL, Compilation of Articles, September 2010), 8–11; and Kurt Weyland, "Latin America's Authoritarian Drift," *Journal of Democracy*, vol. 24, no. 3 (2013),18–32.

47 On the economic front, repeated recessions and debt-induced depressions during the 1970s and 1980s further debilitated LAC economies. Under the ideological influence of the Washington Consensus, the U.S. had been working through the IMF and the World Bank in an attempt to jump-start local economies in the hemisphere by promoting and monitoring neo-liberal economic adjustments in states that had been pursuing ISI strategies for too long and were unable to adequately respond to the new globalizing trends. These

adjustments, while promoting the opening of their economic systems, strained Latin American governments in the middle of their democratization processes, leading to serious economic crises such as the case of Mexico in 1994. For more see Javier Corrales, "Market Reforms," in Jorge Domínguez and Michael Shifter (eds) *Constructing Democratic Governance in Latin America* (Baltimore, MD and London: Johns Hopkins University Press, 2003), 74–99; Judith A. Teichman, *The Politics of Freeing Markets in Latin America, Chile, Argentina and Mexico* (Chapel Hill and London: University of North Carolina Press, 2011); Rosemary Thorp, *Progress, Poverty and Exclusion: An Economic History of Latin America in the 20th Century* (Baltimore, MD: Johns Hopkins University Press, 1998); Gordon Mace, Andrew F. Cooper, and Timothy M. Shaw, "Introduction," in *Inter-American Cooperation at a Crossroads*, ed. Gordon Mace, Andrew F. Cooper, and Timothy M. Shaw (London: Palgrave Macmillan, 2011), 1–19.

48 The summitry process began with the Miami Summit of the Americas in 1994, and continued with the Santiago de Chile Summit in 1998 and the Santa Cruz Summit Conference on Sustainable Development in 1996 and so on. Richard E. Feinberg, *Summitry in the Americas: A Progress Report* (Washington, DC: Institute of International Economics, 1997); The Leadership Council for the Inter-American Summitry, "Advancing Toward Quebec City and Beyond," Policy Report no. 3 (Miami, FL: University of Miami, 2001), 1–25; Gordon Mace, Andrew F. Cooper Mace, and Timothy M. Shaw, eds, *Inter-American Cooperation at a Crossroads*, International Political Economy Series (London: Palgrave Macmillan: 2010); Gordon Mace and Hugo Loiseau, "Cooperative Hegemony and Summitry in the Americas," Inter-Americas Studies Center, 2004: 2–45.

49 Furthermore during the Summit of the Americas in Mar del Plata in November of 2005, the U.S. and LAC began to part ways in a very public forum. The opposition for U.S. foreign policies in Iraq by Chile and Mexico, members of the UN Security Council and the FTAA, emerged as clear responses to Washington's indifference towards LAC.

50 Estevadeordal and Suominen, "Economic Integration in the Americas."

51 Against this backdrop MERCOSUR has pursued a hedging strategy, opening negotiations with other South American nations both to weave a fabric of agreements that allowed for mutual access and to increase leverage vis-à-vis Brazil's leadership has also been driven by its efforts to extend the reach of MERCOSUR and obtain a free trade area with the Andean Community (CAN) and Central America, as well as the Gulf Cooperation Council, the South African Costumes Union, and countries such as India. Such policy direction is evident in the Brazilian efforts to give life to the Union of South American Nations (UNASUR), bringing together the CAN countries with those members of MERCOSUR through initiatives of energy integration and physical structure. It remains to be seen whether the issues presented by Bolivia and Venezuela will challenge the success of the UNASUR project. Even so, the UNASUR attempt to become a geo-economic union of sorts on the basis of an institutional bridge between CAN and MERCOSUR has presented the U.S. with a challenge. As of today, even when considering India or China's economic incursions in the Americas, except for MERCOSUR, most of the region remains highly dependent on the U.S. as a destination for its exports and source of foreign direct investment. Even when bilateralism tends to create an adversarial and competitive strategic alliance between LAC economies, bilateral trade agreements are, for the moment, the only way of locking in benefits on a binding basis with the U.S. Diana Tussie, "Hemispheric Relations: Budding Contests in the Dawn of a New Era," in *Inter-American Cooperation at a*

Crossroads, ed. Gordon Mace, Andrew F. Cooper, and Timothy M. Shaw (London: Palgrave Macmillan, 2011), 23–42.

52 ALBA was put forward in 2004 as an alternative, anti-neoliberal model for regional integration, antithetical to the FTAA and with an emphasis on social issues, solidarity, and cooperation in public service. Originally signed by Venezuela and Cuba, ALBA provided a framework of cooperation between these two countries, with Venezuela providing preferentially priced oil in return for a variety of in-kind resources including health care personnel and education programs. This alliance now also includes Bolivia, the Dominican Republic, Nicaragua, Saint Vincent, and Dominica. Paraguay and Ecuador are also part of ALBA, although they have not yet become fully-fledged members. Honduras became a member six months before the coup that ousted President Manuel Zelaya in 2009. ALBA promotes a socially-oriented trade block rather than one based strictly on market incentives. Instead of the promotion of free markets, ALBA's cornerstone is the Compensatory Fund for Structural Convergence, which manages and distributes financial and economic aid to the most economically vulnerable countries. The program favors endogenous development; rejects the low-quality employment offered by globalized sweatshops; promotes self-sufficient agriculture and the establishment of cooperatives; and opposes intellectual property rights regimes on the grounds that they only protect the areas of scientific and technological knowledge that developed countries control while neglecting biodiversity and the traditional knowledge of peasant and aboriginal peoples. ALBA is ready to support the establishment of the Bank of the South to provide for their financing, which certainly sounds positive, but at the end of the day, all these projects depended on Venezuelan largesse. More importantly, it depended on the good will of former leader Hugo Chavez and its ability to use his "petro-generosity." This is no longer the case, since Chavez is now dead and current oil prices on the global market are so low. Tussie, "Hemispheric Relations," 35–36.

53 For more see Phillip Stephens, "Trade trumps missiles in today's global power plays," *Financial Times*, Comment and Analysis, Friday, November 22, 2013).

10

WE SHOULD CARE ABOUT LATIN AMERICA AND THE CARIBBEAN

> Learn from yesterday, live for today, hope for tomorrow. The important thing is not to stop questioning.
>
> Albert Einstein[1]

Introduction

Today's international environment is changing rapidly. The world is in the midst of a critical juncture, much as it was in the first decades of the twentieth century, after World War II and after the disappearance of the communist threat. While many lessons have (theoretically) been learned, it's still difficult to predict the future trajectory of Latin America. The effects of the financial economic crisis that started in the U.S. (and turned into a global economic recession in 2008/9) were very different for developed versus developing nations.[2]

As discussed in this volume, history shows that transformations tend to be unpredictable. No one can be absolutely sure what the structure of the international system will look like; history tends to make liars out of those brave enough to make predictions. Yet whatever the outcome of these changes, one thing is clear: new winners and losers will eventually emerge.[3]

The National Intelligence Council (NIC) issued a report imagining what the world might look like 20 years from now. They did so with the premise that the international system will be shaped by two big power shifts already taking place: from west to east and from north to south. They asserted that the U.S. will probably remain the most powerful player, or at least retain a dominant role, but it won't be the only player exerting influence in world affairs.[4]

In this brave new world, the question is: what will happen to LAC? Will Latin Americans emerge as winners or as losers? Will LAC nations continue in their roles as rule-takers in the international system, or learn to more effectively wield power in the international system?

It does appear that most LAC states are finally ready to heed the lessons of history and take advantage of their place in the world. Being in close

215

proximity to the U.S. may no longer be just a curse. Countries such as Brazil, Mexico, Chile, Peru, Colombia, Costa Rica, Panama, and Uruguay will never have the military might to coerce the world's stronger powers into action, though that may not matter as much as it did in the past. Most LAC nations have learned to take advantage of the use of power in terms of political economy by seeking ways to improve the efficacy of their internal economic structures.

With notable exceptions such as Venezuela, Argentina, Honduras, Guatemala, Haiti, and Cuba, most of the biggest LAC economies seem to have been able to take advantage of the commodity boom of the twenty-first century. LAC states have finally been able to undergo far-reaching changes, including sustained economic growth, a reduction in poverty, and a fast-paced opening up of their economies. Income inequality has been dramatically reduced in recent years, although the distribution of political and economic benefits remains uneven across LAC (as the example of the Caribbean Basin clearly shows).[5]

Latin American nations seem to have learned to take advantage of an interconnected capitalist system and their place in it, seeking cooperative economic approaches that may serve them to best achieve their goals. The changing nature of arrangements between Canada, Mexico, and the U.S. is a good example. The legacy and future of NAFTA has become part of a global economic strategy with higher ambitions and a greater strategic impact, especially for the U.S. As parts of North America, Mexico, and Canada afford the U.S. a strategic advantage, especially vis-à-vis China, when negotiating two potential regional trade deals: the 12-country Trans-Pacific Partnership (TPP)—which includes the three members of NAFTA plus Chile, Peru and now possibly Costa Rica, and an even bigger EU–U.S. deal, the Transatlantic Trade and Investment Partnership (TTIP).[6]

In addition, the experience of most LAC economies during the 2008 global financial crisis seems to show that history has finally proven to be a good teacher. Given that many of their governments had important macroeconomic policies in place, LAC was more resilient that many other parts of the world.[7] Although the region is still vulnerable to external extreme shocks, the policy improvements mean that many Latin American countries have boosted their resilience. With the notable exceptions of Venezuela or Argentina, the commodity lottery, although still a precarious business, may cease to be a perennial curse for many Latin Americans.

Nevertheless, as covered in this volume, LAC countries have been on the brink of fast-track economic development and progress before. At the end of the nineteenth century and beginning of the twentieth century, LAC was integrated into the global economy and had aspirations of progress, modernization and democracy. Even when adopting import substitution (IS) strategies and authoritarian government to control their populations, which helped initially, their resistance to change and lack of capacity or will to adjust to new circumstances only served to increase their disadvantages vis-à-vis the rest of the world. Time and again, decision-making authorities proved slow to change or adapt to the new realities of increased globalization.

There is no question that LAC still faces many obstacles: the spread of criminal violence associated with drugs and criminal gangs; the need for further development of good governance; the temptation by many governments to impose greater protectionism; and even the unknown consequences of climate change—all have the power to derail any progress LAC societies may be able to achieve in the coming decades.

The future brings uncertainty and will undoubtedly require capable leadership in LAC, the U.S., Canada, and elsewhere. The extent to which LAC leaders take advantage of important factors such as the prime location of the region, the pace of global economic growth, and the demand for Latin American commodities, goods, labor, manufacturing, and other services will ultimately determine whether or not these middle-class societies become part of the higher-income club. But taking a long-term view, many of the largest LAC economies seem to be on the right path.[8]

Although history will be the ultimate judge, political and economic elites will hopefully be wise enough to learn from past experiences. The current critical juncture may prove surprising. One thing seems clear, however: the dominant economies in LAC appear willing to try to break the rigid molds of the past. These aspirations are of no small significance, especially considering that the current crossroads will be mostly remembered by one important game-changing event: a global economic crisis that resulted from financial implosion.[9]

After a thorough examination of the LAC trajectory in the ever-changing international system, this concluding chapter will examine the place of LAC in the contemporary world, and discuss whether or not Latin Americans have learned from past mistakes. Countries that are able to do so will benefit from the lessons of history and finally reach their full potential, poised to take advantage of their place in the international system and their respective roles in world affairs.[10]

LAC: A Tale of Two Economies

Latin America has always depended on commodities to fuel economic growth, so it is not surprising that the natural resources-rich Latin America has done well in the past decade, largely due to demand from fast-growing countries. From oil to gas to copper to soybeans, the insatiable demand for food and commodities in China and other emerging economies helped Latin American countries grow at a rapid pace during the economic cycle that ended in 2008. It is important to remember, however, that the commodity lottery teaches important lessons which some countries seem to have learned better than others.

The easy money that comes with an increasing worldwide demand for commodities is sometimes too tempting. When everyone is experiencing economic growth, all appears well. The global slowdown of the past four years has created a divide, however, between countries that took advantage of their commodity bonanza and pushed a more aggressive free market agenda, keeping a light grip on the public purse and those that retained the bad habit of swelling public coffers with rising commodity prices to support a greater role for government and far too many excesses.

Chile, for example, a country that is heavily dependent on its mineral resources, undertook painful neoliberal reforms during the 1980s and continued them in one shape or another through the 1990s. As a result, Chile is now ranked as an upper-middle-income economy.

In contrast, Argentina, considered one of the world's wealthiest economies a hundred years ago, has suffered from recurring economic crises and sovereign defaults, persistent fiscal and account deficits, high inflation, and public and external debt problems. Argentina serves as the perfect example of a country that has ignored one of the most important lessons of Latin America's past.

The commodity lottery can be both a blessing and a curse. As the events of the 1970s, early 1980s, and start of the twentieth century demonstrated, fast and easy money allows leaders to ignore the need for long-term reforms that lead to sustainable growth.

While it's clear that the Americas did suffer from the 2008 collapse, Latin America's more open economies proved better prepared to face the crisis. Still, as the examples of Venezuela and Argentina clearly show, not all countries have made positive choices regarding long-term growth.[11] Just as in the past, Latin America matters most to the global market in terms of its commodity exports. The 2008 financial crisis, however, exposed two very different economic tracks taken by different countries.

Some countries, such as Ecuador and Venezuela, continued to ride the commodity boom as before. Other countries, such as Mexico and Colombia, have been able to foster something new: the development of light industry and of new consumer markets, thanks to its growing middle class. By these economic strategies, Brazil had lifted between 25 and 35 million people out of poverty by 2009, while Mexico had developed the central lowland region (which hosts a large educated population) and connected it to ports in the U.S, as well as improving its infrastructure. The Bajío area is centrally located and has successfully attracted foreign investment for manufacturing. Overall, Mexico is increasingly becoming an alternative to China as a preferred center of manufacturing for multinational companies looking to supply the U.S.

The reforms that President Enrique Peña Nieto is working to implement would allow Mexico to become competitive in the world economy. If successful, and as part of NAFTA, this would give the U.S. leverage in the

Trans-Pacific Partnership negotiations, which once completed, would deepen international trading relationships with ten other countries: Australia, Brunei, Chile, Canada, Malaysia, New Zeeland, Peru, Singapore, the U.S., and Vietnam.[12]

It follows that Latin America—where light industries and an emerging class are flourishing—is emerging as a more prosperous region with growing influence. Some countries still matter more than others, however, especially to the U.S. as it seeks to manage its foreign policies worldwide. Even considering the trouble spots in the region, the advantages of rapidly expanding economies far outweigh any potential risks, offering opportunities for the U.S. to foster cooperation and free trade.

Latin Americans are no longer the offshoots of the Iberian empires where coups and revolutions continuously overshadow progress. How the U.S. will engage the region is still an open question, but there seems to be little doubt that there are excellent prospects for Washington to do business with its neighbors in a new way.[13] Nevertheless, though they share the same global real estate, a common history, and in many cases a common language, LAC nations seem to be traveling down diverging paths.

Brazil and Mexico: Friends or Foes?

Two titans are currently competing in Latin America to occupy first place as leader: Brazil and Mexico. In 2010, many thought the question had been settled once and for all. The Brazilian economy was more than double the size of Mexico's, growing at a 7.5 percent annual rate compared to Mexico's meagerly near 2 percent. Moreover, in 2001 and thanks to Jim O'Neill, former chairman of Goldman Sachs, Brazil had successfully joined the exclusive BRIC (Brazil, Russia, India, and China) club—though Mexico didn't make the cut. This served as a nod to Brazil, which from then on was seen as protagonist in a new megatrend. Brazil was Latin America's representative of a shift in global economic power away from the G7 economies. Common wisdom at the time dictated that Brazil would step ahead of every other Latin American economy to assume a leadership position, especially for the Southern Cone.

Following the 2008/9 economic crisis, however, the Brazilian economy found itself waddling along at an annual rate of 1.9 percent, while the Mexican economy was set to grow at 3.9 percent. According to Benito Barber, Nomura's Latin American strategist, among others, Mexico is expected to overtake Brazil by 2022,[14] but the matter is far from settled. Between 2000 and 2010, Mexico fell behind Brazil in terms of human capital thanks to competition from Chinese labor, lagging education, and incomplete labor-market reforms. This was amplified by steady emigration to the U.S. By contrast, Brazil benefited from a "formalization" of the labor market as 40 million Brazilians entered the middle class over the decade. A commodities boom led to major investments in Brazil, raising its investment-to-GDP figure from 15 percent to 19 percent.

In contrast, Mexico's dependence on the U.S. economy and a manufacturing sector heavily exposed to China led to disappointing gains from physical capital accumulation and total factor productivity. All this time Mexico's decision to join its destiny to that of the U.S. and Canada through NAFTA seemed to have been a big mistake.

Brazil, so far away from the U.S., was able to do much better. Much of its economic and financial success at that time stemmed from not only its policy efforts but also the Asia-driven commodity boom. This kept the nation going through the worst of the global downturn, while the government's social policies were able to shield the poor.

Cashing in on the rise of China, big offshore oil finds and a boom credit, until recently, Brazil has been considered the region's leader. The high demand for commodity exports, however, has not been enough to sustain Brazil's unprecedented bonanza. By July of 2014, business confidence in Brazil had sunk to an unprecedented low, with inflation expected to reach 7 percent and growth forecasts for 2015 set at 1 percent or less.[15] In addition, the prosecution scandal involving corrupt executives and their misappropriation of billions of dollars from Petroleo Brasileiro SA (Petr4.SA) has hurt not only Brazil's economy but also President Dilma Rousseff, who was chairwoman of the Petrobras board of directors from 2003 to 2010.[16]

While the commodity sector temporarily allowed Brazil to exploit a comparative advantage, many now see limited opportunities for improving total factor productivity, something usually limited to manufacturing. Although Brazil enjoyed a decade of strong government reformations led by Fernando Henrique Cardoso in the 1990s, the last decade has been one of increasing welfare costs rather than additional reform.

For Mexico, on the other hand, despite a slow start during the first decade of 2000, things may be looking up. For one thing, high manufacturing costs in China are improving the competitiveness of and demand for Mexican factories, and the PRI administration has promised to continue the path of supply-side reform pursued by the previous government.[17] In sharp contrast to Brazil, Mexico boasts a friendly investment climate marked by stable foreign direct investment. Moreover, considering Europe's stagnation, Mexico's performance makes the country a notable exception to the slowed global outlook for industrialized nations.

In addition, uncertainty about China's ability to continue importing high levels of commodities could force Brazil to focus more on manufacturing, as well as the country's strong protectionist trade policies. This may prove difficult because, unlike Mexico's export-driven growth model, Brazil relies relatively little on international trade.[18]

As different emerging economies assert their presence on the world stage, power may be shared one way or another among countries, which presents developing and developed societies with both challenges and opportunities. The new international environment will require the U.S. and other Western countries to learn to share power with rising non-Western middle-tier or income states. Some countries will prove better equipped than others to sustain growth and, in the case of Mexico and Brazil, avoid the "middle-income trap" while they secure their leadership role among Latin American countries.[19]

There is no denying that during the next few decades, even considering the changes taking place with the "rise of the rest," the U.S. will continue to adapt its strategies and attitudes and dominate politically, militarily and economically.[20] It follows that a strong relationship with the U.S. is important for any country anywhere, but for LAC specifically, strong political and economic ties with its neighbor (the most powerful country in the world) will have particular perks.

Considering where the two Latin American titans are on the map, one country clearly has an advantage in this respect. Although this has not worked in its favor so far, Mexico is better poised today to take advantage of its powerful neighbor in the North.[21] In light of this, the question remains: why can't Brazil and Mexico behave more cooperatively and leverage their combined strength against the U.S.?

As *Stratfor* points out,[22] the two countries' economic models stem from their contrasting geopolitical imperatives. Because of its proximity to the U.S. and its location in the strategic Caribbean Basin, Mexico has opened its economy by signing dozens of free trade agreements over the past two decades. Through NAFTA, it has shifted towards full integration with the U.S. economy. By contrast, Brazil—which maintains its economic core in the Southern Cone of South America—has adopted a more protectionist approach in order to safeguard its domestic industries and job markets, thus avoiding large-scale economic integration with the U.S. Moreover, the two countries' diverging paths extend beyond national policies. They also lead two distinct Latin American blocks: the Pacific Alliance and MERCOSUR, both of which have different economic philosophies and trade policies.

The Pacific Alliance, comprised of Mexico, Colombia, Peru, and Chile, unites its members in a free trade partnership that limits the role of individual governments in multilateral trade by lowering tariff barriers and harmonizing regulations. MERCOSUR, on the other hand, comprised of Brazil, Argentina, Uruguay, Paraguay, and Venezuela, has been used by its member states as a mechanism with which to periodically negotiate mutually beneficial trade arrangements while otherwise relying on heavy state intervention to shield members from outside competition.

The recent fall in global oil prices has hurt both Mexico and Brazil, yet despite their many similarities, the stark differences and conflicting interests, not to mention their different historical paths and geopolitical realities, will ensure that the two biggest countries in Latin America remain competitors.

Both countries will continue to struggle to overcome their conflicting imperatives (as the bilateral agreement on vehicle exports signed on March 9, 2015, indicates), but their geopolitical and economic realities will keep dividing the two Latin titans.[23]

From a geopolitical perspective, Latin America is not a unified region, and Washington is primarily concerned with Mexico, Central America, and the Caribbean Basin. Everything south of the Amazon, from Brazil and Ecuador to the tip of Tierra del Fuego, might as well be a world away. Brazil is certainly interested in cultivating ties with the U.S., but Mexico has a far greater share of Washington's attention.

Because of its shared history and location, Mexico is—and will continue to be—geopolitically tied to the U.S. In contrast, from its position of relative independence in South America, Brazil's immediate geopolitical concerns involve members of the MERCOSUR, especially Argentina. Thus, even if Mexico is not considered to be a BRIC country, because it is linked to the U.S. by geography and by NAFTA (and thanks also to its sound macroeconomic fundamentals and fast developing manufacturing sector), its economic future seems brighter.

Brazil on the other hand is far from the U.S., its state remains remarkably inefficient, and its hostile bureaucracy considered a barrier to business. As the declining values of Petrobras and Eletrobras indicate, a crumbling infrastructure and the government's high-handed attitude seems to have repelled the very investors it hoped to attract.

In short, while Mexico seems to be successfully diversifying its economy, Brazil is still strongly dependent on exporting commodities and primary goods.[24]

The limits of cooperation between Mexico and Brazil become particularly evident in the energy sector. Until recently, Brazil's wildly successful state-owned energy firm *Petroleo Brasiliero* could (theoretically) have been willing to share expertise with Mexico's ailing *Petroleos Mexicanos* in a joint venture. It's unlikely at this point, however. For the time being, any aspirations for a significant geopolitical partnership between Brazil and Mexico will remain rhetorical.[25]

Latin America and the Caribbean: A Tale of Two Lefts

As a result of the passing of Venezuela's president Hugo Chávez, Latin America's democratic consolidation once again emerged as a topic of discussion. The democratic status of the area is no longer an issue. Indeed, alongside Europe, the Americas are a region where electoral democracy legally binds the states. Excluding Cuba, the only way a leader in the Western Hemisphere can come to power and claim legitimacy is by means of an election.

Latin America's path toward democratic solidification, which began in the late 1980s or early 1990s, has not been easy, but it has been (for the

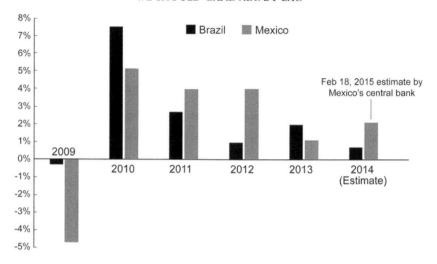

Figure 10.1 Brazilian and Mexican GDP
Source: "Mexico and Brazil Seek a New Trade Deal," *Stratfor*, March 9, 2015.

most part) successful. The achievements of this journey can be measured by the fact that coup d'états, which were a regular occurrence during the 1950s and up to the late 1970s, are now few and far between.

As stated earlier, LAC leaders can only claim legitimacy if they achieve power through electoral means. Yet even when elections take place regularly, a quality of governance problem lingers. Once in office, elected leaders in most Latin American countries find that victory brings serious challenges. For one thing, they find they are accountable to a more educated and vocal society with a growing middle class. This has contributed to the dismantling of many traditional elitist political structures. The new governing elites find it difficult to fulfill their promises and obligations through government structures and institutions that have been severely weakened over the last three decades.

Candidates that come to power demanding accountability often find that the tables are turned. Ironically, whether they are capable or not, they need to respond (or at least be perceived to be responding) to the demands of majorities who will no longer accept disenfranchisement and exclusion, contributing to Latin America's turn to the left. But what kind of left-leaning governments are Latin Americans looking for?

Take Brazil, Latin America's biggest economy, and Cuba, a small island. The two share a common heritage. Both have a history of slavery and sugar, and both are governed by leftist regimes. Yet these leftist governments are very different in at least one respect: socialism has been the only option in Cuba for many decades; in Brazil, however, the left-leaning government has been a matter of choice. These examples illustrate what's happening in the region today: in addition to two distinct economic paths in LAC, there are also two different Latin American lefts, each with its own origins and prospects.[26]

The first left springs from the ideals of classic socialism. This strand heeded the lessons of history and learned from the painful circumstances that brought so much misery to Eastern Europe and contributed to the dismantling of the Soviet empire. As seen in the pragmatic left of Brazil, Chile, and Uruguay, this group aims at achieving economic growth through an open market and the consolidation of democracy while addressing glaring inequalities. They do so through a variety of government-sponsored social programs that aim to lift as many people as possible out of poverty and into the ranks of the middle class.

The second left is born of the great tradition of Latin American populism and emanates from the ingrained *caudillo* tradition. This strand is nationalistic, authoritarian, strident, and closed-minded, and includes countries such as Venezuela, Ecuador, Bolivia, and Argentina. The ideological left claims to represent the disenfranchised and to be on a quest to right traditional wrongs and punish the elitist minority (a goal that they may achieve while their economies suffer). Ironically, some of these goals are gradually being met by the pragmatic left that has more in common with centrist governments in the region (such as the one in Mexico or Colombia) than with their ideological brethren (such as Venezuela).[27]

As explained in Section III, since 2000 the rate of democratization in the countries in the region has been mixed. While democracy is not eroding in Latin America, per se, there are reasons for concern. It is troubling that the advances in democratic governance have not been more widespread in the twenty-first century and that the quality of democracy remains low in a large number of countries. Scott Mainwaring and Aníbal Pérez-Liñán observe, first, that countries with higher levels of socioeconomic development have been more likely to make the journey from transitional to robust democracy—and conversely, that in the poorer countries, fewer people enjoy de facto full citizen rights, and traditional authoritarian patterns of domination tend to be more pervasive. Second, solid states—whether from the left, center or right—underpin robust democracies; in contrast, building democracy in a weak state remains excruciatingly difficult. Third, party systems that are institutionalized and democratic favor high-quality democracy. Such party systems place higher hurdles in the way of political outsiders, who, in the tradition of past *caudillos*, often undermine democracy. Most of LAC's low-quality democracies and competitive-authoritarian regimes are found in poorer countries with weak states and weakly institutionalized party systems where the populist left is increasingly holding to power through authoritarian means.[28] Nevertheless, with all the important obstacles that can still derail their progress, most Latin Americans live in stable democracies with some shortcomings (Brazil, Mexico, Argentina,

Peru, Dominican Republic, El Salvador, and Panama) or in high-quality democracies (Chile, Costa Rica, and Uruguay). Only one dictatorial regime remains (Cuba). These factors matter more than the left or right-leaning slant of an administration.

LAC countries, the U.S., and Canada share the same global neighborhood of the Americas. Since the late 1980s, the Western Hemisphere has aimed to follow a distinctive path. As examined in Chapter 9, nations have, for the most part, been trying to find ways to cooperate by either linking economies through free trade pacts or adopting common norms through the shared principles of democracy. Even though the views of how democracy should work may differ and even considering significant cooperative failures such as ALBA, there has been a trend towards collaboration. This is not to say that the Americas resemble paradise, but that what happens in LAC is important to the global landscape.

Even keeping its flaws and setbacks in mind, Americans in general and Latin Americans in particular are faring better than many others worldwide. More importantly, the U.S. can use its position and influence in the Americas to foster cooperative approaches that could be beneficial to area economies. Washington should take advantage of this potential to strengthen the Western Hemisphere's position in the international system.

There is no question but that serious threats such as weak governments that have allowed organized crime group to thrive, unacceptable levels of inequality and corruption in most countries, weak governments that are not fully accountable to their citizenries or able to control their territories could easily set LAC back once again. Latin America has been on the brink of achieving development before, only to be derailed.

The most likely scenario is that new winners and losers will emerge in the region. For the U.S., this fluid setting will present both challenges and opportunities, and it's important that Washington identifies the "winners" and finds ways to act cooperatively with them. In a world in which the Middle East is unraveling, the power and influence of Europe is declining, China is emerging (yet its economy may be staggering), and Russia is trying to assert its role in their "near abroad," the U.S. can leverage the strength of a relatively peaceful and prosperous neighborhood, and consolidate its position as a leader in world affairs.

Latin America and the Caribbean, and the U.S.

As good neighbors (sometimes reluctantly), the U.S. and Latin America publicly acknowledge the need to find policies that work to advance common interests and solve common problems. In practice, however, they can rarely agree on how to proceed.

Most U.S. presidents begin their terms in office vowing to pay more attention to Latin America. Global crises quickly get in the way, however, and most eventually fail to fulfill that promise. By the time an American president has finished dealing with the Middle East, East Asia, North Africa, or Europe, it is usually time for him to run for re-election or retire, and LAC countries are once again relegated to the sidelines.

On Sunday, January 20, 2013, President Barack Obama was sworn in for his second term. As of 2015, however, other than a promise to work on a thawing of the Cuban embargo, immigration reform, and (maybe) energy cooperation, Mexico and the rest of LAC have failed to garner significant interest from the U.S. Meanwhile, the importance of LAC to the U.S. continues to rise.[29]

Ever since the promulgation of the Monroe Doctrine in the early nineteenth century, U.S. power and influence in LAC has been overwhelming, and continues to be strong today. Yet there is no question that the influence of the U.S. over its southerly neighbors has changed.

For one thing, U.S. trade with Latin America— in terms of both imports and exports—has grown from 18.9 percent of U.S. total worldwide trade to 21.6 percent over the past decade. At the same time, the percentage of trade between the largest Latin American economies—Mexico, Colombia, Venezuela, Brazil, and Argentina—and the U.S. has decreased dramatically. For instance, the U.S. accounted for nearly a quarter of Brazil's overall trade in 2002, but the figure was only 12.5 percent in 2011. Similarly, in 2002 three-quarters of Mexico's overall trade was with the U.S, but this fell to 64.2 percent in 2011. Although this is still quite a high figure, it is remarkable that the overall trade between these two NAFTA members has diminished over time.

As Latin America becomes more important to the U.S. in economic terms, the U.S. becomes relatively less important to Latin Americans looking elsewhere for trade and investment opportunities. The fact that the Nicaraguan government has approved plans by a Chinese businessman to promote the construction of a new canal is a case in point.[30] Whether this ambitious project goes forward or not remains to be seen, but there is no question that Nicaragua's overtures to China and Washington's apparent indifference to these overtures mark a clear departure from the traditional U.S. dominance model in LAC.

It's still fresh in the minds of Latin Americans that Washington has frequently emphasized its exceptional influence and right to consolidate its bastion of power over the Americas. In fact, all through the twentieth century the Western Hemisphere was considered as a "separate sphere" where the U.S. could execute its expanding global power. Different U.S. administrations could try out foreign policies in Washington's own backyard before exporting them to other parts of the globe.[31] Today, Washington seems rather unconcerned about the Americas, an attitude that Latin American decision-makers find disconcerting.

In today's global climate, U.S. authorities seem to be more interested in pursuing economic cooperation with the winners of economic development (and ignoring the apparent losers), which has not always been the case, as described in previous chapters. As long as LAC states don't present a direct threat to the U.S., they've apparently been granted political leeway to decide what kind of government to choose and which markets to cultivate. The fact that a free trade effort like the Pacific Alliance,[32] for example, champions economics over military and security priorities or political ideology, is very telling, especially given strong U.S. support.

In sharp contrast to previous foreign policies pursued by Washington, it seems that current U.S. administrations are no longer interested in directly intervening in LAC's domestic affairs. Furthermore, as the efforts to improve ties with Havana appear to indicate, it seems that Washington is no longer particularly interested in pursuing a common security front or even in further fostering a community of American democracies.

For now, given that it's become "the most peaceful region in the world," Washington seems to trust Latin America to find its own way, and can even afford to disengage from LAC in order to deal with sudden regime changes and serious threats elsewhere.[33]

The question is, where is Latin America heading?

While Washington is trying to find ways to disentangle from Iraq or Afghanistan, deal with Iran or Russia, or face the threat of ISIS and other extremist groups, Latin Americans are navigating an exciting-yet-unsettling new path. In addition to expanding trade horizons, the Americas have been experiencing intriguing developments, especially in terms of common interests and looming threats. With the end of the Cold War, the idea of a communist threat that needs to be confronted has all but disappeared. Furthermore, the U.S. "shale revolution" and cheaper oil, the recovery of the U.S. economy after the recent financial collapse, the death of Hugo Chávez, and the imminent passing of Fidel Castro have all seriously undermined the hard-core Latin American left.

The radical ideology championed by these leaders has been undermined by the success of the moderate left, as well as by the economic reality gradually pushing Argentina toward financial disaster, Caracas toward economic and political disintegration, and Havana toward political moderation. The leftist regimes of Ecuador or Bolivia, for example, and anti-elitist regimes such as Argentina's may need to temper their populist style and message to follow the Brazilian model more closely, and all without overt U.S. intervention.

Secondly, many LAC countries are experiencing profound crises of governability. These crises of rule of law are the unintended consequences of the first generation of market reforms that swept the region during the Third Wave of Democratization in the 1980s and 1990s. Without long-standing U.S. support, Latin American authoritarian regimes began to be replaced by democratically elected regimes that inherited weak institutional structures further affected by the forced downsizing of the neoliberal reforms.

Small and inefficient security forces and government bureaucracies allowed organized crime organizations—such as the drug cartels—to operate with impunity. While they're clearly more democratic, Latin America's government institutions have continued to weaken, affecting their ability to control territories and uphold the rule of law and allowing organized crime groups to fill the void.

Nevertheless, it seems that excluding extreme cases such as Guatemala, Honduras, or Haiti, Latin American societies have learned to live with the drug trade. This has been more necessity than choice since Washington does not see it as an existential threat (as many Latin Americans do), and therefore has not prioritized it.

Take Mexico, for example. In much of the country, especially the industrialized north, drug cartels operate and violence continues. Nevertheless, according to the World Bank, in 2011 Mexico had the world's 14th largest economy and may edge higher in the near future.[34] Mexico is one of the freest trading countries in the world and enjoys a more diversified and more stable economy than most of its commodity-dependent LAC neighbors. Yet at the same time, security threats such as corruption, predatory crimes, and extortion scandals reflect a glaring lack of rule of law and a great deal of social malaise. These contrasting realities reflect where Latin Americans find themselves today, at a critical juncture full of opportunities and difficulties.[35]

Colombia is another case in point. Compared to what is happening in North Africa, for example, the threats of guerrilla warfare that once swept many parts of the Southern Cone seem to be waning. With groups such as the Revolutionary Armed Forces of Colombia (FARC) in clear retreat, the Colombian government now feels secure and strong enough to negotiate with the diminished but still present FARC remnants. In the meantime, however, the current administration has made clear its intention of pursuing a military campaign against the FARC and other organized criminal groups that continue to generate violence. As a result, although the government is still confronting guerrillas, Colombia's economy grew 5.9 percent last year, and will likely grow 4.5 percent or more next year. Furthermore, in spite of persisting violence and security challenges, Colombia has pushed through a range of reforms including a fiscal rule and a change to the way oil and mining revenues are distributed in order to tackle the nation's deficits. In spite of the looming threat of leftist guerrillas and drug cartels, Colombia has attracted billions of dollars in foreign direct investment over the last decade.[36]

Marking a big change in the history of public debt in Latin America (excluding countries such as Venezuela, Ecuador, or Argentina) and in sharp contrast with Europe or the U.S. today, Latin American countries are making every effort to control their public debt.

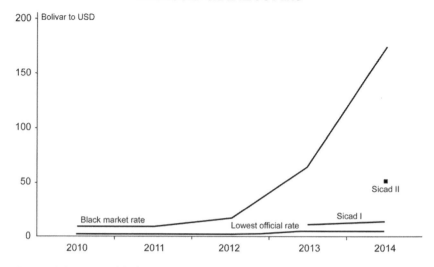

Figure 10.2 Venezuela's foreign exchange rates
Source: *Stratfor*, "Venezuela's Economic Measures Leave Crisis Unresolved," February 12, 2015.

Taking past experiences to heart, Latin American authorities began to improve debt composition well before the 2008 financial crisis, hence they proved less vulnerable to the global shocks in the aftermath of the Lehman Brothers' collapse.

Although there is a much room for improvement, Latin American elites have become more responsible and accountable. But, corruption, very high levels of criminality, and low tax revenues continue to hinder many Latin American governments' capacity to govern effectively—indeed, corruption and a lax approach to the application of the rule of law may be the main culprits behind Latin America's current underdevelopment. And when it comes to the implementation of cooperative policies, these issues have been the main source of distrust by Washington. Despite Latin America's economic growth and diminishing poverty rates, when it comes to corruption, Transparency International still places two-thirds of the region's countries among the world's worst offenders.[37]

This certainly isn't good news, but there is room for hope. In recent years, countries such as Uruguay and Chile (with a perception of corruption score of 73 according to the 2014 Transparency International report, www.transparency.org/cpi2014/infographic/global) seem to be breaking the mold. There is positive momentum toward anti-corruption efforts in Brazil, and in Mexico, civil society seems to be less tolerant of government corruption, as evidenced by the protests regarding the first lady's house and the death of the students.[38] Awareness of the existence of corruption does not in itself solve these problems, but considering the NIC megatrends (namely, the diffusion of power and individual empowerment), the fact that Latin

Americans are becoming more aware and less tolerant of corruption and impunity does have significance. According to the last *Latinobarómetro* report, in sharp contrast with the past, electoral democracy is a right many citizens have come to expect and as a result, governability and accountability is something Latin American citizens not only hope but also, have started to demand. Slowly, economic and political leaders are being forced (especially through the free press and social media) to find ways to avoid overt corruption and abuses of power. They are very much aware that they can no longer easily sweep illegal actions under the carpet, nor can they count on U.S. support to literally get away with murder.[39]

Economist and politicians have become aware that corruption directly affects the quality of their institutions, infrastructure, and education, and influences the decisions of investors who are taking a calculated risk. Decision-makers are realizing that these inefficiencies stand in the way of productivity and economic growth.

Latin American nations with freer trade policies have generally focused on areas where they have a competitive advantage (such as exporting commodities), but many are now exploring new and more dynamic areas.

Peru is a case in point. In spite of a deficit in good governance as well as an insufficient infrastructure and poor education system, the Peruvian economy has been growing by an average of 6.4 percent per year since 2002. Growth in 2010 was close to 9 percent and in 2011 almost 7 percent, due partly to a leap in private investment, especially in the extractive sector, which accounts for more than 60 percent of Peru's total exports. This is not the first time Peru has bet its economic growth on the commodity lottery. It remains to be seen whether Peru will take this opportunity to invest in and develop other sectors of the economy.[40]

While Latin America's economic growth may be the result of a rebound in commodity prices, there is no doubt that the region's strong performance is also the result of well-managed macroeconomic policies. Nevertheless, while attending to their financial stability, these Latin American governments tend to become complacent about ridding their government institutions, security forces, and judiciaries of inefficiencies and corruption, a dangerous stance considering the rapid growth of their middle classes. The countries of Latin America need to address these issues sooner rather than later if they wish to sustain their current growth rate, meet the needs of their populations, and catch up with their East Asian counterparts.[41]

Why Latin America and the Caribbean Matter

If Asian economies like China and India can avoid the middle-income trap and manage their natural resources effectively, it's perfectly possible that they'll grow to become important centers of power. There's increasing competition between the U.S. and China over who will write the rules of the twenty-first century global economy. Beijing's effort to create the Asia Infrastructure Investment Bank (AIIB)—an alternative to the World Bank or IMF—is a case in point.[42]

The AIIB represents a challenge to not only the IMF and World Bank but also the new global economic architecture Washington is trying to forge through the Trans-Pacific Partnership (TPP) (in which the North American countries through NAFTA and Colombia, Chile, Mexico, Peru and recently Costa Rica through the Pacific Alliance have an important role to play), combined with the trade agreement currently in discussion with the EU.

Washington cannot just simply oppose these new institutions, especially when other Western countries (the UK for example) have begun to actively participate. The unipolar moment in which the U.S. dictated all rules of the game seems to be a thing of the past. Nevertheless, the U.S. will likely remain *primus inter pares* among other great powers. Of course, this is dependent on the U.S.'s ability to reinvent the international order and carve out a new role for itself in an expanded and multipolar world. This position will be sustained only if the U.S. can reinvigorate its own economy (and those of its close trade partners) and secure its energy independence—achievable, but challenging, goals.

Washington would benefit greatly if it paid more attention to its own neighborhood, where cooperative arrangements such as NAFTA, the Pacific Alliance, and even established organizations such as the OAS have such important roles to play. At the same time, Washington also needs to pay attention to possible LAC spoilers: the troubled spots in the Andean region, and the weak and failing states in Central America and the Caribbean. If it takes advantage of the good and pays proper attention to the bad elements of the Americas, the U.S. can only advance its position on the world stage. In this scenario, what's good for the U.S. can also benefit LAC states.[43]

The best way for the U.S. to achieve fair free trade with China, India, and other emerging economies is to negotiate from a position of strength. To achieve this position of strength, the U.S. must collaborate with its neighbors. As Robert Pastor correctly asserts,[44] if the NAFTA members (Canada, the U.S., and Mexico, which represent three levels of power and development in the world) decided to approach China together on issues related to currency, unfair trade practices, security, and even climate change, North America would have a much better chance of success than if each nation pursued these issues on their own. The U.S. was able to play the role of world leader during and after World War II largely because President Franklin D. Roosevelt had spent the previous eight years repairing U.S. relations with Latin America through the "Good Neighbor Policy." The same can be said for President John F. Kennedy and the 1961 "Alliance for Progress."

It's true that LAC and the U.S. still face serious problems and security threats, as well as a history of mutual distrust. Moving forward, however, the interests of the most important LAC economies and the U.S. seem to be converging, and working towards collaborative policies would be a significant step forward. Competition for power is still an important element in international relations, but in a fast-changing world it's manifesting itself in many different ways. In this new environment, the U.S. and LAC are no longer fighting for territory or ideological dominance in the region as they did in the past, and this presents a unique opportunity. The U.S. and LAC countries which want to seize this opportunity need to be able to compete for markets worldwide, strengthen their economies, and become less vulnerable to external shocks and violence due to crime, corruption, and possible security threats that come from other parts of the globe.

Washington can achieve more clout on the world stage if it gains the support of other countries in the region, especially if (as in the case of Brazil, and Mexico) they happen to be among the biggest world economies, or (as in the case of Chile, Colombia, Uruguay, Costa Rica, Peru, or Panama) if they can offer a collaborative advantage. Whether future U.S. presidents choose a Latin American cooperative foreign policy, a limited partnership, a unilateral stance, or indifference remains to be seen. Clearly, Washington will be able to more effectively project its power worldwide if it first achieves stable security and a robust economy in its own neighborhood.

Overall, the examples presented in this book show that Latin America and its role in and importance to the international system has changed dramatically for the better. Some of the countries of LAC are significantly more important today—in both global economic and security terms—than at any time in the region's history, and LAC is increasingly able to exercise national and regional autonomy in international affairs.

The challenges that remain have been discussed throughout this volume, and include widespread inequalities, high rates of poverty, a heavy dependence on commodity exports, and a low diversification of key industries. Even considering those elements, however, there are many signs that point towards a brighter future for this significant region.

Whether or not Latin America, led by key countries such as Brazil and Mexico, will achieve its promise in the twenty-first century remains an open question. The evidence presented in this volume points to the possibility that it will. Whether it does or does not, however, one thing is clear: the future of LAC is important to the future of the world.

Main points:

- With the rise of the economies in the Far East, the Americas (Canada, the U.S., and LAC) are now the midpoint of the international system.
- The U.S. has the opportunity to leverage the strength of acting cooperatively with LAC, a relatively prosperous and peaceful neighborhood, especially when compared to other regions in the world.

- Great obstacles for LAC development remain, such as: the ability of all American economies, including the U.S. and Canada, to sustain a rate of economic growth; the inability or unwillingness by LAC state authorities and economic elites to deal with authoritarian tendencies, organized crime, and corruption; the consolidation of LAC democracies through the rule of law; and the lack of investment in infrastructure, health, and education to deal with persistent inequality.
- Whether or not LAC—now more interconnected than ever to the legal and illegal capitalist international system—will benefit from this strategic advantage in the future and whether or not the U.S. will make it a priority to help them accomplish this goal remains to be seen.
- One way or another, what happens in LAC matters greatly to the future of the world.

Notes

1 Read more at www.brainyquote.com/quotes/quotes/a/alberteins125368.html#yTveoUEwRDL7XFvp.99

2 "The Financial and Economic Crisis of 2008–2009 and Developed Countries," United Nations Conference on Trade and Development (UNCTAD) and Hochschule für Technik and Wirstschaft, Berlin, ed. Sebastian Dullien, Detlef J. Kotte, Alejandro Márquez, and Jan Oriewe (December 2010).

3 In the second week of December 2012, the National Intelligence Council (NIC) published its quadrennial report, on how the world could look like twenty years from now. The report, titled "Global Trends 2030, Alternative Worlds" starts by pointing out that the world is rapidly changing and that, as in 1815, 1919, 1945, and 1989, it's at a critical juncture with different possible outcomes. "Global Trends 2030: Alternative Worlds," National Intelligence Council, 2012 (https://globaltrends2030.files.wordpress.com/2012/11/global-trends-2030-november2012.pdf).

4 This report imagines many possible scenarios that could come as a result of important mega-trends such as the diffusion of power, individual empowerment, or the increasing demand for food, water and energy; of game changers such as a volatile global economy and wider regional instability; and choices by leaders and decision-makers responding to these tendencies and major events. For the complete report go to "Global Trends 2030: Alternative Worlds," National Intelligence Council (www.acus.org/files/global-trends-2030-nic-lo.pdf). See also Phillip S. Stephens, "In Tomorrow's World, It's the State Versus the Individual," *Financial Times*, Comment, December 14, 2012, 9.

5 The greater integration of the Americas through Free Trade Agreements (FTAs) with the North America Free Trade Agreement (FTAA) has expanded to multiple regional and extra-regional FTAs, especially via Canada, Chile, Colombia, Mexico, and Peru. With annual real GDP growth averaging 4 percent, the ranks of the middle class have swelled, along with greater economic and political participation by women, indigenous peoples, and minority groups, many of whom have benefited from greater access to education and health services. "Global Trends 2030: Alternative Worlds," National Intelligence Council (www.acus.org/files/global-trends-2030-nic-lo.pdf, 84). See also Robin Wigglesworth,

"Caribbean in Crisis: Checkbook Diplomacy," *Financial Times*, Analysis, December 17, 2013 (www.ft.com/intl/cms/s/0/7f7b0d8e-5ea8-11e3-8621-001 44feabdc0.html?siteedition=intl#axzz2nnJ5jXDN).

6 Zellick points out that the NAFTA partners need to work more closely in order to advance a unified position in global diplomatic and economic debates. They could also cooperate more on security and help each other improve the efficacy of their governments. Of course, not all is said and done. The NAFTA partners need to update and link their energy and border infrastructures, do more to manage human capital and address the prickly subject of immigration, as well as look after environmental resources. Already included in the TPP discussions, Canada and Mexico should also have a role in the EU–US negotiations someday, as Zoellick argues, for clear strategic reasons. The "global weight of three democracies of almost 500 million people," self-sufficient in energy and with an integrated infrastructure as well as interlinked manufacturing and services industries and a common foreign policy outlook would be substantial. With that, North America would be well positioned to contend with 1.3 billion Chinese. For more see Part II and Shawn Donnan, "The Future of NAFTA: World Faces up to an Era of Regional Agreements," *Financial Times*, December 2, 2013 (www.ft.com/intl/cms/s/0/b4371e1e-4c51-11e3-923d-00144feabdc0.html#axz z2mVrxlwRx).

7 The recovery from the "lost decade" aimed to restore some balance to the government's fiscal policies and control inflation. During the 1980s and 1990s, the majority of Latin America governments were able to reduce or eliminate fiscal deficit, an incredible accomplishment, and while not always smooth, in most countries balanced budgets have become the norm. This has allowed central banks in the region to pursue monetary policies more in line with price stability. For more see Javier A. Reyes and Charles W. Sawyer, *Latin American Economic Development* (London and New York: Routledge, 2011).

8 Countries can indeed take advantage of economic crises that come from a financial collapse. For instance, following the Asian financial crisis of 1997/8, South Korea accepted a tough bailout package from the IMF, strengthened its financial system, and increased the flexibility of its labor markets. Soon thereafter it enjoyed an economic boom. In Mexico the economy has performed well since the collapse of the peso and the subsequent 1994 U.S. rescue package. A similar phenomenon took place in other parts of Latin America following the sovereign debt crises of the late 1980s. Although these financial crises were small compared to the 2008 collapse of the U.S. sub-prime crisis, they followed the same pattern, one characterized by allowing a rejection of the old-order capital markets to induce a major economic restructuring. In other words, it is possible to say that Latin America may have finally learned to take advantage of its time and place in history. Roger C. Altman, "The Fall and Rise of the West: Why America and Europe will Emerge Stronger from the Financial Crisis," *Foreign Affairs*, New York, January/February, 2013, 8–13.

9 The international system is at a crossroads today because of a financial crisis that originated in the subprime mortgage market. This made for a slower, longer, and more turbulent economic recovery than would have been the case if the recession had come about as a consequence of a business cycle. Carmen N. Reinhart and Kenneth S. Rogoff, *The Second Great Contradiction: From This time is Different* (Princeton, NJ: Princeton University Press, 2011); Javier A. Reyes and Charles W. Sawyer, *Latin American Economic Development* (London and New York: Routledge, 2011).

10 Reyes and Sawyer, *Latin American Economic Development*, 84–85.

WE SHOULD CARE ABOUT LAC

11 In Venezuela, for example, where just re-elected (but subsequently deceased) President Hugo Chávez had nationalized much of the private sector, the economy was on track to expand by 5 percent in one year, thanks to an election-related government spending spree. As 2013 rolled along, however, government spending decreased and ceased to work its magic. Government interventions and price controls have increased during President Cristina Kirchner's administration in Argentina, which together with a number of controversial reforms (including an initiative to restrict imports unless matched by exports) have damaged even further the nation's prospect for growth and prosperity. In sharp contrast, Peru has been on a remarkable run. In the past ten years it has had the region's highest average annual growth, around 6 percent, which has helped halve the nation's poverty rate to 27 percent over that time, according to government statistics. Chile isn't far behind, growing at an average 4.5 percent clip during the same period. Peru, Chile, and Colombia have embraced free trade and are better for it. They have strong macroeconomics fundamentals and are therefore attracting foreign investment. In contrast, Brazil used its position as commodities exporter to protect local industries with tariffs and regulations, a model that worked very well when commodity prices soared in 2003, but now that prices have fallen, Brazil's economy is slowing. Sara Shaefer Muñoz, "Latin Growth Plays in Two Speeds," *World Street Journal*, December 1, 2012, A10.

12 Reforms to make it easier to hire and fire staff, strip the powerful education union of its power and allow for an evaluation of teachers, implement PEMEX modernization in the energy sector, update the tax system, and overhaul the telecommunications and TV sectors to allow for more competition would all— if implemented—bode well for the future of Mexico. Adam Thomson, "Bloody but Booming," *Financial Times*, Analysis, June 21, 2012, 7; Adam Thomson, "China's Unlikely Challenger," *Financial Times*, Analysis, September 11, 2012, 7; Adam Thomson, "Diverging Paths in Latin America; Early Success for President Raises Hopes for Mexico Economy," *Financial Times*, Word News, March 8, 2013, 4. A deal on the Trans-Pacific Partnership trade pact was reached on October 5, 2015. *Stratfor*, "TPP Deal Reached, Official Says," Pacific Rim, October 5, 2015.

13 During the first decade of the twenty-first century, the balance of power has shifted between Latin America and Europe. Spain and Portugal have been hit by their worst economic crisis in decades and their economies are expected to remain in recession. In addition to the abundance of commodities, a resurgent democracy has helped spur greater stability and investment in Latin America. Seeking trade with Spain and Portugal from a position of strength, Chilean President Sebastián Piñeira said during a November 2012 summit that Latin America is living a true renaissance. Ilan Brat and Patricia Kowsmann, "Iberian States, Latin America Seek Ties in Trade," *Wall Street Journal*, World News, November 19, 2012, 9A.

14 See "Growth: Will Brazil Remain the Country of the Future?" *The Economist*, October 8, 2012 (www.economist.com/blogs/freeexchange/2012/10/growth).

15 See "Brazil's Economy, All Systems Slow," *The Economist*, July 26, 2014 (www.economidt.com/news/americas/21608643-confidence-and-growth-public-spen ding-up-all-systems-slow).

16 Anthony Boadle, "Petrobras' Scandal about to Hit Brazil's Political Class," *Reuters*, February 25, 2015 (www.reuters.com/article/2015/02/25/us-brazil-p etrobras-politicians-idUSKBN0LT2DP20150225).

17 See "Growth: Will Brazil Remain the Country of the Future?" *The Economist*, October 8, 2012 (www.economist.com/blogs/freeexchange/2012/10/growth).

18 Unlike Mexico's export-driven growth model, however, Brazil relies relatively little on international trade. Roughly 10 percent of its $2.5 trillion annual economy comes from exports—a dynamic that stems in large part from the slow but substantial development of Brazil's internal economy. "The Limits of a Brazilian–Mexican Partnership," *Stratfor*, September 21, 2012 (www.stratfor.com/weekly/evolving-latin-america).

19 A preliminary UN report expected that developing countries and economies in transition, such as the BRICs, would continue to fuel the engine of the world economy. Please see "Global Trends 2030: Alternative Worlds," National Intelligence Council, 2012 (https://globaltrends2030.files.wordpress.com/2012/11/global-trends-2030-november2012.pdf).

20 Fareed Zakaria, "How America Can Survive the Rise of the Rest," *Foreign Affairs*, May/June 2008 (www.foreignaffairs.com/articles/63394/fareed-zakaria/the-future-of-american-power).

21 In fact, Mexico is trying to address important issues such as education, tax, and pension reform. Many of these reforms, such as those involving the teachers' union, are generating significant controversy and scattered unrest, and implementing the changes made in the first months of President Enrique Peña Nieto's administration will take years. Nevertheless, it is worth noting that the most important issue facing Mexico in 2013 was energy policy. Over the course of the year, details about Mexico's plans for encouraging the additional investment in the energy sector that is needed to revive flagging production started to emerge. So far, there is sufficient support for the governing Institutional Revolutionary Party (PRI) at the state level to permit Peña Nieto to seriously consider the possibility of a constitutional reform that would allow the country to adopt production-sharing agreements. Meanwhile the government will continue fighting cartels using the military, while Peña Nieto implements organizational changes to law enforcement and the military. Annual Forecast, 2013, *Stratfor* (www.stratfor.com/forecast/annual-forecast-2013#LatinAmerica).

22 "Mexico and Brazil Seek a New Trade Deal," *Stratfor*, March 9, 2015.

23 According to *Stratfor*, "Brazil: Automobile Agreement Signed with Mexico," March 10, 2015; in 2002, MERCOSUR states and Mexico signed the Accord of Economic Cooperation, reducing tariffs on vehicles and auto parts in an effort to encourage automobile trade among the custom union's trade members. These provisions, which turned out to be very beneficial to Mexico, expired in March of 2015. On March 9, 2015, a new bilateral automobile agreement was signed, foreseeing free trade between the two countries within four years. The agreement sets an initial $1.56 billion limit for automobile exports between the two countries, exclusive of import tax, but the amount will increase to $1.7 billion in 2018. In response to Brazil's trade deficit in the automobile sector, Brazil and Mexico signed an agreement in 2012 to limit assembled vehicles from Mexico to Brazil to $1.55 billion per year until March 18, 2015. This bilateral agreement demonstrates how these countries are still struggling to overcome their conflicting geopolitical imperatives.

24 For a complete report see "Global Economic Situation and Prospects 2012: Global Economic Outlook, Pre-release," United Nations, New York (www.un.org/en/development/desa/policy/wesp/wesp_current/2012wesp_prerel.pdf). Also "Stalled: A Long-Awaited Recovery Still Fails to Materialize," *The Economist*, December 8, 2012 (www.economist.com/news/americas/21567945-long-awaited-recovery-still-fails-materialise-stalled).

25 *Stratfor*, "Limits of a Brazilian–Mexican Partnership."

WE SHOULD CARE ABOUT LAC

26 The two paths of the Latin American left were identified first by Jorge Castañeda, "Latin America's Left Turn," *Foreign Affairs*, May/June, 2006 (www.foreignaffairs.com/articles/61702/jorge-g-castaneda/latin-americas-left-turn).

27 Latin America's turn to the left began after the Asian and Russian crises of 1997, when the world's attention was drawn back to the continent. The democratic transition that began in the 1980s had favored centrist governments and the liberal economic policies of the "Washington Consensus." When Russian and Asian economies crumbled, however, Latin America suffered a recession so deep it was called "the lost decade." As a result, poverty rose and the political pendulum swung to the left. By 2009, 20 republics had left or center-left governments. Economically, this could not have happened at a better time. From 2003 onwards the region began to ride a boom in commodity prices, which strengthened government finances and allowed an increase in social spending. The pragmatic left, composed of technocrats and social democrats, followed a path similar to those of other leftist governments after the fall of the Berlin Wall in 1989, acknowledging the failures of the Soviet experiment and choosing to restructure. The ideological strand, rooted in Latin American populism, followed a clientelist model and began spending money with abandon. Closely advised by Havana, Chávez, for example, went so far as to set his sights on a Pan-American revolution against the U.S. by means of ALBA. Interestingly, not many followed his example. Today, after the worst recession in recent memory, about half of Latin American republics are centrist or center-right. This is not to say that the Latin American populist left has completely lost all influence. It is important to keep in mind that these models came to power with the idea of addressing deep societal inequalities. The poor performance of these populist regimes—with Venezuela standing out as a prime example—discredited the Chavista-like model of governance. Particularly in the aftermath of the global economic crisis, this state-centric model is proving to be unsustainable. With Chávez gone, Venezuela in particular is witnessing its potential role as a leader of the region slip away. John Paul Rathbone, "What's Left of the Latin American Left?" *Financial Times*, Analysis, March 9, 2013, 5.

28 Scott Mainwaring and Aníbal Pérez-Liñan, "Cross-Currents in Latin America," *Journal of Democracy*, vol. 26, no. 1 (2015), 114–127.

29 Robert D. Kaplan, "Evolving Latin America," *Stratfor*, December 12, 2012 (www.stratfor.com/weekly/evolving-latin-america).

30 *Stratfor*, "How a Chinese Billionaire Got Invested in Nicaragua's Canal Plan," March 5, 2015.

31 Brian Loveman, *No Higher Law: American Foreign Policy and the Western Hemisphere since 1776* (Chapel Hill, NC: University of North Carolina Press, 2010), 4.

32 The Pacific Alliance is a Latin American free trade block, formally launched in June 2012, with an orientation toward Asian markets such as Singapore. The members of the block are Chile, Colombia, Mexico, and Peru. Associate members are Canada, Costa Rica, Panama, Uruguay, Japan, Guatemala, Spain, Australia, New Zealand, and Portugal.

33 Even when including problematic spots such as parts of Central America, the security environment in Latin America is relatively benign, especially compared to other regions in the Third World. When it comes to this region, the U.S. is more concerned with the disruption that local security and social problems could cause with regard to Latin America's insertion into the new global economy. Arie M. Kacowicz, *The Impact of Norms in International Society: The Latin American Experience, 1881–2001* (Notre Dame, IN: University of Notre Dame Press, 2005); Arie M. Kacowicz, "Latin America and the World: Globalization,

LATIN AMERICA AND THE CARIBBEAN ON THE WORLD STAGE

Regionalization, and Fragmentation," *Nueva Sociedad*, no. 214, March/April (2008) (www.nuso.org/upload/articulos/3513_2.pdf); Robert D. Kaplan, "Evolving Latin America," *Stratfor*, December 12, 2012 (www.stratfor.com/weekly/evolving-latin-america).

34 IMF, "World Economic Outlook," April 2012 (www.imf.org/external/pubs/ft/weo/2012/01/weodata/index.aspx). Mexico's economy used to be marred by tariffs and trade controls, but in 1994 NAFTA eliminated tariffs between Canada and the U.S. and, over time, Mexico's economy became more competitive. Today, Mexico boasts free trade deals with 44 countries, more than any other nation. Multinational corporations seem unconcerned that drug cartels represent a clear and present danger to Mexico's society. German companies turn out electrical components for Europe, Canadian firms assemble aircraft parts, and factory after factory makes televisions, fridge-freezers, and much more. Astonishingly, organized crime does not get in the way of multinational companies, and the looming threat of China's cheap manufacturing is gradually diminishing. Drug wars or not, each year Mexico exports manufactured goods at about the same value as the rest of Latin America put together. "Señores, Start your Engines. Special Report, Mexico," *The Economist*, vol. 405, no. 8812, 5–6. Also Adam Thomson, "China's unlikely Challenger," *Financial Times*, Analysis, September 11, 2012, 7; Adam Thomson, "Bloody but Booming," *Financial Times*, Analysis, June 21, 2012, 7.

35 John Paul Rathbone, "Mexico: Lawlessness Undermines Reforms and Economic Progress," *Financial Times*, March, 3, 2015 (www.ft.com/intl/cms/s/0/2ad7088a-b69c-11e4-95dc-00144feab7de.html#axzz3U6XGQjfE).

36 "Cocaine Complicates Talks in Colombia," *Stratfor*, March 15, 2015.

37 *Transparency International*, "Corruption Perceptions Index 2014" (www.transparency.org/cpi2014/results).

38 This refers to the student protests during the summer of 2012 against the Institutional Revolutionary Party's (PRI) undue influence on the media. The Yo Soy 132 protests challenged the political elite's hold on the TV networks, as well as past PRI corruption and authoritarian practices, making clear that this behavior will no longer be so easily overlooked. For more see, for example, Yo Soy 132, "Por Una Democracia Auténtica" (http://yosoy132.mx).

39 For more detailed information see Latinobarómetro, "Informe 1995–2015" (www.latinobarometro.org/INFORME_LB_2015.pdf); *The Economist*, "The Latinobarómetro Poll: When the Tide Goes Out," The Americas, September 26–October 2, 2015; *Transparency International*, "The Americas: Economies Grow, Democracies Shrink: What Does Corruption Have To Do With It?" December 5, 2012 (http://blog.transparency.org/2012/12/05/the-americas-economes-grow-democracies-shrink-what-does-corruption-have-to-do-with-it/ and "Corruption Perceptions Index 2012," *Transparency International* (http://cpi.transparency.org/cpi2012/results/); Latinobarómetro, "2011 Report" (www.emol.com/documentos/archivos/2011/10/28/20111028141231.pdf), 50–53. Also John Paul Rathbone, "Mexico: Lawlessness Undermines Reforms and Economic Progress," *Financial Times*, March 3, 2015 (www.ft.com/intl/cms/s/0/2ad7088a-b69c-11e4-95dc-00144feab7de.html#axzz3U6XGQjfE).

40 Since 2006, Peru has signed trade deals with the U.S., Canada, Singapore, China, Korea, Mexico, and Japan; concluded negotiations with the European Free Trade Association and Chile; and begun trade talks with Central American and other countries. The U.S.–Peru Trade Promotion Agreement came into play on February 1, 2009, and trade agreements with South Korea, Japan, and Mexico were also signed in 2011. Today, in spite of all the rhetoric, the elected

WE SHOULD CARE ABOUT LAC

leftist leader Ollanta Humalla is committed to continuing down the free trade path. In spite of concerns with its exchange rate and credit-fueled housing boom, not to mention its weak educational system and political fragility, foreign direct investment is flooding into Peru and its economy is growing faster than anywhere else in the region except for Panama. For more see "Annual Forecast, 2013," *Stratfor*, January 7, 2013. Also "Colombia's Economy to Grow Around 4.5 pct in 2013—IMF," *Reuters*, December 11, 2012 (www.reuters. com/article/2012/12/11/colombia-economy-imf-idUSL1E8NBE0A20121211); Peru's Economy Profile, 2012, *Index-mundi* (www.indexmundi.com/peru/ economy_profile.html); "Peru's Roaring Economy: Hold on Tight," *The Economist*, February 2, 2013 (www.economist.com/news/americas/21571162-biggest-threa ts-latin-americas-economic-star-are-overconfidence-and-complacency-hold).

41 Global markets despise opaque and inefficient regimes. A major lesson from the success of East Asia is the value of pursuing longer-term, pragmatic policies based on market principles with clean, transparent, and measured government intervention. It would behoove Washington and LAC governments to support public–private partnerships all over the Americas, where the government would invest in infrastructure and education with the objective of guaranteeing out-comes of increased productivity across regional economies and increased per-capita incomes and decreased inequality. Claudio Loser, "Latin America in the Age of Globalization: A Follower or Force of its Own?" Center for Hemispheric Policy, University of Miami, June 11, 2012; Scott Mainwaring and Anibal Pérez-Liñan, "Democratic Breakdown and Survival," *Journal of Democracy*, vol. 24, no. 2 (2013), 123–137; Sebastian L. Mazzuca, "The Rise of Rentier Populism," *Journal of Democracy*, vol. 24, no.2 (2013), 108–122.

42 It's seen as representing a direct political challenge to the Washington-based institutions in which the U.S. has been the dominant voice since their founda-tion after World War II. For more see Geoff Dyer "Bank Dispute Fuels US-China Rivalry," *Financial Times*, US Politics and Policy, March 13, 2015 (www. ft.com/intl/cms/s/0/f59ed7d4-c90a-11e4-bc64-00144feab7de.html#a xzz3UGhD8J24); and Jonathan Wheatley, "Q&A: the Asia Infrastructure Investment Bank," *Financial Times*, Beyond BRICS, March 12, 2015 (www.ft. com/intl/cms/s/0/bf9c0-c8c8-11e4-b43b-00144feab7de.html?siteedition=intl# axzz3UGhD8J24).

43 The region is still plagued by extreme rates of poverty and continues to present the worst wealth and income inequality patterns in the world. More impor-tantly, its journey toward modern economic development has been encumbered by heavy dependence on primary production of oil, minerals and agricultural commodities, and its limited diversification in basic industries, high technology, and key service sectors such as banking, insurance, and research and develop-ment. Perhaps the major obstacles to Latin America's emergence as a key region are internal and political such as deeply rooted social and political exclusion, criminal violence, and weak political institutions. There has also been some deterioration in democratic practices and institutions in countries like Venezuela, Nicaragua and Honduras, and in such critical issues like freedom of the press. These obstacles could potentially stifle or thwart Latin America's advancement toward a greater role in the global system over the first half of the twenty-first century. For more on the importance of human agency in societies with insti-tutions that are not ambitious in their design, see Steve Levitsky and Maria Victoria Murillo, "Building Institutions on Weak Foundations," *Journal of Democracy*, vol. 24, no. 2 (2013), 93–107. For rentier and plebiscitarian Latin American democracies see Sebastián L. Mazzuca, "The Rise of Rentier

Populism," *Journal of Democracy*, vol. 24, no. 2 (2013), 108–122. And for the evolution of radicalism and normative support for democracy overtime see Scott Mainwaring and Anibal Pérez-Liñan, "Democratic Breakdown and Survival," *Journal of Democracy*, vol. 24, no. 2 (2013), 123–127.

44 Robert A. Pastor, *The North American Idea: A Vision of a Continental Future* (Oxford and New York: Oxford University Press, 2011); Robert A. Pastor, *Exiting the Whirpool: U.S. Foreign Policy Toward LAC* (Boulder, CO: Westview Press, 2001).

BIBLIOGRAPHY

Agüero, Felipe and Stark, Jeffrey, *Fault Lines of Democracy in Post-Transition Latin America* (Miami, FL: North-South Center Press, University of Miami, 1998).

Aguilar Camín, Héctor and Meyer, Lorenzo, *In the Shadow of the Mexican Revolution: Contemporary Mexican History, 1910–1989*, trans. Luis Alberto Fierro (Austin, TX: University of Texas Press, 1993).

Altman, Roger C., "The Fall and Rise of the West: Why America and Europe will Emerge Stronger from the Financial Crisis," *Foreign Affairs*, vol. 92, no. 1 (2013), 8–13.

Archibold, Randal C., "43 Missing Students, A Mass Grave and a Suspect: Mexico's Police," *New York Times*, October 6, 2014.

Arnson, Cynthia J. and Olson, Eric, *Organized Crime in Central America* (Washington, DC: Woodrow Wilson Center for International Scholars, Latin American Program, 2011).

Ashworth, William, *A Short History of the International Economy since 1850*, 4th edition (London: Longman, 1987).

Astorga Almanza, Luis, *Seguridad, traficantes, y militares: El poder y la sombra* (Mexico City: Tusquets, 2007).

Avritzer, Leonardo, *Democracy and the Public Space in Latin America* (Princeton, NJ and Oxford: Princeton University Press, 2002).

Bagley, Bruce M., "The New Hundred Years War? US National Security and the War on Drugs in Latin America," *Journal of InterAmerican Studies and World Affairs*, vol. 30, no. 1 (1988), 161–186.

Bagley, Bruce M., *Myths of Militarization: The Role of the Military in the War on Drugs in the Americas* (Miami, FL: North-South Center Press, University of Miami, 1991).

Bagley, Bruce M., "After San Antonio," in *Drug Trafficking in the Americas*, ed. Bruce M. Bagley and Walker, William O., III (Miami, FL: North-South Center Press, University of Miami, 1996) 61–73.

Bagley, Bruce M., "Políticas de control de drogas ilícitas en Estados Unidos: ¿qué funciona y qué no funciona?" in *La guerra contra las drogas en el mudo andino: Hacia un cambio de paradigma*, ed. Juan Gabriel Tokatlian (Buenos Aires: Libros del Zorzal, 2009), 283–296.

Bagley, Bruce M., "La Conexión Colombia–México-Estados Unidos," in *Atlas de la Seguridad y la Defensa de México 2009*, ed. Raúl Benítez Manaut, Abelardo

BIBLIOGRAPHY

Rodríguez Sumano, and Armando Rodríguez Luna (Mexico City: CASADE, 2009).

Bagley, Bruce M., "Drug Trafficking and Organized Crime in the Americas: Major Trends in the Twenty-First Century," Woodrow Wilson Centre, Update on the Americas, August 2012 (www.wilsoncenter.org/sites/default/files/BB%20Final.pdf).

Bagley, Bruce M. and Horwitz, Betty, "Regional Security in the Americas: Past, Present and Future," University of Miami, 2007 (www.as.miami.edu/internationa lstudies/pdf/Bagley%20BHSecurity%2815%29%20February%204%202007.pdf).

Bagley, Bruce M. and Hernández, Aline, "Crimen organizado en México y sus vínculos con Estados Unidos," in *Seguridad Regional en América Latina y el Caribe: Anuario 2010*, ed. Hans Mathieu and Catalina Niño Guarnizo (Bogotá: Friedrich Ebert Stiftung, 2010), 332–333.

Bagley, Bruce M. and Tolkatían, Juan G., "Dope and Dogma: Explaining the Failure of U.S.-Latin American Drug Policies," in *Neighborly Adversaries: Readings in U.S.-Latin American Relations*, 2nd edition, ed. Michael LaRosa and Frank O. Mora (Lantham, MD: Rowman & Littlefield, 2006).

Barnett, Michael and Finnemore, Martha, *Rules for the World: International Organizations in Global Politics* (Ithaca, NY and London: Cornell University Press, 2004).

Baylis, John, Smith, Steve, and Owens, Patricia, *The Globalization of World Politics: An Introduction to International Relations* (Oxford and New York: Oxford University Press, 2011).

Beittel, June S., "Colombia: Background, U.S. Relations, and Congressional Interest," Congressional Research Service, Report RL3225, November 12, 2012.

Beittel, June S., "Mexico's Drug Trafficking Organizations: Source and Scope of the Rising Violence," Congressional Research Service, Report R41576. July 22, 2015.

Benitez Manaut, Raul, ed., *Crimen organizado e Iniciativa Mérida en las relaciones México-Estados Unidos* (Mexico City: CASADE Colectivo de Análisis de la Seguridad con Democracia, 2010).

Blattman, Christopher, Hwang, Jason, and Williamson, Jeffrey G., "Winners and Losers in the Commodity Lottery: The Impact of Terms of Trade Growth and Volatility in the Periphery 1879–1939," *Journal of Development Economics*, vol. 82, no. 1 (2007), 156–179.

Boadle, Anthony, "Petrobras' Scandal About to Hit Brazil's Political Class," *Reuters*, February 25, 2015 (www.reuters.com/article/2015/02/25/us-brazil-petrobras-p oliticians-idUSKBN0LT2DP20150225).

Bowden, Charles, *Murder City: Ciudad Juarez and the Global Economy's Killing Fields* (New York: Nation Books, 2010).

Brands, Hal, *Mexico's Narco-Insurgency and U.S. Counterdrug Policy* (Carlisle, PA: Strategic Studies Institute, U.S. Army War College, May, 2009).

Brat, Ilan and Kowsmann, Patricia, "Iberian States, Latin America Seek Ties in Trade," *Wall Street Journal*, World News, November 19, 2012, 9A.

Brooke, James, "Drug Spotlight Falls on an Unblinking Cali Cartel," *New York Times*, World, December 17, 1993 (www.nytimes.com/1993/12/17/world/ drug-spotlight-falls-on-an-unblinking-cali-cartel.html?pagewanted=all).

Brown, Chris, Nardin, Terry, and Rengger, Nicholas, *International Relations in Political Thought: Texts from the Ancient Greeks to the First World War* (Cambridge: Cambridge University Press, 2008).

BIBLIOGRAPHY

Bulmer-Thomas, Victor, "Introduction," in *Regional Integration in LAC: The Political Economy of Open Regionalism*, ed. Victor Bulmer-Thomas (London: Institute of Latin American Studies, University of London, 2001): 1–13.

Bulmer-Thomas, Victor, *The Economic History of Latin America since Independence*, 2nd edition (Cambridge: Cambridge University Press, 2003).

Bulmer-Thomas, Victor, *The Economic History of Latin America since Independence*, 3rd edition (Cambridge: Cambridge University Press, 2014).

Bulmer-Thomas, Victor, Coastworth, John, and Cortes-Conde, Roberto, eds, *The Cambridge History of Latin America: Volume I, The Colonial Era and the Short Nineteenth Century* (Cambridge and New York: Cambridge University Press, 2006).

Bulmer-Thomas, Victor, Coastworth, John, and Cortes-Conde, Roberto, eds, *The Cambridge History of Latin America: Volume II: The Long Twentieth Century* (Cambridge and New York: Cambridge University Press, 2006).

Burrell, Jennifer and Shifter, Michael, "Estados Unidos, la OEA y la Promoción de la Democracia en las Américas," in *Sistema Interamericano y Democracia, Antecedentes Históricos y Tendencias Futuras*, ed. Arlene B. Tickner (Bogotá: Ediciones Uniandes, 2000).

Buzan, Barry, *From International to World Society?* (Cambridge: Cambridge University Press, 2004).

Buzan, Barry, Waever, Ole, and De Wilde, Jaap, *Security, A New Framework for Analysis* (Boulder, CO: Lynne Reinner Publishers, 1998).

Cardemil, Leonardo, Di Tata, Juan Carlos, and Frantischek, Florencia, "Central America, Adjustments and Reforms in the 1990s," IMF, Western Hemisphere Department, March, 2000.

Cárdenas, Enrique, Ocampo, José Antonio and Thorp, Rosemary, *An Economic History of Twentieth-Century Latin America, Volume 3: Industrialization and the State in Latin America: The Postwar Years* (Oxford: Palgrave, in association with St. Anthony's College, 2000).

Cardoso, Fernando H. and Faletto, Enzo, *Dependency and Development in Latin America* (Berkeley, CA and London: University of California Press, 1979).

Cardoso, Fernando Henrique, Gaviria, César, and Zedillo, Ernesto, *Latin American Commission on Drugs and Democracy, Drugs and Democracy: Toward a Paradigm Shift* (New York: Open Society Institute, 2008), 7.

Castañeda, Jorge G., "Latin America's Two Lefts," *Project Syndicate*, December 21, 2005 (http://jorgecastaneda.org/nota/2009/06/02/latin-america-s-left-turn).

Castañeda, Jorge G., "Latin America's Left Turn," *Foreign Affairs*, vol. 85, no. 3 (2006).

Centeno, Miguel Angel, *Blood and Debt: War and the Nation-State in Latin America* (Philadelphia, PA: Penn State University Press, 2002).

Center for Economic and Business Research (CEBR), *World Economic League Table, 2015*, December, 2014 (www.cebr.com/reports/world-economic-lea gue-table-2015/).

Cesarini, Paola and Hite, Katherine, *Authoritarian Legacies and Democracy in Latin America and Southern Europe* (Stanford, CA: Hellen Kellog Institute for International Studies, 2004).

Chabat, Jorge, "El Estado y el crimen organizado transnacional: Amenaza global, respuestas nacionales," *ISTOR: Revista de Historia Internacional*, vol. 11, no. 42 (2010), 3–14.

243

BIBLIOGRAPHY

Chaparro, Camilo, *Historia del Cartel de Cali: El Ajedrecista mueve sus fichas* (Bogotá: Intermedio Editores, Círculo de Lectores S.A., 2005).

Chase-Dunn, Christopher, Kaneshiro, James Love, Lawrence, Kirk and Elias, Edwin, "Neoliberalism and the Pink Tide in Latin America," *Department of Sociology and the Research Group on Transnational Movements at the Institute for Research of World-Systems (IROWS)*, preliminary draft v. 4-21/10, April, 2012 (http://irows.ucr.edu/papers/irows58/irows58.htm).

Chew, Sing and Denemark, Robert, eds, *The Underdevelopment of Development: Essays in Honour of Andre Gunder Frank* (Thousand Oaks, CA: Sage Publications, 1996).

Chodor, Tom *Neoliberal Hegemony and the Pink Tide in Latin America: Breaking with TINA?* (London: Palgrave Macmillan, 2015).

CIA World Factbook and other sources, *Honduras Economy*, 2015 (www.theodora.com/global-data/country-data/honduras-gdp-country-report.

Clausewitz, von Carl, *On War*, ed. and trans. Michael Howard and Peter Paret, The Center of International Studies (Princeton, NJ: Princeton University Press, 1984).

Clawson, Patrick L. and Rensselaer, W. Lee, III, *The Andean Cocaine Industry* (New York: St. Martin's Griffin, 1998).

Coastworth, John, "Economic History of Latin America," in *Handbook of Latin American History*, ed. José C. Moya (New York: Oxford University Press, 2010).

Collier, Ruth Berins and Collier, David, *Shaping the Political Arena: Critical Junctures, the Labor Movement, and Regime Change in Latin America* (Princeton, NJ: Princeton University Press, 1991).

Collier, David, "Bureaucratic Authoritarianism," in *The Oxford Companion to Politics of the World*, 2nd edition, ed. Joel Krieger (Oxford: Oxford University Press, 2001).

Combs, Cindy, "*Terrorism in the Twenty-First Century*," 3rd edition (Upper Saddle River, NJ: Prentice Hall, 2003).

Cooper, Andrew F. and Legler, Thomas, "The OAS Democratic Solidarity Paradigm: Questions of Collective and National Leadership," *Latin American Politics and Society*, vol. 43, no. 1 (2001), 103–126.

Cooper, Andrew F. and Legler, Thomas, *Intervention Without Intervening? The OAS Defense of the Promotion of Democracy in the Americas* (New York: Palgrave Macmillan, 2006).

Corrales, Javier, "Why Argentines Followed Cavallo, a Technopol between Democracy and Economic Reform,' in *Technopols; Freeing Politics and Markets in Latin America in the 1990*, ed. Jorge I. Domínguez (Philadelphia, PA: Penn State University Press, 1997), 49–93.

Corrales, Javier, "Market Reforms," in *Constructing Democratic Governance in Latin America*, ed. Jorge Domínguez and Michael Shifter (Baltimore, MD and London: Johns Hopkins University Press, 2003): 74–99.

Corrales, Javier, "The Repeating Revolution: Chávez's New Politics and Old Economics," in *Leftist Governments in Latin America; Successes and Shortcomings*, ed. Kurt Weyland, Raúl L. Madrid, and Wendy Hunter (Cambridge and New York, Cambridge University Press, 2010), 28–56.

Cortés Conde, Roberto, "Fiscal and Monetary Regimes", in *The Cambridge Economic History of Latin America, Volume II: The Long Twentieth Century*, ed. Victor Bulmer-Thomas, John H. Coastworth and Roberto Cortés Conde (Cambridge and New York: Cambridge University Press, 2006), 216.

BIBLIOGRAPHY

Covarrubias Velasco, Ana, "No intervención ersus promoción de la democracia representativa en el Sistema Interamericano," in *Sistema Interamericano y democracia: Antecedentes históricos y tendencias futuras*, ed. Arlene B. Tickner (Bogotá: Ediciones Uniandes, 2000), 51–64.

Craddock, Bantz J., "Posture Statement of General Bantz J. Craddock, United States Army Commander, United States Southern Command Before the 109th Congress Senate Armed Service Committee," U.S. S. Command, Department of Defense, Florida, 2006, 1–27.

Dabène, Oliver, *The Politics of Regional Integration in Latin America; Theoretical and Comparative Explorations* (New York: Palgrave Mcmillan, 2009).

Dahl, Robert, *On Democracy* (New Haven, CT and London; Yale University Press, 1998).

Dávila, Patricia, "La disputa por Ciudad Juárez," in *El México narco*, ed. Rafael Rodríguez Catañeda (Mexico: Planeta, 2010).

Davis, Peter, "Hedge Funds Win Ruling in Argentina Bond Case," *New York Times*, DealBook, August 23, 2013 (http://dealbook.nytimes.com/2013/08/23/hedge-funds-win-ruling-in-argentina-bond-case/?_r=0).

De la Calle, Luis and Rubio, Luis, "Mexico: A Middle Class Society, Poor no More, Developed Not Yet" (Washington, DC: Washington Institute, Woodrow Wilson Center for Scholars, 2012) (www.wilsoncenter.org/sites/default/files/Mexico%20A%20Middle%20Class%20Society.pdf).

Department of the Treasury, *Notice of Finding* (www.fincen.gov/statutes_regs/files/311–ExchHouse-R-NoticeofFinding-Final.pdf).

Devlin, Robert, Estevadeordal, Antoni, and Garay, Luis Jorge, "Some Economic and Strategic Issues in the Face of the Emerging NAFTA," in *The Future of Inter-American Relations*, ed. J. I. Dominguez (New York and London: Routledge, 2000): 153–196.

Diamint, Rut, "Entre el temor y la armonía," in *Sistema Interamericano y democracia: Antecedentes históricos y tendencias futuras*, ed. Arlene B. Tickner (Bogotá: Ediciones Uniandes, 2000).

Diamint, Rut, "A More Secure Hemisphere?" in *Inter-American Cooperation at a Crossroads*, ed. Gordon Mace, Andrew F. Cooper, and Timothy M. Shaw (London: Palgrave Macmillan, 2011): 131–152.

Domínguez, Jorge I., "Constructing Democratic Governance in Latin America, Taking Stock of the 1990s," in *Constructing Democratic Governance in Latin America*, ed. J. I. Domínguez and Michael Shifter (Baltimore, MD: Johns Hopkins University Press, 1996).

Domínguez, Jorge I., "Technopols; Ideas and Leaders in Freeing Politics and Markets in Latin America in the 1990s," in *Technopols: Freeing Politics and Markets in Latin America in the 1990s*, Jorge I. Domínguez ed. (Philadelphia, PA: Penn State University Press, 1997).

Domínguez, Jorge I., "Security, Peace, and Democracy in Latin America and the Caribbean: Challenges of the Post-Cold War Era," in *International Security and Democracy: Latin America and the Caribbean in the Post-Cold War Era*, ed. Jorge I. Domínguez (Pittsburg, PA: University of Pittsburg Press, 1998), 3–38.

Domínguez, Jorge I., Mares, David, Orozco, Manuel, Palmer, Scott, Rojas, David, Aravena, Francisco, and Serbin, Andres, "Boundary Disputes in Latin America",

BIBLIOGRAPHY

Peaceworks, no. 50, ed. Jorge I. Dominguez (Washington, DC: United Institute of Peace, 2003).

Donnan, Shawn, "The Future of NAFTA: World Faces Up to an Era of Regional Agreements," *Financial Times*, December 2, 2013 (www.ft.com/intl/cms/s/0/b4371e1e-4c51-11e3-923d-00144feabdc0.html#axzz2mVrxlwRx).

Doyle, Michael W., *Liberal Peace: Selected Essays* (New York: Routledge, 2012), 195–198.

Dubois, Laurent, *Haiti: The Aftershocks of History* (New York: Metropolitan Books, Henry Holt and Company, 2012).

Dudley, Steven, *Walking Ghosts: Murder and Guerrilla Politics in Colombia* (New York: Routledge, 2004),

Dudley, Steven, "Drug Trafficking Organizations in Central America: Transportistas, Mexican Cartels and Maras," in *Shared Responsibility: U.S.-Mexico Options for Confronting Organized Crime*, ed. Eric Olson, David A. Shirk, and Andrew Selee (Washington, DC: Woodrow Wilson International Center for Scholars and San Diego, CA: University of San Diego, 2010).

Dullien, Sebastian, Kotte, Detlef J., Márquez, Alejandro, and Oriewe, Jan, eds, "The Financial and Economic Crisis of 2008–2009 and Developed Countries," United Nations Conference on Trade and Development (UNCTAD) and Hochschule für Technik and Wirstschaft Berlin, December (2010).

Dunne, Tim and Schmidt, Brian C., "Realism" in John Baylis, Steve Smith, and Patricia Owens, *The Globalization of World Politics: An Introduction to International Relations*, 4th edition (Oxford: Oxford University Press, 2008), 90–103.

Dyer, Geoff, "Bank Dispute Fuels US-China Rivalry," *Financial Times*, US Politics and Policy, March 13, 2015 (www.ft.com/intl/cms/s/0/f59ed7d4-c90a-11e4-bc64-00144feab7de.html#axzz3UGhD8J24).

Eakin, Marshal C., *The History of Latin America: Collision of Cultures* (New York: Palgrave Macmillan, 2007),

ECLAC, *Latin America and the Caribbean in the World Economy: The Region in the Decade of the Emerging Economies* (Santiago, Chile: United Nations/ECLAC, 2010–2011), 21 (http://repositorio.cepal.org/bitstream/handle/11362/1182/S2011521_en.pdf?sequence=1).

Economic and Social Council at the UN, "Global Economic Woes Threaten Efforts to Eradicate Poverty through Decent, Productive Work, Commission for Social Development Told," SOC/4789, February 2, 2012 (www.un.org/News/Press/docs/2012/soc4789.doc.htm).

Economic Commission for Latin America and the Caribbean (ECLAC), *Statistical Yearbook for Latin America and the Caribbean 2011*, Statistics and Economic Projection Division, United Nations/ECLAC, December (2011), 81–82.

Economic Commission for Latin America and the Caribbean (ECLAC), "Preliminary Overview of the Economies of Latin America and the Caribbean," United Nations/ECLAC, 2014 (http://repositorio.cepal.org/bitstream/handle/11362/37345/S1420977_en.pdf?sequence=31).

Engerman, Stanley L. and Sokoloff, Kenneth L., *Economic Development in the Americas since 1500: Endowments and Institutions*, NBER Series in Long-Term Factors in Economic Development (New York: Cambridge University Press, 2012).

Estevadeordal, Antoni and Suominen, Kati, "Economic Integration in the Americas: An Unfinished Agenda," in *Inter-American Cooperation at a Crossroads*, ed. Gordon

246

BIBLIOGRAPHY

Mace, Andrew F. Cooper, and Timothy M. Shaw (London: Palgrave Macmillan, 2011): 81–94.

Feinberg, Richard E. *Summitry in the Americas: A Progress Report* (Washington, DC: Institute of International Economics, 1997).

Feinberg, Richard E., Bergsten, Fred C., Moss, Ambler H., Jr., and Robinson, Nobina, "Advancing Toward Quebec City and Beyond," *The Leadership Council for the Inter-American Summitry* (Miami, FL: University of Miami, 2001), 1–25.

Felbab-Brown, Vanda, Jutkowitz, Joel M., Rivas, Sergio, Rocha, Ricardo, Smith, T. James, Supervielle, Manuel, and Watson, Cynthia, "Assessment of the Implementation of the United States Government's Support for Plan Colombia's Illicit Crop Reduction Components," produced for review by the U.S. Agency of International Development (USAID), April 17, 2009.

Fellmeth, Aaron X. and Horwitz, Maurice, *Guide to Latin in International Law* (Oxford and New York: Oxford University Press, 2009).

Fenwick, C. G., "The Inter American Regional System," *American Journal of International Law*, vol. 50 (1956), 18.

Fenwick, C. G., *The Organizations of American States: The Inter-American Regional System* (Washington, DC: Kaufmann Printing, 1963).

Financial Times, "Brazil Slows Down: The Time has Come for Dilma Rousseff to Change Track," *Financial Times*, Editorial, December 4, 2013 (www.ft.com/intl/cms/s/0/fe25491c-5cdf-11e3-a558-00144feabdc0.html#axzz2nMaJwNSe).

Flores Pérez, Carlos Antonio, *El estado en crisis: Crimen organizado y política. Desafíos para la consolidación democrática* (Mexico City: Centro de Investigaciones y estudios Superiores en Antropología Social (CIESAS), 2009).

Fontevecchia, Augustinio, "The Real Story of How a Hedge Fund Detained a Vessel in Ghana and Even Went for Argentina's 'Air Force One'," *Forbes.com* (https://caneid.miami.edu/cas/login).

Franck, Thomas M., "The Emerging Right to Democratic Governance," *American Journal of International Law*, vol. 86, no. 1 (1992), 48–91.

Garamone, JIm, "Fraser Testifies Before Senate, Says SOUTHCOM Focused on Transnational Organized Crime," *America Forces Press Service, United States Southern Command, Partnership for the Americas*, Editorial, March 14, 2012 (www.southcom.mil/newsroom/pages/Fraser-Testifies-Before_Senate,-says-SOUTHCOM-Focused-on-Transnational-Organized-Crime.aspx).

Garay-Salamanca, Luis Jorge, Salcedo-Albarán, Eduardo, and De León-Beltrán, Isaac, *Illicit Networks Reconfiguring States: Social Network Analysis of Colombian and Mexican Cases* (Bogotá: Método Foundation, 2010).

Garzón, Juan Carlos, *Mafia & Co: The Criminal Networks in Mexico, Brazil and Colombia* (Washington, DC: Woodrow Wilson International Center for Scholars, 2008).

Global Commission on Drug Policy, "War on Drugs," Report of the Global Commission on Drug Policy, June 2011 (www.globalcommissionondrugs.org/Report).

Golob, Stephanie R., "'Making Possible what is Necessary', Pedro Aspe, the Salinas Team and the next 'Mexican Miracle'," in *Technopols; Freeing Politics and Markets in Latin America in the 1990s*, ed. Jorge I. Domínguez (Philadelphia, PA: Penn State University Press, 1997), 94–143.

Gootenberg, Paul, *Andean Cocaine: The Making of a Global Drug* (Chapel Hill, NC: University of North Carolina Press, 2008).

BIBLIOGRAPHY

Grayson, George W., *Mexico's Struggle with 'Drugs and Thugs'*, Headline Series no. 331 (New York: Foreign Policy Association, 2009).

Greenberg, Lawrence M., *United States Army Unilateral and Coalition Operations in the 1965 Dominican Republic Intervention* (Washington, DC: U.S. Army Center of Military History, 2015).

Halperin, Tulio Donghi, "Two Centuries of South American Reflections on the Development Gap between the United States and Latin America," in *Falling Behind: Explaining the Development Gap between Latin America and the United States*, ed. Francis Fukuyama (Oxford and New York: Oxford University Press, 2008).

Hartlyn, Jonathan, McCoy, Jennifer, and Mustillo, Thomas M., "La importancia de la gobernanza electoral y la calidad de las elecciones en América Latina contemporánea," *América Latina Hoy*, vol. 51, April (2009), 15–40.

Hayes, Margaret D., "Building Consensus on Security: Toward a New Framework," in *Governing the Americas: Assessing Multilateral Institutions*," ed. Mace, Gordon, Thérien, Jean-Phillipe, and Haslam, Paul (Voulder, CO and London: Lynne-Reinner Publishers, 2007), 71–96.

Healy, Kevin, "Coca, the State and the Peasantry in Bolivia," Special Issue: Assessing the America's War on Drugs, ed. Bruce Bagley, *Journal of InterAmerican Studies and World Affairs (JISWA)*, vol. 30, no. 2/3 (1988), 105–126.

Hirst, Mónica, "Seguridad regional en las Américas," in *La seguridad regional en las Américas*, ed. Wolf Grabendorff (Bogotá: Friedrich Ebert Stiftung en Colombia-Fescol/Fodo Editorial Cerec, 2003): 25–80.

Holden, Robert and Zolov, Eric, eds, *New Latin America and the United States, A Documentary History* (New York and Oxford: Oxford University Press, 2010).

Holsti, Kalevi J. *Taming the Sovereigns; Institutional Change in International Politics* (Cambridge: Cambridge University Press, 2004).

Horwitz, Betty, "The Role of the Inter-American Drug Abuse Control Commission (CICAD): Confronting the Problem of Illegal Drugs in the Americas," *Latin American Politics and Society*, vol. 52, no. 2 (2010).

Horwitz, Betty, *The Transformation of the Organization of American States: A Multilateral Framework for Regional Governance* (London: Anthem Press, 2010).

Horwitz, Betty, "Cooperation, Security, and the Drug Phenomenon in the Inter-American Context," in *Cooperation and Drug Policies in the Americas: Trends in the Twenty First Century*, ed. Roberto Zepeda and Jonathan D. Rosen (New York: Lexington Books, 2015), 199–222.

Horwitz, Betty, "A Change in the Approach to the Drug Problem in the Americas," in *New Approaches to Drug Policies: A Time for Change*, ed. Jonathan D. Rosen and Marten W. Brienen (London and New York: Palgrave Macmillan, 2015), Ch. 11.

Huber, Evelyn, Pribble, Jennifer, and Stephens, John D."The Chilean Left in Power: Achievements, Failures, and Omissions," in *Leftist Governments in Latin America: Successes and Shortcomings*, ed. Kurt Weyland, Raúl L. Madrid, and Wendy Hunter (Cambridge and New York: Cambridge University Press, 2010), 77–97.

Hufbauer, Gary Clyde and Schott, Jeffrey J. *NAFTA Revisited: Achievements and Challenges* (Washington, DC: Institute for International Economics, 2005).

Hudson, Rex A., *Brazil: A Country Study*, 5th edition (Washington, DC: Federal Research Division, Library of Congress, October, 1998).

BIBLIOGRAPHY

Human Rights Watch, *World Report 2015: Honduras* (www.hrw.org/world-report/2015/country-chapters/honduras).

Hurrell, Andrew, "Power, Institutions and the Production of Inequality," in *Power in Global Governance*, ed. Michael Barnett and Ramond Duval, Cambridge Studies in International Relations, no. 98 (Cambridge: Cambridge University Press, 2005), 33–58.

Ikenberry, John G., *Institutions, Strategic Restraint, and the Rebuilding of Order After Major Wars* (Princeton, NJ: Princeton University Press, 2001).

Ikenberry, John G., *Liberal Leviathan: The Origins, Crisis, and Transformation of the American World Order* (Princeton, NJ: Princeton University Press, 2011).

Ikenberry, John G., ed., *Power Order and Change in World Politics* (Cambridge: Cambridge University Press, 2014).

International Crisis Group (ICG), "Coca, Drugs and Social Protest in Bolivia and Peru," Latin American Report no. 12, ICG, March 3 (2005) (www.crisisgroup.org/home/index.cfm?l=1&id=4775).

International Crisis Group (ICG), "Learning to Walk Without a Crutch: An Assessment of The International Commission Against Impunity in Guatemala," Latin America Report no. 36, ICG, May 31 (2011), 3.

International Monetary Fund (IMF), "World Economic Outlook," April 2012 (www.imf.org/external/pubs/ft/weo/2012/01/weodata/index.aspx).

International Monetary Fund (IMF), "Regional Economic Outlook: Western Hemisphere. Time to Rebuild Policy Space," World Economic and Financial Surveys (Washington, DC: IMF, May 2013) (www.imf.org/external/pubs/ft/reo/2013/whd/eng/pdf/wreo0513.pdf).

Isacson, Adam, *Don't Call it a Model: On Plan Colombia's Tenth Anniversary, Claims of 'Success' Don't Stand Up to Scrutiny* (Washington, DC: Washington Office on Latin America, July 13, 2010).

Isacson, Adam and Poe, Abigail, *After Plan Colombia: Evaluating "Integrated Action: The Next Phase of U.S. Assistance,"* International Policy Report (Washington, DC: Center for International Policy (CIP), December 2009).

Jepperson, Ronald L., Wendt, Alexander and Katzenstein, Peter J., "Norms, Identity and Culture in National Security," in *The Culture of National Security; Norms and Identity in World Politics*, ed. Peter J. Katzenstein (New York: Columbia University Press, 1996).

Kacowicz, Arie M., *The impact of Norms in International Society: The Latin American Experience, 1881–2001* (Notre Dame, IN: University of Notre Dame Press, 2005).

Kacowicz, Arie M., "Latin America and the World: Globalization, Regionalization, and Fragmentation," *Nueva Sociedad*, no. 214, March/April (2008).

Kant, Immanuel, "Perpetual Peace" in *Kant: Political Writings*, ed. Hans Reiss (Cambridge: Cambridge University Press, 1991).

Kaplan, Robert D., *The Revenge of Geography; What the Map Tells Us About Coming Conflicts and the Battle Against Fate* (New York: Random House, 2012).

Kaplan, Robert D., "Evolving Latin America," *Stratfor*, December 12, 2012 (www.stratfor.com/weekly/evolving-latin-america).

Keohane, Robert O., *After Hegemony: Cooperation and Conflict in World Political Economy* (Princeton, NJ: Princeton University Press, 1984).

249

BIBLIOGRAPHY

Keohane, Robert O., "Theory of World Politics: Structural Realism and Beyond," in *Neorealism and its Critics*, ed. Robert O. Keohane (New York: Columbia University Press, 1986).

Keohane, Robert O. and Martin, Lisa L., "Institutional Theory as a Research Program," in *Progress in International Relations Theory, Appraising the Field*, ed. Colin Elman and Miriam Fendius Elman (Cambridge, MA and London: MIT Press, 2003).

Kingstone, Peter, *The Political Economy of Latin America: Reflections on Neoliberalism and Development* (New York: Routledge, 2011).

Klepak, Hal, "Power Multiplied or Power Restrained?" in *US Hegemony and International Organizations*, ed. Rosemary Foot, Neil S. McFarlane and Michael Mastranduno (Oxford: Oxford University Press, 2003), 239–263.

Korzeniewicz, Roberto Patricio, "Democracy and Dictatorship in Continental Latin America during the Interwar Period," *Studies in Comparative International Development*, vol. 35, no. 1 (2000), 41–72,

Krauze, Enrique, "Looking at Them: A Mexican Perspective on the Gap with the United States", in *Falling Behind; Explaining the Development Gap between Latin America and the United States*, ed. Francis Fukuyama (Oxford and New York: Oxford University Press, 2008).

Krueger, Anne, *Crisis Prevention and Resolution: Lessons from Argentina*, Conference on The Argentinian Crisis, International Monetary Fund, National Bureau of Economic Research (NBER), Cambridge, July 17, 2002.

Krueger, Anne, *Argentina: Remaining Economic Challenges* (Washington, DC: International Monetary Fund, American Enterprise Institute, 2004).

Latinobarómetro, *Informe 1995–2015, Latinobarómetro, opinion pública Latinoamericana* (www.latinobarometro.org/INFORME_LB_2015.pdf)

Leahy, Joe, "Appetite for Construction," *Financial Times*, August 29, 2012, 6.

Leahy, Joe and Pearson, Samantha, "Brazil's Economy Turns in Worst Quarter in Five Years", *Financial Times*, Global Economy, December 3, 2013 (www.ft.com/intl/cms/s/0/95c2ef90-5c3b-11e3-b4f3-00144feabdc0.html#axzz2mVrxlwRx).

Legler, Thomas, "Demise of the Inter-American Democracy Promotion Regime?" in *Inter-American Cooperation at a Crossroads*, ed. Gordon Mace, Andrew F. Cooper, and Timothy M. Shaw (London: Palgrave Macmillan, 2010), 111–130.

Legler, Thomas, "El perfil del multilateralismo Latinoamericano," *Foreign Affairs Latinoamerica*, vol. 10, no. 3 (2011).

Legler, Thomas and Burns, Lesley "Introduction," in *Latin American Multilateralism: New Directions*, Compilation of Articles (Canada: FOCAL, September 2010): 6–7.

Legler, Thomas and Kwasi Tieku, Thomas, "What a Difference a Path Make? Regional Democracy Promotion Regimes in the Americas and Africa," *Democratization*, vol. 17, no. 3 (2010), 465–491.

Leogrande, William, "A Poverty of Imagination: George Bush's Policy in Latin America," *Journal of Latin American Studies*, vol. 38, no. 2 (2007), 355–385.

Levine, Daniel H. and Molina, José E., "Evaluating the Quality of Democracy in Latin America," in *The Quality of Democracy in Latin America*, ed. Daniel H. Levine and José E. Molina (Boulder, CO and London: Lynne-Reineer Publishers, 2011), 245–260.

BIBLIOGRAPHY

Levitsky, Steven and Roberts, Kenneth M., "Democracy, Development and the Left," in *The Resurgence of the Latin American Left*, ed. Steven Levitsky and Kenneth M. Roberts (Baltimore, MD: Johns Hopkins University Press, 2011), 1–30.

Levitzky, Steven and Kenneth M. Roberts, eds, *The Resurgence of the Latin American Left* (Baltimore, MD: Johns Hopkins University Press, 2011).

Levitsky, Steve and Murillo, Maria Victoria, "Building Institutions on Weak Foundations," *Journal of Democracy*, vol. 24, no. 2 (2013), 93–107.

Levy, Daniel C. and Bruhn, Kathleen, *Mexico, The Struggle for Democratic Development* (Berkeley, CA: University of California Press, 2006).

Leys, Colin, *The Rise and Fall of Development Theory* (Bloomington, IN: Indiana University Press, 1977).

Linklater, Andrew and Suganami, Hidemi, *The English School of International Relations: A Contemporary Reassessment* (Cambridge: Cambridge University Press, 2006).

Linz, Juan J. and Stepan, Alfred, *Problems of Democratic Transition and Consolidation: Southern Europe, South America and Post Communist Europe* (Baltimore, MD and London: Johns Hopkins University Press, 1996).

López Calva, Luis F. and Lustig, Nora, eds, *Declining Inequality in Latin America: A Decade of Progress?* (New York: Brookings Institutions, and the United Nations Development Programme, 2010)

López-Alvez, Fernando, *State Formation and Democracy in Latin America, 1810–1900* (Durham, NC and London: Duke University Press, 2000).

Los Angeles Times, "Former Drugpin Faces New Charges," March 13, 2003 (http://a rticles.latimes.com/2003/mar/13/world/fg-briefs13.1).

Loser, Claudio, "Latin America in the Age of Globalization: A Follower or Force of its Own?" *The Impact of Globalization on Latin America Task Force Papers* (Coral Gables, FL: University of Miami, June 11, 2012).

Loveman, Brian, *The Constitution of Tyranny: Regimes of Exception in Spanish America* (Pittsburg, PA: University of Pittsburg Press, 1993).

Loveman, Brian, "Introduction: U.S. Regional Security Policies in the Post-Cold War Era," in *Strategy for Empire: U.S. Regional Security Policy in the Post-Cold War Era*, ed. Brian Loveman (Oxford: SR Books, 2004), xiii–xxviii.

Loveman, Brian, *No Higher Law: American Foreign Policy and the Western Hemisphere since 1776* (Chapel Hill, NC: University of North Carolina Press, 2010).

Lowenthal, Abraham F., "The United States and Latin American Democracy: Learning From History," in *Exporting Democracy: The United States and Latin America, Case Studies*," ed. Abraham F. Lowenthal (Baltimore, MD and London: Johns Hopkins University Press, 1991): 261–283.

Lynch, John, *Argentine Caudillo, Juan Manuel de Rosas* (Oxford: Rowan & Littlefield Publishers, 2001).

Lynch, John, *Simon Bolivar: A Life* (New Haven, CT: Yale University, 2006).

Mace, Gordon, Cooper, Andrew F., and Shaw, Timothy M. (eds), *Inter-American Cooperation at a Crossroads* (London: Palgrave Macmillan, 2011).

Madrid, Raúl L., Hunter, Wendy, and Weyland, Kurt, "The Policies and Performance of the Contestatory and Moderate Left," in *Leftist Governments in Latin America; Successes and Shortcomings*, ed. Kurt Weyland, Raúl Madrid, and Wendy Hunter (Cambridge and New York: Cambridge University Press, 2010), 140–180.

Mainwaring, Scott and Soberg Shugart, Matthew, eds, *Presidentialism and Democracy in Latin America* (Cambridge and New York: Cambridge University Press, 1997).

251

BIBLIOGRAPHY

Mainwaring, Scott and Pérez-Liñan, Aníbal, "Democratic Breakdown and Survival," *Journal of Democracy*, vol. 24, no. 2 (2013), 123–137.

Mainwaring, Scott and Pérez-Liñán, Aníbal,"Cross-Currents in Latin America," *Journal of Democracy*, vol. 26, no. 1 (2015), 114–127.

Mainwaring, Scott, O'Donnell, Guillermo and Valenzuela, Samuel J., "Introduction," in *Issues in Democratic Consolidation: The New South American Democracies in Comparative Perspective*, ed. Scott Mainwaring, Guillermo O'Donnell and Samuel J. Valenzuela (Notre Dame, IN: University of Notre Dame Press, 1992), 1–16.

Marx, Karl, *The Eighteenth Brumaire of Louis Bonaparte* (1852) (www.marxists.org/a rchive/marx/works/1852/18th-brumaire/ch01.htm).

Mazzuca, Sebastian L., "The Rise of Rentier Populism," *Journal of Democracy*, vol. 24, no. 2 (2013), 108–122.

Mejía, Thelma, "Honduras Worried About Becoming a Narco-State," *Inter Press Service (IPS)*, October 22, 2010 (www.ipsnews.net/2010/10/honduras-worried-a bout-becoming-narco-state/).

Mendoza-Botehlo, Martín, "Bolivia: The Growth of Grassroots Participation," in *The Quality of Democracy in Latin America*, ed. Daniel H. Levine and José E. Molina (Boulder, CO and London: Lynne-Reinner Publishers, 2011), 137–172.

Mersheimer, John J., *Conventional Deterence*, Cornell Studies in Security Affairs (New York: Cornell University Press, 1985).

Mersheimer, John J., *The Tragedy of Great Power Politics* (New York: W. W. Northon & Company, 2001).

Moffet, Matt, "A Rags-to-Riches Career Highlights Latin American Resurgence," *Wall Street Journal*, Business, November 15, 2011 (http://online.wsj.com/news/a rticles/SB10001424052970204422404576595211776435404?mod=ITP_pageone_0).

Molina, George Gray, "The Challenge of Progressive Change under Evo Morales," in *Leftist Governments in Latin America; Successes and Shortcomings*, ed. Kurt Weyland, Raúl L. Madrid, and Wendy Hunter (Cambridge and New York: Cambridge University Press, 2010), 57–76.

Molzahn, Cory, Rodriguez Ferreira, Octavio, and Shirk, David A., "Drug Violence in Mexico: Data and Analysis Through 2012," Special Report, Trans-Border Institute (TBI), February 2013 (https://justiceinmexico.files.wordpress.com/ 2013/02/130206-dvm-2013-final.pdf).

Moreno, José Antonio, *El pueblo en armas: Revoluvión en Santo Domingo* (Madrid: Editorial Tecnos, 1973).

Movarsick, Andrew, "Liberal Intergovernmentalism," in *European Integration Theory*, ed. Antje Wiener and Thomas Diez (Oxford: Oxford University Press, 2009).

Movarsick, Andrew (with Frank Schimmelfennig), "Liberal Theories of International Law," *Interdisciplinary Perspectives on International Law and International Relations: The State of the Art*, ed. Jeffrey L. Dunoff and Mark A. Pollack (Cambridge: Cambridge University Press, 2012).

Muñoz, Heraldo, "Chile: The Limits of 'Success'," in *Exporting Democracy: The United States and Latin America*, ed. A. L. Lowenthal (Baltimore, MD and London: Johns Hopkins University Press, 1991), 39–52.

Murray, Matt, "Brazil's 2015 Economic Growth Will Be 'Almost Flat,' Says Finance Minister," *Wall Street Journal*, World, January 23, 2015.

BIBLIOGRAPHY

Musto, David F., *The American Disease: Origins of Narcotic Control*, 3rd edition (New York: Oxford University Press, 1999; first published 1973 by Yale University Press).

National Intelligence Council (NIC), "Global Trends 2030: Alternative Worlds," National Intelligence Council, December 2012 (www.acus.org/files/globa ltrends-2030-nic-lo.pdf).

Neruda, Pablo, "Que despierte el leñador" (1948), in *Canto General* (Buenos Aires: Grupo Editorial Planeta S.A.I.C., 2003).

Ng, Eric, "Commodities Super-Cycle is 'Taking a Break'," *South China Morning Post*, July 10, 2013 (www.scmp.com/business/commodities/article/1279041/sup er-cycle-taking-break).

North, Douglas C., Wallis, John J., and Weingast, Barry B., *Violence and Social Orders: A Conceptual Framework to Interpret History* (Cambridge: Cambridge University Press, 2009).

North, Douglas C., Wallis, John J., and Weingast, Barry B., "Violence and the Rise of Open Access Orders," *Journal of Democracy*, vol. 22, no.1 (2009), 55–68.

Ocampo, Jose Antonio, "Latin America and the World Economy in the Long Twentieth Century," in *The Long Twentieth Century, The Great Divergence: Hegemony, Uneven Development and Global Inequality*, ed. K. S. Jomo (New Delhi: Oxford University Press, 2006), 39–93.

O'Donnell, Guillermo, "Modernization and Bureaucratic-Authoritarianism: Studies in South American Politics," Politics of Modernization Series no. 9 (Berkeley, CA: Institute of International Studies, University of California, 1973 and 1998).

O'Donnell, Guillermo, ed., *Counterpoints, Selected Essays in Authoritarianism and Democratization* (Notre Dame, IN: Notre Dame University Press, 1999).

O'Donnell, Guillermo and Schmitter, Philippe C., *Transitions from Authoritarian Rule: Tentative Conclusions about Uncertain Democracies* (Baltimore, MD: Johns Hopkins University Press, 1986, 2013).

Olson, Eric L., Shirk, David A., and Selee, Andrew D., eds, *Shared Responsibility* (Washington, DC: Woodrow Wilson International Center for Scholars/San Diego, CA: University of San Diego, 2010).

Organisation for Economic Co-operation and Development (OECD) and Economic Commission for Latin America and the Caribbean (ECLAC), "Latin American Economic Outlook 2012: Transforming the State for Development" (OECD and ECLAC, 2012) (www.oecd.org/dev/americas/48965859.pdf).

Organisation for Economic Co-operation and Development (OECD), "Latin American Economic Outlook 2014: Logistics and Competitiveness for Development" (OECD, ECLAC, and CNF, 2014) (www.keepeek.com/Digital-Asset-Ma nagement/oecd/development/latin-american-economic-outlook-2014_leo-2014 -en#page1).

Organization of American States (OAS), "17th Meeting of Consultation of Ministers of Foreign Affairs of the OAS," Res/2, Ser/F II.17, Doc 49/79, Rev 2, June 23 (Washington, DC: OAS, 1979).

Organization of American States (OAS), "Protocol of Cartagena de Indias," O.S.P. A.d. (XIV-E/85) (Washington, DC: OAS, 1986).

Organization of American States (OAS), "Report of the Drug Problem in the Americas: Terms of Reference, 2012–2013" (Panama City: OAS, 2013) (www. counthecost.org/sites/default/files/CICAD-Marketing-Document-ENG.pdf).

BIBLIOGRAPHY

Organization of American States (OAS), "Scenarios for the Drug Problem in the Americas: 2013–2025" (Panama City: OAS, 2013) (www.oas.org/documents/eng/press/Scenarios_Report.pdf).

Pastor, Robert A. *Exiting the Whirpool: U.S. Foreign Policy Toward LAC* (Boulder, CO: Westview Press, 2001).

Pastor, Robert A., *The North American Idea; A Vision of a Continental Future* (Oxford and New York: Oxford University Press, 2011).

Perry, Guillermo E. and Fiess, Norbert, "Turmoil in Latin America and the Caribbean," *World Banking Paper no. 3* (Washington, DC: World Bank, 2004) (www-wds.worldbank.org/external/default/WDSContentServer/WDSP/IB/2004/03/23/000090341_20040323143924/Rendered/PDF/281320Turmoil0in0LAC0WBWP0no.03.pdf).

Perry, William and Primorac, Max, "The Inter-American Security Agenda," *Journal of Interamerican Studies and World Affairs*, vol. 36, no. 3 (1994), 111–127.

Piketty, Thomas, *Capital in the Twenty-First Century*, trans. by Arthur Goldhammer (Cambridge, MA, and London: Belkhap Press, Harvard University Press, 2014).

Pion-Berlin, David and Trinkunas, Harold, "Attention Deficits: Why Politicians Ignore Defense Policies in Latin America," *Latin American Research Review: Journal of Latin American Studies Association*, vol. 42, no. 3 (2007), 78–100.

Plattner, Mark F., "Comparing the Arab Revolts; The Global Context," *Journal of Democracy*, vol. 22, no. 4 (2011), 5–12.

Puryear, Jeffrey and Goodspeed, Tamara, "How Can Education Help Latin America Develop?" *Global Journal of Emerging Market Economies*, vol. 3, no. 1 (2011).

Ramirez Lemus, Maria Clemencia, Stanton, Kimberly, and Walsh, John, "Colombia: A Vicious Circle of Drugs and War," in *Drugs and Democracy in Latin America: The Impact of U.S. Policy*, ed. Coletta A. Youngers and Eileen Rosen (Boulder, CO: Lynne Rienner Publishers, 2005).

Rathbone, John Paul, "What's left of the Latin American Left?" *Financial Times*, Analysis, March 9, 2013, 5.

Rathbone, John Paul, "Mexico: Lawlessness Undermines Reforms and Economic Progress," *Financial Times*, March 3, 2015 (www.ft.com/intl/cms/s/0/2ad7088a-b69c-11e4-95dc-00144feab7de.html#axzz3U6XGQjfE).

Reese, Shawn, "Defining Homeland Security: Analysis and Congressional Considerations," *Congressional Research Service*, January 8, 2013 (www.fas.org/sgp/crs/homesec/R42462.pdf).

Rehm, Kathleen T., "Rumsfeld in Nicaragua for Talks with Regional Defense Ministers," *American Forces Press Service*, October 1, 2006 (www.globalsecurity.org/military/library/news/2006/10/mil-061001-afps02.htm).

Reid, Michael, "So Near and Yet So Far: A Richer, Fairer Latin America is Within Reach, But a Lot of Things Have to be Put Right First," *The Economist*, Special Report: Latin America, September 9, 2010 (www.economist.com/node/16964114).

Reinhart, Carmen N. and Rogoff, Kenneth S., *The Second Great Contradiction: From This Time is Different* (Princeton, NJ: Princeton University Press, 2011).

Resende Santos, João, "Fernando Henrique Cardoso, Social and Institutional Building in Brazil," in *Technopols; Freeing Politics and Markets in Latin America in the 1990s*, ed. Jorge I. Domínguez (Philadelphia, PA: Penn State University Press, 1997), 145–196.

BIBLIOGRAPHY

Restrepo, María Elvira and Bagley, Bruce, eds, *La desmovilización de los paramilitares en Colombia: Entre la esperanza y el escepticismo* (Bogotá: Uniandes, 2011).

Reyes, Javier and Sawyer, W. Charles, *Latin American Economic Development* (New York: Routledge, 2011)

Ribando Seelke, Clare, "Mexico's New Administration: Priorities and Key Issues in U.S.-Mexican Relations," Congressional Research Service (CRS), CRS Report for Congress 7-5700, January 16, 2013.

Ribando Seelke, Clare and Finklea, Kristin M., "U.S.-Mexican Security Cooperation: The Mérida Initiative and Beyond," Congressional Research Service (CRS), CRS Report for Congress R41349, February 16, 2011.

Robinson, William I., "Promoting Poliarchy in Latin America: The Oxymoron of 'Market Democracy'," in *Latin America After Neoliberalism: Turning the Tide in the 21st Century?* ed. Eric Hershberg and Fred Rosen (New York and London: The New Press, 2007), 96–119.

Robinson, William I., *Latin America and Global Capitalism* (Baltimore, MD: Johns Hopkins University Press, 2008).

Rodó, José Enrique, *Ariel* (Barcelona: Linkgua Ediciones, 2008; first published 1900).

Rodríguez, Francisco, "Does One Size Fit All in Policy Reform? Cross-National Evidence and its Implications for Latin-America," in *Democratic Governance in Latin America*, ed. Scott Mainwaring and Timothy R. Scully (Stanford, CA: Stanford University Press, 2010), 88–128.

Rodríguez Mondragón, Fernando and Sánchez, Antonio, *El hijo del "Ajedrecista"* (Bogotá: Editorial Oveja Negra, Quintero Editores, 2007).

Romero, Simon, "Brazil's Power Dynamics Shifting Amid Political Scandals," *New York Times*, Americas, April 26, 2015 (www.nytimes.com/2015/04/27/world/americas/brazils-power-dynamics-shifting-amid-legislative-scandals.html).

Rousseau, Jean Jacques, "The Social Contract," in *Democracy: A Reader*, ed. Ricardo Blaug and John Schwarzmantel (New York: Columbia University Press, 1983).

Ruhl, Mark J., "Trouble in Central America; Honduras Unravels," *Journal of Democracy*, vol. 21, no. 2 (2010): 93–107.

Ruiz, Blanco C., "Visiones de seguridad en las Américas," in *La seguridad regional en las Américas: Enfoques críticos y conceptos alternativos*, ed. Wolf Grabendorff (Bogotá: Fondo Editorial CEREC, 2003), 133–160.

Sackur, Stephen, "Honduras counts the human rights cost of America's War on Drugs," *The Guardian*, July 15, 2012 (www.theguardian.com/world/2012/jul/15/honduras-human-rights-war-on-drugs).

Sarmiento, Domingo Faustino, *Facundo o civilización y barbarie en las Pampas Argentinas*, intro. Juan Carlos Casas (Buenos Aires: Stock Cero, 2003; first published 1845).

Scott, Peter Dale and Marshall, Jonathan, *Cocaine Politics: Drugs, Armies and the CIA in Central America* (Berkeley, CA: University of California Press, 1998).

Schaefer, Agnes G., Bahney, Benjamin, and Riley, Jack K., *Security in Mexico: Implications for U.S. Policy Options* (Santa Monica, CA: RAND Corporation, 2009).

Schuman, Robert, "Schuman Declaration and the Birth of Europe," Speech of May 9, 1950 (http://users.belgacombusiness.net/shchuman/9May1950.htm).

BIBLIOGRAPHY

Seligson, Michal A.,"The Rise of Populism and the Left in Latin America," *Journal of Democracy*, vol. 18, no. 3 (2007), 81–95.

Serbin, Andrés, "Old Factors and New Challenges in Regional Multilateralism: A Latin American Idiosyncrasy?" in *Latin American Multilateralism: New Directions*, Compilation of Articles (Toronto: FOCAL, 2010), 8–11.

Shaefer Muñoz, Sara, "Latin Growth Plays in Two Speeds," *World Street Journal*, December 1, 2012, A10.

Shaw, Carolyn M., *Cooperation, Conflict and Consensus in the Organization of American States* (London and New York: Palgrave Macmillan, 2004).

Shifter, Michael, "Latin America; A Surge to the Center," *Journal of Democracy*, vol. 22, no. 1 (2011), 107–121.

Shifter, Michael and Domínguez, Jorge I., eds, *Constructing Democratic Governance in Latin America* (Baltimore, MD: Johns Hopkins University Press, 2013).

Shirk, David A., "The Drug War in Mexico: Confronting a Threat," Council on Foreign Relations Special Report no. 60 (New York: Council on Foreign Relations, March 2011).

Skidmore, Thomas E. and Smith, Peter H., *Modern Latin America* (Oxford and New York: Oxford University Press, 2005).

Slaughter, Anne-Marie, *"International Relations, Principal Theories,"* in *Max Planck Encyclopedia of Public International Law*, ed. Rudiger Wolfrum (Oxford: Oxford University Press, 2011).

Smith, Peter H., *The Talons of the Eagle: Dynamics of U.S.-Latin American Relations* (New York and Oxford: Oxford University Press, 1996).

Smith, Peter H., *Democracy in Latin America, Political Change in Comparative Perspective* (New York: Oxford University Press, 2005).

Solimano, Andrés, *Governance Crises and the Andean Region: A Political Economy Analysis*, Santiago, Chile, Economic Development Division of ECLAC, February 2003 (www.eclac.org/publicaciones/xml/2/12092/lcl1860i.pdf).

Spence, Michael, *The Next Convergence: The Future of Economic Growth in a Multispeed World* (New York: Farrar, Straus & Giroux, 2012).

Stein, Stanley J. and Stein, Barbara H., *The Colonial Heritage of Latin America* (New York: Oxford University Press, 1970).

Stephens, Phillip, "Trade Trumps Missiles in Today's Global Power Plays," *Financial Times*, Comment and Analysis, November 22, 2013.

Steward, Scott, "The Myth of the End of Terrorism," *Stratfor*, February 23, 2013 (www.stratfor.com/weekly/myth-end-terrorism).

Stratfor, "The Limits of a Brazilian–Mexican Partnership," September 21, 2012.

Stratfor, "Annual Forecast, 2013," January 7, 2013.

Stratfor, "Decade Forecast for 2015–2025," February 23, 2015,

Stratfor, "How a Chinese Billionaire Got Invested in Nicaragua's Canal Plan," March 5, 2015.

Stratfor, "Mexico and Brazil Seek a New Trade Deal," March 9, 2015.

Stratfor, "Cocaine Complicates Talks in Colombia," March 15, 2015.

Stratfor, "Improving U.S.-Cuban Ties Create Openings in Colombia and Venezuela," July 1, 2015.

Stratfor, "Pacific Rim: TPP deal reached, official says," October 5, 2015.

Sullivan, Mark P., "Venezuela: Issues for Congress," Congressional Research Service (CRS), CRS Report for Congress R40938, January 10, 2013.

BIBLIOGRAPHY

Sullivan, Mark P., "Hugo Chávez's Death: Implications for Venezuela and U.S. Relations," Congressional Research Service (CRS), CRS Report for Congress Report R42989, April 9, 2013.

Sullivan, Mark P. and Beittel, June S., "Latin America, Terrorism Issues," Congressional Research Service (CRS), CRS Report for Congress 7–5700, August 15, 2013 (www.fas.org/sgp/crs/terror/RS21049.pdf).

Taylor, Alan M., *Latin America and Foreign Capital in the Twentieth Century: Economics, Politics and Institutional Change*, Working Paper no. E-98–91, Hoover Institution, Stanford University, April 1998.

Teichman, Judith A., *The Politics of Freeing Markets in Latin America; Chile, Argentina and Mexico* (Chapel Hill and London: University of North Carolina Press, 2001).

Teichman, Judith A., *The Politics of Freeing Markets in Latin America, Chile, Argentina and Mexico* (Chapel Hill and London: University of North Carolina Press, 2011).

The Economist, "Growth: Will Brazil Remain the Country of the Future?" October 8, 2012 (www.economist.com/blogs/freeexchange/2012/10/growth).

The Economist, "Señores Start your Engines," Special Report: Mexico, November 24, 2012, 5–7.

The Economist, "Stalled: A Long Awaited Recovery Still Fails to Materialize," December 8, 2012 (www.economist.com/news/americas/21567945-long-awaite d-recovery-still-fails-materialise-stalled).

The Economist, "Peru's Roaring Economy: Hold on Tight," February 2, 2013 (www.economist.com/news/americas/21571162-biggest-threats-latin-americas-ec onomic-star-are-overconfidence-and-complacency-hold).

The Economist, "Latin American Geoeconomics: A Continental Divide," May 18, 2013 (www.economist.com/news/americas/21578056-region-falling-behind-two -alternative-blocks-market-led-pacific-alliance-and?zid=305&ah=417bd5664dc76 da5d98af4f7a640fd8a).

The Economist, "Trade, Partnership and Politics: With Negotiations Secret, Optimism About a Path Breaking Trade Deal is Hard to Share," August 24, 2013.

The Economist, "Latin America's Economies: Life After the Commodity Boom," March 29, 2014 (www.economist.com/news/americas/21599782-instead-crise s-past-mediocre-growth-big-riskunless-productivity-rises-life).

The Economist, "Brazil's Economy: All Systems Slow," July 26, 2014 (www.econom idt.com/news/americas/21608643-confidence-and-growth-public-spending-up-a ll-systems-slow).

The Economist, "The Latinobarómetro Poll: When the tide goes out," September 26–October 2, 2015.

The Economist, Bello, "The Poverty Alert: Latin America's Social Progress Has Stopped. What is to be Done?" The Americas, February 21, 2015.

Thomson, Adam, "Bloody but Booming," *Financial Times*, Analysis, June 21, 2012, 7.

Thomson, Adam, "China's Unlikely Challenger," *Financial Times*, Analysis, September 11, 2012, 7.

Thomson, Adam, "Diverging Paths in Latin America: Early Success for President Raises Hopes for Mexico Economy," *Financial Times*, World News, March 8, 2013, 4.

Thorp, Rosemary, *Progress, Poverty and Exclusion: An Economic History of Latin America in the 20th Century* (Baltimore, MD: Johns Hopkins University Press, 1998).

BIBLIOGRAPHY

Thoumi, Francisco E., *Illegal Drugs, Economy and Society in the Andes* (Baltimore, MD: Johns Hopkins University Press, 2003).

Thoumi, Francisco E., "Debates recientes de la Organización de las Naciones Unidas acera del régimen internacional de drogas: Fundamentos, limitaciones e (im)posibles cambios," in *Drogas y prohibición: Una vieja Guerra, un nuevo debate*, ed. Juan Gabriel Tokatlian (Buenos Aires: Libros del Zorzal, 2010), 27–56.

Thoumi, Francisco E. and Jensema, Ernestine, "Drug Policies and the Funding of the United Nations Office on Drugs and Crime," in *Global Drug Policy: Building a New Framework*, contributions to the Lisbon International Symposium on Global Drug Policy (New York: The Senlis Council, 2003).

Transparency International, "The Americas: Economies Grow, Democracies Shrink. What Does Corruption Have to do with it?" (http://blog.transparency.org/2012/12/05/the-americas-economies-grow-democracies-shrink-what-does-corruption-have-to-do-with-it/).

Transparency International, "Corruption Perceptions Index 2012" (http://cpi.transparency.org/cpi2012/results/).

Transparency International, "Corruption Perceptions Index 2014" (www.transparency.org/cpi2014/results).

Tussie, Diana, "Hemispheric Relations: Budding Contests in the Dawn of a New Era," in *Inter-American Cooperation at a Crossroads*, ed. Gordon Mace, Andrew F. Cooper, and Timothy M. Shaw (London: Palgrave Macmillan, 2011): 23–42.

United Nations, "Global Economic Situation and Prospects 2012: Global Economic Outlook, Pre-Release," 2011 (www.un.org/en/development/desa/policy/wesp/wesp_current/2012wesp_prerel.pdf).

United Nations Office on Drugs and Crime (UNODC), *Coca Cultivation in the Andean Region: Survey of Bolivia, Colombia and Peru* (New York: UNODC, June 2006).

United Nations Office on Drugs and Crime (UNODC), *The Globalization of Crime: A Transnational Organized Crime Threat Assessment* (New York: UNODC, 2010).

United Nations Office on Drugs and Crime (UNODC), *World Drug Report, 2010* (New York: UNODC, 2010).

United Nations Office on Drugs and Crime (UNODC), *World Drug Report, 2011* (New York: UNODC, 2011).

United Nations Office on Drugs and Crime (UNODC), *World Drug Report, 2015* (New York: UNODC, 2015).

U.S. Department of State, "Country Reports on Terrorism" (www.state.gov/j/crt/2011/index.htm).

U.S. Department of State, "2013 International Narcotics Control Strategy Report," March 2013 (www.state.gov/documents/organization/204265.pdf).

U.S. Department of the Treasury, "Notice of Finding," FBI Press Release, April 20, 2013 (www.fincen.gov/statutes_regs/files/311–ExchHouse-R-NoticeofFinding-Final.pdf).

U.S. Federal Bureau of Investigation (FBI), "U.S. Government Seized $150 Million in Connection with Hezballah-Related Money Laundering Scheme," press release, August 20, 2012 (www.fbi.gov/newyork/press-releases/2012/u.s.-government-seizes-150-million-in-connection-with-hizballah-related-money-laundering-scheme).

BIBLIOGRAPHY

Valderrama, Mariano and Cabieses, Hugo, "Questionable Alliances in the War on Drugs. Peru and the United States," in *The Political Economy of the Drug Industry: Latin America and the International System*, ed. Menno Velling (Gainesville, FL: University Press of Florida, 2004), 60–61.

Vallejo, Virginia, *Amando a Pablo, Odiando a Escobar* (Bogotá: Random House, 2007), 352–385.

Vasconcelos, José Calderón, *La Raza Cósmica*, Colección Sepan Cuantos no. 719 (Mexico City: Editorial Porrùa, 2007).

Velázquez Flores, Rafael and Lallande, Juan Pablo, eds, *La Iniciativa Mérida: Nuevo paradigma de cooperación entre México y Estados Unidos en seguridad?* (Mexico City: Universidad Nacional Autónoma de México, 2009).

Waltz, Kenneth N., *The State and War, a Theoretical Analysis* (New York: Columbia University Press, 1954).

Waltz, Kenneth N., *Theory of International Politics* (New York: McGraw-Hill, 1979).

Webber, Jude, "Rival contenders for Honduras Presidency Claim Victory," *Financial Times*, World, Latin America, November 23, 2013.

Webber, Jude, "Honduras claims: Worst is yet to come," *Financial Times, beyondbrics*, January 10, 2014 (http://blogs.ft.com/beyond-brics/2014/01/10/honduras-claim s-worst-is-yet-to-come).

Weeks, G., *US and Latin American Relations* (New York: Pearson, 2008).

Wendt, Alexander, "Power is What the States Make of It: The Construction of Power Politics," *International Organization*, vol. 46, no. 2 (1992), 391–425 (http:// ic.ucsc.edu/~rlipsch/Pol272/Wendt.Anarch.pdf).

Weyland, Kurt, "The Left: Destroyer or Savior of the Market Model?" in *The Resurgence of the Latin American Left*, ed. Steven Levitsky and Kenneth M. Roberts (Baltimore, MD: Johns Hopkins University Press, 2011), 71–92.

Weyland, Kurt, "Latin America's Authoritarian Left," *Journal of Democracy*, vol. 24, no. 3 (2013), 18–32.

Wheatley, Jonathan, "Q&A: The Asia Infrastructure Investment Bank," *Financial Times*, Beyond BRICs, March 12, 2015 (www.ft.com/intl/cms/s/0/bf9c0-c8c8-11e4-b43b-00144feab7de.html?siteedition=intl#axzz3UGhD8J24).

Wigglesworth, Robin, "Caribbean in Crisis: Checkbook Diplomacy," *Financial Times*, Analysis, December 13, 2013 (www.ft.com/intl/cms/s/0/7f7b0d8e-5ea8-11e3-8621-00144feabdc0.html?siteedition=intl#axzz2nnJ5jXDN).

Wigglesworth, Robin, "Caribbean Blown by Winds of Financial Crisis," *Financial Times*, Latin American and the Caribbean, December 16, 2013 (www.ft.com/intl/cms/s/2/ead62cda-60ec-11e3-b7f1-00144feabdc0.html#axzz2nnJ5jXDN).

Williamson, John, "What Washington Means by Policy Reform," in *Latin American Adjustment: How Much Has Happened*, ed. John Williamson (Washington, DC: Institute for International Economics, April 1990) (www.iie.com/publication s/papers/paper.cfm?ResearchID=486).

Williamson, Luis and Bértola, Jeffrey G., "Globalization in Latin America Before 1940," in *The Cambridge Economic History of Latin America, Volume II: The Long Twentieth Century*, ed. Victor Bulmer-Thomas, John H. Coastworth, and Roberto Cortés Conde (Cambridge and New York: Cambridge University Press, 2006).

Wolf, Eric R. and Hansen, Edward C., "Caudillo Politics: A Structural Analysis," *Comparative Studies in Society and History*, vol. 9, no. 2 (1967).

BIBLIOGRAPHY

Wolf, Eric R., *Europe and the People Without History* (Berkeley, CA and London: Berkeley University Press, 1997).

Wolf, Eric R. and Hansen, Edward C., "Caudillo Politics: A Structural Analysis," *Comparative Studies in Society and History*, vol. 9, no. 2 (1967), 168–179.

World Bank Group, "Global Economic Prospects: Having Fiscal Space and Using It" (Washington, DC: World Bank Group, January 2015), Ch. 2.

World Economic Outlook, April 2012 (www.imf.org/external/pubs/ft/weo/2012/01/weodata/index.aspx).

Wyler, Lyana Sun, "International Drug Control policy: Background and U.S. Responses," Congressional Research Service (CRS), CRS Report for Congress 7-5700, October 16, 2012 (www.au.af.mil/au/awc/awcgate/crs/rl34543.pdf).

Yo Soy 132, *Por Una Democracia Autentica* (http://yosoy132.mx).

Youngers, Coletta A. and Walsh, John M., "Development First: A More Humane and Promising Approach to Reducing Cultivation of Crops for Illicit Markets," Washington Office on Latin America (Washington, DC: WOLA, March 2010).

Zakaria, Farid, "How America Can Survive the Rise of the Rest," *Foreign Affairs*, May/June (2008) (www.foreignaffairs.com/articles/63394/fareed-zakaria/the-future-of-american-power).

Zaragoza, José, "The Future of the Caribbean Economy," FOCAL Policy Paper (Toronto: FOCAL, 2000) (www.focal.ca/pdf/caribbean.pdf).

INDEX

Entries in **bold** denote tables; entries in *italics* denote figures.

9/11 *see* September 11, 2001

Acapulco Independent cartel 150–1
accountability, horizontal 197, 199, 212n44
ACE (Economic Complementary Agreements) 207n20
Act of Chapultepec 183–4
agricultural products: prices of 62; transportation of 58; *see also* primary goods
Ahmadinejad, Mahmoud 157
AIIB (Asia Infrastructure Investment Bank) 231, 239n42
ALADI (Latin American Integration Association) 207n20
ALBA (Bolivarian Alternative for the Americas) 91–2, 175n80, 196–200, 202–3, 214n52, 225, 237n27
Alessandri Palma, Arturo 77n6, 78n12
Alfonsín, Raúl Ricardo 70
Alliance for Progress (AFP) 51n24, 186, 231
Americas, European discovery of 14–16
Andean Community 197, 207n20, 213n51
Andean Region: coca and cocaine in 146; underground economy in 68; and US supremacy 161, 192
Angostura Congress 182
anti-communism 63, 112, 184–8
anti-coup norms 195, 197, 199, 211n43
anti-drug policies, US funding of 160
anti-poverty programs *see* poverty alleviation
Arab Spring 12n8, 110–11

Arbabsiar, Manssor 158
Arbenz Guzmán, Jacobo 36, 111, 186
Argentina: annihilation of natives 57, 76n3; bureaucratic-authoritarianism in 109; cocaine consumption in 143, 167n12; debt default in 37, 93; economic growth in *132*; entrepreneurial state in 82n26; European migration to 56; export substitution in 83n29; economic growth in 101n20; inflation in 83n33; ISI in 79n14; lost opportunities of 72, 78n11; meat-processing economy in 24; military interventions in 110; recurring economic problems of 218; social conflict in 23, 32n26
Aristide, Jean-Baptiste 212n44
Artistas Asesinos 152
Asian Tigers 67, 70, 85, 96, 121
Association of Caribbean States (ACS) 72
AUC (Autodefensas Unidas de Colombia) 144, 149, 154
Austral Plan 83n33
autarky 101n20
authoritarian backsliding 196–7
authoritarianism: bureaucratic 51n28; LAC predisposition to 23, 45, 182; modernizing 76n1
authoritarian legacies 117n11,118n17
authoritarian regimes: of 1930s 60–1; competitive 224; and economic growth 43; leftist 4; transition to democracy 162, 227–8; US support for 186, 188

261

INDEX

authoritarian republics 25, 58, 76n3,107–8
authoritarian trends 9, 134, 136, 182, 233
autogolpes **112**, 195, 211n43
automobile trade 236n23
Aylwin, Patricio 71, 110
Azevêdo, Roberto 102n20
Aztec empire 16

BA (bureaucratic-authoritarian) state 110, 117n14
Bachelet, Michelle 126
BACRIM (Bandas Criminales) 149, 151, 154
Bajío area 218
Balaguer, Joaquín 4, 12n5
balloon effect 142, 146–8, 152
bananas 24, 68
Banco del Sur 175–6n81, 200
bank lending, decline in 69
Banzer, Hugo 144, 167n17
Barrio Azteca 151
Bay of Pigs 105, 186
Belize 29n10, 31n21, 210n34
Beltrán-Leyva cartel 150
BID *see* Inter-American Bank
bilateralism 213n51
BNDES 128
Bolívar, Simón 22, 30n16, 31n23, 116n5, 182
Bolivia: agrarian reforms in 65; coca cultivation in 144, 146–7, 163; cocaine production in 143–4; in commodity lottery 59; economic growth of *130*; financial liberalization in 83n33; isolation of 58; leftist government in 130–1; peasant associations in 148; US interventions in 212n44
Bolsa Familia 139n28
Bonaparte, Joseph 20
Bonaparte, Louis (Napoleon III) 24
Bonaparte, Napoleon 19
Brady Plan 201
Brazil: bureaucratic-authoritarianism in 110; cocaine consumption in 143, 167n12; colonial society in 17–18; and commodity lottery 59; democracy in 135; economic growth of 4, 6, 96, *127–8*; entrepreneurial state in 82n26; as global actor 11n3; independence of 20–1, 29n14; inflation in 83n33, 84n39; and international trade 236n18; as LAC leader 198, 202, 219–22; leftist government of 131, 133, 223; military interventions in 110; and multilateralism 200; Portuguese conquest of 15, 17; post-colonial upheaval in 22–3; poverty in 127; poverty in 138n16; stability in 90
Bretton Woods system 62, 64, 66–7
BRIC countries 84n39, 96, 219
British Empire 21, 26, 58
British Guiana 25, 33n32 *see also* Guianas
Buenos Aires: conflict with rest of Argentina 23, 31–2n26; Jewish Cultural Center attack in 153, 157
Bush, George H. W. 147, 188–9, 201
Bush, George W. 40, 145, 190–1, 212n44

Cabral, Pedro Álvares 15–16
caciques 18, 107
CACM (Central American Common Market) 207n19
CALC (Latin American and Caribbean Summit) 196, 199
Calderón, Felipe 147, 155–6, 162
Cali cartel 144, 147–9, 151, 168n20
California, Proposition 19 in 164
capital flight 69
capitalism: dynamic of expansion 27n2; and underdevelopment 42–3
Cárdenas, Lázaro 80n17
Cardoso, Fernando Henrique 71, 84n39, 114, 166n2, 220
Caribbean: Chinese investment in 192–3; Commonwealth members in 210n34; economic growth in 71–2
Caribbean Basin: inequality in 216; as strategic location 180, 221
CARICOM (Caribbean Common Market) 13n14, 72, 198–9
Cartagena Manifesto 182
Cartel del Norte del Valle 144
Casa de Contratación de Sevilla 28n6
Castañeda, Jorge 125–6, 138n14, 237n26
Castro, Fidel 175n80, 227
caudillismo: characteristics of 116n8; and dictatorship 117n9; in independence

262

INDEX

movements 20, 106–7; Latin American tradition of 23, 32n32, 55–6, 108; and the left 224; regular overthrow of 30n17
Cavallo, Domingo Felipe 70
CBI (Caribbean Basin Initiative) 72, 193, 201
CEMEX 79n5
Central America: 1970s boom in 68–9; economic growth in 71–2; gangs in 151, 168n25; Mexican drug traffickers in 146–7, 152; 207n22
Central American Federation 22; 31n18
CEPAL (Economic Commission for LACs) 186–7
certification process 164, 175n68, 212
CFE (Comisión Federal de Electricidad) 82n26
Chávez, Hugo: and ALBA 175n80, 237n27; alternative to US leadership 192, 202; death of 222, 227; election of 90–1, 124; military background of 127; and plebiscitary democracy 196; and terrorist groups 155, 157
Chile: in commodity lottery 31, 57, 59; economic growth in 4, *126*; export substitution in 83n29; global profile of 123; and Hong Kong 101n19; middle class in 139n28; military interventions in 110; moderate left in 126, 128, 131; neoliberal reforms in 218; and nitrates 108; and Washington Consensus 70
China: attempted containment of 45; and Brazilian growth 220; development in 70; economic growth in 100n6; global rise of 87, 230–1; "new normal" phase 11n1, 94; and Nicaraguan canal project 226; and Pacific Alliance 192, 203
CHS (Hemispheric Security Committee) 199, 209n28, 210n32
CID (Colegio Interamericano de Defensa) 209n28
Ciudad Juárez 151–2
civil war: in Central America 69, 187; emerging from 162; in post-colonial LAC 30n18
class conflicts 42, 45
Classical Liberalism 39, 44, 56–7
Classical Realists 49n7
clientelism 118n17, 122, 127

Clinton, Bill 145, 188–9, 201, 209n28
coca cultivation 144–8, 163, 167nn8,17, 168n26, 169n30
cocaine: global consumption of 142–4, 167n7; trafficking in Caribbean 193; US consumption of 142
cockroach effect 142, 148, 152
coercive/defensive Realism 35
coffee 25, 59, 68
Cold War: and authoritarian regimes 110, 117n13; end of 112, 201; ideological front in 194; in LAC 62–3, 111, 185–6, 206n17
Colombia: coffee boom 83n28; democracy in 135; domestic terrorism in 154, 157; drug production in 143–7, 169n27; drug-related violence in 145; economic growth of 4, 228; ISI in 79n14; paramilitary organizations in 162
Colombian drug cartels 148–9, 151, 170n39
colonialism, institutional legacy of 55
Columbus, Christopher 14
Comando Vermelho 151
commodity booms: in colonial LAC 17; twenty-first century 97, 131, 216
commodity cycles 73, 128, 179–80, 204n1
commodity exports: countries with large shares of *95*; and imports 96
commodity lottery: and democracy 125, 131; and ISI 82n27; and LAC economic policy 57, 72–3, 216–18; and United States 59; winners and losers 58, 60–1, 68, 79n14
commodity prices, downturn in 91, 93
communism: end of threat 113; fear of 32n26; ideological battle against 193–4; and modernization 51n24; US confrontation of *see* anti-communism
Comte, Auguste 76n1
Comuna 13, Medellín 150–1
Consejo Suramericano de Defensa 199
consequences, logic of 40
Constructivism: and English School 41; and LAC 45; use of term 39–40, 118n20
Contadora and Esquipulas multilateral accords 113, 207n22
Contadora Group 188, 208n23

263

INDEX

contraband 68
Contras 187–8
copper 57, 91, 100n8, 217
CORFO (Corporación de Fomento de la Producción) 79n15, 82n26
Correa, Rafael 124, 134
corruption: in Brazil 128; and drug trade 165; and governability 162, 228; LAC rates of 229–30; in Mexico 134, 162; and terrorism 40; and US loans 78n9; and War on Drugs 175n78
Cortés, Hernán 14–16
cotton 24, 68, 91
credibility, institutional 88
credit rankings 90
criollos 18–21, 29n13, 30n17, 32n27, 106–7, 116n5
Cruzado Plan 83n33, 84n39
Cuba: agrarian reforms in 65; communist regime in 135, 223; independence of 33n32; membership in multilateral forums 196; Spanish rule over 21, 24; sugar industry in 79n14; and terrorism 155; US interventions in 186, 205n9; US thaw with 226–7
Cuban missile crisis 63–4, 193
Cuban Revolution 63
currency over-valuation 67–8

"dance of the millions" 60, 78n9, 79n15
debt: forced collection of 205n10; see also external debt; public debt
debt-induced depressions 212n47
defense, democratic norms in 160
defense capabilities 114, 119n25
deficits, sustainable 87, 98
deinstitutionalization effects 142, 161
demand control failure 142
democracy: and authoritarianism 182; common norms of 225; defense and promotion of 123, 194, 199, 206n15, 212; definitions of 119n23, 211n41; LAC satisfaction with 134, 198–9; and neoliberal reform 121, 123–4; quality of 132, 135–6, 224; variations in 197–8; in Western Hemisphere 112–13, 135
democratic consolidation: and economic development 110, 114, 12n8; and elitism 196; hemispheric cooperation

in 63; and neoliberalism 122; processes of 133–5, 222–3
democratic deficit 133
democratic governance 185, 188–9, 198
democratic institutions: and *caudillos* 23, 32; promotion of 38–9; solidification of 10
democratic participation 60
democratic peace 38
democratic recipes 114–15, 131
democratic rules and norms 45, 194
democratic transitions: authoritarianism during 119n25; defense capabilities during 114; state as arbiter between classes in 65
democratic values 198
democratization: LAC trends in 135; and organized crime 162; "third wave" of 37, 110–12, 135, 200, 227
dependency theory 42–3, 74
developing countries 9, 23, 87, 90
Díaz, José de la Cruz Porfirio 39, 56–7, 117n10
dictatorship: in China 11n1; and liberal economics 56
dirigisme state 51, 87
disputes, lawful and peaceful resolution of 32n27, 107, 111
DMA (Defense Ministerial of the Americas) 191, 209n30, 209–10n32
DOD (Department of Defense): and Guatemalan coup 12n5; LAC security agenda 190–1, 208n25; reports on terrorism 153
dollar diplomacy 59, 74, 79n15
Dominican Republic: attempted Spanish reconquest of 24; coup attempts in 12n5 democratization of 110; exchange rates of 83n28; Trujillo dictatorship in 61; US intervention in 36
drug cartels: growing influence of 40; and neoliberal reforms 228; perils and vulnerabilities of 149; as threat to US 7; and weak states 136; see also Colombian drug cartels; DTOs; Mexican drug cartels
drug consumption, globalization of 142, 165, 166n2
drug control policies 142, 147, 163, 168n26; see also War on Drugs
drug cultivation, areas of 142, 144, 148

264

INDEX

drug decriminalization and legalization 142, 163–5

drug trafficking: and foreign exchange flows 83n28; intermediaries in 148; learning to live with 228; local economic benefits of 160; Noriega regime and 113; routes of 147–8; trends in evolution of 141; and violence 151–2; *see also* DTOs

DTOs (drug-trafficking organizations) 153, 155–6

Duvalier, François 186

EAI (Enterprise for the Americas Initiative) 189, 201

ECLAC (Economic Commission for Latin America and the Caribbean), economic theories of 42–3, 51n25, 81n24

Ecuador: in ALBA 91, 214; and commodity lottery 218; drug trade in 68, 148, 170n35; FARC in 154; GDP of n15 13; leftist movements in 123–4, 134–5, 197, 224, 227

economic crises, taking advantage of 234n8

economic elites: and authoritarian regimes 58, 106–8, 111; growth approach of 56–7; and leftist governments 124; in Liberal approach 39; policy choices of 87–8

economic growth: debt-led 66; and political stability 55; sharing benefits of 58; subordination of democracy to 39, 110, 114

economic power: and LAC 97; state and non-state actors in 141; uses of 8–9, 44, 55–6

elected officials, accountability of 115

elections, external validation of 211n43

electoral choice 115

electoral competition, restricted 108–9

electoral democracies, consolidation of 90, 110, 122

elitist democracy 196

Elliot Management Corporation 132

ELN (Ejército de Liberación Nacional) 153–5, 157, 172n55

El Salvador: civil war in 69, 187–8; economic growth in 71, 79n14; US support for anti-communist regime 112

encomiendas 18

engenhos de açucar 17

English School: and LAC 45; on society of states n3 116; use of term 41

entrepreneurial state 43, 61–2, 64–6, 82n26, 87

EOM (Electoral Observation Mechanisms) 194–5

EP (export promotion) 67–8

Escobar, Pablo 144, 151

Esquipulas Accords 208n23

Estensoro, Victor Paz 37

European immigration 23, 56–7

European Union 97, 102n20, 142, 167n7, 181

exchange rates: in Argentina 72; and export policy 67–8; fixed 66, 80, 83n28; in Venezuela 229; *see also* REER

executive power, concentration of 109–10

export-led model 56–8, 60–1, 64, 67–9, 82n27, 86

export substitution 67–8, 83n29

external debt 72, 95, 218

external shocks: vulnerability to 66, 71; war as 61

Fajardo, Sergio 151

Familia Michocana 150

FARC (Fuerzas Armadas Revolucionarias de Colombia): and coca trade 144–5, 147–8; and ELN 172n55; in neighboring countries 154–5, 157; retreat of 228; terrorist attacks by 153–4

fascism 61–2

Ferdinand VII of Spain 20

Fernández, Leonel 133

financial liberalization 67, 87–8

fiscal discipline 70–2, 115, 123, 136n2, 180

fisiologismo 126

Florida, cession of 29n11

FMLN (Farabundo Martí National Liberation Front) 69, 124

Foreign Direct Investment (FDI) 32n31, 60

foreign reserves 64, 87

Fox, Vicente 110, 149

Foxley, Alejandro 70, 118n22

France, invasion of Mexico 24

265

INDEX

Frank, Adre Gunder 43
Free Trade Agreements (FTAs) 189, 202, 221, 225, 233n5
free trade zones 189, 201, 203
French Revolution 19
Friedman, Milton 70
FTAA (Free Trade Area for the Americas) 192, 201–2, 213n49, 214n52, 233n5
FTOs (foreign terrorist organizations) 154
fueros 18
Fujimori, Alberto 144, 167n17, 195, 211n43
Funes, Mauricio 124

gang violence 150–2, 217
GATT (General Agreements on Tariffs and Trade) 80n20
Gaviria, César 166n2, 211n43
Gente Nueva 152
geoeconomics 45, 96, 141
Germany 59, 77n8, 79n13
Gini coefficient 100n4
global economy: GDP shares in *59*; growth in *94*
globalization, export-led phase of 81n21
gold: exports from LAC 15, 17, 28; from Mexico 24
gold standard 26, 59–61, 77n8, 78n10
Gómez, Juan Vicente 61
good governance 89, 107, 123, 127
Good Neighbor Policy 62, 184, 231
Goulart, João 111
governability, crises of 227
governance: quality of 122; weak 12
government downscaling *see* privatization
government structures *see* democratic institutions; institutional frameworks
Gran Colombia 22, 31n23, 116n5
Great Britain 59, 78n11, 79n13
Grenada, US invasion of 105, 188
guano 24, 58, 108
Guatemala: exports to US of 79n14; US-backed coup in 36, 63
Guianas 29n10, 31n21
Gulf cartel 150, 171
Guzman, Abimael 155
Guzmán Loera, Joaquín 150
GWOT (Global War on Terrorism) 44, 152–3, 190–1, 212n44

haciendas 18, 30n17, 108, 117n9
Haiti: authoritarian regimes in 186; conflict resolution in n25 208; coups and self-coups in 195; democracy in 135; economic growth in 81n23; export promotion in 67; slave revolt in 19, 29n12, 30n17; US aid to 192; US interventions in 212n44
harm reduction 142, 164–5
hegemony, and Realism 35
heroin 142–3, 155, 165, 170n32
Hezbollah 156–9
Honduras: 2009 coup in 90, 135, 193, 197; fruit industries in 79n13; Mexican drug cartels in 171n50; monocultural economy of 58; murder rate in 89, 91; US interventions in 187–8
Hong Kong 67, 101n19
Humalla, Ollanta 124, 133, 239n40
human capital 97, 126, 133, 234n6
human rights, defense of 113, 194–5

IACHR (Inter-American Commission on Human Rights) 194, 206n15
IADB (Inter-American Defense Board) *see* JID
IADC *see* Inter-American Democracy Charter; Inter-American Development Commission
IBRD (International Bank for Reconstruction and Development) 62, 80n19
ICC (International Criminal Court) 191
ideological glue 194–5
IMF (International Monetary Fund): in Bretton Woods system 62; in Bretton Woods system 80n19; debt restructuring in Caribbean 210n34; structural adjustment programs 37; and Washington Consensus 70, 83n32
Incan empire 15–16
independence movements 20–1, 30n15, 106
indigenous peoples 137n4
industrialization: LAC elites and 182; stages of 64, 80–1n21, 82n27
Industrial Revolution 21, 59, 106
inequality: economic 37–8, 110–11, 123; in industrialized countries

INDEX

100n4; in LAC 6, 56, 73, 86; in LAC 13n14

inflation: controlling 70, 83n33, 84n39, 234n7; and deficit spending 60; and export substitution 67–8

infrastructure: Brazilian plans for 11n3; modernization of 56

instability 23

institutional consolidation 5, 7

institutional deficit 136, 163

institutional frameworks: developing 115; erosion of 190; nature of 116n2; strong 90, 98, 106, 134; weak 108, 133, 190

Institutionalism: and LAC 44; use of term of 36–7

institutional mediation 197

institutional reforms 162, 165

Inter-American Bank 36, 63

Inter-American Conference for the Maintenance of Peace 183–4

Inter-American Democratic Charter 195–7, 199, 211n41, 211–12n43

Inter-American Development Bank 184, 189

Inter-American Development Commission 79–80n16

Inter-American instruments of democracy 123

Inter-American System: in Cold War 64; English School on 45; hierarchy of 41; history of 181–3; Institutionalist approach to 44; institutions of 200; LAC in 10, 180; security in 204n3

international law: English School on 41; Institutionalists on 37; Realists on 35–6

international organizations (IOs): in Constructivism 40; imposing conditionality 175n81; LAC interests and 180; US hegemony exerted through 36

International Relations (IR), theoretical approaches in 34, **46–8**

International Republican Institute 212n44

international system: corporate and individual power in 55; LAC in 8, 225, 232

interventionist role of state 65–6, 70, 82n25

investment-friendliness 220

Iran, activities in Latin America 153, 156–8, 173n71

Iraq: ISIS in 7; US intervention in 45, 191, 213n49

ISI (Import Substitution Industrialization): in 20th century 26–7; and commodity lottery 61; and dependency theory 43, 187; and economic recovery 79n14; and export policy 68; golden age of 64–5, 81n24; lack of flexibility 66; re-evaluation of 69; successes of 82n27

Iturbide, Agustín de 30n18, 182

Jamaica: British conquest of 29n10; and CARICOM 13n14

Jesuit order 19

JID (Junta Interamericana de Defensa) 183–5, 191, 199–201, 206n15, 209nn27,28, 210n32

Joumaa, Ayman 159

Juárez cartel 149–50, 152, 171n43

Kelly, John 154, 158

Kennedy, John F. 51n24, 63

Kerlikowske, Gil 164

Keynes, John Maynard 26

Kirchner, Cristina 91, 124, 127, 131–2, 135, 159, 235n11

Kirchner, Néstor 124

Kubitschek, Juscelino 82n26

labor markets 97, 219, 235n12

labor organizations 60, 78–9n12

LAC (Latin America and the Caribbean): barriers to exports from 79n13; colonial societies in 15–18, 28n6; common interests with US 231–2; as community of democracies 194–6, 222; democracy in 111, **112**, 114–15, 117n13, 135–6, 224–5; domestic terrorism in 153; Eastern trading partners of 92, 96–7; elites in *see* economic elites; landowning elites; political elites; foreign invasions and interventions 108; free trade agreements in 189; as global actors 3–4; history of economic growth in 13n12, 33n31, 66, 69, 71–3, 88, *89*, 99n2, 137n10; internal structures of nations 106; in international system 24–7, 56, 86, 97, 179–80, 215–16;

267

INDEX

location of 5–6, 12–13n9; obstacles to growth 4–5, 91, 216–17; outlook for growth in 7, 85–6, 91–5; post-colonial economies in 21–4; pragmatic center in 133; as prospect for investment 90; Realist view of 36; regional integration of 181–2, 186–7, 199, 202; security issues in 210n32, 237n33; theoretical approaches to 43–5; Two Lefts of 125–6, 132, 223–4, 227; unfulfilled promise of 5, 7–8, 10, 27, 72, 87, 98; US aid to 191–2; as US backyard 5, 25, 226

Lagos, Ricardo 124–6
La Línea 152
landowning elites 20–3, 30n17, 32n27, 55–6, 76n3, 107–8
land reform 65, 80n17
La Plata, Viceroyalty of 28n6
latifundios 51, 107
Latinobarómetro 12n6, 134, 198–9, 230
LCB (Lebanese Canadian Bank) 159
leadership: and economic growth 58; of political parties 56
Lebanese diaspora 159
leftist governments 123–5, 127, 131–2, 223, 237n27
legalism, discriminatory 134
Leyes de Indias 28n6
Liberalism: and LAC 44–5, 76n3; use of term 37–9
Lima Declaration 183–4
liquidity shortages 87, 101n8
loans, non-performing 87
Lobo, Porfirio 90, 212n44
López, Francisco Solano 32n30
Los Aztecas 152
"lost decade" 69, 114, 207n21, 234n7, 237n27
Louisiana, cession to Spain 29n11
Lozada, Gonzalo Sánchez 122
Lugo, Fernando 124
Lula, Luiz Ignácio da Silva 124–7

Madrid, Miguel de la 71
Maduro, Nicolas 86, 91, 127, 130, 197, 202
manufacturing: competing with China in 133; elite bias towards 65; in inter-war period 26
maquiladoras 67

Mara Salvatrucha 86, 152
marijuana 142, 155, 164–5
market democracies 189–90
market reforms: backlash against 123–4; as ideological glue 194; and political freedom 113, 121; and state institutions 115, 175n78; technocrats proposing 70; see also neoliberalism
Marshal Plan 63, 80n20, 207n21
Marx, Karl 15, 190
Marxism 8, 41–2, 45, 48, 74, 124
mass protest movements 123
Maximilian, Emperor 24
Medellin, Colombia 150–1
Medellin cartel 144, 147–9
megatrends 219, 233n4
Menem, Carlos 37, 71
mercantilism 17, 28n5
MERCOSUR (Mercado Común del Sur or Southern Common Market) 92, 102, 198–9, 207n20, 213n51, 221–2, 236n23
Mérida Initiative 145–7, 156, 172n61
Mesa, Carlos 122
Mesa de Diálogo 211n41
mestizaje 76n3
mestizos 18, 20, 30n17, 106–7
Mexican-American War 22, 31n22, 105
Mexican drug cartels 90, 147, 149–51, **150**, 168n24, 170n34, 171n43, 238n34
Mexican Revolution 183
Mexicles 152
Mexico: agrarian reforms in 65; in commodity lottery 24, 58–9; debt default of 69, 187; democratization in 135; demographic importance of 5; drug trafficking in 145, 155–6, 162, 172n61, 228; economic growth of 4, 6; energy policy in 236n21; entrepreneurial state in 82n26; as global actor 11n4; heroin production in 143; ISI in 79n15; as LAC leader 219–22; manufacturing sector in 11n4, 92, 218, 238n34; and NAFTA 71; native cultures in 76n3; paramilitary groups in 152; political conflict in 22, 24; post-crisis economy of 234n8; PRI dominance of 109–11; stability in 90; student protests in 238n38; technocratic policies in 56–7

268

INDEX

middle class: challenges of 96; downward mobility of 78n10; global 6, 76, 86, 133, 218, 223; impact of social policies on 139n28; and manufacturing 92; and manufacturing 76n2
middle-income status 86–7
middle-income trap 221, 230
military: corruption in 175n78; in democratic transitions 114, 119–20n25
military coups 31n25, 109, **112**, 193, 206n17
military interventions 25, 36, 44, 63–4, 105, 110
military regimes 83n29, 187
Millennium Challenge Account 212n44
mining 106–7, 117n9, 139n28, 158, 228
ministerial frailty 114, 119n25
MNR (Movimiento Nacional Revolucionario) 137n4, 148
modernization: and institutional arrangements 76n2; passive stance to 108
money supply 67
monoculture 58
Monroe Doctrine 182–3, 185, 226
Morales, Evo 124, 130, 137n4, 147, 163, 202
Movarsick, Andrew 38
Mujica, José 125
multilateralism: economics 201; in LAC 181, 187, 195, 199–200; post-war development of 141; US abandoning 191–2; US support for 184, 189
multinational corporations (MNCs) 38, 50n14, 51n28, 67, 81n23, 90, 238n34

NAFTA (North American Free Trade Agreement): cooperation between members 234n6; and Eastern trade 96–7; economic growth in 71; global importance of 5, 216, 231; and LAC growth 92; Mexico's role in 220–2; signing of 201
Napoleonic Wars 21
Napoleon III see Bonaparte, Louis
narco-dollars 68
National Intelligence Council 215, 233n3

nationalism, corporatist 61–2
nationalization 129–31
natural resources: demand from developing countries for 87, 89, 98; LAC as supplier of 17, 21, 72
neo-colonialism 182
neoliberalism: in Chile 218; and economic growth 71; extreme version of 131; and international business 87; political consequences of 113, 227–8; technocratic imposition of 118n22
Neorealism 35, 41, 49n7
New Granada 28n6, 29n13
New Spain 17–20, 28n6
Nicaragua: agrarian reforms in 65; in ALBA 91; civil war in 69; export prices of 79n14; new canal project in 226; US interventions in 112–13, 183, 187–8, 212n44
NICs (newly industrialized countries) 67
nitrates 25, 32, 59, 108
Noriega, Manuel 113, 118n21, 188
nuclear energy 158

OAS (Organization of American States): and democracy 193–7, 199, 209n27, 211n41; and drug control 163, 165; foundation of 184–5; and Somoza regime 113; and US hegemony 36, 63
Obama, Barack 92, 196, 212n44, 226
the Office (armed group) 151
Office of Coordination of Commercial and Cultural Relations between American Republics 80n16
oil: in commodity lottery 68; exports of 4, 24, 27, 59, 66; expropriation of foreign interests 79n15, 82n26
oil prices, fall in 221
oil shocks 66, 68–9
oligarchic republics 39, 109
oligarchy, competitive 108
O'Neill, Jim 219
organized crime: fragmentation and dispersion of networks 149–50, 152; in Mexico 238n34; and state institutions 73, 161–2, 225, 228; trends in evolution of 141; and violence 90; world attention on 86
Ortega, Daniel 124, 127, 134, 175n80, 197
outward-oriented growth 57

INDEX

Pacific Alliance: Chile in 123; goals of 92, 197, 202–3, 227; Mexico in 221; tariff reduction within 101n20

Pampas region of Argentina 31n19, 32n26

PAN (Partido de Acción Nacional) 109, 162

Panama: FARC in 154; independence of 25, 33n32; US invasion of 1990 188

Panama Canal, US protection of 25, 33n32, 59, 182, 205n9, widening of 5

Pan-American conferences 62, 182–3

Pan-Americanism 182, 204n8

Paraguay: attempted incorporation into Argentina 23, 32n26; isolation of 13n14, 58; smuggling in 68

Pastrana, Andrés 145, 168n22

Paz Estensoro, Victor 144

PED (primary export development) 67–8

Pedro I of Brazil 22, 29n14

Pedro II of Brazil 22, 31n25

PEMEX (Petróleos Mexicanos) 82n26, 222, 235n12

Peña Nieto, Enrique 134, 138n17, 156, 218, 236n21

peninsulares 18, 27

Perón, Isabel 111

Perón, Juán Domingo 61, 65, 82n26

personalism 107, 116n8, 122, 134, 136, 196

Peru: coca cultivation in 144, 146–7, 168n26, 169; cocaine production in 143–4; in commodity lottery 24, 58–9, 108; in democracy 135; economic growth in 230; export substitution in 83n29; FARC in 154; indigenous rebellion in 29; international election monitoring in 39; ISI in 82n27; peasant associations in 148; poverty reduction in 139n28; Sendero Luminoso insurgency in 155, 170n38; Spanish subjugation of 16; trade deals 238n40; Viceroyalty of 28n6

Peru-Colombia air bridge 144, 167n17

Petrobras (Petróleo Brasiliero): corruption scandal in 94, 128, 220; formation of 82n26; value of 222

Picketty, Thomas 38, 50n14

Piñeres, Juan Francisco Gutiérrez 29n13

"pink tide" see leftist governments

Pinochet, Augusto 70, 83n29, 126

Pizarro, Francisco 15–16

Plan Colombia 145, 168n22

Plan Dignidad 144, 167n17

Plano Real 84n39

plebiscitarianism 134, 140n30

political elites: alternative to orthodoxy 61; and authoritarianism 111, 115; and democracy 39, 122–3; during regime transitions 114; and ISI 64, 69; monopolizing electoral competition 117n10

political outsiders 224

political participation, widespread 122

political party systems: institutionalized 135; liberal/conservative 21, 56, 108–9

polyarchy 113–14, 119n23

populism, nationalist 129

populist democracy 122, 196–7

populist regimes 100n8

Portales, Diego 107

Portugal: American colonial empire of 17–18; conquest of Americas 15–16; and mercantilism 28n5; Napoleon's invasion of 19–20

Positivism 76

poverty alleviation 5, 7, 88, 97, 138n16, 208n25

Powell, Colin 105

power: exercise of 105–6; and Realism 35; sharing 55, 220–1

Prebisch, Raúl 81n24, 186–7

presidentialism 107

PRI (Partido Revolucionario Institucional): dominant-party status of 109–10; end of dominance 162; foundation of 61; and pragmatic center 134; recent governments 220, 236n21

primary goods: export of 20–1, 56, 108; and ISI 65; in LAC economies 17, 239n43; processing of 57

privatization 70, 136n2, 187, 189–90

protectionism: in Brazil 220–1; dismantling 70; and economic growth 66; in inter-war period 26, 60–1, 81n21

Protocol of Cartagena de Indias 113, 195

INDEX

public debt: controlling 228–9; levels of 70, 88; maturity profile of 87

public enterprises, income from 65

public goods, impersonal delivery of 122–3

Puerto Rico 21, 24, 33n32, 205n9

Reagan, Ronald 70, 175n78,187

Reagan Doctrine 187

Realism: and English School 41; and LAC 44; and Liberalism 37; use of term 35–6; in US politics 64

REER (real effective exchange rate) 82–3n28

regional integration: and aggregate demand 96; and export policy 68

regionalism: hemispheric 196, 200, 206n15; old 187, 189; open 92

regional security 185, 191, 194, 208n25

regulatory failures 142

representative democracy 134, 196–7, 199, 201, 211nn41,43

Resolution 1080 40, 194–5

Resolution XV 183–4, 205n12

responsible policymaking 100nn4,8

Rio Group 188, 195–6, 199, 208n23

Rio Treaty 36, 184–5, 199

"rise of the rest" 99, 221

Rodó, José Enrique 76n3

Roosevelt, Franklin D. 62, 231

Roosevelt Corollary 182

Rosas, Juan Manuel de 23, 32n26, 107

Rousseff, Dilma 94, 96, 102n20, 125, 128, 220

rule of 72 100

rule of law 25, 27, 107, 109, 111, 123, 134, 162, 227

rule-takers: LAC countries as 8–10, 23, 27, 42; structure creating 106

Rumsfeld, Donald 210n32

rural-urban migration 62

Salazar, Alonso 151

Salazar, António 110

Salinas, Carlos 37, 70

Samper, Ernesto 168n20

Santa Anna, Antonio López de 22, 30n18

Santiago Commitment 40

Santos, Juan Manuel 155

Sarmiento, Domingo Faustin 76n3

"second stage reforms" 70–1

securitization 40, 50n19

security, local implementation of 198

security gap 161, 192

security initiatives, cooperative 160–1

self-coups see autogolpes

self-determination 181, 184–5, 195, 198, 204n3, 205n10, 206n15, 212n43

Sendero Luminoso 147–8, 153, 155, 170n38

September 11, 2001 44, 181, 190–1, 201

Serrato, José 77n6

Seven Years War 29n11

Shakuri, Gholam 158

Shining Path see Sendero Luminoso

SICA (Central American Integration Scheme) 199

Sinaloa cartel 146, 150, 152, 156, 171n43

Singer, Hans 186–7

Singer, Paul 132

slavery 16–20

Smoot-Hawley tariff 79n13

socialism, classic 223–4

Social Progress Fund 63

Somoza, Anastasio 113, 118n21, 186

SOUTHCOM see U. S. Southern Command

Southern Cone: and dependency theory 43; end of military regimes in 187; fascism in 61; financial liberalization in 67; resistance to US 161, 192

South Korea 67; 100, 122–3, 234n8

sovereignty, national 181, 184–5, 198, 204n3, 205n10

Soviet Union: Caribbean influence of 12n5; collapse of 113; support for Cuba 193–4; US countering in LAC 36, 62–4, 111, 187

Spain: American colonial empire of 17–19, 21; conquest of Americas 15–16; Napoleon's invasion of 20; use of silver 28n7

Spanish-American War 25, 33n32, 205n9

Spencer, Herbert 76n1

state capacity 73, 135–6, 165

Structuralism 41–2, 48, 74

structural Realism 35, 49n7

Sucre, Antonio José de 116n5, 182

Summit of the Americas 189–90, 196, 199, 201, 211n41, 213n49

271

INDEX

TCOs (transnational criminal organizations) 156
technocrats 70, 118n22, 237n27
terrorism: Bush administration and 40, 191, 210n32; definitions of 152–3; and drug trafficking 141–2, 153–4; and globalization 38; regional cooperation on 160–1; war on *see* GWOT
Texas, independence from Mexico 22
Thatcher, Margaret 70
Thirty Years' War 18
TIAR (Tratado Interamericano de Asistencia Recíproca) 183–6, 191, 199, 201, 206nn15,17, 209n27
Tijuana cartel 149–50, 171n43
tin 59, 68, 131
Toledo, Alejandro 39
totalitarian regimes 61
TPA (Trade Promotion Authority) 191, 209n30
TPP (Trans-Pacific Partnership) 97, 123, 203, 216, 219, 231, 234n6
trade liberalization 67, 70, 83n29, 88, 99, 136n2
Transparency International 229
Treaty of Guadalupe Hidalgo 31n22
Treaty of Methuen 18–19
tri-border area (TBA) 158–9
Trujillo, Rafael 12n5, 61
Truman Doctrine 185
TTIP (Transatlantic Trade and Investment Partnership) 97, 216
Túpac Amarú 29n13

UNASUR (Unión de Naciones Suramericanas or Union of South American Nations) 13n14, 197–9, 202–3, 213n51
underdevelopment, ECLAC theory on 42–3
underground economy 68
UNHCHR (UN Human Commission on Human Rights) 194
unilateralism 63, 112, 160, 189–90
unipolar moment 201
United States: attention paid to LAC 201–2, 222, 225–7; drug consumption in 142–3; drug control policies of 163–4; economic dependence on 71, 133; global leadership of 3–4, 45, 230–2;

hegemony in LAC 25, 36, 59–60, 111, 182–3; Hispanic population of 92; independence of 18–19; intervention in LAC countries 206n17, 212n44; investment in LAC 80n16; LAC mistrust of 181, 205n9; Mexican criminal organizations in 169n32; Mexican emigration to 219; political quagmire in 94; reaction to 9/11 191; security cooperation with LAC 160–1, 183–6, 188–90; support for authoritarian regimes 63–4, 118n17
UNODC (United Nations Office on Drugs and Crime) 143, 163
UPD (Unit for Promotion of Democracy) 194
Uribe, Álvaro 145–6, 154–5, 168n22
Uriuru, José Félix 61
Uruguay: attempted incorporation into Argentina 23, 32n26; economic growth of 4; export substitution in 83n29; ISI in 79n14; military interventions in 110; moderate left in 131
USAID (U.S. Agency of International Development) 193
US dollar, pegging currencies to 78n10
U. S. Southern Command 154, 158–9, 190
uti possidetis juris 182

Vargas, Getúlio 61, 65
Vasconcelos, José 76n3
Vásquez, Tabaré 124–5
Velázquez, José Abarca 127
Venezuela: 2002 coup in 197, 212n44; in ALBA 202; border dispute with Guyana 25, 33n32; cocaine shipments from 170n35; in commodity lottery 59; economic growth in 101–2n20, *129*, 235n11; FARC and ELN in 154–5; as LAC leader 198; leftist government of 4, 129–30; relations with Iran and Hezbollah 157–8, 172n53

War of 1812 105
War of the Pacific 32n30
War of the Spanish Succession 18–19
War of the Triple Alliance 24, 32n30, 105

272

INDEX

War on Drugs: declaration of 175n78; militarization of 147; partial victories in 144–5; Realist approach to 44; undermining democracy 212n44; unintended consequences of 142; and US aid 192; US demanding LAC adherence in 164

Washington Consensus: adoption by LAC governments 37, 70, 87, 212n47, 237n27; reaction against 125; social consequences of 123; use of term 121

Washington Protocol 195, 211n43

weak states 35, 108, 135–6, 147, 224, 231

Western normative principles 44

Williamsburg Process 191, 199

Wilson, Woodrow 205n10

workforce: democratic participation of 60; education of 58; *see also* labor markets

World Bank: foundation of 62; structural adjustment program 37

World System theories 41–2, 48, 75

World War II 61–2

WTO (World Trade Organization), Doha Round 11n3, 102n8

Yrigoyen, Hipólito 77n6

Zedillo, Ernesto 166n2

Zelaya, Manuel 90, 193, 196, 214n52

Zellick, Bob 96–7, 234n6

Zetas cartel 146, 150, 152, 156, 158–9, 171nn43, 50

eBooks
from Taylor & Francis
Helping you to choose the right eBooks for your Library

Add to your library's digital collection today with Taylor & Francis eBooks. We have over 50,000 eBooks in the Humanities, Social Sciences, Behavioural Sciences, Built Environment and Law, from leading imprints, including Routledge, Focal Press and Psychology Press.

Choose from a range of subject packages or create your own!

Benefits for you
- Free MARC records
- COUNTER-compliant usage statistics
- Flexible purchase and pricing options
- 70% approx of our eBooks are now DRM-free.

Benefits for your user
- Off-site, anytime access via Athens or referring URL
- Print or copy pages or chapters
- Full content search
- Bookmark, highlight and annotate text
- Access to thousands of pages of quality research at the click of a button.

Free Trials Available

We offer free trials to qualifying academic, corporate and government customers.

eCollections

Choose from 20 different subject eCollections, including:

- Asian Studies
- Economics
- Health Studies
- Law
- Middle East Studies

eFocus

We have 16 cutting-edge interdisciplinary collections, including:

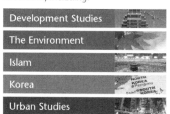

- Development Studies
- The Environment
- Islam
- Korea
- Urban Studies

For more information, pricing enquiries or to order a free trial, please contact your local sales team:

UK/Rest of World: **online.sales@tandf.co.uk**
USA/Canada/Latin America: **e-reference@taylorandfrancis.com**
East/Southeast Asia: **martin.jack@tandf.com.sg**
India: **journalsales@tandfindia.com**

www.tandfebooks.com